Encounter Images in the Meetings between Africa and Europe

Edited by
Mai Palmberg

Nordiska Afrikainstitutet, Uppsala 2001

Indexing terms
African history
Communication
Culture
Culture conflict
Cultural identity
Development aid
Mission history
Prejudices
Racial discrimination
Africa
Europe

Cover photo: Sérgio Santimano
Typesetting: Susanne Östman
Language checking: Elaine Almén
Transcription from taped interviews: Petra Smitmanis and Jenny Thor
© The authors and Nordiska Afrikainstitutet, 2001
ISBN 91-7106-478-8
Printed in Sweden by Centraltryckeriet Åke Svenson AB, Borås 2001

Contents

Foreword

In 1995 the Nordic Africa Institute initiated a research project on cultural aspects of development and Nordic-African relations. One of the aims was to contribute to providing other images of Africa than the negative images of misery, war and catastrophes often conveyed by the mass media. Another was to encourage cultural aspects of change in Africa, and the dynamics of cultural production itself.

It is indisputable that negative images of Africa increasingly dominate everyday reporting and therefore public opinion too. The generalised pessimistic pictures are in stark contrast to what those of us have experienced who have had the opportunity to visit Africa and work there.

It was important not only to encourage alternatives to stereotypes and generalisations, which portrayed Africans as helpless victims, but also to try to understand how and why, and to what extent these images had developed. This was the theme of the first conference organised within the new project on culture, coordinated by Mai Palmberg. This research project was called "Cultural Images in and of Africa", and the seminar dealt primarily with the images of Africa developed in Europe.

A selection of edited papers from this seminar is presented here and we thank the authors for their cooperation. We are grateful that we have also been able to include interviews with two prominent scholars, professor V.Y. Mudimbe and professor Terence Ranger, and texts by one of Africa's most prominent authors, Yvonne Vera, and one of the world's most renowned scholars specialising in African literature, Bernth Lindfors.

The seminar was held in cooperation with the International People's College in Denmark. We thank them, not least the college's international secretary, Garba Diallo, for their warm hospitality and the input of work involved in making the seminar a success. Thanks are also due to Susanne Östman and Petra Smitmanis who contributed to the preparation and organising of the seminar.

The images of Africa are a theme that will have to be revisited many times. This book gives a topical input to the debate through the questions it raises and the simplifications it rejects.

Lennart Wohlgemuth
Director
The Nordic Africa Institute

Introduction

It is something of an axiom that today's images of Africa in Europe are largely negative. Such statements are taken as fact without much questioning. In this book we want to question them. Not that the authors dispute the existence of negative images of Africa. But what does this really mean? How were the images formed, when and why?

The concern with negative images of Africa rests on two underlying assumptions, which can operate independently of each other but are often connected. The first is the observation that what the mass media present us with about Africa are overwhelmingly negative features of today's world: conflict and war, starvation and hunger, flight and despair, corruption and suppression. In sum: misery. The other assumption is that the negative images and stereotyping are as old as the relations between Europeans and Africans. This is questioned in some of the contributions to this book.

A rather general conception is that racism has coloured European images of Africa all along. Often this is asserted without any attempt to define 'racism'. The ideology of racism rests on the thinking that one can meaningfully divide the human species into races, distinguished from each other by different levels of inherited qualities, some belonging to higher 'races', some to 'lower'. In racist thinking, some are hopeless cases by birth due to the 'races' they are born into. In paternalism the case is not hopeless, but those 'less advanced' must be guided by the enlightened (and needless to say, more powerful) into the light of civilisation. If the era of racism as a dominant and accepted ideology in the West seriously declined after the Second World War, the question is whether paternalism is still with us. The many pronouncements on 'partnership' as the new guiding principle bear witness to a recognition that equal terms have not characterised the relationship between Europe and Africa. This is a question of power, but also of the images reproduced.

How do you study images?

Many studies on images are based on "close reading", and a search for the subtext. This also entails reading what is not there—i.e. looking for the omissions.

There is not one single method with which to study images. The variety of approaches was a strength in the conference that brought together the authors of the papers in this book.

The conference was initiated by the research project at the Nordic Africa Institute called "Cultural Images in and of Africa" and was held in Helsingør in Denmark (Elsinore) in November 1996, in collaboration with the International People's College in Helsingør. Papers were presented by scholars based in four Nordic countries (Denmark, Norway, Finland, and Sweden), and in four African countries (the Republic of Congo, South Africa, Kenya, and Nigeria).

Despite the variety of approaches, themes and disciplines there were certain common topics:

1. Probing the assumptions about the relationship between the image and reality.
2. The vacillation between the romantic and the disdainful images of primitive Africa.
3. The genesis of images; the entering onto the historical stage of the hierarchical, disdainful images of primitive Africa as one case in point.
4. The historical context and uses of images.
5. The relationship between negative stereotypes and racism.

None of the papers addresses all of these questions, and many do not address them explicitly.

This book contains material, which is dominated by the historical and literary formulations of images. The intention was to bring out both images of Africa in Europe, and also images of Europe in Africa. However, not much attention is given to the images of Europe in the works produced by African scholars, but hopefully it will in the future.

Most of the papers reproduced in this book are concerned with the two basic approaches or proto-images of Africa: good or bad, true to life or undeveloped.

The papers represent an assemblage of varying academic disciplines and approaches, case studies with a narrow time frame, and more historical studies (Kirkegaard, Magubane, and Lindgren). Some are studies of the images constructed and projected by one single European (Winsnes). The arenas in which they move also span a wide field, from music (Brusila), missionary writing (Mellemsether, Skeie, Simola), development agency material and development aid workers (Løngreen and Wieslander), literature (Martin-Granel), commercial handicraft (Udegbe).

We are also honoured to be able to include two interviews with scholars who have made significant contributions to the debate, Terence Ranger and Valentin Y. Mudimbe, an article by Bernth Lindfors on a bizarre yet historically important cultural phenomenon, and a speech by Yvonne Vera given at the Images of Africa festival in Copenhagen in June 1996.

Images of Africa and the mass media

Let us begin, however, by discussing one topic which we do not cover in this book, generally perceived as synonymous with negative images of Africa, the mass media images. Notwithstanding the fact that there are also alternative images conveyed through responsible and professional journalists, most of the mainstream Africa coverage does promote negative stereotypes. They are characterised by:

1. Emphasis on the sensational.
2. Preference for catastrophes.
3. The use of simplistic notions of conflict causes, notably "tribalism".
4. Focus on the non-Africans as victims or as helpers.

There is a concomitant neglect of slow processes of development. The wide-ranging debate on the proposed New International Information Order (NIIO) in the 1970s was very much about this. The major Western news agencies were seen as the villains.

It is difficult to see, however, how news coverage could ever become development-oriented. Seeing the production and distribution of news in its historical context can help to explain why. International news was born to provide shareholders in Europe with news on conflict areas. Today, transmitting news about catastrophes is still one significant raison-d'être for news production. In addition to this, the newsmakers are competing for a mass market, and their product is hot news. Development-oriented news (whatever that is) must by necessity find other channels.

An anecdotal story can remind us of certain facts. A number of people on the streets of the Zimbabwean capital Harare were asked a few years ago what they associated with Europe. One woman exclaimed:

– Europe? It is awful! I have seen it on TV. I would never ever like to go there, there is only war and misery.

This little story is a healthy reminder of two misconceptions in the debate on images. Firstly, when we talk of images of Africa and the rest of the Third World we invariably think of the negative images of catastrophe, scandals and misery conveyed through the mass media—the story above helps to remind us that it is the normal task of mass media to give priority to drama. To understand how images are formed and changed we need to look at our channels and arenas of image formation. And they do exist.

Secondly, we are reminded of the fact that the sense of distorted images does not come from lies or false representations. The TV that the woman had seen had not lied, there were wars in Europe, but it is the selectivity which performs the trick of distortion, and a heavy dose of generalisation. We can easily identify the source of the Harare woman's information as reports from the wars in former Yugoslavia, possibly also Chechenya and Northern Ireland. While we cannot deny the existence of wars and misery, we hasten to add that this certainly is not all there is of Europe.

We need much more interesting mass media research on the images of Africa. There are many possible explanations for the weakness of mass media research on the news flows from and on Africa. Too often news studies are characterised by the following features:

1. They are highly empiricist, i.e. based on the notion of a simple definition of true as being 'true reflection'. This results in trivial definition of the factual and the true, and completely omits the question of relevance.
2. They are devoted to quantitative counting of units, and neglect meaning and interpretation.
3. They very seldom involve longitudinal studies, or any historical comparisons.
4. When qualitative contents analysis is involved it often entails counting 'negative' or 'positive' statements with little or no discussion on the underlying assumptions.
5. There are few attempts at explaining the causes of such structural patterns as are involved.
6. Mass media are often compared to each other, but hardly ever to an independent analysis of the period or theme in focus.

Window or mirror?

One could also discuss whether an 'image' is a simple reflection of 'reality', as if the image was formed by holding up a mirror in which reality is simply reflected. Although in the most naive understanding of 'objectivity' in the mass media this seems to be the accepted thinking, nobody at our seminar suggested this summary execution of all theories of knowledge.

At the conference a powerful imagery was offered by one of the participants. She drew a simple vertical line on the blackboard to focus the discussion on whether the images were a result of looking through a window, or gazing in a mirror. This goes to the heart of the matter: what is the relationship between the subject ('we'), the object ('them'), and reality?

If we look through a window when we look at each other, then the main questions will be what the window frame leaves out from the angle where we stand, i.e. selectivity in the formation of images.

If we consider the mirror parallel then we look into our own fears and dreams as factors to explain why we form this or that image of 'the other'. In the case of Africa, for example, many researchers have pointed out the contradictory co-existence of two images of Africa, both rooted in the conditions of Europeans rather than in knowledge about Africa: *the romantic Africa* and *the beastly Africa*. 'The noble savage' was the main image for the first, and today perhaps the imagery of Africa as the home of rhythm and dance which has inspired a bushfire movement of 'African dancing' among young people.

The Hobbesian idea of eternal warfare until a social contract was achieved at a certain stage of civilisation stands for the second imagery. This is today illustrated in the notion of tribal warfare lurking around every corner in Africa, a universal explanation for conflicts conveniently obliterating the need for seeking other causes of the conflict development, which could involve 'us' (arms trade and arms exports, protection for mineral resources, colonial traditions of state repression etc.).

Both the window and the mirror image of image formation are needed in the study of images. Excluding one approach leaves too many factors unexplained.

Fruitful as this simple simile was to our discussion the risk is that seeing the line as a window could feed the notion that an image in our mind is just like a picture, capturing reality within the limitations of the window frame and the time frame for registration. The limitation in this case would be parallel to the limitations of a snapshot: both would be 'true' representations of reality, only taken at one particular moment of time, and necessarily leaving out aspects which did not fit into the frame. This would be a misunderstanding of both the concept of image and the mental processes involved, i.e. the construction of knowledge.

Here one of the early writers on the formation of images can be of help. Kenneth Boulding in his philosophical treatise on images stresses that so much more than perception comes into it: "The image is built up as a result of all past experience of the possessor of the image."[1] In a way of reasoning which could place him among post-modernists three decades after his 1956 writing he dismisses the question of whether images are true or not, by saying that the development of images in a society is part of the culture or subculture in which they are developed. And science is just one among many subcultures, and cannot claim to give validity.[2]

Boulding suggests that we should see the images as "transcripts", records which in more or less permanent form are handed down from generation to generation.[3] Perhaps this concept would avoid the pitfalls of empiricism, a simplistic notion of how empirical data are mirrored in our minds. But the concept of 'image' seems to have come to stay.

Sources and maintainers of images

'Image' is one of the fashionable words in today's social science and public debate. It has been used in different ways, and indeed has no firmly accepted scientific definition. Daniel Boorstin[4] used the concept of 'image' in his critique of American society, where reality was not as important as the projected 'images'. He told of the guest who saw the newborn baby of his friend, and was told: Oh, wait until you see the picture. And he told of the now so familiar phenomenon where witnessing an event, such as a sports events, means

[1] Boulding, Kenneth, 1956, *The Image: Knowledge in life and society*, Ann Arbor: University of Michigan Press, p. 6.

[2] Ibid., p. 16.

[3] Ibid., p. 64.

[4] Boorstin, Daniel, 1961, *The image, or, What has happened to the American dream*, New York: Atheneum.

that you see much less than at home in front of the TV. Here 'image' very literally meant 'picture'.

'Image' research has become part of the public relations exercise of modern states, who now and then summarise the 'images' portrayed in the foreign press to gauge their popularity, and see which aspects give the most beneficial interest rating. Few governments are satisfied with the saying of the former Finnish President Urho Kekkonen who said 'no news is good news'.

'Image' has later become more or less synonymous with worldview, and ways of relating and reacting based on the worldview. In Peter Curtin's seminal work on Britain and Africa[5] this is what 'image' means. This is close to my usage of the concept. Among other things, it stresses the point that an understanding of image formation cannot be the superficial summaries of foreign ministries (good for their purposes perhaps), but must be based on an analysis of the historical evolvement of the relationship and its ideological manifestations.

To understand how images are formed, we thus have to study how relationships have developed and changed. Central to this is the study of power relationships. Images of 'the other' have a function in this relationship, but we should not fall into the deterministic trap of believing that the images are simply functions, simply mirrors of the current dominance and legitimacy need. Take for example, the question of racism and slavery. As *Bernth Lindfors* points out in his chapter, there is a strange paradox in the development of racism in England. Just as the abolitionists had won the day, and helped prohibit slavery using arguments on equality and universal human values, racist attitudes of superiority became popularised in the most vulgar ways, for example by touring shows exhibiting physically abnormal Bushmen (women) and 'Kaffirs' (Zulus).

There are other and similar paradoxes in the development of racism, often overlooked in popular thinking. As the Swedish writer Lasse Berg[6] points out, during the long centuries of the devastating and cruel trading in black slaves from the African continent the general attitude towards Africans was in fact quite positive. There were fantastic stories, it is true, about both humans and nature, but also a large degree of respect. At the time of the slave trade the Europeans were simply not superior to the Africans. The men and women taken as captives and sold as slaves were sold to the Europeans by African chiefs and warriors, and there was not then any European arms superiority. On the contrary, Europeans were constantly defeated by nature, especially in West Africa where malaria was a deadly barrier.

---

[5] Curtin, Philip, 1964, *The Image of Africa: British Ideas and Action, 1780–1850*. Madison: University of Wisconsin Press. Curtin claims that the images of Africa were formed during the period he studies, and remained in their essentials as British economic interventions had formed them.

[6] Berg, Lasse, 1997, *När Sverige upptäckte Afrika*, Stockholm: Rabén Prisma.

In the 19th century power relations changed. Berg perhaps overemphasises arms development, but it certainly gave the Europeans the technical means by which to start the partition of Africa. At the same time a racist doctrine was developed in Europe, which declared "other races" inferior, at the very time when the bondage of slavery was being abolished. In the relations between Europe and Africa racism became a legitimising ideology for colonialism, accompanied by the less doctrinaire paternalism.

Some of the papers in this book touch upon this paradox, and reason contrary to the accepted idea that racism was always in their luggage when Europeans stepped on African soil. Where did the idea come from? I can see two possible sources. One is a feeling of guilt over what Europeans have done to Africa, expressed all the more readily when all of Africa has been decolonised, and has a voice. The other is the influence of "afrocentrism" from North America. As Kwame Anthony Appiah has pointed out,[7] early Pan-Africanism in its opposition to colonial oppression in fact accepted the colonialist definition of Africans as a concept based on race. These early Pan-Africanists— Appiah analyses Alexander Crummel, W.E.B. Du Bois and Edward Blyden— even took over some of the colonial views of Africa as an uncivilised continent.

If the early Pan-Africanists wanted to "elevate" Africans to the level of the civilised Europeans, today's Afrocentrists just want to delete and replace some words in the colonial "transcript". Instead of a self-complacent European superiority we find an African-centred superiority, in moral terms if not based on power. In both cases the construction of "us" is based on a notion of a common 'race'.

It can be useful at this point to remind ourselves of the fact that what is wrong with racism is that it is based on false suppositions (the most fundamental being that one can distinguish between different races among human beings). What has been done in the name of racism is another matter. Appiah says that the sadistic slaughter of people during the Nazi era was a horrible crime. Yet the fact that it was committed as a result of racism does not make for moral superiority in the mass murders instigated by Stalin or Pol Pot, where other criteria than 'race' were used.

Annemette Kirkegaard's chapter goes into polemics with the Afrocentrist view that negative stereotypes and images have prevailed as long as Europe has had contacts with Africa. With Basil Davidson she questions the view, exemplified by Hrbek in the UNESCO General History of Africa, Vol. III, who wrote that Africa was identified by Europeans "with the arch-enemy of Christianity":

---

[7] Appiah, Kwame Anthony, 1992, *In My Father's House: Africa in the Philosophy of Culture,* New York & Oxford: Oxford University Press.

> It was already in those early medieval times, that European negative attitudes, prejudice and hostility towards people of black skin first emerged, attitudes which were later to be strengthened by the slave trade and slavery generally.

Her evidence shows something very different, an exchange between Europe, Africa and the Arab world without the characteristics of dominance and hostility. Her own addition to the debate is the part of her paper which deals with medieval music, and especially its Arab influence through Al-Andalus.

Selena Axelrod Winsnes looks at one of the early Danish writers on Africa. She takes the view that we should look for the genesis of images with enduring impact. A complex image as a result of the encounter emerges from her close reading of the trader Ludewig Rømer and his book on the Gold Coast published for the first time in 1760, at the height of Danish participation in the slave trade.

The imagery of light and darkness is there, but not taken to the extreme that Bishop Pontoppidan, who wrote the introduction, wants readers to believe. In fact, Winsnes also finds much curiosity and respect in Rømer's writings. There is a fundamental ambivalence—on the one hand the images of heathenism as darkness, and grotesque stories such as those of monkeys raping Negresses and on the other self-irony in descriptions of encounters and elaborate descriptions of local customs. It is out of this ambivalence that later times could select those stereotypes, which were useful in the nineteenth century as tools to implement both colonialism and missionary activity. But disdain and disrespect did not necessarily accompany the early trade.

Zine Magubane's paper is yet another reminder that racism is not an explain-all device in the analysis of negative images in the encounters between Africa and Europe. She writes on the images of the Khoi Khoi in the debates on labour supply in Cape Province. She points out that one must not mistake all negative stereotypes of Africans as being products of racism. The images of the Khoi Khoi and the stereotypes used about them were not only similar, but in her view, a variant of the images produced in Britain by the upper classes and the owners of capital towards the labourers.

When colonialism partitioned Africa and installed colonial rule, and at the same time racism rose to prominence as sanctioned ideology in Europe and North America, the ideological influence was pervasive. Edward Said has shown us that hardly any intellectual of the time was free from imperialism. He encourages us to look at the individual authors, as he has done with some classical British novelists.[8] Readers swallow their views on the empire with the main story of the book, regardless of whether the book was about the empire. *Yvonne Vera* examines not only what some of the icons of European literature, like Karen Blixen, did write on Africa, but also their silences.

---

[8] Said, Edward, 1994, *Culture and imperialism,* New York: Vintage Books.

In *Mai Palmberg's* chapter the travel writing from a voyage in 1914 by a Finnish journalist and humanist, Guss Mattsson, is analysed. The evidence is not clearly racist at all, but neither is it clearly non-racist, and even less explicitly anti-racist. Light and darkness are here not represented by Christianity and heathenism, but by culture and no culture. There is a hierarchy of European cultures, too, in the satirical portraits of the fellow passengers.

A disquieting question is whether humanism and racism can be reconciled, they at least seem to be mixed here. If by humanism we mean equal value or equality for all members of the human race, humanism and racism are a contradiction in terms—but history shows many examples of compromises with the definitions of membership to humanity. This history of compromise started with the grand document on equality, the US Constitution, which defined the freed slaves as not fully persons for voting purposes.

The intellectual history of colonialism also created what *Valentin Mudimbe* has called "a colonial library". This concept is used by *Björn Lindgren*, who writes on Representing the Past in the Present: Memory-Texts and Ndebele Identity. His objective is not to come to what is true in the very different versions of what happened when the Ndebele king Lobengula was overthrown by the British, but to show how different stories are constructed. The British version, which has generally won the day in written history, is based on and is part of "the colonial library". "History is both ideology and methodology", as Lindgren opens his paper.

Lindgren's study is one of merely two contributions here on an African formation of images. The other is that of *Bolarinwa Udegbe*, who has taken a close look at wooden handicrafts at some selling points in Lagos in Nigeria. She asks not only what Africa, but also what Africans? Men and women are portrayed in various kinds of work and dress, which convey different images to the would-be buyers. The images also feed on notions of the primitive, especially in the nakedness or near-nakedness of figures representing women (a view which, by the way, caused one of the most heated arguments at the seminar).

Two ways of saying primitive

At no time has there existed only one significant type of image of Africa in Europe. Two threads run through history, which both represent ways of saying that Africa is primitive, but with very different connotations.

In one sense of 'primitive' Africa is original, pure, and unspoilt. This is what Africa stands for among the "primitivist" European painters, perhaps the only cultural genre where 'primitive' is seen as an undisputable virtue.

In another sense of 'primitive' it stands for underdeveloped, not sufficiently sophisticated or learned.

Both these image types illustrate how images are formed as in a mirror. The two contrary views of the primitive correspond to views on European industrialisation. A negative view makes for dreaming about an unspoilt past. A positive view lends itself to a view of the world where "European civilisation" is highest on an assumed development ladder. Those societies are primitive which are low on the ladder.

Africa as a symbol for dynamic life unfettered by industrial civilisation and bourgeois manners has lived on in musical life, and can be seen today perhaps best in the subcultures of African dance in a variety of forms, that have been sweeping like a wave over the Western world.

This kind of primitivism is in focus in *Johannes Brusila's* paper, a primitivism where romantic ideas are mixed with condescension, not least in the reaction to the appreciation of African or Africa-inspired music.

He includes two instances of massive import of Africa-inspired music, jazz and world music. In the reception of jazz after the First World War, according to Brusila, the ideological aspects of the 'acculturation process' had from the start so little to do with the musical facts, that this clearly shows how the external meanings of music were created. The African and Afro-American music was seen as "a spontaneous, primitive force, and as something sexual, corporeal and ecstatic".

"World music" was born in a different milieu and the term itself coined by British music people in 1987 for music with a rather heterogeneous character. But again this is "the Western bourgeoisie looking for an 'Other'", something thrilling in their boredom. World music makes old images be reborn in new contexts, rather than changing the trend.

The missionaries and the double discourse

If anywhere, we would expect to find disdainful images of culture in Africa in the writings of the missionaries. A rich field of research can be found here, because missionaries spent a lot of time and effort writing reports, impressions and letters. There is often the possibility to study two levels, writings for public consumption, and correspondence.

The public writing of the missionaries could be expected to present the plight of the Africans and their deplorable primitiveness in stark colours, so as to encourage the congregations back home to support the work for the salvation of the Negroes. This poses the same kinds of questions as in the discussion on images used for emergency fund-raising, in a different setting and in the age preceding mass produced pictures. This debate was particularly intensive in the 1970s, following the development of the so-called "Biafra syndrome" of starving children. While appealing to pity and donors' generosity these pictures also appealed to an image of the non-Africans as the only possible source of help in the misery. African initiatives were ruled out *a priori*.

The missionary gaze is not as simple as one might expect. *Karina Hestad Skeie* studies two types of missionary material in the Norwegian Image of the Malagasy. The reports from the field in the Norwegian Missionary Magazine

1866–1895 constitute one category. A number of books by a missionary author, Johannes Einrem, constitute the other category.

She does not quite find that missionaries, as Comaroff says, functioned as "agent, scribe, and moral alibi" in the colonising project. Certainly, there is an imagery of how light conquers darkness. What is noteworthy is the fact that there are other images as well, which contradict those images. She forwards the thesis that there is another story altogether than that of European domination and superiority. This is a story of negotiation with give and take on both sides. Einrem, too, in his books gives a complex and many-sided account of the Malagasy people, and even a deep understanding of the religion and culture. She warns for a stereotype of the missionaries' images. There is no single one.

Hanna Mellemsether includes another dimension in her study on gendered images. Her study of what one Norwegian female missionary, Martha Sanne, wrote on the Zulus along with other missionary writing does not, however, show gender markers. The Christian notion of Christian brotherhood and equality transcends gender divisions.

There is an interesting difference between Sanne's public texts, and her private letters, where she talks about Africans and Zulus as being lazy, sly, untrustworthy, dirty, demanding, and ungrateful. In the public texts it is heathen culture which darkens the souls and hearts. With Sara Mills, Mellemsether assumes that her public texts are devoid of disdain because feminine discourse demanded women to be or appear to be caring and sympathetic.

Popular culture

Raisa Simola, however, sees no nuances in the very stereotypical and simplistic images of Namibians published in a booklet by the Finnish Missionary Society as late as 1993. This booklet is produced as a strip cartoon, and one might say that this genre compels its special features of simplification, contrast, and simple dramaturgy. Yet, it gives no answer to why the genre is chosen or accepted as a vehicle for communication, and why it is done like this.

Nicolas Martin-Granel also looks at popular culture, but of a secular kind. He examines some global best sellers, which mix a brew of all prejudices, with no second-thoughts. They are well written in their genre, and often best sellers. Africa is not really the subject but the place for the thrilling events. They are not read by many critical minds, and are misunderstood by some—I had seen one of the stories Martin-Granel tears apart as a film, and thought it was satire, whereas it appears to have been an uncritical reproduction of colonial images.

This is a paper on the darkest pits of Western ideas about the primitive, which is not only undeveloped, but close to the apes. His claim is that the Congo has always served as the source for terrifying darkness and impenetrable jungles, where man and monkey are roughly the same thing.

The developers

Another major group of image mediators remains to be mentioned, and deserves to be studied much more. The missionaries have created a constituency, but the developers have not. We can easily identify missionary thinking, but we often mistake developmentalism for common sense, and not ideology.

Hanne Løngreen has written a paper on Danida information material on development aid. She talks of a Development Gaze that is very similar to the Tourist Gaze. Both are directed towards features which are pre-modern and which separate them from Western ways of living. The difference is, she says, that unlike in the case of tourism there is an obvious power relationship between "Us Here" and "Them Out There".

Anna Wieslander has done what few others have embarked upon. She has carried out a number of interviews to find out how the counterparts and aid recipients see it all. More such studies are obviously needed, and one wonders whether we will soon be able to find records of notes, diaries, letters etc. of Africans involved in development cooperation to constitute the same kind of research material as the missionary archives.

Who are 'we' and 'they'?

Lastly, let us admit that the construction of the concept and delimitation of "we" in itself needs closer examination. In foreign ministry-sponsored studies "we" is simply defined in nationalist terms—the Swedes, the British, the Germans, the Norwegians etc. The nationals are cells in the organism, not all those who inhabit the territory, but all those who are citizens and "real" Germans etc. An analogy between an organism and a nation runs as a broad theme through European 19th and 20th century history.

How to relate to other 'cells' of different origin who happen to live in the territory defined by the nation has been an ongoing problem and object of debate. Assimilate, let live or chuck out are, colloquially speaking, the options. All of which presuppose that there is an easily defined "us" and "them" to begin with. Whether there is constitutes the dilemma in the whole notion of multi-cultural societies. For some the ability to define "us" and "them" is the cornerstone of multi-cultural societies ("we" must be kind and generous to "them"). For others the whole exercise of defining "us" and "them" is an inclusive-exclusive manner of thinking foreign to the basic ideas of "multi-cultural societies", which should be inclusive and non-hierarchical in their concept of cultures.

On the global scale the "spontaneous" identification of "us" and them" is often, as we have seen, based on ideas of race, whites against blacks. To some extent these and other constructed identities are "facts to be considered" because the constructions have been accepted. *Terence Ranger* and *Valentin Mudimbe* both take this stand while maintaining the importance of being critical in the analysis.

Two studies carried out by the undersigned on the image of Africa in Swedish schoolbooks in the 1980s and 1990s illustrate an identification of a Swedish "us" with the European colonisers of Africa. One could have expected that the Swedes would be taking the opportunity to distance themselves from the colonialist scramble for Africa that Sweden did not take part in.

The construction of "us" and "them" is itself a highly ideological exercise, and one that must be addressed in any intellectual endeavour to understand the images of the other. As the anthropologist Peter Rigby points out, "the other" is in fact seldom or never the white, European or North American male (one might add, heterosexual male) who is posited as the normal and normative creature. "The other" is those people whose peculiar differences from this normative creature need to be explained and come to terms with. As Patrick Brantlinger[9] asks, "how does it come about that [the terms race, class and gender] are perceived in the dominant culture [of the West] as relevant to minorities, instead of to majorities?"[10] When in fact "one obvious characteristic women share with both the working class and racial 'minorities' is that they are in actual fact a majority. Or how Michael Ondaatje describes the Indian sapper when he is in London as being "an anonymous member of another race, a part of the invisible world".[11]

Brantlinger wonders:

> How has the map of the world become so distorted in, for example, traditional humanities fields that questions of class, gender, and race seem marginal, "special" topics for seminars and graduate courses, perhaps, but not for the main agenda?[12]

The discussion on European images of Africa must continue for the simple reason that there is a constant reproduction of images and stereotypes, and also stereotypes about images. At the same time, along with *Terence Ranger*, we agree that the way Africans present themselves should be on the agenda now. In the research project on "Cultural Images in and of Africa" this is being done through the subtheme "Cultural Dynamics of Contemporary Africa", which examines African representations of Africa in its multitude of identities.

Mai Palmberg, Dalsbruk, Finland, June 2000

---

[9] Brantlinger, Patrick, 1990, *Crusoe's Footprints: Cultural Studies in Britain and America*, New York: Routledge.

[10] Quoted from Rigby, Peter, 1996, *African Images: Racism and the end of anthropology*, Oxford: Berg, p. 1.

[11] Ondaatje, Michael, 1992, *The English Patient*, London: Picador, p. 196.

[12] Brantlinger, loc. cit.

Questioning the Origins of the Negative Image of Africa in Medieval Europe

Annemette Kirkegaard

Thesis

In this paper I wish to explore as far as possible the influence of African peoples in the cultural history of the medieval world. I also hope to shed some light over the contribution of musicological research on the images of Africa as it must have appeared in medieval Europe.

My initial assumption[1] is that in the Middle Ages, i.e. roughly in the years from the Muslim invasion of the Iberian peninsular to the coming of the Renaissance, the African, Arab, and European—at least the Southern European —cultures are connected and that they to a very high degree constitute a common cultural area. Cultural areas can be defined by a common religion or by common cultural forms. In this paper the presence of Islam defines the cultural area whether the populations converted or not. In this way even parts of Christian Europe and the non-Muslim African region would be part of the hegemony of emerging Muslims.[2]

There are conflicts, unrests and upheavals and there are differences in viewpoints and powers, but generally within this common cultural area the image of the African or Arab was different from the post-renaissance attitudes which came to dominate for centuries. The notion of division by skin colour or ethnic origin—to use a contemporary phrase—was not yet present. Wealth, prestige, and good manners held higher priority in the social ranking.

This is for example visible if you look to the portraits in gothic and early renaissance art paintings. Here you will notice that the Black peoples are depicted loyally and truly without any trace of the racism, which later fuelled European attitudes towards people of other complexions and physiognomy.[3]

There are of course different angles on this issue. If you look at the view presented in the General History of Africa published by UNESCO in the 1980s you will see that the focus is directed towards establishing that European racism and ethnocentricity started early on in European civilization.

---

[1] This paper is part of a research project which came about by coincidence. I have been working with Muslim musical cultures in East Africa and European courtly song in the Middle Ages, and suddenly I realized that the two cultures were connected—both socially and in rather strict musical terms. The paper is in this way a provisional result of the research.

[2] Africa in this respect is primarily the parts in contact with the Arab or Muslim World. This is North Africa, the ancient Sudan and the coast of East Africa.

[3] See for instance the paintings of Paolo Uccello, Piero della Francesca or even Mathias Grünewald.

Because the authors interpret the penetration of Islam in North Africa and Southern Spain as a breaking up of a hitherto united cultural area around the Mediterranean into two culturally diverse zones—a European or Christian, and an Arabo-Berber or Muslim zone—they attribute hostility to the involved parties:

> ... it is not surprising, therefore, that Africa was identified [by Europeans] with the arch-enemy of Christianity and that its inhabitants, irrespective of their colour, were regarded and treated accordingly. Europe's lack of any direct contacts with Africa beyond the Muslim sphere was bound to lead to the emergence of a very distorted image of the continent, and especially of its black inhabitants. Some recent studies have clearly shown how both this ignorance and the presumed identification of black Africans with Muslims fashioned the European image of them as the personification of sin, evil and inferiority. It was already in those early medieval times, that European negative attitudes, prejudice and hostility towards people of black skin first emerged, attitudes which were later to be strengthened by the slave trade and slavery generally.[4]

If you on the other hand look to, for instance, the works of Basil Davidson who expresses an equally political view, the aim of the writing of history is clearly to describe an African past in which the skin colour and the ethnic origin were of lesser importance. This viewpoint is marketed under the catch-phrase of 'different but equal'.[5]

Davidson uses the evidence of interdisciplinary research in stating that the relationship between the two zones was marked by respect—even across the frontiers of the Crusades—and that the admiration on the part of the Europeans was historically founded in the indisputable superiority of the Arabs in all fields of life.

The statement presented in UNESCO's history in my view refers to a general historical image, which might cover attitudes of later historical phases, but which is not valid in relation to early medieval history.

I am in other words more in agreement with Basil Davidson and I shall in the following describe some selected features in the history of the area, and propose some musical facts, which contribute to the discussion of the European image of the Arabs and Africans. I shall rely on historical sources and musicological knowledge, and by a juxtaposition I hope to broaden our somewhat limited knowledge of early medieval culture.

---

[4] Hrbek, I., "Africa in the context of World History", in Hrbek, I. (ed.), *The UNESCO General History of Africa*, Vol III: Africa from the Seventh to the Eleventh Century. London 1992, pp. 9–10.

[5] See Davidson; *The Story of Africa*, London 1984, pp. 19ff and 46.

Islam and Europe in the middle ages

After the founding of Islam in 622 the Muslim expansion during the following 100 years took place at a very rapid pace. In 711 Muslim military forces crossed the Mediterranean at Gibraltar and progressed into the Iberian Peninsular to be stopped only by the height of the Pyrenees.

During the penetration of the Arab forces the only serious resistance was delivered by the Berbers of North Africa, but due to a combination of military force and political slyness the Berbers eventually converted to Islam and made a strong alliance with the Caliphate.

In fact, Tariq ibn Ziyad who led the Arab invasion army which in 711 crossed the narrow straits of Gibraltar (after the name djibal al-Tariq = tariq's mountain) was Berber by birth, but had converted to Islam. The main part of his relatively small army of between 5,000 and 7,000 warriors were also of Berber stock.[6]

The Muslims brought along the knowledge and skills of the Arab and Oriental worlds and their impact was vast. In all aspects of life they brought renewals and seemed in all fields superior to Christian Europe. I shall give a few examples.

First of all the urban character of the Muslim world and civilization was profoundly different from the social order of the Christian West which was dominated by the rural dynasties and the great migrations.[7]

The backbone of the urbanization of the Arabs was technological innovations such as irrigation, gardening, and building-construction, and architecture dominated by arches and a *horror vacui*, which resulted in a huge amount of ornamentations and decorations.

Another important influx from Islam to Europe was in the field of medicine. The Arabs brought along knowledge of plants and decoctions, which had previously been unknown to the Northern inhabitants. The plants were often brought from all around the 'known world'—i.e. from Asia or Africa. The Arabs also commanded astronomy—the knowledge of the stars—which was essential to the peoples who carried out the trans-Saharan trade and transportation.

The knowledge of algebra based on the so-called Arabic numerals[8] was transmitted to Spain by the Arabs and so was the crucial new technique of paper making, orginally invented in China, adopted by the Persians, and finally through the advent of Islam spread to Europe. This product was to

---

[6] Bæk Simonsen, Jørgen in von Folsach 1996, p. 218.
[7] Hrbek 1992, p. 2.
[8] The Arabs themselves called them Indian numerals, thereby acknowledging their origin. Hrbek 1992, p. 3.

have far-reaching consequences for the development of a civilization increasingly dependent on written documentation.[9]

The cultural influence of the Arabs is further more prominent in a long row of loan words, and if one acknowledges that the word normally follows the object this bears witness to an enormous exchange of products.[10]

Words like magazine, tariff, arsenal, syrup and alcohol all have Arab origin.

And finally influences also became clear in fashion, in games—predominantly chess[11]—and in music through the instruments, the scales and the social and aesthetic setting of the musical events, to which I shall return.

The Arabs had a long tradition of poetry and literature—for instance *Tales from the Thousand and One Nights*[12]—and perhaps most interesting to this thesis they brought with them a strong interest in history and discovery. Thus it is from Arab travellers, geographers, historians, and chroniclers that we have the first recordings in writing of the peoples south of the Sahara—the great empires visited by Arabs as early as the 10th century.

Another important group of chroniclers were the Jews. One of their contributions to world history is the so-called Geniza files. Geniza is a Jewish concept referring to a secret chamber in the Synagogue, where archives are kept. The Geniza files were found in Cairo and consist of almost 10,000 sources written in Hebrew but in Arab characters. These writings report minutely the trade routes within the different parts of the Arab World,[13] and they are the foremost source of our knowledge of the size of the trade in trans-Saharan goods. The files accurately mention numbers, prices and amounts of gold, ivory and slaves, and they cover the years between approximately 900 and 1492.[14]

Evaluating the impact of the Muslims it seems however likely that rather than being inventors and innovators, the Arabs worked as a kind of cultural brokers or middlemen attracting and accumulating knowledge, skills and fashions from all over the area they controlled. Therefore a discussion of the peoples in contact with the Arabs is appropriate.

---

[9] Hrbek 1992, p. 3.

[10] Frisch 1973.

[11] The game of chess originated in India, and was adopted by the Persians, who named it after their Shah, and was brought to Europe by the Arabs. The first depictions date from manuscripts from around 1200. Frisch 1973.

[12] Tales from the *Thousand and One Nights* are actually a collection of folktales within a given frame-story believed to originate in India. It is the most celebrated Arabian literature in Europe but with a much lower rating amongst the literates of the Orient. Stig T. Rasmussen in von Folsach 1996, p. 132.

[13] Davidson 1984.

[14] Bæk Simonsen, Jørgen in von Folsach 1996, p. 207.

The cultural and ethnic situation in Al-Andalus

After the rise of Islam and the conquest of the large areas around the Mediterranean the Muslim offensive stopped at the Pyrenees. The invaders found a loyal ally in the Jews who were fighting the Visigoth kings and rulers in order to avoid forced conversion to Christianity. The political situation stabilised, control over the Iberian Peninsular was eventually divided and the Muslim parts of it were named al-Andalus.

Al-Andalus, however, soon broke away from the rulers in Damascus and established an independent emirate—later to proclaim itself a Caliphate—in Cordoba.

During the times of the Umayyad caliphs in Islamic Spain from 756 to 929[15] the culture of al-Andalus flourished greatly, and due to its degree of urbanity it outshone the cultures of the surrounding Spanish dynasties.

Accordingly, the city of Cordoba became a centre of Muslim civilization and knowledge. Around the year 900 it had almost half a million citizens, 28 suburbs, 113,000 houses, and almost 3,000 mosques.[16] Cordoba also had several hundred public baths, the so-called *hammams*.

Literacy was strong in al-Andalus and in the 9th century Cordoba had no less that 37 libraries. Among them was a university library containing 400,000 volumes.

Who were the peoples benefiting from and contributing to this sophisticated culture? Generally it was a very mixed group of people, but the Berbers again, in particular, held a significant position. After the invasion of Tariq ibn Ziyad thousands of Berbers followed as soldiers. They reached as far as Southern France and after the decrease in the fighting they settled and married both Arab and Ibero-Roman women. They in fact became the Muslim Andalusians. It has been estimated that around 70 per cent of the population in Islamic Spain had Arab or Berber fathers.[17]

Throughout the 9th and the 10th century Muslim Spain was a uniquely tolerant society, where Jews, Christians and Muslims lived side by side and benefited from their meeting.[18] The Christian and Jewish peoples in Spain and North Africa were free to maintain full inner autonomy, i.e. their own cultural, legal and religious traditions. The price for this autonomy was the paying of taxes to the Muslim superiors.[19]

---

[15] Bæk Simonsen, Jørgen in von Folsach 1996, p. 219.

[16] Frisch 1973, p. 258.

[17] Hrbek 1992, p. 128.

[18] Bæk Simonsen, Jørgen in von Folsach 1996, pp. 219 and 342ff.

[19] Not all religions were treated equally generously. While Islam was generally very tolerant towards the other monotheistic religions—i.e. the Jews and the Christians—the polytheistic or pagan religions were met with harshness and reprisals if they resisted conversion. Bæk Simonsen, Jørgen in von Folsach 1996, pp. 219 and 241ff.

One of the outstanding results of the tolerant society in al-Andalus, however, was that the Europeans in this way became acquainted with the great works of antiquity. Many of these books were Arabic translations of antique and predominantly Greek works.[20] The books were made the objects of budding European curiosity and this is believed to be one of the major agents behind the so-called revival of the antique wisdoms and ideas—i.e. the Renaissance.[21]

When Spain was initially invaded it was, as already mentioned, a result of the joint forces of Arabs and Berbers, but for the first 300 years the rule was in effect in the hands of the Arabs.

A renewed struggle for power, however, started in the 11th century and as the Christian European powers gained still stronger grounds in Spain—finally resulting in the fall of Granada in 1492—the tolerance was gone. During the *reconquista* both Jews and Muslims fled the country; the Muslims to settle in North Africa and the Jews in present day Balkan.

After a shift of power from Arabs to Berbers around the 11th century the so-called Moors dominated the area. This term, which later was used derogatorily by the Europeans for all inhabitants of Muslim Spain, was in fact the name for the mixed population, who were descended from Berbers, Arab and Africans.

In the 12th and 13th centuries, the Muslim areas in Spain together with large areas in North Africa came to be controlled by Berber dynasties. With centres in the Moroccan cities the Berbers established themselves as rulers of the Western Muslim world.

The role of the Berbers was twofold. As their traditions were basically egalitarian they preferred the Muslim sects which were consistent with this structure. As a result the Berbers gave rise to the Almoravid religious movement and they had a strong influence in the proliferation of the Sufi brotherhoods.

The second important result of the political dominance of the Berbers was the fact that they brought Islam to Sub-Saharan Africa. All along the trading routes the religious and cultural ideas of Islam were gradually accepted by the commercial class and later at the court of the African rulers.

The large-scale trans-Saharan caravan traders of the Berber dynasties sold the majority of the goods from Africa to merchants and dealers in North Africa and Spain.

---

[20] Bæk Simonsen, Jørgen in von Folsach 1996, p. 342.
[21] Bæk Simonsen, Jørgen in von Folsach 1996, p. 219.

Africa

The area south of the Sahara was known to the Muslims, Berbers, and Arabs as Bilal al-Sudan. Hence the nominal confusion around the name of Sudan, which is today a nation-state not of the same geographical position. In those days it was a huge belt stretching from present day Senegal to the Niger Delta and Chad.

Islam had reached West Africa through the big caravans around the year 900. But the Sudan was never conquered by the Arabs or other Muslim peoples, and it never became part of the Caliphate. It was, however, exposed to Muslim culture through the commercial contacts,[22] and in the process a number of Africans converted.

Generally the African empires welcomed Islam. They were kind and obliging, but normally only the kings or rulers converted, while the common people stuck to their old religion. There was simply no stimulus to convert, since Islam in those early days was so very much a matter for the upper layers of society.[23]

What we know of the African World at this time in history was—as mentioned above—primarily brought down to us by Arab and Jewish writers, who travelled to the kingdoms of the Sub-Saharan empires.

And what they describe are some very strong links between Africa, Muslim Spain, and the rising European courts—the strongest perhaps being the gold trade which brought the mineral from the rich ores of the Sub-Saharan mines in ancient Ghana and later from the empire of Mali.

The importance of the gold to the rise of Europe cannot be underestimated. As the resources within Europe had already been drained by the end of antiquity, gold had to be brought in from other sources. It was due to the alliances between the Arabs and the Berbers, who possessed the knowledge and technique for crossing the Sahara, that gold was brought from the rich mines in Africa. From that time on the trade was counted in the African dinar and it had almost the same universality as the dollar has in the 20th century.[24]

From around the year 1100 the total world trade was based on the high-quality gold, which was shipped across the Sahara from the port of ancient Ghana to the northern port of Marakesh.

As it was the powerful African rulers who provided the gold for this important exchange, it seems highly unlikely that they were looked down upon. Quite to the contrary their ways and mores might have influenced and even impressed the rulers of Europe—as they certainly did the Arab travellers, who visited the locations. The following examples demonstrate how the visitors admired both the wealth and the traditions of the black African rulers.

[22] Hrbek 1992, p. 4.
[23] Simon 1983—with reference to Trimingham 1969.
[24] Hrbek 1992, p. 2.

In 1068 the Muslim historian and geographer al-Bakri of Cordoba wrote his 'Book of the Roads and Kingdoms'.[25] It is a geographical guide, but al-Bakri also found social aspects interesting.

Although he never set foot on African soil he collected an amazing material based on the works of other scholars and travellers, and his stories are studied intensely today. Among his contributions are some very unique observations from the kingdom of ancient Ghana, an empire rare in splendour and refinement.

> The king adorns himself like a woman [wearing necklaces] round his neck and [bracelets] on his forearms, and he puts on a high cap (*tartur*) decorated with gold and wrapped in a turban of fine cotton. He sits in audience or to hear grievances against officials in a domed pavilion around which stand ten horses covered with gold-embroidered materials. Behind the king stand ten pages holding shields and swords decorated with gold. ... At the door of the pavilion are dogs of excellent pedigree who hardly ever leave the place where the king is, guarding him. Round their necks they wear collars of gold and silver studded with a number of balls of the same material. The audience is announced by the beating of a drum they call *duba*, made from a long hollow log.[26]

The famous traveller Ibn Battuta of Morocco who in 1352 visited the Mali Empire tells another example. He lists what he approved and disapproved of amongst the people of Sudan in the following way:

> One of their good features is their lack of oppression. They are the farthest removed of people from it and their Sultan does not permit anyone to practice it. ... Another is their assiduity in prayer and their persistence in performing it in congregation and beating their children to make them perform it. ... Another of their good features is their dressing in fine white clothes on Friday.[27]

The music of the medieval world

Al-Andalus

While we know that Cordoba was the Spanish centre of Muslim knowledge, wisdom, and literacy, Sevilla, however, was the centre of Muslim instrumental knowledge, and it was here that instruments of the new kinds were constructed.

The influence is clearly demonstrated in the intensive use of Arab instruments throughout Europe from the early Middle Ages and onwards.

This concerns the use of violin (the rebec), the lute (the Arab Ud) and the drum called Naqqara (naker, a small kettledrum of clay or metal).

---

[25] Or 'Book of the Routes and Realms' as it is sometimes translated.
[26] Hopkins 1981, p. 80.
[27] Hopkins 1981, p. 298.

These instruments were to become the backbone of much European instrumentation and especially the violin—but also the guitar—came to be the quintessence of art and art music.

The Muslims not only brought with them the instruments, they also provided learned treaties on music, which were translated from the Arabic to Latin in Toledo—and later brought to the North.

The influence of these treatises should not be underestimated as they had taken over much Greek theory on music—a feature later to thoroughly affect European music theory. Thus the learned Al-Farabi—a 10th century philosopher who wrote extensively on music—is often mentioned in manuscripts from the 13th century.

Likewise the Arabs founded music conservatories, the first actually set up by the famous musician Ziryab who after controversies in the Baghdad court had fled to Spain in 822.[28]

The impact of the Muslim music schools was so radical that Christian Spanish courts in the 13th century often employed Muslim musicians[29] for their exquisite instrumental skill, which is clearly documented in contemporary miniatures and manuscripts.

Even the people of the church reluctantly enjoyed the 'minstrelsy of the Moors' for example at the pilgrim cathedral of Santiago de Compostela, where instruments supported the religious chanting and singing.

According to the rules regarding the legal position of music making[30] it is important to notice that folk-song was treated in a specific way within Islam. While there was a clear tendency to homogenize the strictly religious music i.e. the chanting of the Qur'an, on the other hand a relative liberalism ruled concerning the performing of local music such as domestic entertainment and social ceremonies. This could point to the fact that not only Arab music but also the musics of the Berbers and other black African peoples were brought to Spain.

We know very little about the music of medieval Africa. But it seems that the desert peoples who came to be specialists in nomadic life and cross-Saharan transportation and who controlled the ports, the Bedouins and the African peoples, gradually developed a singing tradition, which in many ways resembled that of the European courtly singers, the troubadours.

When Ibn Battuta in 1352 visited the Mali Empire—the heir after the demise of the empire of Ghana—he wrote of the singers and musicians, thereby at least giving a hint of the traditions surrounding courtly music:

---

[28] Trærup, Birthe in von Folsach 1996, p. 240.
[29] These musicians are generally in the manuscripts referred to as Moorish.
[30] A hierarchy of musical genres regulating the proper use of music within Islam. See al-Faruqi 1986/87 or Kirkegaard 1996.

Dūghā the interpreter comes with his four wives and his slave girls. ... A seat is set up for Dūghā and he sits on it and plays the instrument which is made of reed with little gourds under it, and sings poetry in which he praises the sultan and commemorates his expeditions and exploits and the women and slave girls sing with him and perform with bows.[31]

In another paragraph Ibn Battuta recounts how he saw poets—the Jalis or *griots*—reciting for the Sultan and how their leader after having finished the recital of the nation ascended to the Sultan and put his head in the Sultan's lap. Ibn Battuta was informed:

... that this act was already old before Islam, and they had continued with it.[32]

The important message here is of course that what Ibn Battuta witnessed were musical traditions claimed to be pre-Muslim.

Until now I have proposed several issues which could point to a common origin of the courtly manners in Muslim Spain and in Africa. I shall now address the possibility of the connection of this kind of music to European courtly song, and to some of the problems and controversies reigning in the field.

In the 1920s the musicologist Henry G. Farmer proposed a theory of Arabian influence on European music. It was generally acknowledged that the eastern tradition of chanting was related to the emergence of Western plain-song. It was however not agreed that eastern musics could also influence other musical forms.[33]

As there is—apart from Mozarabic chanting[34]—no musical evidence, i.e. no manuscripts of early Arab or Andalusian songs, most scholars in the 1950s and 60s rejected any kind of assumption which gave Arab—let alone African—music a role in the development of early European court music, which has traditionally been regarded as the cradle of Western art music. They found that the connection was accidental and based on speculation. That musical events and instruments which appeared in miniatures and paintings did not give any evidence of the sound, let alone style of the actual musics.[35]

---

[31] 'Dūghā' means interpreter, and is a dignified title. The instrument he plays is an ancient kind of the present day balafon. Ibn Battuta in Hopkins 1981, p. 293.

[32] Ibn Battuta in Hopkins 1981, p. 293.

[33] Burstyn 1990, p. 120.

[34] The Mozarabs were the resilient Christian Spaniards who during Arab/Muslim domination continued an independent liturgy.

[35] While I believe that it is true that the evidence of instrumental use and exchange can give a hint to a musical development, it is, however, equally true that it does not prove that music as such was brought with it. Many examples exist of how the instruments are tuned differently in the new culture and on a general scale brought to comply with the aesthetic values of the receiving culture. For the general critique see for instance works by the musicologists F. Gennrich and Gustave Reese from the 1940s.

The Spanish musicologist Julian Ribera, on the other hand, proposed a close relationship between the cultures: actually he advocated that Arab music was the source of European troubadour song. But he has been severely criticised, because his argument was based on the poetic verse, not on the music.

Ribera was particularly discussing the so-called *Cantigas de Santa Maria*, a codex dating from the second part of the 13th century. It is a collection of 413 songs devoted to the Virgin Mary, and their texts are likely to have been composed by the King of Castile, Alfonso X the Wise. The songs are composed in the courtly manner—inspired by the troubadours who side by side with musicians from the Arabian world, from Africa and from Muslim Spain—formed the highly diverse group of entertainers and performers at the court of Alfonso.

We know for instance that nine years after the death of Alfonso a source relates that the court of his son included 27 paid musicians. Of these 13 were of either Arab or Moorish ancestry: two were women and one Jewish. The musicians were apparently inherited from Alfonso.[36]

The codex includes 41 miniatures which show musicians of all three faiths and more than 44 different instruments of both Arab and Spanish origin.

On the basis of these miniature paintings it has been assumed that the *Cantigas de Santa Maria* are in fact now lost songs of the Moors. As there are no transcriptions of the music of the Moors it is unlikely ever to be proved either false or true.[37]

Nawba

Much of the controversy in the debate is founded in the fact that researchers have differed in the interpretation of the oral nature of both transmission and composition in all medieval musical culture, be it African, Arab or European.[38]

Generally researchers are today increasingly interested in evidence found in living musical traditions, which are likely to have had contact with historical —now extinct cultures.[39]

One such surviving musical genre is the North African *nawba*.[40] It is also of prime interest in the present discussion on musical exchange between the European, African, and Arab cultures. Originating in al-Andalus and being a product of the uniquely tolerant cultural society there, it is held to be the

---

[36] Sadie 1980, Spain and Mozarabic music.

[37] Sadie 1980, Spain.

[38] See Burstyn 1990.

[39] See for instance Jeffrey, Peter, *Re-envisioning past Musical Cultures. Ethnomusicology in the study of Gregorian Chant*, Chicago 1992, and the works of René Clemencic, for instance cover notes to the cd-set of 'Troubadours—Cantigas de Santa Maria' 1995.

[40] *Nawba* according to Sadie, 1980 is an Arab term for a suite of songs or pieces. (*Nawba* means 'turn'.)

ers and the handclaps of the audience or co-singers. If a song is just to be re-cited liberty reigns both in relation to tempo (rubato) and ornamentation.[44]

These rhythmical features have traces of African musical practices and can hardly be seen as unconnected. That the music of the troubadours is believed to have been performed in a unison—or even heterophone—manner might also indicate a common point of departure with Muslim musical culture.

The last issue which I want to raise is connected to the topic of the lyrics for the courtly singing. Beside the praises, the news-telling and the genealogy, the courtly singers—in Africa, Arabia, and Europe—also sang of love. One theme in this love-singing was the languishing for the loved one. The theme is said to originate with the Bedouins—for instance the Berbers—of the desert, and it addresses the fact that nomadic people are continuously departing. This separation can no doubt be seen as a parallel to the languishing which fol-lowed in the wake of the Crusades, which provided one of the main themes for early troubadour song.[45]

The Crusaders and their contact with Africa and the black world

The events of the Crusades which dominated European medieval societies from 1095 to the middle of the 13th century brought Europeans into close contact with Arabs and Africans in still another way.

First of all the Europeans on their way to the Holy Land found an enemy much stronger, wiser and civilized than they had imagined. They were im-pressed by the military powers and knowledge of the 'Barbarians'.

A direct influence of the musics of the Muslims is found in the military bands. The Muslims troops used a sound which was intended as a deterrent to the enemy. It was produced by the use of kettledrums and trumpets.[46] This feature was adopted by European bands and has made an impact in Western military music for some time.

Even though the Muslims were the prime enemies of the crusaders—the relationship was not all that biased. The Europeans were impressed by what they saw and the respect is even demonstrated in relation to one of the Arab heroes in the times of the Crusades. Saladin or Salah al-Din al-Ayyubi defeated King Richard the Lion Heart, who was by the way himself a famous trouvère singer,[47] and a renowned crusader. Saladin is therefore in the Islamic part of the world rightly remembered as the person who broke the Christian crusaders. Even so he is also in medieval Europe mentioned with awe and

---

[44] Sadie 1980.

[45] A famous example is the so-called Palestina-song by the German singer Walter von der Vogel-weide.

[46] Shiloah 1995, p. 79.

[47] Trouvère was the name for the courtly singers in northern France—as opposed to troubadour in Provence.

respect; he is thought to have been a noble warrior and a just ruler.[48] This bears witness to the fact that the impact of the Muslims went beyond the triviality of war and religion.

When Saladin defeated the Normans and expelled them from the Holy Land in 1187 he, however, also cut off a faithful ally of the Westerners.

The Aswan Dam today hides the ancient city of Faras, in which many frescos were found during the excavations. They depict the Ethiopian and Nubian Christians, who were partners of the European crusaders on equal terms with them.[49]

The partners are shown in the full armour of chivalry and they are believed to have had a powerful role in the European victories until defeated by Saladin.

Afterwards the Christians in Black Africa were left without contact with the Mother Church, and this is believed to be the direct background to the isolation, which as a side effect has preserved the cultural and musical elements of Coptic and Falashi religion almost intact to the present day.

However, before the disastrous break of the alliance the image of the noble partner in black Africa had made its mark in Western culture. In 1240 a statue of Saint Maurice in the church in Magdeburg was erected, and the figure for the first time appeared with full African features. The saint had always been known to come from Africa, but until that day he had always been depicted with white European features. The statue now showed an authentic black person and a new kind of reverence, it is a representation of an ally—a fellow crusader. The theme was repeated in many paintings and it is truly a representation of the African as 'different but equal'.[50]

Conclusion

So what can be conclude. Nothing is known for certain, except that the total denial of the connection between cultural expressions of Islam, Christianity, and the African World is false. As I have shown with cases from music, there are too many common features.

So in my view the splitting up of the Mediterranean in two cultural zones like the authors of the UNESCO history tell us actually happened later.

I favour the view that the European courts looked to the mixed—i.e. the Arab or African—cultures in southern Spain where poetry, musical skill and refinement reigned, and later to the successful warlords of the East for knowledge and inspiration.

---

[48] Bæk Simonsen, Jørgen in von Folsach 1996, p. 163.
[49] Davidson 1984, pp. 42–43.
[50] Davidson 1984, p. 46.

And I have come to agree with Basil Davidson that a community which in so many ways copied the material, emotional, philosophical, and musical ways of the ruling Arab or Berber could not have looked down upon him with the scorn and disdain which is the key element of the later view of the African in European history.

In my view the racism of Europe started exactly when it was needed, i.e. when the Portuguese began to colonize and conquer both the New World and the ancient lands of Africa. Until then it was neither practical nor necessary.

In this way a provisional conclusion might be that exactly the cultural features brought to the Europeans by Muslims of both Arab and African descent —the economic conquest of the gold and the knowledge of antiquity with the subsequent rise of the Renaissance—also brought about an image of 'the other' which for centuries to come ruined the relationship between the peoples of the Mediterranean.

References

al Faruqi, Lois Ibsen, 1986/87, "Music, Musicians and Muslim Law", *Asian Music*, 17, 1.

Brincker, Jens, Finn Gravesen, Carsten Hatting and Niels Krabbe, 1982, *Gyldendals musikhistorie*, Vol. 1. Copenhagen: Gyldendal.

Burstyn, Shai, 1990, "The 'Arabian Influence' Thesis Revisited", *Current Musicology*, Nos. 45–47.

Davidson, Basil, 1981, *A History of West Africa 1000–1800*, first published 1965. 4th edition. London: Longman.

—, 1984, *The Story of Africa*, London: Mitchell Beazley.

Davis, Ruth, 1996, "Arab-Andalusian Music in Tunisia", *Early Music*, August.

Frisch, Hartwig, 1973, *Europas kulturhistorie, bind 2: Fra Rom til Renæssancens Gennembrud*, 5th edition. Copenhagen: Politikens Forlag.

von Folsach, Kjeld, Torben Lundbæk and Peder Mortensen (eds), 1996, *Sultan, Shah og Stormogul. Den islamiske verdens historie og kultur*. Copenhagen: Nationalmuseet.

Hopkins J.F.P. and Nehemia Levitzion (eds), 1981, *Corpus of early Arabic Sources for West African History*, Cambridge: Cambridge University Press.

Hrbek, Ivan (ed.), 1992, *General history of Africa. 3: Africa from the seventh to the eleventh century*. London: Currey; Berkeley: University of California Press; Paris: UNESCO.

Irgens-Møller, Krister, 1989, "Jali-musikken hos Mandingoerne i Mali, Senegal og Gambia", *Den jyske historiker*, No. 49.

Kirkegaard, Annemette, 1996, *Taarab na Muziki wa densi. The popular musical culture in Zanzibar and Tanzania seen in relation to globalization and cultural change*. Unpublished Ph.D. thesis, Copenhagen University.

Pacholczyk, Josef, 1983, "The Relationship between the Nawba of Morocco and the Music of the Troubadours and Trouvères", *The World of Music*, Vol. XXV, No. 2.

Sadie, Stanley (ed.), 1980, *The New Grove Dictionary of Music and Musicians*, articles on Arab Music, Mali, Mozarabic music, Spain, and Troubadours.

Salmen, Walter, 1983, *Der Spielmann im Mittelalter*. Insbruck: Edition Helbling.

Shiloah, Amnon, 1991, "Round Table IV (15th Congress of the IMS): The meeting of Christian, Jewish, and Muslim musical cultures on the Iberian Peninsular (before 1492)", *Acta Musicologica*, Vol. LXII.

—, 1995, *Music in the World of Islam. A socio-cultural study*. Aldershot : Scolar Press.

Simon, Artur, 1983, "Islam und Musik in Afrika", in Simon, Artur (ed.), *Musik in Afrika*. Berlin: Museum für Völkerkunde, Reiter Drück.

Widdess, Richard, 1996, "Editorial", *Early Music*, August.

An Eye-Witness, Hearsay, Hands-On Report from the Gold Coast

Ludewig F. Rømer's *Tilforladelig Efterretning om Kysten Guinea*[1]

Selena Axelrod Winsnes

Our study of Images should deal not only with identifying and demonstrating their existence and spread, but with their origin and persistence. We should look for early appearances and, above all, reasons for their creation, and it is with that aspect I am concerned. The early sources not only reified the images of the African for their own time, but they were undoubtedly used by later generations to buttress concepts useful to European activity in Africa. The early sources were the 'primary sources'—they were, after all, based on personal experience.

I am writing here about a Danish primary source from the eighteenth century. The author was a merchant, a slave trader for Denmark–Norway, and his book has been much used since its publication in 1760. It was certainly an important source for the formation of opinion and belief about Africa and things African, not only for the eighteenth century reader in Denmark but even for an uncritical reader today.

Experience comes through the senses and can be discussed in those terms. A person who had actually lived and worked in Africa was considered a reliable, authoritative source, and what he saw, heard, and felt would undoubtedly have been accepted without question. Therein lies the trap. The writer placed his own interpretations on his experiences and I feel certain that few, if any, of his readers would have analysed or criticised those interpretations. Undoubtedly, in company with the pure reporting, the explanations, interpretations, and conclusions would have been given equal importance and acceptance. I have selected material which could be accepted as eye-witness reports; things told to the author by others based on their own eye-witness or hearsay reports; and the author's personal experiences in his close contacts with Africans—hands-on reports. My intention is to show how the received material and the author's own interpretations probably contributed to the construction of an African image in the minds of those readers. I shall also point out cases where, in my opinion, the author revealed his own attitudes indirectly, and inadvertently, by the things he did *not* write about or say.

---

[1] Ludewig F. Rømer, *Tilforladelig Efterretning om Kysten Guinea* [A Reliable Account about the Guinea Coast] published in Copenhagen in 1760.

My original intention was to present a survey of images taken from a number of the Danish primary sources, but it was soon evident that this would have resulted either in a book or simply a tiresome congeries. Thus, this paper will be concerned with the images as received from one book, that written by Ludewig Ferdinand Rømer, merchant, about his experience of West Africa during the period when the slave trade was at its height. There is a total of ten books by men employed by the various Danish Companies during the two centuries when Denmark–Norway was involved in the trade. I am concentrating on Rømer's book because he had the longest stay on the Coast—ten years—and he had the most intimate contact with the people there.

First, a brief historical background. Denmark–Norway [hereafter D–N] was involved in the triangular slave trade—Europe to West Africa to the West Indies and back to Europe—from the mid-seventeenth century to 1850. D–N was a late-comer to the trade but remained to become one of the three European nations that maintained establishments on the Gold Coast, from the seventeenth century and the beginning of the trans-Atlantic slave trade, until the nineteenth century and its abolition. The D–N headquarters, in the mid-seventeenth century, was Fort Fredriksborg at Amanful near Cape Coast. This fort was sold to the British in 1685 and the Danes moved to an earlier lodge at Osu, in Ga country, present-day Accra. Here they established Christiansborg Castle, which remained their headquarters until all their possessions were sold to the British in 1850. It is now the seat of government of the Republic of Ghana.

A number of the men who were stationed at these headquarters published books about their experiences in Africa.[2] These books were written apart from the official documents and reports the Company servants had sent home—the books were meant for public consumption, and it is in that light that we must consider them.[3]

One of these men was a merchant and trader, Ludewig Ferdinand Rømer, who lived on the Coast for ten years, a longer period than any of the others. I shall use excerpts from his book in the discussion of encounter images. Rømer wrote his book a number of years after he had returned to Copenhagen, and published it in 1760, ten years after he had left the Coast. He was then very well established with his own sugar refinery in Copenhagen. Now married and with a very large family (13 children in 15 years, of whom only 4 survived him), he published the book, based on notes and memory.

The material from Rømer's book shall be treated from the three aspects stated above: as an eye-witness report; as information gleaned from hearsay; as images created from day-to-day, personal contacts—a hands-on experience.

---

[2] See list of publications at the end of the article.

[3] Note that three of the books—those of Rask, Wulff, and Carstensen were published posthumously, using their diaries, notes, and letters, so the image of the author consistently writing with an eye to his public does not apply.

Throughout I try to view the material from the viewpoint of the European readership; its probable impact on the European imagination; and the images brought into being—images which were strikingly enduring, as well as useful for political and economic purposes. I have selected incidents and descriptions, which I felt best illustrated the building of images. I have also included excerpts which, in my opinion, reveal, indirectly, and probably unintentionally, attitudes on the part of the author that the reader may not have discovered.

Rømer's status is confirmed by the Introduction to the book by one of the leading literary/religious lights of his day, Bishop Erik Pontoppidan, and it is with this Introduction I shall start.[4] It is important to our purposes that we understand the standpoint of the expected readership of the book Rømer had written. Pontoppidan, writing the Introduction, establishes Rømer's status first, as "… this good man, who is now one of our most esteemed and excellent citizens". We are informed that we shall read about strange and singular things; about the wars of "barbaric nations"; about their "superstitions" and the already famous 'fetish worship'. He tells us that:

> … the disorder, the insecurity, and the coarse barbarism of these nations is one [sic] of the chief truths, which, along with many others, are presented in a perfect light in the following pages …, [which, in turn] … renewed that great truth that heathenism is indeed far more miserable than the absolutely worst degree of Christianity …[5]

Our good bishop has, of course, to confront the fact of the slave trade. Admitting that, from a moral point of view, it does seem to be in conflict with the spirit of Christianity, he does present two important points to justify it. The first is "… that the condition of the Guinea slaves in their own land, even including the bodily aspects, is so decidedly miserable that it can never be worse, more uncertain and inhuman; that they steal from one another; mistreat, even murder each other so that, as Mr. Rømer shows us, the Nation is nearly extinct, and the beautiful land will soon be quite deserted."[6]

The second point is this, that unless the Africans hear and see much that is disgraceful in the behaviour of the Christians, the latter can provide a role model in giving them a better understanding of God and his kingdom. Conversion to Christianity is the answer:

> … since even among the absolutely wildest and coarsest Negro slaves, who seem to have lost all humanity in their own land, there are to be found many examples of such honest and lasting conversion. [Once converted, the slaves] … neither lie,

---

[4] Erik Pontoppidan (1698–1764), a Lutheran minister, who, besides holding a number of important posts, such as Bishop of Bergen and Chancellor of the University of Copenhagen, also wrote treatises and books on subjects varying from theology to history and natural science.

[5] See Introduction b 7.

[6] Ibid. a 7. Even Pontoppidan did not read the book very carefully because Rømer states just the opposite on p. 115.

steal, rebel, nor do anything evil, but become their master's most capable and best workers.[7]

Pontoppidan, enjoying almost universal respect in D–N, has provided the model, giving us a perfect picture of the image he himself had derived from Rømer's book. The stage has been set, and the reader knows what to expect.

Rømer's reliable account

Rømer was in an excellent position to sell the book to a large [and credulous?] group of readers. But one does not have the impression that he was in desperate need of augmenting his income, as was the case with Monrad in 1822.[8] He was simply out to relate his experiences both as he saw them during his stay in Africa, but also through the new cultural window of a bourgeois citizen of Copenhagen.

What did he tell his readers? And how might they have reacted? Since Rømer was a trader and was at Christiansborg, voluntarily, in order to earn money, much of his material treats of aspects and details of trade, and his eagerness to inform the Company of ways to improve trade—basically by removing their monopoly and allowing private trade. But, since he was also a close friend of an important African priest and a number of other Africans, he was interested in all aspects of their lives; religion, culture, history are described and commented upon.[9]

Eye witness report

It is necessary to point out that the term 'eye witness' is not literally so at all times. I have found, in a number of instances, that when Rømer reports something that reads as if he had seen it himself, a check on dates shows that the incident(s) occurred before he had even arrived in the Gold Coast. But I shall handle the material as if it were an actual eye witness report, because that is the way the readers in Denmark and Germany would have encountered it, as they did not have access to the dates, or were not interested in a close analysis.

Reports on religion

We shall treat of religion first because this was the great concern of the Europeans who wrote about Guinea. Rømer did in fact witness religious ceremonies, such as the Ga annual Homowo,[10] a number of times. He took guests to

---

[7] Ibid. b 1.

[8] See list of sources section 8.

[9] All parentheses marked with ( ) are from Rømer's text; editorial comments are marked with [ ]. I have substituted modern orthography for the proper names in the text.

[10] This is the 'New Year' festival celebrated by the Ga people in August–September; a time of purification, of righting wrongs, of preparation and prayer for an auspicious year to come.

see it, too. In his descriptions it is important to note his choice of terms, especially adjectives: the ceremonies are 'peculiar, queer'; the dances are 'capers'; the dancing in front of the most sacred drum are 'sacred capers'; the movements of the devotees are 'particularly ridiculous gestures'.[11] Rømer tells of his friend, Chief Priest Kpoti, whom Rømer sees in his private shrine where:

> ... he sat for an hour among these knick-knacks and rummaged among them. One cannot count all the bric-a-brac they have there [in the 'fetish' hut].[12]

It is with mild amusement he tells of a particular stone, which Kpoti toys with while they speak. Kpoti tells him that he had found the stone at a propitious moment and since then always kept it in his hand when he was involved in a serious case, etc. Rømer was not the kind of person who could, or would, make comparisons with habits among Europeans that were comparable to what he found in Africa.

To his credit, Rømer includes a detailed description of Anansi the Spider, of the stories and performances of this corpus of oral literature which were, and are, an important part of life among the people in the Gold Coast. Other writers had ignored or ridiculed this. He had evidently seen performances in the evenings of some of the many tales, which were stories with a moral, stories in which Anansi, the trickster, usually outwitted himself. As such they were important in child-rearing, as well as first-rate entertainment. Rømer admires the theatrical ability of the storyteller, but cannot refrain from moralising. In speaking of the performances, which were in the evening, he says of the people "... they have nothing to do but sleep during the day and gather together in the moonlight ...". He knew perfectly well that the people worked during the day—during the cooler hours of the morning, late afternoon, and evening, and that rest in the heat of midday was practically *de rigeur*. Unfortunately, it is just such sweeping statements that were picked up by the readers, reinforcing the stereotype of laziness.

On wars

Rømer tells of a war between two kings at Cape Mount. He hears, with amusement, that the cause of the war was a conflict over which king had the greater right to rule, and that the war was considered bloody by the participants because a total of eight people had been killed.[13] Why the mocking tone in a man from a Europe recently recovering from the all-encompassing War of the Spanish Succession and the Great Nordic War?[14] Was it to show the Afri-

---

[11] pp. 63–67.
[12] p. 68.
[13] pp. 13–14.
[14] The War of the Spanish Succession (1702–13) involved all of Europe in a struggle for power in Europe, supremacy on the seas, and control of American territories. The Great Nordic War

cans as less advanced, less able to mount a proper war? The rival kings came to an amicable agreement and all was well. Did it strike the reader that these people were remarkably peaceable? Rømer went on to describe the joy with which one of the kings purchased a grenadier's hat and an officer's [lace?] collar and gave it to his daughter. She put them on and the father declared that she was now more beautiful than before.[15] Again we sense Rømer's mild mockery—from a man whose compatriots in Europe wore powdered wigs, and whose women would soon arrange hair styles requiring door openings to be built higher to enable them to go through them.

We are told that a particular king of Akyem stopped stealing and killing people and changed his tactics. "He no longer sent his people out to catch slaves, but sent people with gold to buy them in Crepe."[16] Thus, since the Akyem *purchased* slaves for re-sale:

> ... we Europeans at Accra could, to a degree, be called tradesmen, and we could, with quite good conscience, carry out our commission, when, in earlier times, we had been called 'fences', and accomplices to murder and robbery.[17]

Here is a prime example of rationalisation. And the European readers might have nodded in approval. But Rømer's unease is implicit.

Rømer spends some time decrying what he sees as the Africans' restlessness, that they cannot live in peace and security but carry on with altercations and clashes between factions vying for power. Never does he turn around to look at European conflicts for the same reasons. Did his readers ask: "Wherein lies the difference?" Some may have, certainly, but most, I fear, would read with the distinct feeling of 'the other'—always doing things incorrectly or badly. Rømer goes on to prophesy what the political/military situation in Gold Coast would be in future. The Asante would eventually grow to be all-powerful; the Fante and Akyem would not be able to withstand them;[18] wars will result; and:

> When this happens there will be delightful times on the Coast for 6 months, and longer, since one can expect to buy a slave for a bottle of brandy, as in the year 1733, the time when the Akwamus were beaten.[19]

(1700–09) was that in which Peter the Great of Russia in his western thrust, defeated Sweden at the Battle of Poltava.

[15] p. 15.

[16] p. 169.

[17] Ibid.

[18] The Asante are a people living in the forest region of Gold Coast/Ghana; the Fante are a coastal people based west of Accra; the Akyem are an inland people living north of Accra. Although all three belong to the same larger ethnic group, the Akan, they were in constant conflict, with varying coalitions, in the eighteenth century. The wish to control coastal trade was an important component in these conflicts.

[19] p. 237.

There we have it in a nutshell: war among the Africans is deplorable—and exceedingly profitable for the Europeans. And this is what it was all about. Profit was their sole reason for being there.

The Christian work ethic

"I feel that God must first change the Blacks' nature before one can bring them to an understanding and worship of God."[20] He proposes the establishment of a school for children from the age of seven. The school would be located on an island in the Volta River where the children, isolated from their parents, would stay until grown. There they would not only be taught Christianity but "... they must also learn to work ... since if they do not become accustomed to work they will soon begin to live in the manner of their forefathers again, which can in no way exist alongside Christianity."[21] Here we have the Christian work ethic, which the Europeans felt they must instil in the Africans. The Africans are lazy; they sleep all day and play at night; they only cultivate a small portion of land and leave the rest fallow; they are not rushing to learn the Christian religion. In other words, they are not like us—in fact they are the exact opposite. Yet, in the following paragraph Rømer warns that newcomers should learn to understand the nature of the people, otherwise "... they will measure everything according to European *Alen*, which will truly fall short."[22] Isn't this exactly what our excellent merchant is doing?

Colourful and exaggerated reports

Finally, I shall relate a couple of examples of his play to the gallery. The lurid account was expected and the readers must not be disappointed. Pointed teeth, whether naturally so, or filed, always aroused comment, usually with the assurance that the owner was a cannibal. Rømer wrote of such people as having:

> ... wild nature, a physiognomy like a tiger, and with comparable teeth in their mouths. We have had them among other slaves, and they have sneaked up to one and bitten a large piece of meat from his arm or thigh, and have eaten it quite greedily.[23]

Conceivably, if a man is bound hand and foot and wishes to escape, or defend himself, using his teeth is perfectly logical. As for his making a light lunch of his neighbour, I feel safe in placing this claim among other equally bizarre statements, which we find in Rømer.

---

[20] p. 326.
[21] p. 327.
[22] The *alen* is an old linear measure equalling 63 cm.
[23] p. 21.

Another tabloid type of report is that of the French ship captains tearing small children and babies out of their mothers' arms and throwing them on the beach to be eaten by wild animals.[24] Rømer's intention was to besmirch the reputation of the French at every opportunity because they were such successful competitors, and in so doing he managed to contradict himself later by stating that "… they buy anything black."[25] In fact, the French did not refuse to take children along with their mothers, and during the time Rømer was in Africa fully one-quarter of the French slave cargoes consisted of children.[26]

Hearsay report

'Hearsay' is also a slightly ambiguous term here. It could be material that went the rounds on the Coast—claims, fantasies, assertions, gossip—or it could be material lifted from earlier written sources, because most of these writers had read works of their predecessors on the Coast. I have had problems about the placement of the material I am presenting, because lines cannot be finely drawn between 'eye-witness' and 'hearsay'. The text is rarely clear about sources of information, apart from the direct reception of Ga historical material. I hope, then, that this will not distract from the main line I am trying to draw.

An early instance of hearsay is admittedly so. Rømer retells what 'an Englishman' told him about Benin. Benin is described in all its former glory and wealth:

> Iron was for them much more rare than gold, and when they could not get iron they had to smith gold in order to have hoes and cutting knives …[27]

This is one of Rømer's more baroque statements, and one wonders how many of his readers would have taken issue, aware, as most of them should have been, that gold is far too soft a metal for such use.

Still writing about what he calls 'the Benin period':

> … none of them had any need to steal foodstuffs from any other because the one in need was given, at his request, as much as he wanted. The Negroes still hold to this [system].[28]

Rømer, as did other authors, credits the Africans with sharing amongst themselves. There were positive reports, too.

---

[24] p. 240.

[25] p. 319.

[26] See David Geggus, "Sex ratio, age and ethnicity in the Atlantic slave trade", *Journal of African History*, 30 (1989) 23–44.

[27] p. 115.

[28] Ibid.

We are told that land was easy for the European to acquire for a very low payment—a pot of brandy, and the African leaves it to work in another place. This was a frequent assumption among Europeans, and the cause of much argument as to which of them held the right of ownership. In fact, none of them really did because what was 'sold' was the usufruct. Ownership of the land was always in the hands of the Africans.

One particular area on the Guinea Coast [western Côte d'Ivoire] was called the 'Coast of the Bad People' [*Malos Gentes*] and the neighbouring section [eastern Côte d'Ivoire] was the 'Coast of the Good People' [*Bonos Gentes*]. These terms were accepted as proper, being found on the seventeenth century maps and even earlier. The Bad People were said to be cannibals, but the trade with their people was unusually good, particularly for ivory, so all the ships stopped in the roads outside that area. Notably, no one actually went ashore; they only saw the traders who came out to the ships, and proof of cannibalism could never be shown. It is conceivable that the terminology was propaganda to ward off competitors. And it makes a good story.

In writing of their being plagued by mosquitoes, particularly around the Volta delta, Rømer tells us:

> These vermin are worse at night than in the daytime, and all the city people, grown and small, go outside of their towns to the seashore, and bury themselves in the sand, leaving no more than a bit of their faces uncovered.[29]

This is incredible, bordering on the ridiculous. Surely the Africans used the smoke of their fires to ward off insects; and they had concoctions with which to anoint themselves to protect them against bites, at least to a degree.[30] But a universal exodus every night is wild beyond imagining. However, Rømer's readers could have swallowed it whole.

There is a long and interesting dialogue, quoted in its entirety, between Noy, the Danish ambassador to Asante, and Opoku Ware I, the great king of the Asante. The King is purported to have boasted greatly of his wealth and power over the entire world, and Noy replies obsequiously, bowing and scraping throughout the ordeal, while hating and fearing the King. The King is made to appear absolutely ridiculous.[31] A close look at this section reveals several stages of filtering: the King speaking to Noy in Twi, the language of the Asante, while Noy's own language was Ga; the speech was being delivered through an interpreter; Noy repeated it to the Danes in Portuguese; Rømer

---

[29] p. 289.

[30] Such concoctions and medications are described in books on plants in West Africa. See F.R. Irvine, *Woody, Plants of Ghana*, Oxford 1961; Daniel K. Abbiw, *Useful Plants of Ghana*, Kew 1990.

[31] pp. 194–97. Actually it was not the rodomontade Rømer tried to make it seem. The entire dialogue followed an established pattern of sumptuousness always used in discourse with the King of Asante.

wrote it down in Danish for the amusement of his readers in Copenhagen. Did anyone stop to wonder what could have been left of the original conversation?[32] In one place he writes:

> At Fredensborg [the fort at Old Ningo] I have often heard that the fetish's message has not been anything other than these words, 'Be obedient to your Whites. Do what the Whites tell you to do.' One can well imagine how welcome such an oracle is for us Europeans, who at all times suffer mischief from malicious and stupid Negroes, especially in that place.[33]

Subsequently he frequently gave brandy to the priestess so she could continue her possession and exhortation. Were the Africans 'stupid', or were they playing the situation for all it was worth?

As did all the other authors of books from West Africa, Rømer described natural phenomena: weather, climate, insects, plants, fish, birds, and animals. He goes into a long description of the 'monkey society', where I think he must have meant larger primates, like chimpanzees or mandrills. At the end of his description he makes the bold statement: "One has often had examples of monkeys having raped a Negress."[34] This claim was well entrenched in the mythology Europeans constructed on the Coast. It was oft repeated, even depicted pictorially.[35] Not until Isert came on the scene in 1788 was it challenged in the Danish sources.[36] The writers could feel fairly free to let their imaginations run wild in telling tales to audiences back home. There was often, in their behaviour as well, an attitude of 'anything goes'. The phrase they used was 'Heaven is high, and Europe is far away.'

Hands-on report

'Hands-on' is to be treated here in the figurative sense of close personal contact. The literal, physical sense was, of course, very much a part of the picture during the slave trade. Slaves were very carefully examined to discover imperfections that would result in fixed discounts on the sale price. That is another story—a tale of tragedy.

---

[32] Subsequently, my own translation, into English, forces the conversation through yet another linguistic filter.

[33] p. 73.

[34] p. 343.

[35] See J.N. Pieterse, *White on Black*, Yale University Press, 1992, p. 38.

[36] See P.E. Isert, *Letters on West Africa and the Slave Trade*, Oxford University Press 1992, p. 121. Isert vehemently refuted this kind of myth, theorising that the dark skin came from exposure to the sun, and that in intelligence the Africans were, if not better than, at least equal to, the Europeans.

Friendship and respect

Rømer's ten years on the Gold Coast, and his own personality, as I interpret it, brought him close personal contacts among the Africans. Not only were there peer relationships—a trader among traders—but there were real friendships and mutual respect. Chief among these friendships was that which Rømer enjoyed with Kpoti, the Chief Priest and leading personage among the people of Labadi. Kpoti was his informer on all matters, were they religion, custom, or history. And it is in Rømer's recording of the information thus gleaned that we can glimpse what I see as his ambivalence. Expected as he was to ridicule the 'heathen' religion and practices in general, he still had doubts, precisely due to his respect for Kpoti. Kpoti is represented as dignified, intelligent, never obsequious, and always honest. And the respect and trust appeared to be mutual. Note the following situation:

"Kpoti has told me something which he swears is true, that no secular Negro knows ...", which was a tale of a time during a certain war when it was necessary to hide the Labadi 'fetish' before fleeing from the enemy. Those who had hidden it, secretly, died before the people could return home at the end of the war, but two other priests found the 'fetish' while in a state of spirit possession. Rømer's reports this seriously, with no comment nor aspersions, but acceptance.[37]

Rømer tells his readers that the Africans believed in a supreme spirit, Dzemawong, but it was with the intermediate spirits that the people were most concerned:

> All the Blacks are agreed on there being creatures (spirits) who are between God and man (according to what Kpoti claims) who were created during the time God created the first people, and that they were created for the purpose of teaching the people to live piously and virtuously, and who also, with God's permission, tell them what good and evil are in store for them.[38]

Where are Pontoppidan's 'barbaric heathens'?

It was not only Kpoti who was represented as a man of dignity. "Out there I once offended our broker Adoui."[39] Rømer had just written that the people did not like to speak of death, which, to them, was evil. Adoui had become ill and asked for a drink of brandy. Rømer, ready to serve him, asked him, clumsily, who would succeed him in service after his death. "He became quite upset at this, stood up and answered, 'God has sent me to the world with many years on my head. Do you think that I am like the Whites, who come and go?[40] But, since you wish to know, don't you know my brother Atte?' He did

---

[37] pp. 91–92.

[38] p. 58. The parentheses are Rømer's.

[39] p. 102.

[40] The Europeans experienced an extremely high mortality in West Africa.

not wait for his brandy but went his way." End of statement, no further comment, neither on brandy nor death. I read respect into this presentation, and perhaps some chagrin on Rømer's part.

In the following case Rømer showed his understanding of the feelings of the people. A French priest[41] claimed to have destroyed 'fetishes' at a shrine and have given the people small crosses instead. Rømer's comment was that:

> ... it is certain that if the above-mentioned good Father had treated a Negro's fetish thus, he would undoubtedly have got a bloodied head, and the Father would then have become wiser.[42]

He also wrote:

> We shall have been a long time on the Coast before a Black will give an answer to our questions about his religion. Furthermore, we shall, in fact, have been there for several years without anyone having seen us laugh at their ceremonies, or, when they have answered our questions, without a European having ridiculed them. If we do that, and say 'It is nonsense, etc.', they then answer, 'That may well be, believe what you will', and even laugh with us.[43]

Would the European readers have recognised an inherent respect here?

A sardonic European

There are, certainly, and frequently, cases of the back-of-the hand. Rømer tells of Kpoti that he was all of eighty years old and "... has spent his entire lifetime in this study (if one can call it that)."[44] There was irony, there was derision. This is not surprising, given Rømer's Copenhagen frame of reference during the writing. But I feel that it is in his omissions that we find a dimension worth examining. Several have been noted above. It is when we expect a derogatory comment—having been so directed in the Introduction—and it is absent, that we sense Rømer's ambivalence. I shall give a final example of the hands-on aspect, to be found in the following description of miscegenation.

Mixed marriage

Rømer, having described the marriage customs among the Africans, goes on to mixed marriage.[45] He goes into detail on the pros and cons, the "good and evil of these marriages". The good is seen in the concern the African wife

---

[41] Probably Villault de Bellefond himself. See Villault, *Relation des Costes d'Afrique, Appellées Guinée*, Paris 1669, pp. 269–75.
[42] pp. 3–4.
[43] p. 50.
[44] p. 99.
[45] pp. 245–46.

would have for her husband's health, since the death of a young person would be seen as unnatural and the result of witchcraft; she would be held responsible. [One can imagine how important this 'insurance' would be to Europeans seeing their compatriots sickening and dying in great numbers.] The African wife would be able to purchase foodstuffs more cheaply—a great advantage, considering the meagre salaries of the soldiers and employees of the Company. The evil is concentrated on the dilemma of the African woman in the event she is unfaithful to her European husband, particularly with an African man, knowing that "… if she brings a black child into the world the European will sell her and her lover, if her parents do not ransom her."[46] Rømer informs us that Bishop Worm of Copenhagen had decreed that all the Danes at Christiansborg "… are allowed to take to themselves a black woman, yet NB [*nota bene*] not more than one …", on two conditions: that she be converted to Christianity; and that she be taken with her husband back to Denmark, if she wished to go. "On these conditions each one of our nation has his mistress."[47] No further comment on this. Rømer does not except himself. The omission is telling.[48] However, the report does include two aspects, which are inherent in the entire matter: *Firstly*, the Europeans were seriously plagued by melancholia and homesickness—symptoms which were certainly ameliorated by marriage on the Coast; and, *secondly*, quite simply, they fell in love, established families, and had children whom they loved.[49] Rømer may have felt constrained to soft-pedal this information, his new situation being what it was, so he adds that, if the European is wealthy, the African wife would take care to use her time to cheat him of his money, which she indeed does adequately.[50]

African encounters with Europeans

It would be interesting to speculate on the African reaction to the Europeans. They saw the Europeans as they traded; as they feasted—and drank too much; as they competed for trade using fair means and foul; as they fought with each other; as they sickened and died. And trade was the leitmotif for both Africans and Europeans. It would be naïve to think that the Africans did not use every means at their disposal to come out ahead in trade. But the Europeans, inquisitive about African life, were also often impudent and rude. So Africans probably learned to keep a certain distance between themselves and the newcomers.

---

[46] p. 247.
[47] Ibid.
[48] See Nørregård, Georg, *Danish Settlements in West Africa 1658–1850*, Boston University Press 1966, p. 106 for an unsubstantiated claim that Rømer was married to an Akwamu princess.
[49] p. 334.
[50] Ibid.

When a woman was possessed "... the Blacks, when they can, immediately form a circle around the old crone, and do not allow any European to enter it, out of fear that he will mock both the fetish and her."[51] When Rømer asked his friend Kpoti why there were such widely divergent ideas about life after death among the people Rømer had questioned on the subject, Kpoti answered, "Sir! I have never been dead and come back to life, so that I can debate with such certainty about the other life, as did your holy man [during] the time he was here."[52] Rømer made no rejoinder. Was Kpoti being ironic?

African leaders often acted as mediators between the Europeans when the latter were locked in conflict. The Akwamu King offered to mediate once, but even after "... he had taken bribes from both sides, there was still not achieved any compromise between us and the Dutch."[53] In another instance, the Fante 'fetish' is reported as saying "You shall not follow the example of the Blanke (Europeans) since although they have God's pure word before them, as you (the Blacks) do not, so are they damned after their death because of their evil ways."[54] Strangely, the 'fetish' is speaking in suspiciously Christian terms, but Rømer's informer was a mulatto, born on the Gold Coast, and educated to the ministry in Denmark. Was he, perhaps, seizing the opportunity to make his own statement?

Rømer tells of two high Dutch officials having a fight, throwing things at each other, and all the servants came to see this battle "... which was not edifying." He was concerned that the misbehaviour of the Europeans would debase them in the eyes of the Africans, and Rømer evidently cared what the Africans thought. Rømer concludes his book by stating that "... we all ... believe that God blesses what we have earned with good conscience, and that God lays his curse on what we have brought about to the ruin and destruction of other people."[55]

Rømer's images

Rømer was not out to create images. His purpose was twofold. The first was to show trade practices and convince the government to give up its monopoly and allow private trade. The second, the one that concerns us here, was to share his experiences with the readers in a lively and colourful manner. He chose dramatic, sensational incidents and practices that would make a good read, but his choice was largely based upon what he knew his readers (such as Pontoppidan) already believed. And he 'improved' his tales by using poetic licence freely. There were indeed few people who could, or would, argue with

[51] p. 73.
[52] p. 105. Reference is to the Danish Chaplain Elias Swane.
[53] p. 148.
[54] p. 61.
[55] p. 348.

him. Moreover, in contradistinction to most of the earlier writers, he *liked* Africa; he *cared about* his friends; he *respected* a number of individuals; he *enjoyed* his work there and found it challenging. As I read him, his personal feelings constantly forced their way to the surface. It is in his omissions, as I have pointed out above, that these positive attitudes are revealed.

Conclusion

The usual stereotypes of Africans, by mid-eighteenth century, had become part of the mental baggage of the Europeans who went to Africa to work; who wrote books in which they reinforced the stereotypes; whose readers comfortably recognised the stereotypes. The Africans were lazy, thieving, inhuman [less than human?]. They were heathens whose religion and all its accoutrements were simply 'fetish'. As the European saw it, the slave-trade was providential by giving the slaves the opportunity of converting to Christianity, thus saving them from the horrors of their lives in Africa; all the while providing sugar and profits. But it is important to look carefully at this book by Rømer, and to read the other dimension. He knew the people, as people, and as equals in friendship and business. He was certainly troubled by what he was doing; but he could do no more than vacillate between what he knew and felt, and what was expected of him.

Nonetheless, the stereotypes won the day for staying power, and they were useful in the nineteenth century as tools to implement both colonialism and missionary activity. We still stumble over them today.

Danish published sources

NB: Take note of dates of stay and dates of publication. A long hiatus may affect the reliability of the material.

1. Hans Jacob Zur Eich. 1659–69. The book was written in German, no title given in Jones. He worked for the Glückstadt (Danish) Company for ten years as a locksmith, and witnessed the establishment of Frederiksborg Fort, above Cape Coast, as the Danish headquarters. He plagiarised most of his material from his colleague Müller (see no. 2). English critical translation in Adam Jones *German Sources for West African History 1599–1669*, Wiesbaden 1983.

2. Wilhelm Johann Müller. 1662–69. This book, published in 1673, was also written in German. Müller was a Lutheran pastor who was employed by the Glückstadt Company as chaplain for the Danish establishment at Frederiksborg in Fetu. He was not sent as a missionary, but revealed a great desire to evangelise and convert the Africans. Extremely rich in detail, the book covers and comments on all aspects of life among the Fetu, and includes an extensive vocabulary list. English critical translation by Jones (op. cit.).

3. Erick Tilleman. 1682–1698. *En kort og enfoldig Beretning om det Landskab Guinea og dets Beskaffenhed* published 1697. This is the first source written in Danish.

Tilleman was a military officer, trader, and he was knowledgeable about sailing along the West African coast. He made several voyages to the Gold Coast between 1682 and 1698 and lived at Christiansborg Castle (new headquarters for the Danes after the loss of Frederiksborg to the English in 1684) for a total of nine years. His book is largely a 'post description', full of detailed information about sailing, anchoring, trading places all along the west African coast He also gives ethnographical information on the Akwamu, Akyem and Ga people, their customs, etc., and most particularly he has guides to trade. The material is brief because his target readership consisted of people who would be going to the Coast themselves and, consequently, could fill in details at will. English critical translation by S.A. Winsnes *A Short and Simple Account of the Country Guinea and Its Nature,* Madison 1994.

4. Johannes Rask. 1708–13. His book *En kort og sandferdig Rejse-Beskrivelse til og fra Guinea* was published in 1754. Rask was given a parish in Sør Folla in Norway. The book was written from his notes after his return home, possibly also while in Norway. It was published posthumously in Trondheim and contained a long preface by Frederic Nannestad, Bishop of Trondheim. Rask was also a pastor, and sent to the African establishments to minister to the Danish staff. He covers a good deal of ground on the Akwamu and Ga peoples, customs, nature, with the text constantly punctuated by yet another European death and funeral. Rask had almost nothing good to say about Africans. Translated into New Norwegian by Jostein Øvrelid *Ferd til og frå Guinea* Fonna Forlag 1969. It is not a critical translation, but it has a few footnotes, some of which are unreliable.

5. Ludewig Ferdinand Rømer. 1739–45/1745–49 or –50. The book *Tilforladelig Efterretning om Kysten Guinea* was published in Danish in 1760. Rømer was a trader. His contacts with the people during his ten years on the Coast were close and lively. He lived, thus, among fellow-traders, friends, family (he is said to have married an Akwamu princess) and his book is rich in detail—and fantasy. He tells a great deal about the history of the peoples around Accra, and is an excellent source of oral history. The book is prefaced by Eric Pontoppidan presenting a long discussion of the value of converting the heathen African. Rømer translated the book himself into German (actually his mother tongue) in 1769. There is also an annotated French translation *Le Golfe de Guinée 1700–1750* by Mette Dige-Hess, L'Harmattan 1989; and a critical translation into English by S.A. Winsnes is in progress.

6. Paul Erdmann Isert. 1783–87/1788–89. The book (written in German) *Reise nach Guinea und den Caribäischen Inseln in Columbien in Briefen an seine Freunde* was published in 1788. Isert was a botanist and medical doctor who was employed by the Danish West India and Guinea Company as surgeon to minister to the European staff, and to examine the slaves. His purpose in going was his desire to explore. He was not interested in trade of any kind, he was not out to make a fortune. But he was keenly interested in his pursuits in natural science. However, once on the Coast he felt that he was obligated to write a detailed description of the people, their lives, customs, etc. So he, too, produced an ethnographic work, with the great difference that his attitude toward the Africans was unstintingly positive. He returned to the Gold Coast in 1788 (after the publications of his book) to start a plantation that would make the trans-Atlantic slave trade redundant. This project resulted only in his death and the deaths of his wife and new-born child a few months after their arrival. The project deteriorated. There has always been a good

deal of interest around this man, and his book has been translated into several languages from the very outset (Danish, Swedish, French 2 editions, German again, Dutch twice). There is a modern (1989) reprint of the French 1793 edition with an introduction and footnotes by N. Gayibor, and a critical translation into English by S.A. Winsnes *Letters on West Africa and the Slave Trade* OUP 1992.

7. Andreas Riegelsen Bjørn. Worked on the Gold Coast for many years, finally 1789–93 as Governor of the Danish establishments. He wrote *Tanker om Slave-handelen* published in Copenhagen 1806. This is a short apology for the continuation of the slave trade.

8. H.C. Monrad. 1805–09. His book *Bidrag til en skildring af Guinea Kysten og dens Indbyggere* was published 1822. Monrad was also a pastor, also sent to be chaplain at Christiansborg Castle. He held a positive view toward the Africans, was keenly observant, wrote well. His book, as befitted his time, was anti-slave trade and pro-Christianising. (The Danish government had just made the trans-Atlantic slave trade illegal.) Monrad's book has been translated into German and partially into French.

9. Carl Behrens, ed. *Da Guinea var Dansk: Wulff Joseph Wulffs Breve og Dagbogoptegnelser fra Guldkysten 1836–1842.* pub. Copenhagen 1917. This book contains the letters and diary of W.J. Wulff who lived on the Gold Coast for six years. He established a family there, built a fine house, and died shortly after that. The family continued and is very active today, with names combined with Wulff. Wulff himself was buried in the basement of his house. It has a fine location, near The Castle [Christiansborg] and with a balcony overlooking the sea.

10. Georg Nørregård, ed. *Guvernør Edward Carstensens Indberetninger fra Guinea 1842–1850.* These are the despatches of the last Danish governor on the Gold Coast. His stay ended in 1850, with the sale, for £10,000, of all the Danish settlements to the English.

For other, shorter, books and articles, see J. Reindorf, *Scandinavians in Africa*, Oslo 1980, pp. 127–29.

Other (not Danish) critical translations:

1. Pieter de Marees *Description and Historical Account of the Gold Kingdom of Guinea (1602)* trans. and ed. by Albert van Dantzig and Adam Jones (OUP) 1987. This is a Dutch source.

2. *Barbot on Guinea: The Writings of Jean Barbot on West Africa 1678–1712* trans. and ed. by P.E.H. Hair, Adam Jones, and Robin Law, London 1992. This is an English source originally written in French.

3. William Bosman *A New and Accurate Description of the Coast of Guinea (1705)*, ed. by J.D. Fage and R.E. Bradbury, Frank Cass 1967. This is a Dutch source.

4. *The Founding of the Castelo de São Jorge da Mina: An Analysis of the Sources* P.E.H. Hair, Madison 1994. This is a discussion of two Portuguese sources followed by extensive and highly informative annotation.

Hottentot, Bushman, Kaffir
The Making of Racist Stereotypes in 19th-Century Britain

Bernth Lindfors

In her perceptive study of scientific racism in Great Britain, Nancy Stepan notes that

> a fundamental question about the history of racism in the first half of the nineteenth century is why it was that, just as the battle against slavery was being won by abolitionists, the war against racism in European thought was being lost. The Negro was legally freed by the Emancipation Act of 1833, but in the British mind he was still mentally, morally and physically a slave. (Stepan 1982:1)

Answers to this question have been sought in the intellectual climate of that period, particularly in the shifts of thought that marked the transition from a revolutionary Romantic age to an imperialistic Victorian one (Curtin 1964, Cohen 1980, Gilman 1982, Frederickson 1971). The tendency has been to examine the words and deeds of the leading thinkers, policy makers and adventurers of those times—the scientists, the statesmen, the explorers and travelers—and to trace through them the evolution of a distorted image of black peoples that both attracted and repelled the fair-skinned, reinforcing irrational assumptions of fundamental racial difference. Throughout Europe native Africans were stereotyped as brutish, dimwitted, naive, emotional, undisciplined, uncultured—in short, children of nature who needed to be civilized and domesticated. British abolitionists sought to protect them from gross exploitation, while the British government aimed to harness their raw energy for the development of colonial commerce, an enterprise deemed beneficial to Africans themselves, for it would give them useful employment, raise their standard of living, and thereby help to refine their ways. The paternalistic relationship between colonizer and colonized was thus perceived as a necessary symbiosis that was morally correct. At an abstract intellectual level British racism after the Enlightenment may have been largely benign, or intended as such, even while its concrete effects were often malignant in the extreme.

Racial stereotypes were also powerfully conveyed to the common man through the popular literature of the day, especially the adventure fiction set in various corners of the colonial empire. A study aptly titled *The Africa That Never Was* documents the role imaginative literature played in disseminating farfetched racist ideas to English readers (Hammond and Jablow 1970). Such value-laden discourse, directed at a mass audience, probably did more collective harm than the published papers of scientists, many of whom in the latter half of the nineteenth century became increasingly preoccupied with formulating "objective" racial theories based on comparisons of quantitative data derived from precise measurements of various anatomical parts, especially the skull (Gould 1981). But the subjectivity of the pop writers and the objectivity of the scientists pointed toward the same conclusions because they were based on the same premise: that Africans were by nature inferior to Europeans.

Among men and women of conscience it was believed that this inherent difference in biological status made certain moral demands upon the superior race. Clearly it was unethical to enslave an inferior, but it was considered perverse to marry one. In dealing with subnormal human beings some balance had to be achieved between enforcing total social control and allowing absolute personal freedom. Blacks had to be released from oppressive physical captivity yet kept strictly confined to their proper biological niche at the bottom of the natural human ladder. The civilized and the savage had to remain distanced from one another, if only to prevent disastrous taxonomic confusion. For otherwise the neat, color-coded distinctions that marked significant gradations in varieties of mankind could become blurred and indecipherable. It would then be impossible to distinguish at a glance between the Self and the Other.

One very effective method of distancing Africans from Europeans was though visual images. Even the illiterate masses could understand a picture, and the picture didn't have to be accurate to convey a powerful impression. Indeed, before the advent of photography, hand-drawn sketches of black people functioned as a kind of ocular shorthand, reducing complex human beings to a pattern of schematic lines meant to represent their essence. Some of this racial iconography aspired to exact representation undistorted by bias or overstatement, but much of it consciously or unconsciously expressed a bigoted attitude toward the individual or group depicted, emphasizing differences that set this race apart from others. Blacks were thus made to appear less than fully human at precisely the time their full human rights were being secured through legislation. The paradoxes of British racial paternalism are indelibly inscribed in the visual arts of the nineteenth century, particularly in those arts that forthrightly aided and abetted racist thinking.

Racial arguments were advanced in media ranging from careful illustrations in scientific texts to highly exaggerated political caricatures and lampoons, from picturesque portraits in travel books to grotesque images on posters and handbills advertising ethnic entertainments. Some of the best examples of this graphic tradition can be found in depictions of three southern African peoples: the Khoikhoi, the San and the Zulu, popularly known throughout the nineteenth century as the Hottentot, the Bushman and the Kaffir. What may have made these three African ethnic groups more visible in British art than others was the fact that specimens of each occasionally were conveyed to England and displayed publicly as examples of uncivilized humanity. The artists who drew them therefore did not have to rely on tall tales or hearsay for their impressions but could record their own responses to living creatures they could see with their own eyes, close up, and in the flesh. The various distancing devices these artists adopted to portray such subjects tell us something about racial attitudes in Britain in the nineteenth century, a century that began with attempts at exploration of selected parts of Africa and ended with Europe's aggressive expropriation of the entire continent.

The Hottentot Venus

The most famous African performer on the British stage in the early nine-teenth century was Sartjee Baartman, a woman who made her debut in Lon-don in September 1810 and remained on display in cities and towns through-out the British Isles and Europe until her death in Paris in December 1815 (Kirby 1949, Altick 1978, Gould 1982). Billed facetiously as the "Hottentot Venus," she had one remarkable attribute, a steatopygous rump, that made her an anatomical curiosity. Her manager, a Boer farmer from the Cape, sought to add further novelty to her exhibition by having her emerge from a cave, perform rudimentary tasks on command, sing, dance, and play a few melodies on a simple stringed instrument. But the big attraction for those who came to see her was her enormous bottom, the authenticity of which some skeptics insisted on testing by patting, pinching or poking with a cane or para-sol. To spice up her act, she was outfitted in a skintight, skin-colored garment that made her appear nude under her native ornaments. So this outlandish Venus offered the British public at least three kinds of sideshow stimulation: she was part freak, part savage, part cooch dancer.

The degrading nature of her exhibition did not please everyone who wit-nessed it. Members of the newly formed African Institution, led by the famous abolitionist Zachary Macaulay, took her manager to court, charging that this woman could not possibly have consented to being displayed in this humili-ating manner, that she therefore was being kept in a condition of involuntary servitude, and that under protection of British law she ought to be released from her captivity and repatriated to Africa. The petitioners also claimed that the show was indecent, but they chose to contest only the legality, not the morality, of the exhibition. Her manager flatly denied all the charges (Lindfors 1985).

To settle the matter, the presiding magistrate arranged for the woman to be interrogated for several hours in low Dutch in the presence of witnesses for both sides. To the surprise of the plaintiffs she testified in support of her man-ager, swearing she had willingly agreed to the terms of the contract she had with him, that she was under no restraint but was well treated and earning good money, and that she wanted the show to go on. On the strength of this testimony the magistrate had no alternative but to dismiss the suit and allow Sartjee Baartman to continue her show business career.

The resolution of this unusual case, which was remarked on in all the London papers and picked up quickly by the provincial press, added immeasurably to the notoriety of the Hottentot Venus, making her a household word throughout the British Isles. Ballads, doggerel verse, quips and jokes inspired by the incongruity of her situation began to make the rounds. Several humor magazines published letters in broken English purportedly written by her, and comic artists quickly joined in the fun, graphically inflating her strange tale. To sustain such hilarity, crude caricature became the dominant verbal and iconographic idiom (Lindfors 1984).

The best-known burlesque image of Sartjee Baartman was an aquatint by Frederick Christian Lewis used to advertise her exhibition (Figure 1). Its emphasis rested squarely on her buttocks, which protruded like oversized basketballs from an erect frame seen in profile. Sander L. Gilman, in a suggestive essay on the iconography of female sexuality, advances the idea that "when the nineteenth century saw the black female, it saw her in terms of her buttocks. ... Female sexuality is tied to the image of the buttocks, and the quintessential buttocks are those of the Hottentot" (Gilman 1985:90–91). Using Sartjee Baartman as a spectacular case in point, Gilman finds that "it is indeed in the physical appearance of the Hottentot that the central icon for sexual difference between the European and the black was found" (Gilman 1985:83). One could go further and argue that to the European mind the pronounced steatopygia of the Hottentot Venus not only made her appear sexually different from white women but also placed her much closer to the animal world both literally and symbolically. Her buttocks were an outward sign of her primitive nature as well as an emblem of her unbridled lust. By exaggerating a trait presumed to signal corporal and cultural atavism, Lewis was adding flesh to a racial myth that dehumanized Africans.

Another physiological peculiarity of Hottentot females that increased their reputation for voluptuousness, further exciting the curiosity of European scientists and laymen, resided in their genitalia. Early traveler in southern Africa had reported that these women possessed an "apron" of tissues that dangled between their legs to extraordinary lengths (Cowley 1960:105–06, Ten Rhyne 1933:47, Kolb 1731:118–19). Le Vaillant's *Voyage dans l'intérieur de l'Afrique par le Cap de Bonne-Espérance* even included an illustration of a woman with such appendages extending halfway to her knees (Le Vaillant 1790:349, Figure 2). This characteristic was cited as further evidence that Hottentots were more closely akin to apes and chimpanzees than to human beings. Their primitive organs pointed toward primitive origins.

It is not known whether the Hottentot Venus exposed her genitals to the spectators who flocked to her shows. It is unlikely that this would have been tolerated in the British Isles as part of her public routine, but private viewings may have been arranged occasionally behind the stage curtain, especially in Paris. One French scientific source states that Sartjee Baartman was reputed to

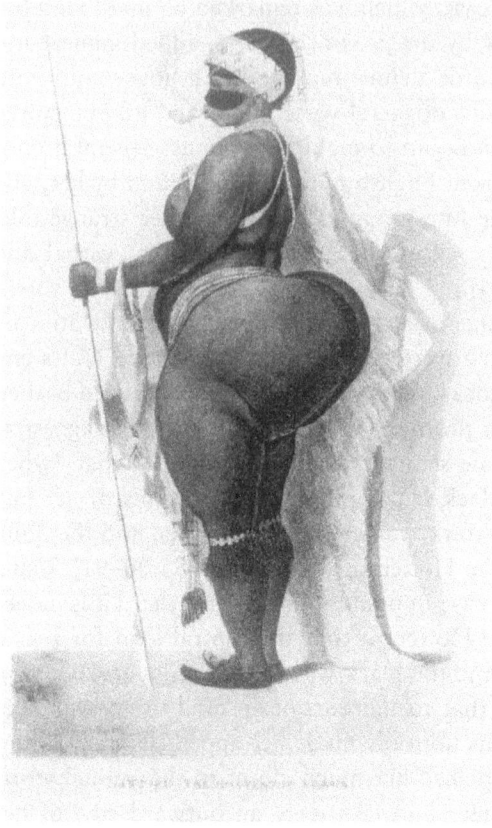

Figure 1. Frederic Christian Lewis, "Sartjee, the Hottentot Venus," an aquatint used to advertise her exhibition. This copy is from the British Museum Collection of Prints and Drawings. For further information see the brief discussion in Mary Doroth George (1978), *Catalogue of Political and Personal Satires in the Department of Prints and Drawings in the British Museum*, Vol. 8, No. 11602, p. 959.

have been a woman of amorous disposition who "did not scorn those of her admirers who had the kind of morals that made Sodom famous" (Verneau 1916:178).

Yet she is also reported to have been so modest when posing in the nude for a team of French anatomists and figure painters that no one afterwards could say with assurance whether or not she possessed any kind of genital anomaly, even though several casual attempts had been made to discover if she did (de Blainville 1816:183–90). It wasn't until the most eminent comparative anatomist in France, Baron Georges Cuvier, dissected her body a year later and published a classic scientific paper on her buttocks and genitalia that the full truth became known. Indeed, Cuvier must be credited with having finally unraveled the mystery of the Hottentot apron, identifying it correctly as consisting of nothing more than hypertrophied nymphae. Yet his elaborate description of her person and personality is remarkable for its tendency to compare her quite matter-of-factly to an orang-outang. Cuvier is known for his belief in the fixity of species and his resistance to evolutionary theories, but apparently he was tempted to view Sartjee Baartman and her kind as constituting a marginal species, half-animal and half-human. Without going so far as to say so directly, he hinted through his comparison that he regarded her as some sort of missing link (Cuvier 1817:259–74).

Figure 2. François Le Vaillant (1790), *Voyage dans l'intérieur de l'Afrique par le Cap de Bonne-Esperance*, Vol. 2:349.

Many of the European scientists who subsequently made use of Cuvier's discoveries or who independently took measurements of her skull, skeleton or other carefully preserved remains were equally convinced that she represented a lower order of being, perhaps a transitional one in human evolution. In a textbook diagram of craniometrical variation, her skull was placed midway on a continuum between European man and the wolf (Cloquet 1821:80). The shape and size of her skull relegated her to this humble position.

Images of Sartjee Baartman were also used to illustrate early ethnological studies, sometimes being placed beside idealized images of European beauty such as the Venus de Milo or the Venus de Medici (Luschka 1864:8, Figure 3). European viewers could be left to draw their own conclusions from such contrasts. In addition, she turned up regularly in illustrated encyclopedias on the races of mankind and once even made an unexpected appearance in a comprehensive study of world costume (Racinet 1888). In most of these "scientific" uses of her body there was a very deliberate attempt at verisimilitude, at faithful and exact reproduction of her physical characteristics. This was science, after all. No obvious distortions of surface phenomena could be permitted in an unbiased quest for truth. But the strategy underlying the selection and placement of her image often betrayed blatant racist assumptions. Objec-

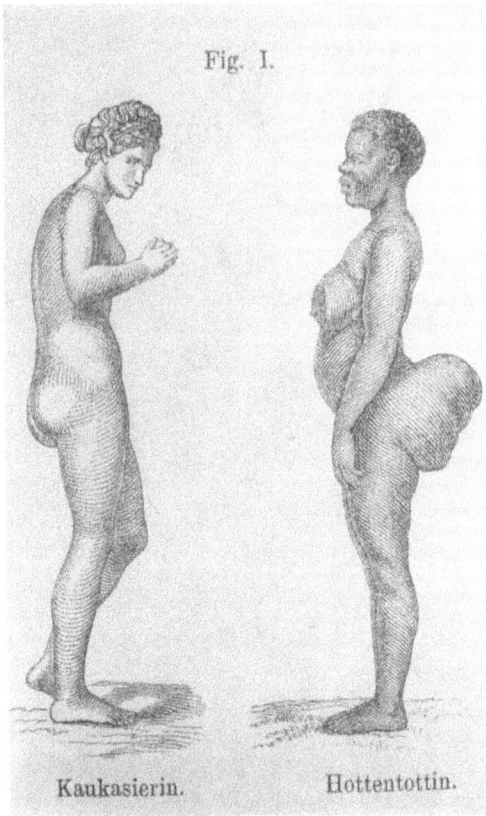

Figure 3. Hubert von Luschka (1864), *Die Anatomie des menschlichen Beckens,* Vol. 3 of Die Anatomie des Menschen in Rücksicht auf die Bedürfnisse der praktischen Heilkunde, Tübingen: H. Laupp, Vol. 2, p. 8.

tive portraiture only served to buttress highly subjective notions about natural gradations in the variety of the human species.

Caricature, an art based on flagrant distortions of reality, fed on the same assumptions and used ironic juxtapositions of European and African figures to make unspoken racial points. In the earliest political cartoons based on the original Lewis aquatint, Sartjee Baartman was placed rump to rump with Lord William Wyndham Grenville, a former Whig prime minister who in 1810–11, when George III was showing clear signs of irreversible mental illness, favored forming a broadly based coalition government under the Prince Regent. Grenville and his backers therefore had come to be known popularly as "Broad Bottoms," a term that "connoted the comprehensive character of the Ministry and the bulky posteriors of the Grenvilles" (George 1978, Vol. 8:410), so naturally they became easy targets for graphic satire. In one unsigned engraving entitled "A Pair of Broad Bottoms" the playwright Richard Brinsley Sheridan is shown half-kneeling between the mirrored figures, measuring Sartjee Baartman's bottom with calipers and exclaiming that "such a Spanker beats your Lordship's hollow" (George 1978, Vol. 8:948). In other words, here was a lowly Hottentot who had outstripped Lord Grenville in fundamental excellence; she was by far the broadest of the Broad Bottoms. The humor sprang from an inversion of accepted notions of Hottentot inferiority and backwardness. Indeed, the absurdity of juxtaposing Sartjee Baartman and Lord Grenville rested on an implicit assumption that Hottentots and English noblemen were so radically different from one another as to be incomparable. Africans, especially Hottentots, could not be placed on the same footing as Europeans, much less elevated above them. The very idea was comical.

The same sort of humor informed caricatures that dealt with Sartjee Baartman's potential as a love partner. The word "Venus" in her title was enough to trigger numerous mock-romantic visions of hearts and cupids (George 1978, Vol. 10:338). But perhaps the best illustration of this kind of visual gag can be found in Charles Williams's travesty of the Duke of Clarence, who in 1811 was striving to find a very wealthy woman to marry. He had proposed six times to a young heiress and then had relentlessly pursued a number of others, all of whom had turned him down. He was averaging about one marriage proposal per month when Williams's engraving entitled "Neptune's Last Resource or the Fortune Hunter Foiled, a Sketch from Heathen Mythology" appeared depicting him as a long-bearded admiral trying to seize Sartjee Baartman's money bags (George 1978, Vol. 9:38–39). The Hottentot Venus was represented as spurning his suit, having divined his true motive for approaching her. Even the rudest barbarian, it was suggested, could see through the clumsy advances of the Duke of Clarence.

The portrayal of Sartjee Baartman as a young woman financially well-endowed and mindful of the value of her assets may be indicative of public awareness of her remarkable success in show business. Occasionally one finds in the press of that period waggish suggestions that she might now make an advantageous match for an ambitious suitor: "The damsel, it is said, has picked up some cash, and may become a desirable object in the eyes of some of our minor fortune hunters" (Lysons n.d.). The image of her as a female worthy of amorous attention was, of course, something that the satirists continued to exploit. But in Williams's caricature of the Duke of Clarence, the comic accent was on money rather than love. Any nobleman desperate enough to marry an African for financial gain clearly violated English norms of acceptable elite behavior. A duke's marriage with a Hottentot was unthinkable for it would be a betrayal of all the verities of race, class and gender.

So the iconography of Hottentots in early nineteenth century England emphasized their biological incompatibility with Europeans. They were regarded not just as social and intellectual inferiors but as a breed apart, a throwback to earlier evolutionary times, a rudimentary link in the great chain of humanoid beings. And this closeness to nature, manifested in their strange anatomy and raw vitality, made them fascinating and attractive to scientists, travelers, artists, and the ordinary man on the street. They were the exotic, primitive Other against whose arrested development one's own progress could be measured. The Hottentot Venus was therefore much more than a living icon of sexual difference; she was Otherness personified—a singing, dancing, jiggling incarnation of one extreme in a rigidly hierarchical taxonomic paradigm. She gave body to racist theory.

The "Bosjesmans" and the Earthmen

The San who were exhibited in the British Isles were also assumed to be among the very dregs of humanity. The first troupe, consisting of two men, two women and an infant, arrived in 1846, shortly after P.T. Barnum's Tom Thumb had stormed Europe, popularizing the display of unusual small people.[1] In newspaper advertisements the manager of the "Bosjesmans" claimed that these dwarfish folk and their few crude implements

> show how very nearly sentient beings may sink to, or rather have never risen above, the condition of animals unendowed with reason to guide or govern their instinctive propensities. ... They are supposed to belong to one of the numerous tribes of their benighted country which have not yet emerged from absolute barbarism.[2]

Apart from their small size and odd facial features, what appears to have made the Bosjesmans particularly fascinating was their life style, which was utterly different from that of any people the British had ever encountered before: they owned very few possessions, used only the simplest tools, built no permanent structures, and wore hardly any clothing. All these traits could have been traced to the fact that they were a hunting and gathering people and therefore had no need for belongings or paraphernalia that would impede their mobility, but the British interpreted a lack of things as a lack of culture and thought less of the Bosjesmans as a result. Commentators tended to agree with the oft-quoted assessment offered by the learned traveler Dr. Lichtenstein that

> there is not perhaps any class of savages upon the earth that lead lives so near those of the brutes as the Bosjesmans;—none perhaps who are sunk so low, who are so unimportant in the scale of existence;—whose wants, whose cares, and whose joys, are so low in their nature;—and who are consequently so little capable of cultivation. (Lichtenstein 1928:244)

In short, the Bosjesmans were presumed to be an utterly hopeless lot.

Nonetheless, thousands of spectators turned out to see them, if only to confirm at an intimate but safe distance xenophobic prejudices against brutish

---

[1] Tom Thumb's first European tour had started in London in 1844. At the end of the summer of 1845 two "Bushmen Children" had been exhibited in London for a short time, but they do not appear to have made much of an impact and vanished quickly from the stage; a sketch of them was published in the *Illustrated London News*, 6 September 1845, p. 160. The Bosjesmans, on the other hand, remained on tour for several years and were a very popular attraction. There is evidence to suggest that they were abandoned in Rouen by an unscrupulous manger in December 1853 (Goblot 40).

[2] *Liverpool Mail*, 14 November 1846, p. 3.

beings from the Dark Continent. Charles Dickens probably summed up the public reaction best when he wrote:

> Think of the Bushmen. Think of the two men and the two women who have been exhibited about England for some years. Are the majority of persons—who re-member the horrid little leader of that party in his festering bundle of hides, with his filth and his antipathy to water, and his straddled legs, and his odious eyes shaded by his brutal hand, and his cry of "Qu-u-u-u-aaa!" (Bosjesman for some-thing desperately insulting I have no doubt)—conscious of an affectionate yearn-ing towards that noble savage, or is it idiosyncratic in me to abhor, detest, abominate, and abjure him? I have no reserve on this subject, and will frankly state that, setting aside that stage of the entertainment when he counterfeited the death of some creature he had shot, by laying his head on his hand and shaking his left leg—at which time I think it would have been justifiable homicide to slay him—I have never seen that group sleeping, smoking, and expectorating round their brazier, but I have sincerely desired that something might happen to the charcoal smouldering therein, which would cause the immediate suffocation of the whole of the noble strangers. (Dickens 1853:337–38)

Dickens was debunking the Romantic myth of the Noble Savage but he wasn't entirely joking. Believing as he did that the Noble Savage's "virtues are a fable; his happiness is a delusion; his nobility, nonsense" and that "the world will be all the better when his place knows him no more," Dickens recommended more than half-seriously that it would be "something highly desirable" for all such people to be "civilized off the face of the earth". If this wasn't a cry for literal genocide, it must at least be recognized as a call for cultural genocide, which perhaps amounts to the same thing.

Dickens wasn't their only detractor. Pictorial representations of the Bosjesmans in the media of the day were not at all flattering, the consensus among observers being that these were exceedingly ugly creatures who differed as much from Europeans in appearance as in intelligence. To heighten the contrast between savage and civilized, some illustrated papers such as the *Pictorial Times*[3] and *Sportsman's Magazine* printed sketches of the Bosjes-mans dancing wildly while their fashionably dressed exhibitor stood sedately in the background looking on (Figure 4). For the show itself a large poster was prepared, illustrated with scenes said to be typical of Bosjesman life: "Quarrels of Bushman," "Fight of Bushman," "Tracing the Footsteps of the Enemy," "Killing the Puff Adder," "Preparing for Dance," etc. Significantly, the borders between the vignettes were lurid with snakes and animal heads.

---

[3] The sketch (fig. 4) is from the *Pictorial Times*, 12 June 1847, p. 376, and the gentleman in the background is identified as Dr. Knox. The same sketch appeared in *Sportsman's Magazine*, 10 July 1847, p. 319, with the gentleman in the background identified as Mr. J.S. Tyler. Knox, an Edinburgh anatomist who had been involved in the notorious Burke and Hare scandal, gave an anthropological lecture as part of the show; Tyler was the manager who accompanied the Bos-jesmans on their tour. The *Illustrated London News*, 12 June 1847, p. 381, printed a similar sketch of the group and identified the gentleman in the background as Tyler.

THE "BOSJESMANS" FAMILY
PERFORMING, UNDER THE DIRECTION OF DR. KNOX, A NATIVE DANCE *(see page 376.)*

Figure 4. *Pictorial Times,* June 12th 1847, p. 376.

Less sensational images of the women and child in the troupe were used in the fourth edition of a leading ethnological textbook, James Cowles Prichard's *The Natural History of Man,* but even these "scientific" plates did not make them look attractive. David Livingstone may have been right when he said of the Bosjesmans that "the specimens brought to Europe have been selected, like costermonger's dogs, on account of their extreme ugliness." But one wonders if he was justified in making a still more demeaning comparison: "That they are, to some extent, like baboons is true, just as these are in some points frightfully human" (Livingstone 1875:35). Whether this was a fair assessment or not, British artists and illustrators who drew the Bosjesmans evidently agreed with it entirely.

This is not to say that the British eye was incapable of appreciating Bushman beauty. The public reaction several years later to the exhibition of a fourteen-year-old boy and a sixteen-year-old girl misleadingly identified as "Earthmen from Port Natal" was quite favorable, in part because they were much better-looking specimens than their predecessors. Several papers carried handsome sketches of them, and the *Illustrated London News* (Figure 5) noted with approval their "pleasing hue ... lustrous black eyes ... perfect docility and mildness of disposition ... good natural faculties ... [and] excellent ear for music ... Martinus is a fine little savage, beautifully formed, and with well developed muscles. Flora is also a nicely-made child, of more slender and

Figure 5. *Illustrated London News*, November 6th 1852, p. 372.

delicate frame, but perfectly healthy."[4] A handbill for one of their shows claimed that they were "the only Specimens of this Extraordinary Race ever beheld in Europe," but this was questioned by a number of informed spectators. They had been dubbed "Earthmen" because in South Africa they were alleged to have slept in hollows in the ground made by burrowing; however, members of the English Ethnological Society, noting their resemblance to the Bosjesmans, preferred to classify them as "Bushman-Troglodytes, or Troglodyte-Bushmen" (Latham 1856:149, Conolly 1855:27–28).

Like other human curiosities before them, Martinus and Flora danced, sang and mimed to entertain their customers, but their "act" differed in one important respect: they performed entirely in English. They were able to do this because they had lived for two years with a British family in Croydon before being put on stage. During that time they had acquired a fluency in English, had learnt to play the piano, and had built up a repertoire of songs that included "Buffalo Gals," "I'm Going to Alabama," "Annie Laurie,"

---

[4] *Illustrated London News*, 6 November 1852, p. 372.

"Britons Never Shall be Slaves," and a number of black American tunes. Their musical talents were much admired, but audiences were most impressed by their mastery of a "civilized" tongue. One provincial paper reported that "the most interesting part of the *séance* is found to consist in the sprightly conversation they carry on with their visitors,"[5] and another exclaimed that "their knowledge of the English language, together with their musical proficiency, is very remarkable for the time they have been in this country, shewing even a greater intelligence than that evinced generally by the more civilized children of our own country."[6] To such observers Martinus and Flora were miracles of transformation, savages turned to some extent genteel, base Earthmen transmuted within two years into reasonable facsimiles of pure English folk. More than anything else, it was their ability to chatter and sing in English that made them recognizable as fellow human beings; such lively interlocutors could not possibly be mistaken for baboons, orang-outangs or other species of monkeys. Soon Martinus and Flora were being hailed as "a direct Contradiction to the Theory lately set forth, of the Impossibility of Rendering the Savage a Thinking, Feeling Being."[7] Given this high degree of enthusiastic public acceptance, it is not surprising that these youngsters were treated more kindly by graphic artists than the Bosjesmans had been. Their basic humanity was never in question.

The Zulu Kaffirs

During the same month of 1853 that the Earthmen were first exhibited, another troupe of South African performers arrived on the London scene. These were the "Zulu Kaffirs"—eleven men, a woman and a child—who performed events alleged to be representative of the tenor of their brutish life. Of all South African peoples, the Zulus may have been the most notorious abroad for their warlike ways. Reports of the military prowess of this "wild and formidable race"[8] had been filtering back to England ever since the reign of Shaka thirty years before. After England annexed Natal in 1843, emigration to the new colonial territory was encouraged, and within ten years thousands of British settlers found themselves sharing an unstable frontier with Zulu farmers and herders. So there must have been considerable curiosity back home about the aggressive natives who inhabited this remote corner of the empire and occasionally made trouble for kith and kin.

But even without such a reputation, the Zulus would have been an interesting novelty in Victorian England, for they put on an exciting show, dis-

---

[5] *Brighton Guardian*, 5 October 1853, p. 5.
[6] *Brighton Examiner*, 11 October 1853, p. 5.
[7] Regent Gallery Handbill, hand-dated 22 August 1853, in the John Johnson Collection, Oxford University.
[8] *The Court Journal*, 7 May 1853, p. 300.

playing themselves and their traditions with uninhibited energy yet with remarkably professional stage presence. The *Times* gave the spectacle a rave review:

> Now the Caffres are at their meal, feeding themselves with enormous spoons, and expressing their satisfaction by a wild chant, under the inspiration of which they bump themselves along without rising in a sort of circular dance. Now the witchfinder commences his operations to discover the culprit whose magic has brought sickness into the tribe, and becomes perfectly rabid through the effect of his own incantations. Now there is a wedding ceremony, now a hunt, now a military expedition, all with characteristic dances; and the whole ends with a general conflict between rival tribes. The songs and dances are, as may be expected, monotonous in the extreme, and without the bill it would be difficult to distinguish the expression of love from the gesture of martial defiance. Nevertheless, as a picture of manners, nothing can be more complete; and not the least remarkable part of the exhibition is the perfect training of the wild artists. They seem utterly to lose all sense of their present position, and, inspired by the situations in which they are placed, appear to take Mr. Marshall's scenes for their actual abode in the vicinity of Port Natal. If all English actors could be found so completely to lose themselves in the characters they assumed, histrionic art would be in a state truly magnificent.[9]

The reviewer for *The Spectator*, equally impressed, maintained that "the exhibition transcends all others we have witnessed of the kind. ... As for the noises—the howls, yells, hoots and whoops, the snuffling, wheezing, bubbling, groveling and stamping—they form a concert to whose savagery we cannot attempt to do justice."[10] The *Illustrated London News*, which carried a sketch of the performers in action (Figure 6), praised some of the same scenes and sound effects and concluded that "the Zulus must be naturally good actors; for a performance more natural and less like acting is seldom if ever seen upon any stage."[11]

Indeed, it was a performance by this very troupe that prompted Dickens's comic diatribe on "The Noble Savage," for he found much to ridicule and nothing to admire in their dramatization of Zulu life. Parts of the exhibition, he asserted, were totally incomprehensible to a cultivated mind:

> What a visitor left to his own interpretings and imaginings might suppose these noblemen to be about, when they give vent to that pantomimic expression which is quite settled to be the natural gift of the noble savage, I cannot possibly conceive; for it is so much too luminous for my personal civilisation that it conveys no idea to my mind beyond a general stamping, ramping, and raving, remarkable (as everything in savage life is) for its dire uniformity. (Dickens 1853:338)

---

[9] *Times*, 18 May 1853, p. 8.
[10] *The Spectator*, 21 May 1853, p. 485.
[11] *Illustrated London News*, 28 May 1853, p. 409.

Figure 6. *Illustrated London News,* May 28th 1853, p. 409.

Dickens went on to recount in hilarious detail the customs and traditions he saw enacted before him—everything from murder and mayhem to witchcraft and weddings—and concluded that "if we have anything to learn from the Noble Savage, it is what to avoid".

Dickens of course was also to some extent playing a theatrical role himself: that of an impatient Victorian pragmatist eager to puncture inflated Romantic notions of the dignity of "primitive" peoples. For him the Zulus were simply a convenient case in point, a group so far removed from Europe in custom and culture that they could easily be held up as examples of an underdeveloped race obviously in need of moral improvement and mental refinement. Yet it is interesting to note with what contempt he and other humorists viewed Zulu traditions and institutions, for underlying such ethnic satire was a broad streak of undisguised racism, a belief that Zulus were in every way inferior to Europeans. The numerous comments on their smell, their bizarre modes of dress (and undress), their noises, their monotonous songs, rabid incantations, and wild, demoniacal dances, betray an arrogant assumption that the Zulus were overgrown children of nature who had not yet developed the inhibitions, self-discipline and polite manners that distinguish more civilized folk. They were savages pure and simple, primitives in the raw.

Zulu savagery became an iconographic cliché later in the century, especially during and after the Anglo-Zulu wars. Issues of the *Illustrated London News* and other pictorial mass media in 1879 were full of gory battle scenes displaying heroic British soldiers and settlers struggling manfully against ferocious hordes of spear-wielding warriors. The popular adventure fiction of H. Rider Haggard, G.A. Henty, Bertram Mitford and others, while sometimes respectful of Zulu courage or chivalry, contained illustrations reinforcing the notion of such people as militaristic and fiendishly dangerous. Perhaps the single exception to this iconographic tradition was the Spy portrait in *Vanity Fair*[12] of the deposed Zulu monarch Cetewayo, who lived for a time in London; he was shown dressed rather modestly in a grey suit, cravat and blue slippers, and seated quietly on a divan. But his enormous bulk and toothy grin connoted that he was still an unpredictable force to be reckoned with. His seemingly innocuous appearance contrasted all too sharply with his reputation for barbarism. The Spy cartoon thus played upon a perceptual incongruity: here was a notorious savage deceptively clad in civilized costume.

Fed by such media images, public curiosity about Zulus peaked in the last two decades of the nineteenth century, and well-known writers and showmen tried to capitalize on their trendiness. George Bernard Shaw included Cetewayo and his retinue in *Cashel Byron's Profession* (Shaw 1886), a novel about boxing; and P.T. Barnum was so eager to obtain Zulus for his shows that he offered Queen Victoria's government $100,000 for permission to exhibit Cetewayo for five years, a petition that did not amuse the Queen (Wallace 1959:111). A rival showman outdid Barnum by putting on display not only three of Cetewayo's nieces (whom he billed as the chief's daughters, true "Zulu princesses") but also a baby, another Zulu chief, and twenty-three warriors who had surrendered to British authorities in South Africa; it has been reported that "their arrival in London was greeted by over one hundred thousand people on the docks and as far up the street as the eye could reach" (Coup 1901:166).[13] Other showmen couldn't ignore such palpable signs of popularity, and soon spears, shields, feathers and war paint could be found in abundance in every carnival sideshow as well as in circus "specs" or opening pageants. Any subterfuge that could be of advantage was used: a handbill for an exhibition of "Farini's Friendly Zulus" at the Royal Aquarium in September 1880 brazenly quoted accolades from the *Times* review of the 1853 Zulu Kaffirs as if these praises had recently been bestowed on the Farini troupe (Figure 7).

Needless to say, many of the Zulus hauled up for public display were frauds. More than one circus veteran has commented on this in his memoirs:

> I recollect at the time of the Zulu war how one showman conceived the idea of exhibiting a number of Zulu warriors. There was only one drawback—not a

---

[12] *Vanity Fair*, 26 August 1882.

[13] The same show may have gone to the United States, for a poster for W.C. Coup's United Monster Shows at the Great Paris Hippodrome in Chicago in 1881 advertises "Princess Amazulu, King Cetewayo's Daughter and Suite." A newspaper advertisement for the same circus the following year bills "Zulu Princess Amadage, daughter of King Cetewayo, and her maids of honor". These women were also said to be "the only Female Zulus who ever left Zululand and the only genuine Zulus in America." These materials can be found at the Circus World Museum, Baraboo, Wisconsin.

Figure 7. *Royal Aquarium handbill hand-dated 28 September, 1880.*
(From the author's collection of ethnic iconography.)

single Zulu was at that moment in the country. But drawbacks do not exist for the born showman and a party of ordinary niggers were easily made up into Cetewayo's savage soldiery. (Walker 1922:130)

Managers in this kind of show business quickly learned that pseudo-Zulus were far easier to handle than real ones. When James Lloyd engaged a dozen *bona fide* tribesmen for a show that toured Ireland, he found that

> Their wildness [in performing dances] was disturbingly genuine; this being one of the disadvantages encountered by showmen who, with more honesty than aesthetic perception, prefer Nature to Art. Nature, it has been said, is pulling up on Art; but she has still a long way to go before she produces savages who are equal to the other for show purposes. (McKechnie n.d.:210)

By the end of the century it appeared that Art had overtaken Nature, that painted Irishmen or indigenous British blacks were now displacing true Africans in British show business.

The pseudo-Zulu eventually became a stock comic character like the "nigger minstrel," a humorous stereotype recognized and accepted as a gross exaggeration. Almost anybody could play the part. James T. Tanner, in his 1896 musical "My Girl," took the unusual step of casting a "genuine negro (Mr. W. Downes)" in the role of a pseudo-Zulu prince who performed an athletic "witch-song and dance."[14] The drama ended with the other characters discovering that this negro in savage dress was neither a Zulu nor a prince but a brazen imposter who was not as black as he seemed. Such an ending reveals that the stereotype had already taken on a life of its own, spawning a tradition of humorous inauthenticity.

But then in 1899 an extravaganza called "Savage South Africa," certainly the biggest spectacle of its kind ever presented to the British public, opened at the Empress Theatre in London. Organized by Frank Fillis, a South African circus man, it included two hundred genuine "natives" who, along with twenty Boers, re-enacted episodes from the Matabele Rebellion. These performers also participated in the Greater Britain Exhibition at Earl's Court in May of that year, and some of them later were recruited for supporting roles in a Boer War Exhibition that toured Europe and made a sensation at the 1904 World's Fair in St. Louis. In England there was public concern voiced in the media about the friendliness of some of these African men toward British women and vice versa:

> ... why do so many women take pleasure in touching and patting and even stroking these black persons? These blacks do not represent the highest, but the lowest in man. If the Earl's Court savages were a collection of astronomers or physiologists, if they were in any way noted for their brain power they would create no interest at all among women of this kind. Minds weigh not at all against matter with many women. It is not a pleasant thing to say; but this Earl's Court show has not tended to show the niceness of women. (Shephard 1984:40)

Another paper, after noting that "grown women not only shake hands with them but stroke their limbs admiringly," joined the masculine chorus of disapproval:

> Nothing is left undone by certain misled English females to gratify the vanity of these miscellaneous African natives in whose delightful manners and customs this show is presumed to instruct us. The Kaffir Exhibition at Earl's Court has in fact degenerated into an exhibition of white women visitors, and a very disgusting exhibition it is. These raw, hulking and untamed men-animals are being unwillingly and utterly corrupted by unseemly attention from English girls. (Scobie 1972:124)

---

[14] *Times*, 14 July 1896, p. 11.

Figure 8. Dudley Hardy, "Kaffirs Booming". (A caricature from the author's collection.)

The situation got worse in July when there was an actual attempt at marriage between the leader of the Matabele troupe, "Prince" Peter Lobengula, and a white woman, Miss Kitty Jewell, daughter of a Cornish mining engineer who had emigrated to South Africa (Shephard 1984:36–41). The managers of "Savage South Africa," the local vicar, the Chancellor of the Diocese of London, and Kitty's mother closed ranks and succeeded in thwarting the marriage, but not before the affair had generated heated vituperations in the press against the evils of miscegenation. A milder critique of such heterosexual comingling appeared in a caricature by Dudley Hardy entitled "Kaffirs Booming" (Figure 8). If nothing else, this well-publicized incident exposed another of the obvious dangers in importing true "native warriors" to the British Isles for ethnological shows: clearly it wasn't only their vaunted military prowess that intrigued spectators. How could an appropriate distance between civilized and savage be maintained in such close quarters? The stereotype of the African as a lower form of humanity had taken such firm hold of the British imagination by the end of the century that xenophobia was inspired by the very thought of race mixing.

The iconographic record of the nineteenth century thus tends to confirm in popular culture the answer Nancy Stepan gave to her own question about the rise of racial thinking in the West: why at the time of abolition, and after, was the war against racism in European thought being lost? Her conclusion was that the long tradition of scientific racism, which extended well into the twentieth century, testified to "the deep psychological need Western Europeans, scientists among them, seem to have felt to divide and rank human groups, and to measure them negatively against an idealized, romanticized picture of themselves" (Stepan 1982:189). The same kind of taxonomic impulse, the same sorting and sifting of human groups into hierarchical categories, the same tendency toward self-congratulation, can be seen in European visual arts of the nineteenth century that depicted Africans and other non-Western peoples. It didn't seem to matter how much more one had learnt about such peoples over the years or how many specimens of each could been seen and inspected firsthand. Graphic stereotyping persisted and grew, feeding upon its own traditions of bias, distortion and caricature. The visual image, a form of ideational shorthand, simplified what it represented, reducing complexities and concealing contradictions so as to reaffirm prevailing preconceptions.

In Britain the Hottentot, the Bushman and the Kaffir were all assumed to be savage races, but important distinctions were made between them so each could be distinguished from the others and placed in its own barbarous pigeonhole. The Hottentot, morphologically deviant yet sexually potent, represented man's link to the animal world. The Bushman, stunted in stature and devoid of culture, stood as an example of human degeneration. The warlike Kaffir symbolized mindless anarchy, bloodshed and brutality. The three together could thus be viewed as emblematically recapitulating stages in the eternal life cycle: Birth, Decline and Death. Only the Earthmen escaped this kind of inexorable reductionism, and one is justified in asking why. Could it possibly have been because these young people, singing and dancing to a new tune, approached the English public through the ear rather than primarily through the eye? Could familiar sounds in the mouths of such strangers have made them appear less alien? Could comprehensible utterance alone have made the crucial difference, undoing the effects of years of racial stereotyping? In searching for a plausible explanation of why the Earthmen were treated so humanely and given a far friendlier reception than any of the other African peoples in the British Isles in the nineteenth century, one returns inevitably to their most remarkable singularity: their ability to speak directly to their audiences in English. For the average Englishman a few words may have been worth a thousand pictures. Language may have spoken louder than racist iconography.

This chapter has been published in a slightly different form in the *Nordic Journal of African Studies* 5(2), 1996. It is printed here with permission of the editor, Arvi Hurskainen.

References

Altick, Richard D., 1978, *The Shows of London*. Cambridge, Mass., and London: Belknap Press of Harvard University Press.

Cloquet, Jules Germain, 1821, *Anatomie de l'homme*. Paris: C. de Lasteyrie, Vol. 1.

Cohen, William B., 1980, *The French Encounter with Africans: White Response to Blacks*. Bloomington: Indiana University Press.

Conolly, John, 1855, *The Ethnological Exhibitions of London*. London: John Churchill.

Coup, William Cameron, 1901, *Sawdust and Spangles: Stories and Secrets of the Circus*. Chicago: Stone.

Cowley, Ambrose, 1960, "Voyage Round the World 1683–1686", in Kemp, P.K. and Christopher Lloyd (eds), *The Brethren of the Coast: The British and French Buccaneers in the South Seas*, pp. 105–06. London: Heinemann.

Curtin, Philip, 1964, *The Image of Africa: British Ideas and Action, 1780–1850*. Madison: University of Wisconsin Press.

Cuvier, M.G., 1817, "Extrait d'observations faites sur le cadavre d'une femme connue à Paris et à Londres sous le nom de Vénus Hottentote", *Mémoires du Museum d'Histoire Naturelle*, Vol. 3, 259–74.

de Blainville, M., 1816, "Sur une femme de la race hottentote", *Bulletin des Sciences par la Société philomatique de Paris*, 183–90.

Dickens, Charles, 1853, "The Noble Savage", *Household Words*, 11 June, 337–39.

Frederickson, George M., 1971, *The Black Image in the White Mind: The Debate on Afro-American Character and Destiny, 1817–1914*. New York: Harper and Row.

George, Mary Dorothy, 1978, *Catalogue of Political and Personal Satires in the Department of Prints and Drawings in the British Museum*. London: British Museum, Vols. 8–10.

Gilman, Sander L., 1982, *On Blackness without Blacks: Essays on the Image of the Black in Germany*. Boston: G.K. Hall.

—, 1985, *Difference and Pathology: Stereotypes of Sexuality, Race and Madness*. Ithaca and London: Cornell University Press.

Goblot, Laurent, 1983, "L'Image du noir d'un peuple à l'autre", *Peuples Noirs, Peuples Africains*, No. 31, 40

Gould, Stephen Jay, 1981, *The Mismeasure of Man*. New York: Norton.

—, 1982, "The Hottentot Venus." *Natural History*, Vol. 91, 20–27.

Haggard, H. Rider, 1887, *Allan Quatermain*. London: Longmans, Green.

—, 1892, *Nada the Lily*. New York: Longmans, Green.

Hammond, Dorothy & Alta Jablow, 1970, *The Africa That Never Was: Four Centuries of British Writing about Africa*. New York: Twayne; reissued in 1977 as *The Myth of Africa*. New York: Library of Social Science.

Henty, G.A., 1885, *The Young Colonists*. London: George Routledge and Sons.

Kirby, Percival R., 1949, "The Hottentot Venus", *Africana Notes and News*, Vol. 6, 55–62.

—., 1953, "More about the Hottentot Venus", *Africana Notes and News*, Vol. 10, 124–34.

Kolb, Peter, 1731, *Present State of the Cape of Good Hope*. London: W. Innis.

Latham, R.G., 1856, "Ethnological Remarks upon Some of the More Remarkable Varieties of the Human Species, Represented by Individuals Now in London", *Journal of Ethnological Science*, Vol. 4, 149.

Le Vaillant, François, 1790, *Voyage dans l'intérieur de l'Afrique par le Cap de Bonne-Espérance, dans les années 1780–85*. Paris: Leroy. Vol. 2.

Lichtenstein, M.H.C., 1928, *Travels in Southern Africa in the Years 1803, 1804, 1805 and 1806*. Cape Town: Van Riebeeck Society. Vol. 2.

Lindfors, Bernth, 1984, "The Bottom Line: African Caricature in Georgian England", *World Literature Written in English*, Vol. 24, 43–51.

—, 1985, "Courting the Hottentot Venus", *Africa* (Rome), Vol. 40, 133–48.

Livingstone, David, 1875, *A Popular Account of Missionary Travels and Researches in South Africa*. London: John Murray.

Luschka, Hubert von, 1864, *Die Anatomie des menschilichen Beckens*. Tübingen: H. Laupp.

Lysons, Daniel, n.d., "Collectanea; or a Collection of Advertisements and Paragraphs from the Newspapers, Relating to Various Subjects," unpublished scrapbook, Vol. 2 (British Library 1881.b.6).

McKechnie, Samuel, n.d., *Popular Entertainments Through the Ages*. London: Sampson, Low, Marston.

Mitford, Bertram, 1893, *The Gun-Runner: A Tale of Zululand*. London: Chatto and Windus.

— 1894, *The Luck of Gerard Ridgeley: A Tale of the Zulu Border*. London: Chatto and Windus.

Prichard, James Cowles, 1855, *The Natural History of Man*. 4th ed. London: H. Baillière.

Racinet, Auguste, 1888, *Le Costume historique*. Paris: Firmin-Didot.

Scobie, Edward, 1972, *Black Britannia: A History of Blacks in Britain*. Chicago: Johnson Publishing Co.

Shaw, George Bernard, 1886, *Cashel Byron's Profession*. London: Modern Press.

Shephard, Ben, 1984, "A Royal Gentleman of Colour", *History Today*, April, 40.

Stepan, Nancy, 1982, *The Idea of Race in Science: Great Britain 1800–1960*. London: Macmillan.

Ten Rhyne, Wilhelmi, 1933, "Scediasma de Promontorio Bonae Spei: ejusve tractus incolis Hottentotis (1686)", in Schapera, I. (ed.), *The Early Cape Hottentots*, p. 47. Cape Town: Van Riebeeck Society.

Verneau, R., 1916, "Le centième anniversaire de la mort de Sarah Bartmann", *L'Anthropologie*, Vol. 27, 178.

Walker, Thomas (Whimsical), 1922, *From Sawdust to Windsor Castle*. London: Paul.

Wallace, Irving, 1959, *The Fabulous Showman: The Life and Times of P.T. Barnum*. New York: Knopf.

Labor Laws and Stereotypes
Images of the Khoikhoi in the Cape in the Age of Abolition

Zine Magubane

Introduction

This paper examines images of the Khoikhoi in the period between 1800 and 1850. During this time there was a tremendous amount of debate in Britain and the British colonies around the issue of free and unfree labor. The aim of the paper is to investigate how the Khoikhoi were represented with regard to issues of labor and the economy during, the popular debates of the time. From the time that John Barrow first reported on the condition of the Khoikhoi in his much cited *Travels into the Interior of South Africa* the issue of the Khoikhoi, their propensity (or lack thereof) for labor, and the reasons for it were the subject of a (great deal of discussion. This discussion was resumed with renewed vigor in the wake of the abolition of the slave trade in 1807, the Caledon Code of 1809, the Apprenticeship Act of 1812, Ordinance 50 of 1828, emancipation, and the proposed Vagrancy Legislation of 1834. Each time a change was introduced into the labor market provided an opportunity for the issue of the Khoikhoi as laboring men or women to be debated publicly.

These discussions are fascinating in that they contain layer upon layer of subtext. It is clear that the Cape colony suffered a generalized labor shortage. The abolition of the slave trade and emancipation served only to exacerbate the situation. Farmers had always relied on a combination of slave and (nominally free) Khoikhoi labor, and used whatever legal and discursive devices they could muster to secure continued access to that labor. Hence, it is not difficult to see why an image of the Khoikhoi as "vagrant" and "Idle" emerged in the settler press. Debates over interventions in the labor market provided arenas wherein these images crystallized and were disseminated to the wider public.

Representatives of the London Missionary Society who were not only involved in preaching the Gospel but also in the fight against slavery saw thin as rather differently. Although they, too, represented the Khoikhoi as idle, they were at pains to show how the slave economy of the Cape was ultimately responsible for Khoikhoi deficiencies. Thus, agitating for the civil rights of the Khoikhoi was always deeply implicated the fight against unfree labor generally.

However, the way in which these two very different groups of British represented the Khoikhoi goes much deeper than a simple fight over what kind of labor system (slave or free) should rule the colony. That was just the "top layer" so to speak. Underneath the conflict over labor systems lay a conflict between two fundamentally different world views. These world views had been shaped not only by, experiences at the Cape, but more importantly, by experiences that were carried over from Europe. Thus, these debates were as much about how the Europeans saw and experienced one another, as they were about how they saw and experienced the Khoikhoi. Largely due to the work of post-modernism and post-colonial studies it is well accepted that the colonial encounter involves, amongst other things, a process of transference whereby the Colonized Other becomes a screen upon which negative elements of the self-image of the Colonizer are projected. In the early 19th century when issues of class struggle, hierarchy, and status loomed large in British sensibilities, it was not a simple case of the Khoikhoi acting as a screen upon which settler fantasies were projected. In the case of the missionaries and other representatives of the rising middle classes, the Khoikhoi functioned as proof positive of the power of self improvement and reform as well as the viability of the capitalist social order. For the conservative eastern Cape settlers the Khoikhoi were the line of demarcation between a host of binary oppositions; slave/free, civilized/savage, elevated/degraded, and, of course, white/ black. They were in need of this kind of reinforcement because of the extremely insecure position in which they found themselves given the fluidity in class, caste, and status amongst whites that both precipitated and characterized the 1820 settlement scheme.

Labor legislation at the Cape

The Caledon Code of 1809 required Khoikhoi to have certificates of residency and passes: this enabled local officials to distribute Khoikhoi labor to anyone they chose. From the date of Caledon's law onwards all Khoikhoi living in the colony were regarded as being subject in every, respect to the colonial courts of law. The practical effect of the law was to require all Khoikhoi laborers, upon leaving their place of service, to report to the field coronet of their district from whom they received passes and directions to find a new master. The passes were only valid within the field cornetcy, arid the length of time given to the laborer to find new employment was also subject to the discretion of the field coronet. If a laborer wished to go beyond the limits of the pass he or she was required to make an application to the *landdrost* for permission. Neither the field coronet nor the *landdrost* was subject to any type of control in his dealing with the Khoikhoi laborers. An investigation into abuses in the pass system at Uitenhage showed the following:

> The period allowed in the passes varies and Hottentots are required to find masters immediately. The field coronets and landdrosts have been disposed generally to abridge the period as well as the distance to which their permissions have extended, with a view to monopoly of labor in their particular district. The result of these regulations has been that of creating a perpetual obligation in the Hotten-

tots to enter into service, for although it was declared that, at the expiration of his engagement a Hottentot was free to make another or to act in any manner that the laws of the colony, admitted, yet in the event of his not making a new engagement he was liable to be apprehended as a vagrant thrown in a gaol, and a master provided for him.[1]

The Caledon measure had the practical effect of coercing all Khoikhoi into the service of the colonists. Without a pass A was illegal for anyone of Khoikhoi descent to be anywhere in the colony at all. The colonists—particularly Its local officials like he *landdrost* and Field coronet—controlled the issuing of passes and thus gained the right of total control over the mobility of all Khoikhoi within the colony. The Caledon Code was followed by two others dated 1812 and 1819. The first of these, passed by Governor Cradock, stipulated that Khoikhoi children who had been maintained by their parents' employer up to the age of eight years should be apprenticed to that employer for a further period of ten years without remuneration, save food and clothing. If the employer refused or was found unfit to carry out the responsibility the *landdrost* was authorized to bind the children in question as apprentices to another "suitable" employer within the district. This principle was extended by the proclamation of 1819 which decreed that any Khoikhoi child whose mother died or was unable to care for him would be "apprenticed to Christian inhabitants of known and acknowledged humane disposition and good character until age 18".[2] As a result of the law the extremely derogatory and insulting term "Hottentot" came to be synonymous with thievery and vagrancy.

In 1828, however, as a result of a strong campaign by John Philip in Britain the acting Governor of the Cape, Richard Bourke, promulgated Ordinance 50 which served to guarantee for the Khoikhoi the same freedom and protection as any other British subject. It ended compulsory labor except for that to which whites were also liable. Ordinance 50 altered the status of colonial Khoikhoi and limited the legal authority of white employers. The law decreed that it was no longer necessary for the Khoikhoi to have a fixed place of abode, carry passes, or be subject to pass laws. Khoikhoi children could no longer be forced into service. Oral contracts of service were henceforth to be binding for one month only and registered contracts for a maximum of one year. Domestic punishment of servants was no longer admitted in law, but penal sanctions could be invoked against the servant for breach of contract. In the law the Khoikhoi were granted legal equality and, formally, the right to buy land. This meant lifting the slavery-like restrictions which prevented the free movement of labor. The opposition to Ordinance 50 was widespread

---

[1] W. Colebrooke, Report upon the State of the Hottentots and Bushmen of the Cape of Good Hope (Cape Town, 1829), p. 20.
[2] Ibid., p. 24.

amongst the settler population. In May of 1834 in the wake of the Emancipation Act, this generalized discontent crystallized in the form of a Draft Ordinance to reinstate vagrancy legislation. This Ordinance, however, never became law.

Images and counter-images of Khoikhoi labor 1800–1850

From the time that the first British humanitarians explored the Cape, they decried the idleness of the Khoikhoi which they saw as an inevitable result of the slave economy of the Cape. The Dutch settlers were chastised for treating the Khoikhoi no better than chattel. It was this unhealthy relationship that induced sloth and idleness in both black and white. Barrow represented the Khoi as being the "most wretched of the human race." He continued

> duped out of their possessions, their country, and their liberty, they have entailed upon their miserable offspring a state of existence to which that of slavery might bear the comparison of happiness ... their extreme poverty, scantiness of food, and continual dejection of mind, arising from an inhuman and unfeeling peasantry who have hitherto exercised, in the most wanton and barbarous manner, an absolute power over these poor wretches whom they had reduced to the necessity of depending upon them for a morsel of bread.[3]

John Campbell continued in this tradition when he wrote:

> Many of the Boers have four or five stout sons, who, in consequence of the crowd of Hottentots in the house, have no occasion to put their hands to any work. ... In this way their days and years pass on in miserable idleness. Perhaps the only thing which a Hottentot will have to do during the whole day is to bring his master's whip from the next room; another will have to bring his mistress's fire box and place it under her feet; a third, to bring two or three times wood from the fire to light the master's pipe. In this way the Hottentots have their habits of idleness confirmed and increased.[4]

The missionaries saw that the relationship between the Khoikhoi and the Boers was tantamount to slavery. Because the missionary enterprise was so closely related to that of the abolitionists, the movement for the liberation of the Khoikhoi quite naturally became closely allied with that of anti-slavery. The missionaries agitating for Khoikhoi emancipation used the same kinds of moral and economic arguments that the abolitionists did. Slavery and forced labor were seen as both economically inefficient as well as leading to the moral decline of both servant and master. The missionaries made considerable efforts to demonstrate that the Dutch (and later the eastern Cape settlers) held the Khoikhoi as virtual slaves. This, in turn was responsible for their current state of degradation.

---

[3] J. Barrow, *Travels into the Interior of Southern Africa* (London, 1801), Vol. 11, p. 93.
[4] J. Campbell, *Travels in South Africa* (London, 1815), p. 110.

However, they were confident that freeing their souls and freeing their labor would kick off a process of rapid transformation. An article in the *Methodist Magazine* challenged those opposed to the mission enterprise to

> show in any part of the world, a people more capable of being improved than the abused Hottentots of South Africa, or attempts at civilization more complete in their success than what may now be seen at Bethelsdorp.[5]

Another missionary concurred when he wrote:

> It is pleasing beyond expression to behold the success of our feeble efforts in the instruction of the rising generation of Hottentots. Little more than four months have elapsed since their admission into the school., nevertheless the most promising and encouraging effects already appear. ... We have *now* the unspeakable pleasure to see them desirous of being taught the truths of Christianity, which ever inculcate habits of cleanliness, order, and decorum.[6]

The most famous exposition on the moral and spiritual uplift attendant upon the abolition of bonded labor and the entrenching of capitalist labor relations was, of course, the oft quoted *Researches in South Africa* which was published in the same year that the so-called "Magna Carta" of the Hottentots or Ordinance 50 was passed.

> Make the colored population in your colony free ... permit the natives to choose their own masters—secure to them, inviolate from the grasp of colonial violence, the right which God and nature have given to their offspring—allow them to bring their labor to a free market, and the farmers will no longer have occasion to complain of a want of servants.[7]

It is clear that Philip and others were trying to fix an image of the Khoikhoi in the minds of their fellow settlers and the colonial administration. Their view on Khoikhoi character and destiny was based on three premises. The first was that the Khoikhoi were the potential equals of the European; with the proper degree of education and 'civilization' they could some day be entrusted with similar rights and responsibilities. The second was that the Khoikhoi, far from being hopeless and degraded by nature were in actuality noble; they only needed the proper environment to uplift them. The final premise was that Christianity and free labor held the key to Khoikhoi advancement; conversion to Christianity was the means by which the Khoikhoi could come to take their place among other civilized men. The freeing of their labor would raise them to the level of any other British subject. The Liberal position is summed up in the oft quoted passage by John Philip who said that all men are savage until given the proper degree of instruction.

---

[5] February 1823, p. 129.

[6] *Methodist Magazine*, January 1824, p. 201.

[7] J. Philip, *Researches in South Africa* (London, 1828), p. 329.

> We are all born savages, whether we are brought into the world in the populous city or in the lonely desert. It is the discipline of education, and the circumstances under which we are placed, which create the differences between the rude barbarian and the polished citizen—the listless savage and the man of commercial enterprise—the man of the woods and the literary reclusive.[8]

In the wake of Ordinance 50 and emancipation, therefore, the Khoikhoi would naturally return to their former state of grace. The key to Khoikhoi uplift lay in their conversion to Christianity and their acceptance of European habits of industry.

> [They are] an acute, active, and enterprising race of men, but their unhappy condition as a degraded caste, and the irregular sort of life they had led, in some respects ... was not favorable to the formation of habits either of steady industry or strict morality.[9]

The Dutch and British settlers as well as the first three Cape governors, Cradock, Caledon, and Somerset were completely opposed to Khoikhoi emancipation, the abolition of slavery, and humanitarian reform. They were mired in the hierarchical society of the Cape colony and saw the missionaries as advocating a form of society that was dangerously fluid. In the aftermath of Ordinance 50 and emancipation they became even more outspoken in their characterization of the Khoikhoi as "idle" and unable to cope with independence. They were at pains to represent the Khoikhoi as hopelessly idle, drunken, and addicted to thieving. One settler described the Khoikhoi as a

> degraded and vicious population, they plunge into the grossest intemperance, indulge in the most shameless debauchery, disgrace our streets by their drunken brawls and pollute the car by their obscene language and imprecations; they people our jails, and they wander through the country in idleness, and prey upon the industry of those who are exerting themselves to promote their own and the general welfare.[10]

Just as the missionaries were at pains to demonstrate that freedom and free labor led naturally to moral uplift, the settlers were at pains to prove the opposite. In the wake of the Emancipation Act and the blocking of the Vagrancy Legislation of 1834, considerable time was spent discussing the evils attendant upon free labor. The same settler went on to list the evils attendant upon emancipation:

> Ungathered vintages, fallow fields, crops rotten on the ground, unserved tables, and labor-lacking warehouses—these were some of the evils sustained by the colony and the colonists; but still more pitiable was the state of the helpless victims, bound to the horns of the great idol Liberty. ... Another change ... soon followed

---

[8] Ibid., p. 319.
[9] T. Pringle, *Narrative of a Residence in South Africa* (London 1835), p. 111.
[10] J. Chase, *The Cape of Good Hope* (London, 1842), p. 233.

the Emancipation Act—the bye-alley, the low reeking roof, the close straw hut, were visited by disease. Intemperance had prepared the way and pestilence followed in her rear ... The rod fell chiefly ... with a hundred fold severity on the emancipated slave and Hottentot, crowded and I impoverished as they were left by their sudden enfranchisement. ... Emancipated from slavery they were also emancipated from the kindest guardianship.[11]

Napier concurred when he wrote:

It would appear that the real cause of the diminution of the Hottentot race may be therefore in great measure attributed—not to the reasons usually alleged—but to the effects of accidental disease, aggravated by natural habits of improvidence, filth, and intemperance, evil effects probably not a little increased by that spirit of indolence—or rather thorough idleness—so shamefully countenanced and encouraged at most of the missionary establishments within the limits of the Colony. Here, under the false pretense of being instructed—and, generally speaking, by most incompetent instructors—in the doctrines of Christianity, the Hottentot leads a life of, to him, *dolce far niente*; during which his manual labor (with the remuneration for the same) is not only lost, but those habits of idleness, which invariably beget vice, are here a hundredfold increased. These hotbeds of laziness have been ... converted into nurseries for harboring deserters and vagabonds of every description; and with the germs of discontent and suspicion, most injudiciously planted, have produced the evil fruits of enmity against the Colony.[12]

Bowker argued explicitly against the equation of free labor with moral salvation when he argued that had the settlers had their way and Vagrancy Ordinances been kept on the books:

Savageism would long ere this been fast fading away before civilization,—the animal propensities would have begun to give place to the moral; filial attachment, gratitude for parental care, sense of propriety, domestic honor, charity, love, piety, might possibly have been developed among men whom that system would have sternly taught to distinguish between right and wrong—to respect life and property, and to work for their own maintenance.[13]

Clearly, a very serious debate was being waged over the future labor system at the Cape. However, if we return to our metaphor of "pulling back" layers of analysis, it is also clear that what we are witnessing is a clash between two different experiences of being British.

The British in South Africa: How, why, and where from?

The humanitarian reform movement, which spawned both abolition and the missionary movement, is curious and contradictory. In some ways it represented the most progressive forces that England had to offer. In other ways it

---

[11] Chase, loc. cit.

[12] E. Napier, *Excursions in South Africa* (London, 1852), p. 112.

[13] J. Bowker, *Speeches, Letters, and Selections from Important Papers* (Grahamstown, 1864), p. 209.

was shockingly conservative. The reform movement is difficult to analyze because it contained so many strands and because it underwent so many changes. It has been accused of being a cover for the forces of Jacobinism and Thomas Paine. It has also been accused of being the agent by which Europe conquered Africa. It was home to both radicals and conservatives, wealthy merchants and struggling artisans. Therefore, in order to understand the lens through which the Khoikhoi were viewed, it is important to look critically at the life experiences of the men who eventually became missionaries (the rank and file) as well as the elite class of men who led the movement. Specifically, it is important to examine their life experiences as they related to issues of social status and labor

When we look at South Africa in the period between 1800 and 1830 when John Philip, Johannes van der Kemp, and James Read were the most vocal and outspoken, the issue at the forefront of every humanitarian's attention was that of slavery and abolition. These men need to be understood as having come of age with the abolition movement. Thus, although they were not necessarily abolitionists, they recognized the interrelated nature of Khoikhoi emancipation and emancipation generally. They were also subject to the ideological vicissitudes of the abolition movement.

Enlightened abolitionists attacked slavery from the 1760s to the 1780s. This reform cause went on to gather radical support in the early 1790s. The radical support was such that some conservatives were led to denounce the abolition movement as a Jacobin front.

In the early 19th century, however, the movement pulled away from the Painite radicals of the early 1790s and won legitimacy from government ministries in the years 1806–07. Soon after it was penetrated by wealthy merchant philanthropists and British political and social elites who were generally obsessed with the fear that social reform would lead to revolution.[14] William Wilberforce, for example, was the son of a rich Hull merchant. Thomas Fowell Buxton was a partner in a brewery concern.

The rank and file of the missionary movement were not from such prestigious backgrounds. John Philip, for example, was an artisan who was able to advance due to the period of economic prosperity in Scotland that coincided with his youth and young manhood. James Kitchingham, one of the first missionaries to come to South Africa, was a shoemaker before being ordained and was "acutely conscious of his humble origins, the inadequacy of his education, and his lack of sophistication."[15] James Read was a carpenter who had received little formal education. Neither Robert Moffat nor David Livingstone had benefit of much formal education. Moffat was apprenticed to a gardener

[14] D. Davis, "Reflections on Abolition and Ideological Hegemony" in T. Bender, *The Anti-Slavery Debate* (University of California Press, 1992).
[15] B. le Cordeur, *The Kitchingham Papers* (Brenthurst Press, 1976), p. 9.

while Livingstone, though trained as a doctor, came from an extremely disadvantaged background and was put to work at the age of ten as a piecer in a cotton factory.[16] For these men who had made their ways unsteadily into the ranks of the middle class, involvement in the church conferred not only respectability but also a measure of social security, despite its limited financial rewards. Thus, they placed a high value on achievement and respectability as well as on education and discipline. David Livingstone summed up this attitude best when he reflected back on his humble upbringing:

> Looking back now on that period of toil, I cannot but feel thankful that it formed such a material part of my early education; and were I to begin life over again, I should like to pass through the same hardy training. I never received a farthing from anyone.[17]

The missionaries believed in the improvability of all men, at least in part, because of their experiences in Europe. Their belief in the capacity of the Khoikhoi for self improvement reflected their own commitment to self improvement through diligence and sacrifice. Their understanding of history and society was based on Adam Smith's understanding of the world. The general good of everyone, so the argument went, would be served by everyone working hard and following their economic opportunities. "These men and women had 'got on' because of their Christian faith and the dedication to hard work and the virtuous 'life that accompanied such faith in their milieu. In Africa they believed that in turn, the Khoi, the Griqua, the Xhosa could also 'get on' by following the same path."[18] To espouse such views in a slave oriented society ruled by *ancien regime* Tories was dangerously radical. However, there were serious limits to this radicalism. In important ways their brand of radicalism functioned to maintain social and political inequality, not to overthrow it. They saw civilized society as essentially a *class* society. There would be rich and poor, employers and employees. The Khoikhoi were to be given the same legal rights and obligations as any other proletarian in Britain or the empire. Their greatest hope was to transform the Khoikhoi into cheerful and obedient wage laborers. They assumed that the British system of free wage labor achieved a good balance between order and freedom and could "serve as a norm against which all other labor regimes could be measured."[19] They were always careful to maintain a sharp distinction between the evils of the slave world and the "free" institutions that had been imperiled by French tyranny and Jacobinism.

---

[16] G. Seaver, *David Livingstone; His Life and Letters* (Lutterworth Press, 1957).

[17] D. Livingstone, *Missionary Travels and Researches in South Africa* (London, 1912), p. 5.

[18] R. Ross, *John Philip (1775–1851): Missions, Race and Politics in South Africa* (Aberdeen Press, 1986), p. 80.

[19] D. Davis, op. cit., p. 165.

84

The settlers, on the other hand, had profoundly different experiences prior to and in the immediate aftermath of emigration. Unlike the missionaries who had experienced life as a steady stream of upward mobility, they had fallen victim to a steady stream of failures and setbacks. The same economic forces that inspired the rising middle class with confidence and led to their economic triumphs, had driven the settlers to financial ruin in England. The tremendous loss in social status that accompanied this financial misfortune was a key factor in the decision to emigrate.

As was mentioned previously, in 1819 the British Government promulgated a scheme to assist approximately 4,000 emigrants to settle at the Cape. This was not the first time the British government had sponsored an emigration scheme. However, this scheme differed quite profoundly from other such schemes for two reasons. First, it attracted a record number of applicants. Second, it drew applicants from a class of British society that had not been involved previously. The terms of this scheme stipulated that free passages and grants of land would only be granted to men of sufficient means to sponsor and settle a work force of ten or more laborers. The official position of the government was that no applications from individual settlers and their families who lacked the capital to employ laborers would be accepted. In actuality, a number of people wishing to do just that banded together in groups of the required number and selected a nominal head to apply on their behalf. The land grant their leader received in the colony was to be divided among them. These joint stock parties were contrary to the letter and spirit of the scheme, nevertheless they made up the bulk of the settlers.

According to official policy pauper parties were *not* to be admitted. Paupers were only to be allowed as subordinate laborers, not as independent emigrants. Thus, the great majority of emigrants fell somewhere between the two categories of substantial capitalists and paupers. Roughly, there were three different classes of people represented in the scheme. The first were the declining gentlemen, the very persons the scheme was designed to attract. Such men had a small amount of capital and could afford to pay the expenses of the passage to the Cape and settle themselves and a number of impoverished laborers who were, in effect, their indentured servants. These men who became the leaders of the "proprietary parties" were members of the respectable classes who emigrated to avoid facing the prospect of reduced social status at home. Such reductions in status came about as a result of either revolution from below, changed economic relations, or both. Miles Bowker, a Wiltshire farmer who was one of the first to apply, stated the following reasons for his desire to emigrate.

> I have twice in my life been worth £14,000 or upwards, and twice by necessary political arrangements had that sum nearly annihilated. I am presently upon a large farm where I can make a living, but cannot provide for a family of eight sons and one daughter without reducing them to the lowest ranks in society

which ill accords with their previous knowledge of being descended from the first.[20]

The administrators in the Colonial Office supported the scheme of granting land primarily to men like Bowker because "it held out the expectation of stability in binding upper and lower classes in a legally-enforceable master-servant relationship; and it kept the ownership of land in upper class hands".[21]

The second group of emigrants consisted of joint stock parties. These parties were made up of men of respectable rank (though perhaps not quite as respectable as the proprietary heads). They were merchants, professional men, or half pay officers with limited funds who could not commit themselves to the responsibility of taking out and maintaining a party. By joining forces with other would-be emigrants in similar circumstances they were able to make up the required numbers and funds. The admission of this class of men profoundly influenced the future of the scheme. Opening the door to a larger number of settlers with education and means had the effect of increasing the number of potential employers without introducing a proportionate number of laborers in an area where labor was already in desperately short supply. These men were to eventually clash not only with the autocratic colonial state but the "would-be gentry" that were the leaders of the proprietary parties.

It appears that the emigration scheme was doomed from the start. There were far too many men with the ambition to lead and far too few with the desire to labor. The problem reached alarming proportions shortly after the settlers arrived at the Cape. The labor shortage throughout the colony afforded the poor artisans the opportunity to return to their trades and the high rate of wages that prevailed in the colony made many of the indentured servants break their agreements. Indeed, it was the agricultural servants and the mechanics who came to the colony as paupers who soon found their condition improving and those of the "better classes" who found themselves in the most dire of circumstances. In *Some Account of the Present State of the English Settlers in Albany South Africa* Pringle reported that the mechanics and laborers had generally improved their condition by emigration to the financial detriment of the party heads:

> The remnant of the English Emigrants consist chiefly of the heads of parties, and of the independent families who expected to establish themselves on their several allotments by the aid of their own funds, or the exertions of their own industry. These two classes have been by far the most unfortunate, if not the exclusive sufferers, by the result of the emigration. The mechanics and laborers found sufficient and profitable employment on the locations, so long as the funds of the superior settlers lasted. ... The great body of them gradually abandoned the settle-

---

[20] Theal, *Records of the Cape Colony*, Vol. XII (Cape Town, 1902), p. 119.
[21] M. Nash, *Bailie's Party of 1820 Settlers* (A.A. Balkema, 1982), p. 13.

ment and quietly dispersed themselves throughout the colony when the means of their employers failed and the free rations and local restrictions were alike withdrawn by the colonial government.[22]

Finding themselves in even further reduced circumstances and unable to force their indentured servants or the Khoi to labor for them the "Albany gentry" as they came to be called, borrowed and adapted from discourses at home about the poor and the working classes. Here we locate the source of such pejorative words as "indolence," "thieving," and "lack of self control". Indeed it was the mechanics and laborers who first came under censure and were described as "indolent". Pringle, for example, reported that the white laboring classes in the colony had "conducted themselves with much reprehensible idleness, improvidence, and presumption".[23] Another settler complained that the "lower orders have been corrupted through idleness".[24] While yet another protested that government rations had allowed the servants to "continue in a state of idleness".[25]

These settlers had brought with them to South Africa a whole baggage of class prejudices and practices which dated back to the Elizabethan poor laws which "provided work for those that would labor and punishment for those that would not".[26] According to McClintock:

> Beginning in sixteenth century Britain, an intricate discourse on idleness had emerged, not only to draw a distinction between laboring classes but also to sanction and enforce social discipline, to legalize land plunder, and to alter habits of work.[27]

Thus, the discourse surrounding the Khoikhoi was not so very different from the discourse that had surrounded white labor for centuries. The Albany settlers came from a hierarchical, class-conscious social order wherein inequality was part of the natural order of things. On occasion, writers on the servant question referred to domestics not as a distinct class but as a separate race. And the "civilizing mission" first referred not to the rule of Europeans over Africans but to the wealthy over the poor in Britain itself.

These notions only became rigidly racialized when "a white skin became the essential mark of a gentleman".[28] This change, in turn, was spurred by the paradox of life in the colonies where the ordinary extremes of behavior of British domestic life were exaggerated, while the extremes of social distance were infinitely reduced. Francis Hutchins made the following observation

[22] T. Pringle, *Some Account of the English Settlers in Albany South Africa* (London, 1824), p. 33.
[23] Ibid.
[24] Theal, *Records of the Cape Colony*, Vol. XIV, p. 105.
[25] Ibid.
[26] G. Himmelfarb, *The Idea of Poverty* (Alfred Knopf, 1984), p. 27.
[27] A. McClintock, *Imperial Leather* (Routledge, 1995), p. 252.
[28] D. Lorimer, *Colour, Class and the Victorians* (Oxford Press, 1978), p. 15.

about India which applies equally well to South Africa in the 1820s and 1830s:

> The viceroy of noble birth and the disorderly soldier were united by a bond which would not have existed in England. The official Englishman could not dismiss vulgar Englishmen with the contempt the aristocracy would have employed at home, for the simple reason that his own pretension rested on the same grounds as that of the common soldier. The English nation, in its entirety was depicted as an aristocracy with respect to India; the whole English nation was 'the aristocracy of nature.' While the official Englishman might deplore the conduct of the vulgar Englishman he was trapped by the realization that if he sacrificed the vulgar specimens among his countrymen he was jeopardizing his own position.[29]

The gentlemen settlers like Bowker and Chase were acutely aware that their claims to aristocratic status were becoming more and more tenuous as time passed. First, the middle class British men of lesser means who had come out as members of joint stock parties soon became engaged in mercantile or commercial activity. Very soon they surpassed the upper class settlers in wealth and influence. Even more upsetting was the fact that the servants who broke their labor agreements were able to find employment in town and, as a result, were quickly improving. It was "the persons who had formerly been in a respectable situation of life in England and had brought out some property with them who suffered the greatest privations and calamities."[30] One settler complained to Earl Bathurst that:

> Combination and mutiny have changed the face of servitude, they have broken the bonds of indenture, servants have become bold plunderers! And masters have become mere slaves![31]

Another settler made an appeal to Somerset for relief based on the fact that the better classes were sinking below the status of the servants they had brought out. He wrote:

> Born of honorable Parents, descended from ancestors conspicuous for their public and private virtues untainted with vice, I now call on my Lord Bathurst and yourself to do justice to my injured feelings, to rescue my name and that of my amiable wife, a lady of one of the highest families in Ireland, and our six children, from the stigma, the stain thus thrown on the settlers generally.[32]

Yet another settler complained to Somerset that the indentured servants he had brought out had "behaved in a manner unbecoming their station". He protested that his servants, upon hearing how easy it was to obtain a higher

---

[29] F. Hutchins, *The Illusion of Permanence* (Princeton University Press, 1967), p. 111.
[30] *Report of the Committee of the Society for the Relief of the Distressed Settlers at the Cape of Good Hope* (London, 1824), p. 30.
[31] Theal, *Records of the Cape Colony*, Vol. XIII, p. 212.
[32] Theal, *Records of the Cape Colony*, Vol. XIV, p. 190.

station in the colonies, had become insolent and outspoken. In a letter to Somerset he decried his situation:

> They actually said that the laboring Men were better off in this country than their Masters and subordination was completely at an end as soon as they heard how the heads of parties were treated.[33]

The heightened sensitivity to race also stemmed from the new, harsher attitudes towards social status that emerged out of the politically and socially disturbed times.

Hutchins noted that the increased emphasis on social status and rank was related, not only to the growing competitiveness of the international situation in Europe, but also to changes in the social and political position of the British middle classes. The advancing specter of inter-race equality prompted many mid-Victorian gentlemen to nurture far greater consciousness of distinctions in status. What the "respectable classes" realized was that their class position no longer guaranteed them the privileges it had previously, they emphasized race as yet another factor distinguishing them from the lower orders. "Much of the talk about barbarism or darkness of the outer world was a transmuted fear of the masses at home."[34]

Thus, the Eastern Cape settlers were products of a profoundly different social experience than the missionaries. Therefore, where the missionaries saw the liberation of the Khoikhoi as further affirmation of the triumph of their world view, the settlers viewed this same process as further affirmation that theirs had been eclipsed. The legal elevation of the Khoikhoi to the same status as any British subject and the emancipation of the slaves brought greater fluidity (whether real or imagined) to social hierarchies at the Cape. This fluidity was extremely disconcerting to a group that had already experienced a profound degree of social dislocation.

No discussion of images of the Khoikhoi would be complete without some mention of how the "objects" of discussion engaged with this process. The Khoikhoi were well aware of the near continuous assaults on not only their liberty but their character. After a particularly vitriolic assault on the Khoikhoi that appeared in the *Grahamstown Journal* one missionary made the following observation which appeared in a *Missionary Register* of January 1828:

> An attack has been made upon us in a paper published at Cape Town; the writer, who calls himself Rusticus, seems very angry, and repeats his unfounded charges, the absurdity of which is manifest to all acquainted with the Mission. Yet such calamities tend to distress us, and ... disturb the minds of our Hottentots.[35]

---

[33] Ibid.
[34] V. Kiernan, *The Lords of Human Kind* (Oxford Press, 1972), p. 33.
[35] Ibid., p. 28.

The Khoikhoi vigorously protested the negative images being put forth and devised a variety of different strategies for broadcasting an alternative image to the public. Khoikhoi people organized meetings to oppose vagrancy ordinances as well as to draw up memoranda to the colonial and British governments. At each and every mission petitions opposing vagrancy legislation were drawn up. 401 Kat River residents supported by the London Missionary Society sent a letter to Sir Benjamin d'Urban that protested against the proposed Vagrancy Ordinance of 1834. The petition protested that the legislation would "seal the degradation" of the Khoikhoi as well as "present such a barrier to their improvement as will for ever prevent their rising in the scale of society."[36]

The petition demonstrated the intensity of the Khoikhoi opposition to the proposed vagrancy ordinances. It is clear that the Khoikhoi understood very well that they were being singled out on account of their race. They were also cognizant of the fact that the proposed vagrancy legislation was yet another assault in a long line of racial assaults stretching very far back into the past. The petition was careful to point out the long-standing and irrational nature of discrimination by whites against Africans and to highlight the danger of giving discriminatory behavior the force of law. The Khoikhoi then went on to present an image of themselves as a race undergoing rapid improvement thanks to the introduction of Christianity, Civilization, and Commerce amongst them. Indeed, the second paragraph of the petition clearly demonstrates the extent to which their self-definition had been influenced by the writings and speeches of the missionaries. The final sentence of the second paragraph which states "the memorialists came to the mission institutions without morals, without Bibles, without any knowledge of the white man's God, without property, and without any clothing, except the sheepskin kaross, but now have schools and Bibles, a knowledge of the Supreme Being, houses of their own, and can appear in public and at church clothed in British manufactures",[37] appears to have been lifted almost directly from Philip's *Researches in South Africa*.

The petition, however, presents the emerging Khoikhoi self concept M only the most embryonic of terms. It is in the speeches given at the protests against the Vagrancy Act of 1834 that we see the Khoikhoi represent themselves in the most clear and articulate fashion. These protests were the strongest, most sophisticated, and well planned in Khoikhoi history. At Theopolis the protest against the Vagrancy Act took the form of a day of prayer and fasting. There were also extremely large and well attended meetings at Phillipus Mission during August and October of 1834, the full proceedings of which were

---

[36] J. Sales, *Mission Stations and the Colored communities of the Eastern Cape, 1800–1852* (A.A. Balkema, 1975), p. 131.

[37] Ibid.

splashed across the pages of *The South African Commercial Advertiser*. These meetings were modeled on the May Meetings of Exeter Hall. Accounts of them were also published in the *Missionary Chronicle*. Elbourne writes that "experience with the London Missionary Society made the Khoisan aware of the benefits of a particular type of publicity".[38]

The Khoikhoi self concept was extremely sophisticated and based on their understanding of their own history and the role European conquest had played in bringing about their current degraded state. One of the strongest and most frequently repeated themes in Khoikhoi speeches and writings was that of the inherent equality of all men before God; regardless of race. The Khoikhoi presented their arguments so clearly and elegantly that 1 will allow them to speak for themselves.

James Read Junior, the offspring of the Reverend James Read and an African woman, made the following pronouncement at a meeting held at Philipton on August 5, 1834. His speech was reprinted in full in *The Advertiser* of September 3, 1834.

> The equality of the government was adopted from the equality of the race—all our fellow citizens are brethren of the same parents—therefore we regard ourselves not as slaves and masters, as we are in every respect equal.

Closely related to the idea that the Khoikhoi and the settlers were equal was the idea that they deserved the same treatment in the areas of government, society, and economy. At the same meeting Andries Pretorious, one of the most outspoken of the Khoikhoi made the following observations:

> [The Hottentots] became vagrants on account of hard treatment and bad pay. For the most all they got was six ewes a year, and even now many of us get only 6d per day. What could they make of six ewes? Could they farm with them? Or the 6d per day? Could they buy clothes with it? Or a spade? Let the Boer hire the settler for that, or the settler the Boer and let him see what he will make of it.[39]

Andries Stoffels, a Khoikhoi man who had been taken to England by John Philip and who was later to give testimony before the Select Committee on Aborigines in 1836 was even more adamant that black and white were equal and, therefore, deserved the same treatment in the polity and economy. He makes the point that the settlers were in an even more degraded state than the Khoikhoi when they first arrived in South Africa and it was only with the help of the government that they were able to raise themselves. He said the following in the course of a speech he made at a meeting at the Kat River Settlement on July 30, 1834:[40]

---

[38] E. Elbourne, *To Colonize the Mind* (London, 1991), p. 315.
[39] *South African Commercial Advertiser*, Sept. 3, 1834.
[40] *SACA*, Sept. 3, 1834.

When the settlers came out they asked where the Hottentots were that they heard of in England. ... The settlers were without horse or cow or sheep or hen. ... But the Hottentots lowered the prices of their horses out of compassion for them for they were very poor. Now the government supports them. ... There are people here in this meeting that carried some of the settlers! ... From the first to the last settler is provided for,—from the first to the last Boer is provided for—but the greatest number of the Hottentots are not.

The Khoikhoi had a complex understanding of their own history and the consequences of their oppression by the British and Dutch settlers. This knowledge strongly influenced their self-concept. The Khoikhoi are frank in their acknowledgment of the degraded condition which they found themselves in by mid-century. However, they are careful to demonstrate the extent to which this condition was the result of the depredations they had suffered, rather than being innate to them because of their color. They also stressed the degree to which they had improved and continued to improve. On August 16, a letter signed "A Hottentot" appeared in *The Advertiser.*

Sir, I came here ... in the year 1834 when he [Stockenstrom] said that the government had given the Kat River Settlement to the poor Hottentots. As it was [because] I was poor I came. ... I then commenced to labor ... but when I and my comrades were ready to make water-courses, the field coronet came with his men, broke my house to pieces, and drove us away stating it was by order of the government. 1 then settled in the field like a vagrant.

Sir I did not expect that this should happen, after I had good intention to labor. ... Sir, tell the governor not to make a vagrant law. ... It is but to give us a bad name. ... I have suffered enough. ... I fear I shall become a worse vagrant. ... I am an oppressed vagabond.

At the August 5 Philipton protest the speakers adamantly defended the Khoikhoi character as they asserted the rights of the Khoikhoi, as the original inhibitors of the land, to live in peace and dignity. A man from Phillipolis stood up and said:

The Hottentots are a poor people; but we have reason to thank God the he has raised men to plead their cause. If the word of God had not come the nation would have been extinct. The Vagrant Act may be well meant but it may be bad in its operation. We hear the people speak of sheep and cattle stealing and that the Hottentots are thieves. But we have to thank God that the Hottentots have been taught to write, and to defend themselves.[41]

Another speaker argued passionately for the Khoikhoi as the original inhabitants of South Africa:

Our fathers occupied the land from the Scout River to the Great Kay River. We see the land but cannot possess it. Our fathers had abundance of cattle and sheep,

---

[41] SACA, Sept. 3, 1834.

and then there were no vagrants, for they could support themselves. Then [we] became weak and lost our property, and were obliged to enter in the service of the farmers ... and become vagrants on account of hard treatment and bad pay. ...The government gives us freedom but ... no money, so that we must become vagrants.

Andries Botha was

at a loss as to know the sins of the Hottentot nation that they should have deserved such oppression ... he had never heard that the Hottentot nation possessed or had taken another people's land, or had oppressed them ... He was also greatly at a loss to account that the same people (the British) who had sent the Hottentots the Gospel, should now wish to throw them back into the hands of the Boers, from whom they had already suffered so much.[42]

The majority of the outspoken Khoikhoi were those that had gone through the mission system. They had been through mission schools, listened to numerous sermons, and some, at the behest of missionaries, had traveled overseas to tell their stories. It was quite natural, therefore, for them to seize on mission rhetoric and religious doctrines. In arguing for their equality they appealed to the ideal of the equality of all men before God. They presented themselves as devout Christians seeking neither more nor less than any other of their brethren. They argued against the settlers' portrayal of them as uncontrollable savages living in squalor as a result of their wanton and slovenly behavior. They acknowledged their degraded condition but located the source of their degradation not in their color, but in the circumstances in which white men had placed them. They were careful to point out the extent to which they had risen above their previous degraded condition and to acknowledge the important role that British missionaries had played in their transformation. Thus, they seized on the rhetoric of both the missionaries and the liberals—arguing that they had already demonstrated not only their common humanity but also their capacity for improvement. Their argument, however, stressed one very important element that neither the missionaries nor the Cape Liberals dared to touch. That was their insistence that they were the original inhabitants of the land. The idea that it was they and not the white men who were the rightful heirs to South Africa was an extremely important element in the Khoikhoi construction of their self-concept. They saw themselves as the aboriginal inhabitants of South Africa and demanded certain rights based on that fact. The Khoikhoi more than anyone understood the power of these images and thus sought to actively engage in their construction.

---

[42] SACA, Sept. 3, 1834.

Conclusion

The debates that took place around the Vagrancy Ordinances of 1809, 1812, and 1834 and the emancipations of 1828 and 1834 are not only debates around the relative merits and demerits of the proposed legislation, but also debates about particular ways of life. The missionaries and eastern Cape settlers had very different reasons for leaving England and arrived with very different experiences and expectations. These experiences profoundly colored their reactions to the potential disruptions to Cape society attendant upon both "emancipations". The Khoikhoi, however, refused to remain objects of discussion and seized on the extant narratives as vehicles for their self-representation.

This chapter has previously been printed in *South African Historical Journal*, Vol. 35, May 1996, pp. 115–34. It is reprinted with the kind permission of the journal.

References

Barrow, John, 1801, *Travels into the Interior of Southern Africa.* London: A. Strahan, Vol. 11.

Bowker, J., 1864, *Speeches, Letters, and Selections from Important Papers.* Grahamstown: G. Greig.

Campbell, John, 1815, *Travels in South Africa.* London: Black, Perry and Co.

Chase, J., 1842, *The Cape of Good Hope.* (Reprint: Cape Town: C. Struik, 1967).

Colebrooke, W., 1829, *Report upon the State of the Hottentots and Bushmen of the Cape of Good Hope,* (Cape Town).

Davis, David Brion, 1992, "Reflections on Abolition and Ideological Hegemony", in Bender, Thomas, *The Antislavery Debate.* Berkeley: University of California Press.

Elbourne, E., 1991, *To Colonize the Mind: Evangelical Missionaries in Britain and the Eastern Cape.* Ph.D. diss., Oxford University.

Himmelfarb, Gertrude, 1984, *The Idea of Poverty.* New York: Alfred Knopf.

Hutchins, Francis G., 1967, *The Illusion of Permanence.* Princeton: Princeton University Press.

Kiernan, Victor, 1972, *The Lords of Human Kind.* London: Oxford Press.

le Cordeur, Basil 1976, *The Kitchingham Papers.* Johannesburg: Brenthurst Press.

Livingstone, David, 1912, *Missionary Travels and Researches in South Africa.* London: John Murray.

Lorimer, Douglas A., 1978, *Colour, Class and the Victorians.* London: Oxford Press.

McClintock, Anne, 1995, *Imperial Leather.* New York: Routledge.

Methodist Magazine, January 1824:201.

Methodist Magazine, February 1823:129.

Napier, E., 1852, *Excursions in South Africa.* London: William Shobert.

Nash, M.D., 1982, *Bailie's Party of 1820 Settlers*. Cape Town: A.A. Balkema.

Philip, John, 1828, *Researches in South Africa*. London: James Duncan.

Pringle, T., 1824, *Some Account of the English Settlers in Albany South Africa*. London: T. and G. Underwood.

Pringle, Thomas, 1835, *Narrative of a Residence in South Africa*. (Reprint: Cape Town: C. Sruik, 1966).

Report of the Committee of the Society for the Relief of the Distressed Settlers at the Cape of Good Hope. London, 1824:30.

Ross, Andrew, 1986, *John Philip (1775–1851): Missions, Race and Politics in South Africa*. Aberdeen: Aberdeen University Press.

Sales, Jane, 1975, *Mission Stations and the Coloured communities of the Eastern Cape, 1800–1852*. Cape Town: A.A. Balkema.

Seaver, G., 1957, *David Livingstone; His Life and Letters*. London: Lutterworth Press.

South African Commercial Advertiser, Sept. 3, 1834.

Theal, 1902, *Records of the Cape Colony*, Vol. XII. Cape Town: C. Greig.

Theal, *Records of the Cape Colony*. Vol. XIII.

Theal, *Records of the Cape Colony*. Vol. XIV. London: 1897.

[Note: The records of the Cape Colony from 1793–1823 were copied for the Cape Government from the manuscript documents in the Public Record Office, London, by George McCall Theal.]

"A Gentleman Went to Zanzibar"
Racism and Humanism Revisited

Mai Palmberg

"If ever a universal talent was born to us it was Guss Mattsson", wrote Gunnar Castrén in his obituary about his journalist colleague Guss Mattsson who died much too young in 1914.[1] He became somewhat of a legendary figure in Finnish cultural life and in the Swedo-Finnish and Nordic history of journalism, concludes literary critic Sven Willner in his contribution on Guss Mattsson in a series of portraits of great Swedish-speaking Finns.[2]

Guss Mattsson was well versed both as a humanist and a natural scientist. Although by profession a chemist, he was extremely well read, and followed closely contemporary European cultural development. He presented the latest findings in technological development in accessible articles to a wider public, and he wrote about cultural anthropology and the psychological theories of Freud and others. His musicality was renowned, and he was an unusually accomplished amateur pianist. His knowledge of world politics was probably greater than that of any of his contemporaries in Finland, and he followed newspapers in several languages. While knowledgeable about politics he remained aloof from emotional attachment to any of the ideologies of the time. To sum up, if ever there was in the pre-World War I period in Finland a cultured person with an internationalist perspective and, in a philosophical and political sense, a humanist outlook, it was Guss Mattsson.

Guss Mattsson was in the process of editing his letters from his last trip, a sea voyage to Africa, when he died from his life-long illness, tuberculosis. The book "A Gentleman went to Zanzibar" did appear shortly after his death and became a household item in the Swedish-speaking homes in Finland, and was reprinted seven times.

In 1995 I took part in a radio programme on Guss Mattsson and Africa. I had selected some parts of the text to be read *verbatim* from the book as an illustration and as a basis for the discussion between the cultural editor and me. The actor who had been asked to read the selected texts exclaimed: "This man was a damned racist." This was contrary to Sven Willner's view in a previous radio programme on Guss Mattsson that "he was not a racist". In this paper I want to show that both of them were both right and wrong.

---

[1] Gunnar Castrén in *Nya Argus,* autumn 1914, quoted by Willner 1966.
[2] Willner, p. 8.

Guss Mattsson—the man and the country

Guss Mattsson's active period in the late 19th and the beginning of the 20th century coincided with an intense political period. Finland had since 1809 been a Grand Duchy under the Russian Czar (after many centuries as part and parcel of the kingdom of Sweden), and the autonomy had allowed the development of industry, transport, education against a background of strong Finnish nationalism. But at the turn of the century a Russification policy put a halt to this. How to meet this pan-Slavic offensive gave rise to heated debate, a passive resistance developed (including mass petitions, and refusals to respond to the military call-up) and occasional calls for a struggle for full independence from the tutelage of the Russian Czar were heard. Guss Mattsson died three years before Finland's independence in 1917.

Born in 1873 Guss Mattsson (whose real name was Gustaf) was the son of a Swedish-speaking sea captain of the second generation from Kimito, the biggest island in the Swedish-speaking archipelago in southwestern Finland. His mother's father was also a sea captain (from Nykarleby in Ostrobothnia, further north on the similarly Swedish-speaking western coast of Finland), and her mother was Irish. But the mother died when Guss Mattsson was only one year old.

Guss Mattsson was a researcher and university teacher in chemistry, but he was also after 1897 a contributor of opinion columns, and travel reports to various daily papers, and he popularised natural science in periodicals. In 1902 he was employed on a part-time basis for a daily paper (*Helsingfors Posten*) to summarise the most important articles in the Finnish-language dailies in the capital, Helsinki. From then on he was always a part-time journalist in addition to his work in chemistry teaching and research, and a few years in politics (1904–1906). From 1911 to 1914 he was responsible for a new daily paper, *Dagens Tidning*.

His style was "devoid of pathos, sentimentalism and moralising",[3] to borrow Willner's words. Perhaps his scientific research had led to relativism, a view that everything was in a state of flux and change. Although active in politics he was never a party man. He was more radical than his colleagues on the suffrage issue, and had signed a petition for full suffrage for women (which was achieved in 1906 when Finland as the first country in the world adopted universal suffrage). Although the Swedish-speaking press in Finland, where he wrote, then as now was dominated by the bourgeois Swedish People's Party (Svenska folkpartiet) Guss Mattsson did believe that the party should be bilingual. He was sceptical towards the Finnish social democrats because of their refusal to join the campaign for a mass protest against Russification in 1899.

---

[3] Willner, p. 23.

Guss Mattsson is best known for his witty columns, called "Today" (*I dag*), commenting on life and views in the capital. Apart from his doctoral dissertation in chemistry his name is on only two full-length books, both of them based on letters from travels, first published in a Helsinki newspaper. The first was based on a trip in 1907 to the Canary Islands, *En sommarfärd till de lyckliga öarna* ("A summer journey to the happy isles"), where he had travelled in the footsteps of Humboldt. The second piece of travel literature is the one we want to examine here.

Africa in the margin

It is one of the axioms in the modern discussion on travel literature that one travels from rather than to a place. In Guss Mattsson's case this is the banal truth. He travelled from his sickness, in the hope of curing or alleviating his lung ailment in a leisurely atmosphere, away from stress, and in a warmer climate. He also welcomed a break from his life as chemist *cum* newspaper editor. The latter job at *Dagens Tidning* had become intolerable when the financial backer, Amos Andersson, had withdrawn his support and Guss Mattsson had been forced to go to possible financiers to beg for money. He did agree to join the staff of a new paper, *Dagens Press*, which was a merger between *Dagens Tidning* and *Nya Pressen,* but his main contribution to this paper was the letters from his Africa trip.

The trip came as a gift from heaven to Guss Mattsson. One day in early May 1914 he received a note from a bank telling him that he had received a gift for a trip from an anonymous lady, 4,000 Finnish marks. He writes to his father on May 6, 1914 about his plans to use this for a voyage around Africa on a German ship from Hamburg, adding that this is a trip he has dreamed about ever since his trip to the Canary Islands, undertaken on a German ocean cruiser which then continued around Africa.[4] Guss Mattsson prefers a German ship, where he knows that passengers come from many different countries; he believes that only Englishmen travel on the British ships, and feels that his command of English is not good enough.

The trip as a cure and the achievement of being able to round Africa are thus what he looks forward to:

> I met two in 1907 who had done this trip and they said that especially the Eastern part was very enjoyable. One is all the time on the same ship. For both lungs, throat and nerves one cannot think of a better sanitary cure than a long and comfortable ocean voyage in warm areas. The food is excellent, and so are the cabins, this I found already on the trip to the Canary Islands.
>
> I very much look forward to this trip. It should give me back a great deal of what the last pressing years have taken from me. And it does not entail any hard-

---

[4] Letter from Guss Mattsson to his father May 6, 1914, quoted in Jung 1942, pp. 487–90.

ships. To be able to round the Cape and remember that my dear parents in their happy youth succeeded in doing the same will be a special treat to my soul.[5]

One can assume, however, that he had not only been dreaming about the trip, but also talking about it and preparing himself mentally and by reading. But we have few clues about what Africa meant to Guss Mattsson, or where he found his sources. He does not speak of Africa in his letters.[6]

In *Dagens Tidning* that he edited from 1911 to 1914 articles on Africa are few and far between. The exceptions to the rule that Africa is absent include

- Some articles on the revolt in Morocco and the difficulties France experiences in its "necessary pacification and civilisation exercise".[7]
- An article about "the revolt of the Hindus" in South Africa in 1913.
- An article on new Egypt in October 1913 which says that national radicalism in Egypt has no friends in England and supports Rhodes' and Curzon's "great programme" to join both South Africa and India into Egypt/Arabia "for the strength and glory of the empire".[8]
- An article entitled "The future sea in the Sahara" on an idea of how to create an interior lake in the Sahara desert, which bears the marks of Guss Mattsson's fascination with technology "in this dawning time of giant canals".[9]
- An article about "the Zanzibar issue" and the British plans to accede the island to Germany in exchange for other areas or concessions in Africa. The article states that the British do not want to give it up, because they do not want to give up any conquests, and because they have proud memories of putting an end to the slave trade on the East coast of Africa through the conquest of the Zanzibar sultanate, and lastly because the island is an important trading place, from which the Arabs, who are "extremely skilful businessmen" bring goods from the African interior.[10]
- A short report on "the familiar car trip" from the Cape to Cairo where the readers are told that the road between Pretoria and Bulawayo was extremely bad, but the expedition under captain Kelsew continues, and Wankie has now been reached.[11]
- A detailed story based on British papers about Captain Fox's expeditions against an American elephant poacher in the Sudan.[12]

[5] Ibid., p. 489 (same letter).
[6] The Åbo Akademi University in Åbo/Turku, Finland has a large collection of letters to and from Guss Mattsson, which I have kindly been permitted to consult.
[7] *Dagens Tidning*, Aug. 20, 1912.
[8] *Dagens Tidning*, Oct. 26, 1913.
[9] *Dagens Tidning*, Aug. 25, 1912, p. 1.
[10] *Dagens Tidning*, Oct. 16, 1913.
[11] *Dagens Tidning*, Nov. 11, 1913.
[12] *Dagens Tidning*, Aug. 31, 1912.

Africa and the Africans were of marginal interest to Guss Mattsson, while the Africa voyage was of central and vital interest to him. When looking at the newspapers from Africa that he picked up on the way in various ports of southern Africa, and which have been preserved in the Åbo Akademi University library, I get the feeling that the Europeans living in southern Africa were even less interested in Africa and Africans except as a continent of natural resources to exploit and from which they could live a good life. In these papers (*Cape Times*, July 8, 1914; *The South African News*, July 8, 1914; *Südwest* (Windhoek), June 30, 1914, No. 52; *Illustrierte Wochen-Chronik* (Windhoek), no date (most probably June 1914), printed in Berlin; *Deutsch Südwestafrikaniske Zeitung*, June 27, 1914; *Lüderitsbuchter Zeitung*, July 3, 1914; *De Zuid-afrikan* (Cape Town), July 7, 1914; *Lourenço Marques Guardian*, July 16, 1914) there is no mention at all of Africans in the area. Considering this it is remarkable that Guss Mattsson does write at all about Africa and Africans. The book could have been written as a report of an all-white affair.

"A gentleman went to Zanzibar"—the work and the trip

The voyage started in Hamburg in mid-June on m/s Tabora of the German East India Company, with Lisbon as the first stop. The first port off the European mainland was the Canary Islands, whereupon the ship followed the African coast line to Lobito and Mossamedes in Portuguese Angola, Lüderitz and Swakopmund in German South West Africa (Namibia), Cape Town, Port Elizabeth and Durban in South Africa, Lourenço Marques (Maputo), Beira and the city of Mozambique in Portuguese Mozambique, the British protectorate Zanzibar and Dar es Salaam in German East Africa (Tanzania).

The outbreak of the first world war cruelly interrupted the dream of travelling around Africa, and sailing through the Suez canal, which Guss Mattsson's grandfather had been the first Finnish sea captain to accomplish.[13] In Dar es Salaam the British authorities seized the German ship. Guss Mattsson managed, as a Russian citizen, to get permission to return to Zanzibar, and could there start the journey back home, but under such miserable conditions that his tuberculosis only got worse. If he only could have communicated with back home he would rather have stayed with the natives in Tanganyika, he wrote in a letter, perhaps more a sigh at the hardships than a real option.

He wrote his travelogue while on board the ship, and sent dispatches home to be published in a newspaper in the *Dagens Press* in Helsinki. They did not, and were never intended to, form an in-depth study of Africa. What he saw were some coastal cities, and not least he observed his fellow travellers in first class, some of them colonialists and some fortune-seekers. He was the only

---

[13] Letter quoted by Sven Willner, p. 51.

passenger who had embarked in order to round Africa as an adventure in itself.

What Guss Mattsson wrote on the Africans

This section summarises how Guss Mattsson wrote about Africa and Africans. I have chosen to group his views under a number of headings, by which I attempt to summarise his views and attitudes. The translations from Swedish are mine.

Negroes as curious animals

South of Cap Vert (on the mainland) the heat met the ship. Everybody was suffering from the heat, but once, in the middle of the night, a tropical rain shower poured down, and Guss Mattsson went out on deck, in pyjamas. He writes:

> A large number of passengers gathered by and by on deck, and it was a show in itself to see the Negroes and the Arabs on the bow lying like snails stretched out in the open air exactly the way they had fallen asleep at about ten. The rain did not seem to wake them up, and their thin clothes wrapped their bodies like wet silk paper. The dog Petrus whined at times when it poured too viciously, but there was not much change there either.[14]

Unspoilt children

Innocence is one of the traits GM believes he finds in the Africans. In his first encounter with Africa, in Lobito, he notes that:

> none of the blacks had their homes out there on the reef, or even at all in the vicinity. They dwell here only as port or railway workers, live crammed in some corrugated iron shacks and live their poor lives as toilers under the command of mulattos or whites by name. Among almost all of them I saw the good, surprised children's gaze, which characterises the unspoilt Negro.[15]

GM also finds a blessedly innocent attitude towards money matters. The people are not touched by "global commerce", he writes about his first encounter with blacks in Lobito, "there is a total lack of persistence, nobody called out any goods, nobody forced themselves upon us as guides or interpreters, no child begged."[16] He tells about three women who discreetly and quietly walked around with fruit baskets, from which the European visitors could take what they wanted and then be told how much it cost by the women holding up their fingers to indicate the price. A fellow passenger paid with 100

---

[14] Mattsson 1921, p. 64.
[15] Mattsson 1921, p. 79.
[16] Mattsson 1921, p. 79.

reis for bananas worth 80, and tried to show that the woman could keep the rest.

> The woman did not smile gratefully, but followed us a long way. When we stopped, she quietly extended her copper coin. I took it. She looked at me with surprise, and then pointed at the right owner. "It is his". When he kept on refusing, she took the coin from his hand, hesitated a moment and then took four bananas from the basket and tried to give them to K. He was curious about what would happen next, and again refused. The she bowed down and put the four bananas on the ground, drew a ring around them with her index finger, rose and walked away.
>
> A lesson in natural law. In any case, the Negro woman was the winning party, and the Europeans who had been making difficulties, looked puzzled at the bananas on the ground.[17]

They passed the place two hours later, and found the bananas still there. So they learnt that the ring meant taboo, these fruits have an owner and nobody else may touch them. GM writes:

> This is, as I said, a virgin place. In one or two years there will not be much of this left. Perhaps we saw one of the last rings in the sand.[18]

In another anecdote the innocence of the Africans is displayed as ignorance of sophisticated Western civilisation. This is one of the few places where he uncritically conveys stories that his fellow passengers have told. The story is occasioned by a statue in Lourenço Marques raised in 1910 in honour of the Portuguese governor Antonio Ennes, and told with the irony that GM often bestows on other Europeans:

> ... Below the plinth a Negro woman raises the ever-present palm leaf of peace with a broad smile. Above her the man himself stands with a long coat and a *pince-nez*. ... The Antonio Ennes statue is original in that the main figure who holds a book in his left hand, leans on a full, small book cupboard with his right hand. There has apparently been a wish to show that this Portuguese governor, he had books, and he even read them. One does not register the intended impression without being moved.[19]

Then he goes on to say that:

> I have not heard what the Negroes think about the woman with the leaf, but they are said to lack every capacity for allegorical expression. Thus the Germans in both East and West have made the psychological blunder of raising statues of groups intended to be symbolic. The Negroes make constant fun of them. In Daressalam [sic] the main figure in the Wissman monument high up on a cliff wears a German military uniform. Further down there is a fallen lion, and a

---

[17] Mattsson 1921, p. 80.
[18] Mattsson 1921, p. 80.
[19] Mattsson 1921, p. 149.

Negro soldier who lowers the flag over it. The blacks say: that one on top has fled from the lion and the Negro has killed it.

In Windhuk [sic] again there is a German war monument with one standing and one fallen German. I am told that no two blacks will pass by without saying: that one was killed by my father, my brother, myself, or: we will one day do that to all of them. The constant reiteration shapes opinion, and above all it has not the least in common with respect or fear.[20]

In the context of music GM adds to his remarks on what the Africans "are really like". The setting is Lourenço Marques and its botanical garden, "a little paradise". In one cage ostriches are walking around, and nearby a band is playing, with black musicians and a white conductor, and *a white drummer* (GM's emphasis). GM tells why, again retelling somebody else's story:

A local tells me that this function used to be performed by Negroes, but they found it so indescribably fun to beat the base drum and could not possibly be prevented from banging away all through the pieces with all their power. On both musical and economic grounds then this function had to be taken away from the black race.[21]

Exploitation of Africans

Perhaps surprising to a modern reader is the fact that in some passages GM notes in no uncertain terms that Africans are being exploited, which he observes in his detached style, but implicitly with strong disapproval. In his first letter from African soil he observes:

The pale fat ladies of Lobito made the Negroes do many miles long marches [over the mountains to the high plateau] to bring soil for the meagre flower beds on the sand reef.[22]

When GM writes about Beira he notes in passing that the whole system is based on exploitation:

The most remarkable thing about Beira is the fact that the city and a large part of its surroundings are not administered by the Portuguese government, but by a share-holding company, Companhia de Moçambique, whose manager seems to be Portuguese and whose money is English and French. Almost the entire colony of Mozambique, as large as Scandinavia, is in this way leased to private syndicates (besides the above-mentioned, Companhia de Njassa, C. Zambezia, C. Inhambande and C. de Gaza). These pay yearly leasehold to Portugal and have no other interest than to exploit the country and its black population.[23]

---

[20] Mattsson 1921, p. 150.
[21] Mattsson 1921, p. 151.
[22] Mattsson 1921, p. 77.
[23] Mattsson 1921, p. 159.

In the city of Mozambique GM mixes remarks on exploitation with ironical remarks on racial mixing:

> There was an apparent lack of Europeans in this little old place. The Portuguese, just like the Boers, do not object to mixing with the natives, and the production of bastards has long gone on without limitation, although the whites and half-whites are great oppressors of the Negroes, and even though the sound of the slave traders' whip still belongs to the natural sounds. A loving, middle-aged plantation owner on the mainland next to the isle of Mozambique has 178 children, all half-blood. When these lines are published this information will, however, be out-dated.[24]

Notes on racial discrimination

As with exploitation, GM notes racial discrimination. Sometimes he implies that he finds it ridiculous, as when he says about a female passenger, Mrs Hartmann that "she died a couple of times because a Negro had brushed against her".[25]

When he visits Camps Bay in Cape Town he records that there is a sign on a secluded part of the beach, out of reach for sharks, saying "Only for European children".[26]

In the city of Beira he contrasts the extreme discrimination of Africans with what he saw in South Africa:

> The Negroes here act as they did a hundred or two hundred years ago, that is, timidly like slaves. In the Cape and Natal they walk on the pavements like the whites. Here they can walk on the pavements only to get into a building and back out. In Beira no Negro can come forward to a counter in a shop or a post office as long as a white is standing there.[27]

Intelligent Negroes, stupid tourists

Only two black persons in the whole book have a name, and one of them even has the honour of being quoted. They are Hassan and Ali Noa. The first is:

> a young, not very handsome but clever and reliable Arab, who assists in the making of fine dishes in the kitchen, and sometimes carries specialities around. I have seen him fall headfirst with a big pile of plates on the stairs of the saloon, and rise up again with obvious bruises but with all the plates undamaged. Hassan is a splendid man.[28]

The other is Ali Noa:

---

[24] Mattsson 1921, p. 180–81.
[25] Mattsson 1921, p. 111.
[26] Mattsson 1921, p. 100.
[27] Mattsson 1921, p. 159.
[28] Mattsson 1921, p. 135.

who belongs to the large tribe of the Suaheli, is deep black—which Negroes seldom are—has seventeen years behind him and moves in his attractive white costume so gracefully and at the same time shyly, that I believe that ladies would among themselves call him 'very sweet.' Ali Noa attends in the officers' mess. He is an alert character.

GM goes on to tell the story of how one of his fellow passengers once remarked to Ali Noa:

"Ali Noa, you have turned out really black." The young boy stopped politely, smiled and asked: "Bwana, what do you think I should do about that?"[29]

There are other passages where a certain admiration for Africans is displayed. In Mozambique he and three other male passengers watch African women carrying things on their heads. Out of 200 "Moçambique-negritas", he claims, 182 were noted as more beautiful than most European women they had seen. The other 18 were tired or old:

This eternal carrying and this constant attention paid to balance foster an inimitable way of walking and a posture that would make thousands of pale princesses pale even more.[30]

In contrast to these instances of idealisation of African women and the admiring remarks on the skill and wit of the two black servants we find a number of quite condescending and ironical remarks about his fellow passengers.

In Lobito he wanted to take the train to Catumbela and Benguela. But the excursion was cancelled as not enough passengers signed up:

But at the same time an enormous majority rushed away to Restaurant Lobito to drink beer from bottles—more expensive, of inferior quality and warmer than on board, where dark and light Bier from the barrel was available at a decent price all the way around Africa.

Funny people, the majority. Here they have agonised for twelve restful days about how to put an end to the monotony of the ocean voyage. And, now when a rare and valuable change is presented as on a silver platter, they do not respond, but sit down to drink beer, on the finest desert coast the Atlantic still has. Some blamed it on the 6 Rmk for the train trip. This objection could have been respected, if these economical characters could not be expected with all certainty to drink champagne this evening, too, from many, and large, glasses.

I hate them with all my heart, these jewels, because they have kept me from visiting the world's most famous slave owners' den, where, in times past, ever since the times of the great seafarers, the live black ivory was taken on secret caravan trails, and in secret and under false labels they were shipped out to plantations and mines on many coasts. These are things one wants to sniff the scent

---

[29] Mattsson 1921, p. 135.
[30] Mattsson 1921, p. 178.

of, because they belong to the great saga of the conquistadors, whose shadows still cross the oceans.[31]

A similar contempt for the banalities of the majority's pastime preferences is found in his description of an excursion to Amanzimtoti north of Durban, a place "to which foreigners are accompanied to see the jungle and nigger life *in natura*":

> Soon we arrived at the big kaffer kraal. The number that followed was no success. The men were just like those in the city, only more impertinent, the old women were terrible to look at and the younger ones announced that they could take off the sweater they had put on when the guests arrived, for 1 shilling per hyena—a proposal which to their surprise had no effect at all. Earlier tourists had apparently a more developed sixth sense than the gentlemen from Tabora.
>
> For 5 shillings they would let themselves be photographed. In short, I do not advice anybody to go to the big and famous kaffer kraal at Amanzimtoti. Of course, it has had its time of virginity, but now it stinks with no end. The river is beautiful and remains in the memory as a forecourt, beyond whose farthest gate one should not have trodden.[32]

Racism and humanism

Let us return to the question whether Guss Mattsson was a racist. Could it be possible that the actor who read texts by Guss Mattsson and exclaimed that he was a damn racist came to this conclusion because Mattsson talked about "Negroes" (alternately with 'blacks')?

But whatever 'racism' is, we cannot meaningfully deduce 'racism' from the use of certain words. The usage of words is so culture-bound that it only tells us what time and context a person lives in. Certainly one can argue that there is political power in words, but the blame can be laid on individuals only if there is public consciousness of the connotations of given words, and good alternatives.

In the time of Guss Mattsson 'Negro' and 'black' were practically synonymous, both having as their stem a word for 'black'. The disrepute of the word 'Negro' is a much later development, and probably an effect of its derogatory form, 'Nigger'.

We need to penetrate into the patterns of thinking to come closer to the question of racism.

Guss Mattsson and the Jews

In the radio programme *Reflektion* ("Reflection") on the Finnish radio in 1995, author and critic Sven Willner explained to the listeners that Guss Mattsson was not a racist, and hastened to add, "at least not anti-semite". He

---

[31] Mattsson 1921, p. 78–79.
[32] Mattsson 1921, p. 131–32.

is clearly right in the qualified sentence, but this is not necessarily the same as being an anti-racist or non-racist.

In a letter dated May 20, 1903 from the sanatorium in Zurich where he is trying to cure his lungs, Guss Mattsson tells his father that he met a Jewish Finn, Engel, and learnt from him how Jews were discriminated in Finland:

> He told me in good Swedish that there is no civilised country, Russia included, where the legal stipulations on the Jews are so hard and merciless as in Finland. ... I had on my part little to object with and felt quite ashamed. We can thank our glorious priests and our enlightened landowners for the Law of the Jews from 1889.[33]

In his work as a journalist he often brought eminent Jews to the readers' attention. For example, on November 20, 1913 we find a headline "A learned Jewess" ("En lärd judinna"), with a picture and all—something that was relatively rare in the paper—and a text that tells us that these are the features of the first female professor at the Charité hospital in Berlin, medical doctor, miss Rachel Hirsch.[34]

In 1913 Guss Mattsson wrote a long article on the Zionist project of colonisation in Palestine, expressing admiration and support.[35]

Biological ideas about race

Racism narrowly defined is the doctrines, purported to be scientific, which categorise people into inferior and superior races on the basis of inherited biological traits. Such quasi-scientific doctrines were developed in 18th and 19th century France and Germany, as a concomitant of the rivalry between these European powers. The question then was whether the French or Germans were superior, a rather ridiculous question since both nations were (as most) quite ethnically mixed and the whole project should have been ruled out as foul on the basis of the absence of racial purity in the first place.

These doctrines were developed by such men as Gobineau and Chamberlain, and also attracted many followers in Scandinavia, particularly in Sweden.

There are no traces of these doctrines of race biology in the letters from Guss Mattsson's encounters with Africa. Sven Willner assumes that as a scientist GM was hesitant to utter definitive and ill-founded conclusions.

Yet in an article in *Dagens Tidning* in 1912 we find a puzzling discussion on "Big heads. How the English believe they can prove their increasing intelligence".[36] The article is not signed, but we know that Guss Mattsson with his

[33] Letter by Guss Mattsson to his father May 20, 1903, Åbo Akademis bibliotek, the manuscript section.

[34] *Dagens Tidning*, Nov. 20, 1913.

[35] "Zionismen och Palestina", *Dagens Tidning*, Dec. 28, 1913 (reprinted in Mattsson 1918, pp. 171–78).

[36] *Dagens Tidning*, Sept. 15, 1912.

energy and wide reading was responsible for a great majority of the material (and in any case as chief editor he was responsible). The English claim was that their skulls had grown in ten years by a quarter of an inch. This is virtually impossible, the article claims, quoting an article from a paper in Sweden, where the 'prominent scientist in the field', a doctor Beckman at Uppsala University points out that the methods of measurements are questionable. The claim was thus unscientific, not irrelevant. "It is in general difficult to draw any conclusions about an individual's gifts from the form of the skull, in general or specifically", the author writes, but continues in a slightly ironical style which sounds very Mattssonian:

> Even if the findings of the English scientist should prove tenable, which does seem unlikely, there is no need for us, the paper says, to feel in any way distanced by the English. ---No less than 87 per cent of the Swedes are long-skulls, which shows a greater homogeneity than any other European people. This shows nothing with full certainty, but as far as research now has reached it is the best accessible criterion of positive qualities in the contents of our skulls.[37]

The article thus ends ambiguously, but still not clearly questioning the basic idea of skull measurements, and the division of people into "long-skulls" and "short-skulls".

The core of racism

Yet the core of racism is not the specific quasi-scientific doctrines on skulls or other expressions of race biology, but a much broader strand of thought. Leon Poliakov has pointed out:

> It seems as if the West, perhaps out of shame, perhaps out of fear to seem racist, has selected a few lesser personalities (Gobineau, H. Chamberlain) as scapegoats. In this way a big chapter in the history of Western thought has been blotted out and the omission results in a massive collective repression of awkward memories and uncomfortable truths.[38]

The core of racism as an ideology is the division of human beings according to group categories into superior and inferior, higher and lower groups. Racism is one of the *ideologies of hierarchisation.*

This makes racism a cousin of other constructions of hierarchical scales which are supposed to inform us who is worth more than others. There is, for example, the classification of the male and female sex as superior and inferior,

---

[37] Loc. cit. It is interesting to note that the author (GM, I presume) here seems to identify himself with the Swedes in Sweden. Later genetic research has shown that the Swedish-speaking Finns have more in common genetically with the Finnish-speaking Finns than with Swedes in Sweden, because of the long social and biological mixing since the first people from Sweden settled in Finland in the 10th–12th centuries.

[38] Quoted by Stephen Wilson, *Ideology and Experience* (1982), here taken from Sven Lindqvist 1995, p. 9 (my translation from his translation into Swedish).

and the hierarchical order into which we often without reflection sort languages and language forms, what sociolinguist Tove Skutnabb-Kangas calls *lingvicism.*[39]

The American cultural anthropologist Ruth Benedict in a classic book on race and racism first printed in 1942, joins the above-quoted Jacob Katz when she writes that racism did not develop as a legitimation of the slave trade or the genocide of Indian peoples in North America. The European expansion overseas meant extermination and subjugation on a massive scale, but according to her:

> The dogma of racial superiority and inferiority, however, even under these drastic conditions, did not arise for more than three centuries. Natives were outside the pale of humanity, but this was regarded as a consequence of the fact that they were not Christians, not of the fact that they belonged to darker races.[40]

Ruth Benedict's definition of racism is this:

> Racism is the dogma that one ethnic group is condemned by nature to congenital inferiority and another group is destined to congenital superiority.[41]

In South Africa, for instance, according to Benedict, the old division of the human race, with which the whites legitimised their conquests and exploitation of the blacks, was a division into "believers" and "unbelievers". When many freed slaves and also many slaves became Christians a dilemma arose:

> The time was ripe for a new theory of superiority and inferiority, and people began to talk of natives as sub-human, as related to apes rather than to civilised man.[42]

I think the definition Benedict offers is too narrow, and too much tied to "the lesser personalities" of count de Gobineau and Houston Chamberlain. Their racist theories were not the beginning of racism, but one historical variant of the ideologies of hierarchisation of groups into superior and inferior.

The narrow definition of racism leaves out the pervasive ideas about a hierarchy of cultures or civilisations, which often puts African societies on the lower steps of the ladder. If this is not racism then we need another term to cover these ideas of superiority.

Similar to what is the case with the concept "ethnic groups" there have always been two tendencies when defining boundaries, one based on ideas of

---

[39] The very word 'dialect' is often used as a lower form of a standardised 'high' form of a given language. In Latin America we find that many who see themselves as descendants of the Spanish use 'dialects' for the languages of the Indian population in the Andes, such as Amyará and Quechua.

[40] Benedict 1983, p. 107.

[41] Ibid., p. 97.

biological differences, one based on cultural differences.[43] In contemporary discussion there is a tendency to believe that we are moving from an old biological concept of race to a culturally based race concept. But the latter is not new. Already at the beginning of the 20th century ideas were in vogue in Europe to think of the superior white race, followed by the brown races, and at the bottom the dark races. This was concomitant with ideas of their level of culture.

In the notes from Zanzibar which have been used to provide the text for the last chapter of Guss Mattsson's book we find this kind of thinking, in his admiration for the Arabs and disdain for the blacks:

> The Portuguese, who loyally had followed the wake of Vasco's ships, made Zanzibar theirs in 1503. But these were not pious poor kaffirs, who gaping took what came to them. Here they met Islam. After centuries of ceaseless struggle with the Arabs, the Portuguese lost their hold in 1729, and Zanzibar became Arabic.[44]

Humanist or racist?

Guss Mattsson appears to many, not least to his present-day admirers in Finland, as a true humanist, although I have not found that he ever gives this, nor indeed any other ideological label, to himself. Perhaps his expression in an article on the Armenian question, "contemporary humanitarian cosmopolitanism", comes closes to a self-definition.[45]

The Swedish philosopher Alf Ahlberg, while admitting that it has been understood historically in many different ways, defines 'humanism' as an ideology which postulates as a belief the superior value of the human being.[46] He mentions as proponents of humanism, among others, Grillparzer and Ellen Key, both of whom were highly regarded by Guss Mattsson.

We come closer to the truth, however, if we conclude that Guss Mattsson in some respects comes close to humanism, in others he moves towards the ideas of racism. In his detached scientific attitude, resistance to pompous expressions of sentiments, in his curiosity, his humour and self-irony, and in his broad-minded perspective on life he came close to humanism. But in his elitist attitudes, his assimilation of attitudes of looking down on the uneducated and to him uncivilised blacks, and not least in his admiration of the British empire, he comes closer to the camp of racism.

---

[42] Ibid., p. 109.

[43] du Toit, 1982, points out that in the scientific discussion on ethnic groups the British anthropologists have tended to include conceptions of race and biological descent as central variables, whereas in American anthropology culture has more often been the defining criterion.

[44] Mattsson 1921, p. 187.

[45] Mattsson 1918, p. 163.

[46] Ahlberg 1992, pp. 17 and 23–25.

When one reads what GM writes about German, or Portuguese colonialism and colonialists one can begin to believe that he was an early anti-imperialist. But there is a notable exception in his critique and astute observations on exploitation. In his admiration for the British empire Guss Mattsson completely lost his detachment.

Mattsson and Rhodes

When Guss Mattsson arrives in Cape Town he pays a visit both to Cecil Rhodes' mansion, Groote Schuur, and to the recently erected Rhodes Memorial. He says that one would need at least a day to look at the study and the library of Cecil Rhodes, and he tells the story of how Cecil Rhodes came to South Africa, condemned to death by his lung disease. It seems as if Guss Mattsson here identifies himself with Cecil Rhodes, but also entertains the dream of the Great Man and Leader:

> The large head [of the Rhodes statue in the memorial] is inclined against one hand, the eyes gazing over the equestrian statue, out into the open landscape, where behind valleys, ridges and plains the interior of South Africa fades away. It was here that Rhodes staked new, immensely expanded frontiers for the empire, and did it *alone*.
> ... The era of Rhodes is for him who has paid it attention something so tremendously great, manly and above all, British, that you can never leave it behind.[47]

He says he will never forget the stories about Rhodes coming to the wilderness near Bulawayo and convincing the warriors of Lobengula of the advantages of "a free existence under British protection",[48] or how the Matabeles brought the dead body of Rhodes to Matapos and grieved over him "as their greatest chief". And he quotes Kipling's dreams:

> "I dream by rock and heath and pine of Empire to the northward. Ay, one land from Lion's Head to Line."[49]

In some of his newspaper writing Guss Mattsson did note the aspirations of the oppressed people of the colonised world, if he did not understand and identify with them. In one article in 1913 called "The bomb in Hanoi" he quotes what the Vietnamese Phan Chan Trinh has written in *Le Journal* about events in Indochina, where he asks the French to show more individual respect to the natives, and adds that the situation is serious. Mattsson adds, with a reference to Multatuli's protests against the Dutch regime on Java:

---

[47] Mattsson 1921, p. 105.
[48] Loc. cit.
[49] Ibid., p. 106.

His [Multatuli's] good Javanese did not posses any bombs, but in Hanoi in 1913 they have bombs, just as in New Delhi last year. As foreboding signals from an awakening, foreign world their dark tone rolls in westwards.[30]

But in the British empire Guss Mattsson has heard of no native protests. It is striking that he, who in Finland supports the struggle against the Russification attempts of the Russian Czar, sees no parallels with the colonised peoples in Africa. Instead he praises the civilising mission of the British.

In Guss Mattsson's world the African natives have no culture worth mentioning, and perhaps none worth defending. In Amanzimtoti GM deplores that untouched African life can no longer be seen, but nowhere in the book does he speak of African culture with admiration or even recognition. When he arrives on the African continent, in Lobito in Angola, he describes the town as "a strange rag of half-culture, only some decade old, and without imprint of the uninhabited coast".[51] On the coast of Mozambique, in Beira, he has the same feeling of emptiness beyond the European foothold:

Beira has about the same form and extension as Kaskö [a coastal town in Finland]. The fathers of the town have laid out a narrow park of tamarind trees, which stand out against the sea as a curtain. Behind it there are no expectations, but flat Africa begins without compliment. Like the remnants of a formerly rich head of hair a thin palm stubble reaches up in the air, but apart from that there is nothing but the untouched miles long steppe, where in the foreground one can see some Negroes lumber, and in the background smoke from small fires is seen in the glaring sun.[52]

It does not occur to him that there could be cultures beyond the eye and reach of European settlements.

Concluding remarks

How do we handle the question of Guss Mattsson's humanism after these examples of his identification with the colonialist mission? Is he not a humanist after all? Or do we perhaps have to question whether humanism and racism are mutually exclusive?

The justification of violence, to the point of advocating extinction, is a logical but not necessary sequence of racism. The Swedish author Sven Lindqvist has shown how the belief that the 'lower races' will die out, and how the 'higher races' should help history carry this out, was an integral part of European intellectual history from the 19th century until well into the 20th century.[53] This was inspired by the strong movement of social Darwinism, the

---

[30] Quoted in Willner, p. 26 (no date given).
[51] Mattsson 1921, p. 75.
[52] Ibid., p. 160.
[53] Lindqvist 1992.

attempts by Herbert Spencer and others, to use the evolutionary ideas of Darwin and especially his dictum about the survival of the fittest in the development of new and higher biological forms, on humankind.

On this score, GM was influenced by the ideas of the time that people could be divided into races, and that the races could be judged in terms of superior to inferior. But there is no proof that he was an advocate of violence or the extermination of the 'lower races'.

GM is thus not a Spencerian kind of racist. Yet this does not make him a humanist. Between extreme racism and extreme humanism there are many shades.

We saw that humanism, according to Alf Ahlberg, as a world view, is based on the belief in the inalienable value of the human being. But does this entail all human beings? In reality, I am sure that many of the great humanists have restricted themselves to thinking of all individuals in their given culture or group. In a world in which there is any intolerance and any racism a humanist, according to the definition above, should by necessity be a fighter against racism and intolerance. How many are?

We must also consider another possible compromise with the absolute ideal of the inalienable value of each human being. Can a humanist be a person who does think of people and groups as lower and higher, but believes that those of less value shall be treated humanely? Some would say no, and claim that the recognition of differing degrees of power and capacity is the result of other than inherent factors. Yet, the paternalism, which is an important element in colonial ideology, not least in British colonialism, combines an assertion of equal values with an even stronger assertion of the right and capacity of some to decide for others. The above-mentioned "humanitarian cosmopolitanism" that Mattsson views favourably, can accommodate this.

The limitations to Guss Mattsson's humanism illustrate the extent to which racism cannot sufficiently be explained in terms of psychology. Racism does not come from within, as a response to the stimuli of a certain personality trait or individual history. It is not an endogenously but an exogenously derived belief in 'natural' inequality, and as such can be explained only in a historical analysis. It is the society not the individual which needs racism, but it is through individuals that it is verbally expressed. And it is not reflected mechanically.

If we want to be able to replace the principle of a hierarchy of values with the principle of equality we need to repeat the intellectual surgery that Edward W. Said has performed on some of the English-language classics.[54] This is what I have attempted to do here. More studies are needed on our popular

---

[54] Edward W. Said, *Kultur och imperialism*, Ordfronts förlag, Stockholm 1995 [*Culture and Imperialism*, 1993].

culture, mass media, and literary heritage, and we must not be afraid to scrutinise the heroes and geniuses of our culture.

References

Ahlberg, Alf, 1992, *Humanismen.* (First published 1953). Ludvika: Dualis förlag.

Benedict, Ruth (1983) *Race and Racism.* (First published 1942). London: Routledge & Kegan Paul.

Dagens Tidning (Helsingfors) 1912, 1913.

du Toit, Brian M. ed., 1982, *Ethnicity in Modern Africa.* Boulder: Westview Press.

Jung, Bertel, 1942, *Guss Mattsson berättar om sig själv.* Helsingfors: Holger Schildts förlag.

Liebkind, Karmela, 1988, *Me ja muukalaiset—ryhmärajat ihmisten suhteissa* ["Us and the strangers—boundaries between groups in interpersonal relations"]. Helsinki: Gaudeamus.

Lindqvist, Sven,1992, *Utrota varenda jävel.* Stockholm: Bonniers.

—, 1995, *Antirasister, människor och argument i kampen mot rasismen 1750–1900.* Stockholm: Bonniers.

Mattsson, Gustaf, 1918, *Stormakter och små folk* ["Great Powers and Small People"]. Valda skrifter af Gustaf Mattsson, Vol. 8. Helsingfors: Holger Schildts förlag.

—, 1921, *En herre for till Zanzibar* ["A Gentleman went to Zanzibar"], Sjunde upplagan (7th edition). Helsingfors: Holger Schildts förlag.

Said, Edward W., 1995, *Kultur och imperialism* [Translation of *Culture and Imperialism,* 1993]. Stockholm: Ordfronts förlag.

Willner, Sven, 1966, "Guss Mattsson", in *Kulturbärare,* Finländska gestalter V. Ekenäs: Ekenäs tryckeri aktiebolags förlag.

Wuolijoki, Hella, 1947, *Kummituksia ja kajavia. Muistelmia Eino Leinosta ja Gustaf Mattssonista.* Helsinki: Tammi.

A Voyeur's Paradise ... Images of Africa

Yvonne Vera

'When we really did break into the natives' existence, they behaved like ants, when you poke a stick into their ant-hill; they wiped out the damage with unwearied energy, swiftly and silently—as if obliterating an unseemly action.'

Karen Blixen, *Out of Africa*

Of course, colonialism was not a playful, flirtatious poking at anthills, but a determined, patterned effort at domination. This passage, from Blixen, reveals several tendencies in colonialist writing, one of deliberate dehumanisation and the other of projection, or perhaps, dehumanisation through a process of projection.

One of the most urgent tasks in the issues of development in Africa, is the construction of primary images of Africans; these are visual, written, and lived expressions of identity: most of them have been biased and misinforming. In literature, and in the visual and artistic communities in Zimbabwe, the restoration of dignity is a main preoccupation. Our development means the control of personal history and independence.

In Blixen, the act of invasion is defined, minimally, by this expression—'when we really did break into the native's existence.' There is a mystery about the action performed, a mystification, with 'really' carrying all the emphasis of the accompanying violence. The 'break' above means only a successful entry, not at shattering. The anthill image Blixen offers accepts there being some order, some preoccupation, some living. Some.

What is the so called 'native's existence'—a being there, really, in a kind of absence, perhaps. It means being available, merely, to be poked at, but nothing more. Joseph Conrad in a more amorphous mood describes this existence of the African more confidently; 'a suspicion of their not being inhuman'.

Accompanying this mode of colonialist writing is the creation of a myth of Africanness captured in the words 'swiftly and silently,' each of which suggests an incomprehensible determination on the part of the African to recover from disturbance. They work 'swiftly and silently,' without communication, I suppose, for like the ants, they are not heard to speak. Their language is incomprehensible. The anthill image removes from the Africans the possibility of language and grants them instead, a telepathic effort.

The 'desire to forget' is projected as another characteristic and this is achieved through Blixen's expression that the Africans are like ants hastily engaged in 'obliterating and unseemly action.' They engage in 'forgetting' another's shameful act, not concerned with thinking through the damage, assessing it, or even questioning the other's action, but uniformly 'acting' to forget. Yet remembrance is essential to any recovery.

The Africans are granted no ancestral rites of memory, or as Malawian poet Jack Mapanje writes in the poem "Your Tears Still Burn at My Handcuffs"—they have not even 'dead roots to lean on.' This is the loss of memory, when roots have lost their ability to heal. Mapanje acknowledges that we must begin among these dead roots. The image of ants offers only the ability to forget, to banish the shameful evidence of having been disturbed. But this image offers only a consoling myth to the invader who reduces the act of invasion to child play, to poking at anthills.

However, it is the power to remember which is crucial to restoring identity. It is an understanding what has happened, in knowing where the rain began to beat us, that we begin to find again our autonomy. As Milan Kudera in *The Book of Laughter and Forgetting* tells us: 'The struggle of man against power is the struggle of the memory against forgetting.'

Edward Said's *Orientalism* (1978) is based on a theory that challenges language as power where a strategy of inclusions and exclusions becomes paramount. Meanings and descriptions become dependant on binary oppositions where one group is voiced, another silenced. This is a play of power and subjugation as a central theme, this poking at anthills, this theme I have mentioned above.

Through the projection of oppositions, one artificially describes and categorises the world, at the same time generating other concepts which do not serve to enlighten, but bar reception of the 'known' object. Knowledge of any kind is sacrificed by deference to the over-determined ideal. Africa is an absence on which particular images are built.

To circumscribe and dominate Africa as an Edenic space depends on the elimination of the African as actual human presence, again this is Africa as an anthill. In a recent and popular Hollywood film "The Bridges of Madison County" Clint Eastwood's character Kincaid seduces Meryl Streep by telling her tales of Africa, much like Othello does to his Desdemona, except Eastwood whispers, very alluringly, very provocatively that 'Africa is a voyeur's paradise.'

A photographer, Eastwood's character has seen Africa mainly through his camera, captured it, preserved it even. Such things can be done to a place which is understood only as an image, a visual experience, an anthill merely. As Kincaid/Eastwood explains there is no place like Africa to satisfy the act of observing, of watching, without the gaze being returned. This is what one does to anthills. Africa as a voyeur's paradise. One watches without interruption, anonymous. One pokes as much as one desires, for this is a place where there are no systems of ethics, no restrictions.

Definitions arising from binary oppositions are arbitrary constructions, and willed rather than real. Colonialist descriptions consist of wilful projections based on the devaluation, transformation and domestication of African peoples. A series of repeated rhetorical moves fashions an elaborate guise of realism. The idea of nullity is also integral to the function of colonialist writing, there being no Africa 'named' or 'defined' before the outsider. This belief in absence is accompanied, paradoxically, by the illusion of pre-existing essence—an essential essentialism.

Essentialism, understood as a belief in the real, invariable and fixed properties which define the essence of a given entity, structures most of colonialist discussion and nurtures its language and images. The so called 'essence' of Africa is frequently encountered as a negation. Through repeated rhetorical moves Africa becomes and absence, yet still knowable.

Essentialism, as an approach to knowledge of any entity, radically undercuts the cultural, psychological and social complexities that underlie differences: It denotes that which is irreducible, unchanging, and therefore constitutive of a person or thing. The 'African,' as defined in colonialist writing, is an essentialist construct.

The African essence is circumscribed before being actually encountered. To the observer, it has existed as image, rather than actual. Colonialist descriptions have been nurtured from the maps of Ptolomy (which represented Africa as a shapeless, mythological ground), through the ages of discovery, the colonial period and the present. However, the present at least offers competing images. One can be exposed to writing, film, art and argument from competing sources.

The most significant factor in the formulation of Africanist descriptions and images was the unequal relation between coloniser and colonised. I speak of a form of colonising in which the identity of one being is controlled, even created by another in an oppressive relationship.

The colonial venture in Africa consisted of the act of creating out of a perceived absence—out of nothing. The native was the 'blank' out of which this creation was to be moulded, in the image of the transported civilisation. A new identity would be inscribed. Some of the inscription on the 'blank space' that the native occupied took the form of speculation.

Having defined the dark race in opposition to civilisation with industrial culture, the native was therefore perceived as being 'purer', nearer to the origin of man. By inscribing this romanticised, limiting and limited idealistic identity of the African, the emotional, psychological and social interests of the colonialist inscriber would be served. This form of anthropomorphic inscription is indicated in the anthill image Blixen's writings on Africa provides.

The imperial presence successfully disseminated among its members a partial, self-serving image of Africa. It was not until the 1950s that Africans, as writers, were themselves able to voice their discontent with the image offered by the imperial culture. Colonial texts functioned as objects of power and channels of authority. Their influence on the Western conception of Africa was immediate and unquestioned.

The texts were not interrogated for their fidelity by those from the imperial centre who 'consumed' the literature. Colonial texts were in fact objects of power. While most of them adopted conventions of fictions, they claimed empirical validation. In most cases the writings, and the images they proposed, functioned to argue the legitimacy of imposed social structures (the civilising mission with all its paraphernalia of churches, schools and government offices).

The literature represented a strategy for ideological struggle, interrupting contemporary history even as it reflected it, and registering the exploitative transformation of that social order. Far from being mere linguistic entities, whose meaning resides in the transcendental or universalistic aspects, the texts operated as ideological forces to justify change or invasion itself, this poking at anthills. The texts were strategically positioned within colonial history for maximum utilisation in social action. The writings of Joyce Cary each identify an aspect of the colonial objective—from the installation of administrative structures to religious patterns.

In *Heart of Darkness* Marlow says that Africa is no longer the 'blank space' on the map: 'it had ceased to be a blank space of delightful mystery—a white patch for a boy to dream over. It had become a place of darkness'. The darkness was validated by an antithetical opposition of values. The myth of darkness rose out of a self-justifying moralising authority capable of interfering and displacing the lives of independently existing peoples by recourse to an economically, religiously and politically sanctioned set of sustaining principles.

This self proclaiming civilisation, in an effort to privilege its own effort, denies the African as an actual self-defining and self-legitimising presence. The African is asked to fit into a projected definition, to become an absence.

In Doris Lessing, as in Conrad, several references are made to the African as an emptiness or a text to be read: The African man Moses has a 'blank look' which the colonial settler Mary attempts to read. The text reads: 'Now the oblong of light was blank; Moses was not there.' The Africans are not given a voice in Lessing's narrative but only exist as 'other'. We are told too that natives reside, within the society and within the text 'Silently and unobtrusively'. The African becomes an unexplainable presence, an obsessive 'thing' that can not be comprehended. Described only as an 'amorphous mass'. The inception of the African into a multifarious abstraction to be feared, denies his existence as a human being. While Lessing's *The Grass is Singing* questions the dominant settler ideology, it does not sufficiently present the African as a fully formed human presence.

The parallel between the reading texts and 'reading' the native is made apparent in the manner in which the text foreshadows future events through Mary: ... her mind wandered as she determinedly turned the pages; and she realised, after she had been reading perhaps an hour, that she had not taken in a word. She threw the book aside and tried another but with the same result. For a few days the house was littered with books in faded covers. Mary goes through several servants, discarding each one of them as she fails to under-stand them or find ways of establishing and fixing their identities in ways that are comfortable for her. She does not know how to 'read' the native till she meets Moses, who is the only figure to emerge from the haze, creating a shape or outline.

She reads him because she has 'inscribed' her own mark on his face: 'the scar on his cheek, a thin, darker weal across the black skin'. This mark or writing becomes the basis of her reading of the native, and leads to his gaining a permanent position in her household, and to the eventually disastrous nature of their relationship. The blood that he sheds as she 'marks' him with the whip, drips like red ink into his clothing. The whip is not only the instrument of inscription, but of effective domination. Moses has no identity beyond the one she has initiated by her inscription. The scar that Mary inscribes speaks more eloquently in the text, that does Moses himself as a character, as an African. I have often thought that Lessing has the good humour to describe this same Moses as a 'powerful black man'.

In the 1940s a white woman's desire for a black servant was a theme as taboo to a novelist in Rhodesia as it was for general conversation. In writing about the taboo of her society, Lessing questions the whole basis of white Rhodesia's system of values, and their image of Africans. We see Moses al-most exclusively through the eyes of Mary and other whites who 'colour' him in accordance with their own prejudices and apprehensions. he is always coming in and out of shadows, and is insubstantial and empty and dark as any of those shadows. His resignation of all attempt to flee after the murder is reported with the same characteristic indifference: ... *what thoughts of regret, or pity, or perhaps wounded human affection were compounded with the satisfaction of his completed revenge, it is impossible to say. For, when he had gone perhaps a couple of hundred yards through the soaking bush, he stopped, turned aside, and leaned against a tree 'on an ant heap'. There he would remain, until his pursuers, in turn came to find him.*

There is still the surprise of the African mind that goes along with the ani-mal-like motions and the predominance of instinctual reasoning. The choice of the anthill as a final location of the African (as in the end of Cary's *Aissa Saved*, though less brutal) suggests the passivity of the character. Moses is 'suspected' by the author or narrator of 'perhaps wounded human affection'. The author's refusal to probe, and the tendency of a Conradian speculation upon the incomprehensible workings of the 'native' mind are all evident. Africa represents the lapse of consciousness.

I speak of three qualities—inscription, marking and mythologising: When we really did break into the natives' existence they behaved like ants, when you poke a stick into their anthill they wiped out the damage with unwearied energy, swiftly and silently—as if obliterating an unseemly action. [Karen Blixen, *Out of Africa*]

Africa must restore its symbols and identity, and confirm and initiate more fulfilling images. Africa, whole and imaginative. Not this poking; not this voyeur's paradise.

[This text was originally delivered at the Images of Africa Festival in Copenhagen June 1996.]

Representing the Past in the Present

Memory-texts and Ndebele Identity

Björn Lindgren

Introduction: Memory-texts, Ndebele identity and the colonial library

History, we may say, is both ideology and methodology. It is ideology in the sense that it is written in a selective way from a specific perspective. It is positional, as Jonathan Friedman (1992a:194) writes, "that is, it is dependent upon where one is located in social reality, within society, and within global process". At the same time, however, it is methodology in that it follows internal logical rules about sources, causality and linearity which are presented in a specific narrative form. Ideology may of course be regarded as embracing methodology since values form rules, but in contrast to ideology these rules are accepted as more or less universal by most historians. While ideology often diverges various historians' representations of a particular past, methodology often conforms them.

In this paper I deal with the history of the Ndebele in Zimbabwe as ideology. I suggest, firstly, that a lay or academic historian's conscious and unconscious ideology is most evident when he or she is dealing with politically important questions and when the past at the same time is difficult to reconstruct according to the discipline's methodology, that is when evidence is contradictory. I suggest, secondly, that such important and contradictory reference points of the past, on purpose or not, are used to construct and deconstruct Ndebele identity. And I suggest, thirdly, that ideology apart from these reference points of the past is used to describe Ndebele mentality, and that different authors use different images of the Ndebele which strengthen or weaken Ndebele identity.

To "make" history in this way is to construct and deconstruct identity in that it "produces a relation between that which supposedly occurred in the past and the present state of affairs" (Friedman 1992b:837). However, since I deal with history as ideology rather than methodology, and since I treat history as the past described in the present rather than as the past forming the present, I follow V.Y. Mudimbe (1991:89ff) and refer to different oral and written representations of the past as memory-texts. A memory-text, Mudimbe (1991:97f) writes with reference to Claude Levi-Strauss (1966), is beyond the difference between history and myth. It may be considered, Mudimbe writes (1991:89) as a

> theoretical discourse which validates a human geography, its spatial configuration, and the competing traditions of its various inhabitants, simultaneously

cementing them via this retelling of the genesis of the 'nation' and its social organization.

A memory-text is according to Mudimbe (1991:91)

> both a legend and a dream for political power. In effect it links words and names to possessed things and spaces, designating motions of ancestors ... according to processes of appropriations of power and governance over new lands.

In the following, I first present a memory-text by education officer Pathisa Nyathi who has written a book on the Ndebele past in his mother tongue isiNdebele (Nyathi 1994). I met him the first time in the spring of 1993 at the Swedish Embassy in Harare where he gave a lecture entitled "The Ndebele History 1820–1893". The speech was a translation of parts of the book and delivered in the hope of getting financial aid to publish it. Two years later I saw the book in many bookstores and libraries in Bulawayo as well as in rural Matabeleland. I present Pathisa Nyathi's memory-text as I heard it in the form of a summary in the first person. I have surrounded the summary with two paragraphs of quotes where Nyathi with some emphasis tells the reasons for giving his view on the Ndebele past. The summary, as well as the quotes, is based on a tape recording of his speech and follows the chronological order in which he delivered it. Thereafter, I compare three debated issues that Pathisa Nyathi takes up with memory-texts written by Europeans, European settlers and their descendants. Finally, I compare an image of the Ndebele used by Pathisa Nyathi with some images used in other memory-texts and sources.

These memory-texts and sources are widely spread and often referred to. They are with two exceptions (Lye 1985 and Cooke 1992) published before independence in 1980 (between 1835 and 1978), and I regard them as belonging to what Mudimbe calls "the colonial library". This library, Mudimbe (1994:xii) writes

> represents a body of knowledge constructed with the explicit purpose of faithfully translating and deciphering the African object. Indeed, it fulfilled a political project in which, supposedly, the object unveils its being, its secrets, and its potential to a master who could, finally, domesticate it.

Pathisa Nyathi's memory-text is very much a reaction against this domestication, but it is also a reaction against the dominating Shona perspective in national schoolbooks.[1] However, before I present Pathisa Nyathi's memory-text, I need to give a short description of how the Ndebele has been categorised by linguists and anthropologists in relation to Southern Bantu and Shona peoples, and I need to say a few words on Ndebele identity in relation to other identities.

---

[1] Interview with Pathisa Nyathi in Bulawayo, 29 March 1997

Basic linguistic categorisation of Southern Bantu and Shona peoples

The Ndebele are categorised by linguists and anthropologists as a Southern Bantu people in contrast to the Shona speaking peoples in Zimbabwe—that is the Zezuru, Korekore, Manyika, Ndau, Karanga and Kalanga (e.g. Bourdillon 1991:16ff, von Sicard 1975, Murdock 1959). They number perhaps a little over one and a half million people while the Shona peoples together consist of about eight and a half million of the total Zimbabwean population of ten and a half million (Census 1992). Most authors divide the Southern Bantu peoples into four different groups primarily on linguistic grounds: the Nguni, the Sotho-Tswana, the Venda and the Tsonga. The Nguni, in turn, are often divided into four sub-groups: the Xhosa, the Swazi, the Transvaal Ndebele and the Zulu. The latter often include the three Nguni offshoots: the Ngono, the Shangana and the Ndebele (Kuper 1982:5ff, Breutz 1975, N.J. van Warmelo 1974, but see Murdock 1959). The Ndebele, with whom I am here concerned, were the last of these off-shoots to leave Zululand and they eventually ended up in what is today south-west Zimbabwe (Beach 1990:52ff). They were probably given their name during their migration north by Sotho-Tswana people who called them *Matebele* (Hughes & van Velsen 1954) and they should not be confused with the Transvaal Ndebele who have a completely different history and who have lived in what is today Transvaal in South Africa since the seventeenth century (Breutz 1975).

As Pathisa Nyathi writes in his memory-text, the Nguni who left Zululand were later on reinforced during their migration north by among others Sothos and Tswanas. Still later, even more people were incorporated, notably Shonas (Kalangas and Karangas). In effect, the Ndebele today consist of people from many different origins. A person living in Matabeleland may both be a Zimbabwean, a Ndebele, and, for instance, a Nguni, that is a Ndebele of Nguni origin. Apart from Zimbabwean national identity and Ndebele ethnic identity, we may therefore talk about different sub-ethnic identities, e.g. Nguni and Shona, and even about sub-sub-ethnic identities, e.g. Zulu and Kalanga (see Lindgren 1998). These and other identities are all used and come into play in different situations. In this paper I concentrate on one of these identities, namely Ndebele ethnic identity, which I also regard as being the politically most important one in Matabeleland today.

The Ndebele genesis 1820–1893: A memory-text by Pathisa Nyathi

"I am here in defence of a manuscript, in defence of a people, in defence of the survival of a people", says Pathisa Nyathi. He looks out over the mainly European audience attending his lecture. "As Ndebele people we do not have a comprehensive book on Ndebele history, in *isiNdebele*, in our own language", he continues. "Yes, we do have a few works in English." "They obviously present this history from the victor's point of view and never from the vanquished's point of view. We are making efforts therefore, funds permitting,

to rewrite our own history in our own language and giving it our own perspective." "It is not just Ndebele history which is not written. Even our own
culture remains unwritten. One or two authors may have written on our culture, but it is really just scratching on the surface. So the Ndebele people remain to be discovered, and there is no man or woman who shall discover
them. They will discover themselves. We are going to present ourselves to the
world." "The Ndebele will present themselves to the world the way they want
to be presented and not the way they have been portrayed by other peoples."

The Ndebele state was an off-shoot from the Zulu state, Nyathi continues.
The founder of the Ndebele state was Mzilikazi, who was a chief under the
Zulu king Shaka. But Mzilikazi had an independent mind. He broke away
from Shaka, not because of greed, as some people tell us, but because of the
love for independence. He left Zululand in about 1820 with a small group,
largely consisting of his own people, the Nguni section. Shaka, of course, sent
some of his regiments to stop him, but they could not. Mzilikazi continued
and more people joined him. You realise this is east of the Drakensberg,
Nyathi continues, and the people who joined Mzilikazi were largely of Nguni
stock. However, the nation that Mzilikazi created was from a number of diverse disparate ethnic groups. From amongst the Nguni themselves there were
several sub-groups. When Mzilikazi crossed the Drakensberg he was getting
more people from non-Nguni stock, largely from the Sotho and the Tswana.
Mzilikazi had that capacity of moulding a homogenous state from a number
of diverse ethnic groups. Obviously they abandoned their cultures. Now, when
Mzilikazi left he was a chief. As a chief he could not have gone far, so they
had to elevate him to the level of king. This happened to the west of the
Drakensberg.

From the west of the Drakensberg the Ndebele continued to the Pretoria
area where they came into contact with Robert Moffat and other missionaries.
At this time Shaka was killed by his brother Dingane who sanctioned a follow-
up operation after Mzilikazi. They forced Mzilikazi and his people to move on
to western Transvaal. This was in the early 1830s. At the same time the Boer
moved north because of the establishment of British rule in the Cape area. The
two groups met. Obviously, they could not live together, Nyathi explains. The
Ndebele say you cannot have two bulls in the same kraal [homestead, cattle-
byre]. One bull has to be kicked out. The Boer moved quicker and had arms.
In 1836 the Ndebele could not take this any more. They had to move again.

Mzilikazi split his people into two parts. Mzilikazi and his regiments
formed one part, while women and children, with a few men, formed the
other. All my oral sources claim that Robert Moffat told the Ndebele where to
settle next, Nyathi says, even though some authors claim he did not [e.g.
Rasmussen 1978]. The first group settled by a mountain. The other group,
however, never showed up. Some people say Mzilikazi got lost, but the Ndebele do not think so. They say he was surveying the land. The truth is difficult
to determine, but after two years without a king the group by the mountain

installed Mzilikazi's first-born son as king. However, Mzilikazi was still alive and he came back. There cannot be two suns in the sky at the same time, Nyathi continues. This is an important Ndebele philosophy, which has implications even today. There will never be two political leaders in Matabeleland at the same time. When Mzilikazi came back his son was probably sent south to live with his uncles in Zululand. Some people say he was butchered. This was in about 1839/1840. Mzilikazi regained his position as king, which he held until his death in 1868. The only serious threat against the Ndebele during the rest of his life was the Boer who tried to invade the Ndebele from the south in the 1840s.

With Mzilikazi's death came the issue of succession. Some people favoured Mzilikazi's first-born son who was sent to Zululand, while others favoured the son Lobengula, who eventually became king in 1870. Now, Nyathi explains, a king cannot rule from the town from where his father ruled so Lobengula established his own town. He named the town Bulawayo because he was rejected by a section of his own people, the section that had favoured Mzilikazi's first-born son. Fortunately, Nyathi adds, the name lives today even though the Whites took over the country. They never changed the name, they just got the wrong meaning of it. The name Bulawayo means both to kill and to be persecuted. It should be interpreted with the last meaning. The same year Lobengula became king, Cecil Rhodes landed in Durban. At this time missionaries, traders and hunters were already active in Ndebele territory. In 1854 Moffat visited the country, in 1859 a mission station was opened up and the same year the first school in Zimbabwe. Meanwhile, in Berlin in 1884, the colonial powers agreed on the rules of the game of colonisation and it did not take long before Cecil Rhodes and the British South Africa Company arrived in the area.

There are some mischievous people who say Lobengula sold out the land, Nyathi says. Lobengula signed a document, but he had no idea of the significance of this, and, let us be frank, whether Lobengula signed it or not does not matter. The country would have been colonised anyway. In 1890 Cecil Rhodes sent an invading force, calling themselves the Pioneer Column, into Matabeleland. Cecil Rhodes wanted to have a direct confrontation with Lobengula, but the British High Commissioner in Cape Town found out about the plans and demanded that the column withdraw. The column continued to Salisbury [Harare] in Mashonaland instead. People thought Mashonaland was an El Dorado where they could find gold, but they were disappointed. So they thought Matabeleland was probably the El Dorado where King Solomon's mines were. They wanted war and now they were looking for a pretext to attack Matabeleland.

If you want to provoke the Ndebele you must know how to provoke them, Nyathi continues. If you steal cattle from the Ndebele, then you provoke them. Some people in Mashonaland outside Fort Victoria [Masvingo] had stolen telegraph wires going to Salisbury, so the British created an incident which has been called the Victoria incident. The British went to punish the chief who had stolen the telegraph wires. They took the cattle, Nyathi argues, and they knew that some of these cattle were held for the king. Lobengula sent a party to investigate what had happened. The Ndebele party was confronted by Captain Charles Lendy who told them to leave since they had crossed a border that they did not know existed. On 18 July in 1893 about 30 to 40 Ndebeles were killed.

Starr Jameson, who worked for the British South Africa Company and was now in Fort Victoria, telegraphed to Cecil Rhodes that he wanted to make war on the Ndebele. Cecil Rhodes agreed by a quote from the bible. They had then the Maxim machine gun, which had been developed by the engineer Hiram Maxim in the United States and now needed field-testing. There had been no serious wars since its invention and they were all excited about the war against the Ndebele and how it would work. Yes, Nyathi says, they tested it, and yes, it succeeded. In September the forces were ready. A first column left Salisbury, a second left Fort Victoria and a third came from the south. In Fort Victoria a service was held where they prayed to God to give the Christian soldiers strength to defeat the Ndebele state, or, actually to destroy it. On 1 November 1893 Lobengula's best regiment lost an important battle. The spear was no match for the Maxim machine gun. But the Ndebele died fighting, because among the Ndebele a wound in the back meant that you were fleeing, and such men were worth nothing more than food for vultures. However, Lobengula left Bulawayo before the columns reached the city.

"Now, the Ndebele people are secretive people", Pathisa Nyathi says at the end of his lecture. "They do not want to tell the truth." "This is the case with Lobengula's fate. It is very clear that there were people with him. The field commander was there and came back. He knew exactly what happened to the king, but he never told them anything." "In any case", Pathisa Nyathi continues, "the Ndebele knew and believe that if you capture the king there is no chance again in the future of resurrecting that chieftainship or kingship. It was therefore very important for Lobengula to flee rather than be captured. You have only defeated a people when you have captured their king. This is why the Ndebele say the Whites never defeated them, because they never captured Lobengula."

Writing against the colonial library

Pathisa Nyathi takes up several debated issues in his memory-text. He argues that the Ndebele are an off-shoot from the Zulu rather than from the wider category Nguni, that Mzilikazi broke away from Shaka because of love for independence and not because of greed, and that people joined him during his migration rather than were taken by force. He says that Moffat was involved in where the Ndebele should resettle, that Mzilikazi was surveying land rather than being lost, and that his first-born son was sent to Zululand and not killed. He writes that Bulawayo means being persecuted and not to kill, that Lobengula did not sell out the land but was fooled, and that the Ndebele were attacked by an invading force rather than a Pioneer column. He emphasises that the English found a pretext to legitimise their war against the Ndebele, that Lobengula did not die but escaped, and that the Whites in this sense never defeated the Ndebele. Pathisa Nyathi is on these issues writing against the colonial library, which is vast indeed regarding the Ndebele past. I will illustrate this with a short comparison of three of Nyathi's statements with some European memory-texts: that Mzilikazi left Shaka because of love for independence, that Mzilikazi's eldest son who was made king in his father's absence was sent to Zululand, and that Lobengula did not die but escaped and therefore never was defeated.

Firstly, while Nyathi says that Mzilikazi broke away from Shaka because of love for independence and not because of greed, the two anthropologists A.J.B. Hughes and J. van Velsen (1954:47f) write that Mzilikazi after a raid failed to hand over cattle to Shaka, an act of treason punishable by death, and had to flee. The retired colonial officer Harold Child (1969:6) likewise writes that Mzilikazi was entrusted with a mission which included the raiding of Sotho tribes:

> The mission was successful and Mzilikazi returned with much booty in cattle but refused to hand them over to Tshaka [Shaka] as was customary. As a result of this in the same year he decided to flee the country with his people and possessions.

The historian Kent Rasmussen (1978:2, 20ff), whose first priority in his reconstruction of Ndebele history is "to get the facts straight", gives a similar story adding that:

> The flight of the Khumalo from Zululand is the first Ndebele national epic. It is the story of the birth of the nation; as such it has been subjected in Ndebele accounts to patriotic distortions.

Secondly, Nyathi states that when Mzilikazi came back to his people in 1840 and found that his son, Nkulumane, had been installed as king, Mzilikazi probably sent the son south to live with his uncles in Zululand, although "some people say he was butchered". Hughes and van Velsen (1954:49) write that when Mzilikazi came back he immediately executed a large number of those responsible for electing his son to king, including the son himself. "To keep this murder secret", they continue, Mzilikazi "spread the rumour that his sons had been sent to Zululand for reasons of safety". Kent Rasmussen (1977:33) likewise writes about Nkulumane that: "It is probable that Mzilikazi had him executed, but many Ndebele continued to believe Nkulumane was alive, and in exile in South Africa", and historian Julian Cobbing (1976:258) states about Nkulumane and his brother Buhlehlo:

A tradition associated with Mzilikazi's eventual successor, Lobengula, has them strangled on Mzilikazi's orders; another has them escape south of the Limpopo. ... It is practically certain, however, that he was dead [at the time of Mzilikazi's death in 1868 and Lobengula's installation as king in 1870]. The man who claimed to be Nkulumane after 1868 was an impersonator. Nkulumane was never after 1835 positively identified; and there is no single contemporary reference to his existence between 1841 and 1868.

Thirdly, Nyathi states that Lobengula did not die in the war but escaped and that the Whites in this sense never defeated him or the Ndebele. Hughes and van Velsen (1954:52) write about Lobengula that

the most probable and generally accepted story is that he died somewhere near the Kana River, either by his own hand or as the result of the dropsy from which he suffered; the site of his alleged grave has been declared a national monument. But the Ndebele mostly hold that he did not die here, but survived somewhere in the north, a story which is also current among the Fort Jameson Ngoni.

The colonial officer N. Jones (1945:19) writes under the pseudonym Mhlagazanhlansi that "from the full story, as it has come to us through the official investigation, it is possible to reconstruct the circumstances and conditions of the King's end" and concludes that Lobengula poisoned himself and was buried in a now known grave in Matabeleland. The historian Stafford Glass (1968:238) refers to an author of a colonial report who "confirmed that Lobengula had died of fever about 22 or 23 January [1894], some 30 or 40 miles south of the Zambezi river", and the Curator of Antiquities C.K. Cooke (1992:16) writes in the National Museums and Monuments of Zimbabwe's guide to the Matopo Hills that Lobengula

died as a fugitive and was buried at Malindi having, it was said, taken poison. How sad it is to think that only the grave, far from the haunts of the ancestral spirits, may be all that remains of Lobengula, second and last king of the Amandebele.

History as ideology and methodology

These three reference points of the past are politically important ones both for Ndebeles and Europeans since they deal with the birth of the Ndebele nation, a succession crisis within this nation and the end of, if not the Ndebele nation as an idea, at least the Ndebele state as a functioning body. They are events incorporated both in Ndebeles' and Europeans' memories. In this sense we may say that history is ideology since different authors use various ideologies and present their altering representations of the past as history. However, the reason why Nyathi can put forward his interpretation of the three issues as a (lay) historian within the same historical discourse as the colonial library is that the different interpretations partly are based on contradictory evidence. Both Nyathi and the other authors use (Ndebele) oral sources as well as (European) written sources, although Nyathi, perhaps together with Cobbing, uses oral sources to a larger extent than the others and definitely treats them more seriously. In this sense we may say that history is methodology since rules about sources, causality and linearity also form what is presented as history. While ideology diverges various historians' representations of the past, methodology conforms them.

Pathisa Nyathi and the other authors referred to above are thus not only guided by their ideology to a larger extent in these three cases than in others because they are politically important issues, but because the past simultaneously is difficult to reconstruct according to the discipline's methodology. In the first example the difference is more a question of how to describe what happened than different opinions on what actually happened. Pathisa Nyathi says that Mzilikazi *broke* away from Shaka because of love for independence and *left* Zululand in about 1820. Hughes, van Velsen, Child and Cobbing, on the other hand, describe how Mzilikazi *failed* to hand over cattle to Shaka, an act of *treason* punishable by death, and had to *flee* from Zululand. In the first interpretation Mzilikazi is the deciding and acting agent, in the second it is Shaka. In the other example, however, Nyathi builds his interpretation on certain sources and Hughes, van Velsen, Rasmussen and Cobbing on others, although they all are aware of the existence of contradictory evidence. In the third example Nyathi makes a point that nobody officially knows what happened to Lobengula, while Hughes, van Velsen, Jones, Glass and Cooke build on different sources and give different interpretations of Lobengula's death.

Memory-texts and Ndebele identity

When Nyathi says that Mzilikazi left Zululand because of love for independence, that his son Nkulumane probably was sent south to Zululand, and that Lobengula did not die, since he did not die a public death, and that the Ndebele therefore never were defeated by the Whites, he is with the other statements in his memory-text constructing Ndebele identity by representing a shared Ndebele past in a favourable way. He is as an education officer and author identifying himself with the Ndebele and his memory-text reinforces an Ndebele-speaking listener's or reader's identification with the Ndebele, and not, for instance, with the nation-state Zimbabwe, nor with sub-groups among the Ndebeles based on Nguni, Sotho, Tswana, Shona or other origins. His memory-text "validates a human geography, its spatial configuration and the competing traditions of its various inhabitants", as Mudimbe states, and "it is both a legend and a dream for political power".

Similarly, the European authors do not only state that Mzilikazi was forced to flee from Zululand, that Nkulumane probably was executed, and that Lobengula died, but explain how, where and when Lobengula died—even though they differ internally regarding the cause, time and place of Lobengula's death. These authors are identifying themselves with superior nation-states and superior academic communities. They are, as Mudimbe writes about the colonial library, fulfilling a political project by "faithfully, translating and deciphering the African object" and thereby domesticating it. Their memory-texts are reinforcing national and academic identities as well as the existing power relations between these nation-states and communities, on the one hand, and the Ndebele, on the other. In effect they are deconstructing Ndebele identity. This is also true for Cook's text from 1992.

For instance, when Hughes and van Velsen write that the site of Lobengula's alleged grave has been declared a national monument although the Ndebele mostly hold he died somewhere else, they are talking about the nation of Southern Rhodesia and they are making Lobengula's death public in consistence with a British victory over the Ndebele. Since then, after independence in 1980, there has been an interest by the government and people regarding themselves in the first instance as Zimbabweans to shape national unity rather than ethnic conflict. Cooke, as an example, concludes in the official National Museums and Monuments guide of Zimbabwe, not only that Lobengula died as a fugitive by taking poison and that he was buried at Malindi, but that he was the second and *last* king of the Ndebele. This down playing of a Ndebele perspective of the Ndebele past in current national literature is by some Ndebeles seen as the majority Shona speaking peoples' oppression of the Ndebele as well as the nation-state Zimbabwe's oppression of them.

Images and counter-images

Apart from conflicting interpretations of specific reference points of the past, Pathisa Nyathi and authors represented in the colonial library use different images of the Ndebele. These images are not only used in memory-texts, defined as the "retelling of the genesis of the 'nation' and its social organisation", but in writings referred to as sources. An often used image of the Ndebele within the colonial library is the image of the Ndebele as cruel warriors. This is a description of "the other" which also has been taken up by some Ndebeles and used in their self-identification, albeit with the more positive aspects of being a warrior emphasised. Although some authors (e.g. Cobbing 1976) have tried to balance the image of the Ndebele as cruel warriors by explaining the Ndebele migration with political, economic and social factors, many authors have since the 1830s and onwards explicitly or implicitly described Ndebele mentality by using this image.

Thus, when Pathisa Nyathi gives the image of Mzilikazi as a man with the "capacity of moulding a homogenous state from a number of diverse ethnic groups" who people "joined" while "they abandoned their cultures", it is to a large degree a counter-image to the images used within the colonial library. The missionary Robert Moffat (1940[1835]:6f), for instance, describes how the Ndebele defeated the Griqua in a battle before they left Transvaal in South Africa with the words:

> The Matabele, with the groaning and hissing signals of death, marched onward, levelling all they met with. In a few minutes the rout was general, when every Griqua and Bechuana who was still alive sought safety in flight. Of these, many took wrong direction, and as the day approached fell prey to their exasperated conquerors, who seemed determined not to let a single soul escape.

Hughes and van Velsen (1954:49f) likewise write of Mzilikazi's later migration into the highlands north of the Matopos in Zimbabwe:

> It was from here that Mzilikazi directed his conquering and raiding expeditions. The Kalanga who remained in the area were incorporated into the Ndebele political organization, along with captured women and youths of some tribes which were raided. ... His most profitable source of booty and young soldiers were the Shona, whose country became his favourite raiding ground.

Missionary David Livingstone (1857:10f) similarly describes the Ndebele as "the most cruel enemies the Bechuanas ever knew", anthropologist Isaac Schapera (1953:15) writes about a period of chaos among the Tswana due to "mainly to the successive onslaughts of invaders from the east", among them "Moselekatse's Tebele (1825–37)", and N.J. van Warmelo (1974:76) states that "the Tswana seem to have multiplied and prospered until in 1825 Mzilikazi appeared on the scene and began slaughtering them wholesale".

These images helped to justify the war in 1893 and thereafter colonisation, but they are still referred to, used and spread—also within the academic world. The historian William Lye writes for instance in a text-book (1985:32f):

> Even though the Ndebele were few in numbers, they struck terror in the minds of their neighbours. ... Their usual technique was haughtily to warn their foes of their coming, and then surround them by night. At dawn they would drum their heavy shields like thunder to startle their sleepy victims. Then they stormed the village, stabbing their short assegais into everyone in sight and firing the huts. No one survived except the young men who could be drafted into the regiments and young maidens who could reward the valour of the fighters.

This passage is not even a description of a certain event of the past, but is a general description of the Ndebele's "usual technique" of fighting, that is a description of how the author William Lye imagines the Ndebele as cruel warriors. In the same way as conflicting interpretations build upon and react against each other, images and counter-images of the Ndebele mirror and change each other. Conflicting interpretations, images and counter-images are all used in memory-texts and they represent a past and construct identity in that they produce a relation between the past and the present state of affairs.

Conclusion: Conflicting memory-texts and the power to represent the past

The construction of Ndebele and other identities does not only depend on communication in face-to-face situations within *social groups*, that is given sets of people at certain times in certain places, but on communication of *social categories* through different kinds of printed and electronic media. The construction of identities within social groups and via media are not, of course, mutually exclusive. On the contrary, the interface between face-to-face situations and media is of utmost importance, since a social category can be communicated to, interpreted and then used in a social group, and vice versa. One of several social categories, however, is at a certain time often more important than others in being used by people in social groups and thereby in forming collective identities. The category *Ndebele* is to a certain extent such a social category today. This category is used and interpreted in different ways for different ends, but many Ndebeles use it consciously or not to reinforce Ndebele identity. An important way to strengthen Ndebele identity through media is to write about a shared Ndebele history. This has been done by some Ndebeles in recent decades, often partly in opposition to Europeans who have written about the Ndebele since the first half of the nineteenth century.

In this paper I have compared one such Ndebele representation of the past with some European representations. I proposed that history is ideology and methodology in that different historians use various ideologies in their diverging representations of the past while at the same time following conforming methodological rules about sources, causality and linearity. I focused mainly on history as ideology by referring to different representations of the Ndebele past as memory-texts, the European ones belonging to the colonial library. I suggested, firstly, that a lay or academic historian's conscious and unconscious ideology is most evident when he or she is dealing with politically important questions and when the past at the same time is difficult to reconstruct according to the discipline's methodology, and I gave three examples to show this. I suggested, secondly, that such important and contradictory reference points of the past, on purpose or not, are used to construct and deconstruct Ndebele identity, and I described how different authors with various arguments help to construct different identities. I suggested, thirdly, that ideology apart from this is used to describe Ndebele mentality and that different authors use different images of the Ndebele, which strengthen or weaken Ndebele identity, and I showed how Pathisa Nyathi used a counter-image in contrast to the images used within the colonial library.

These conflicting memory-texts should not be regarded as a game in opposition to real life. "It is not a question of semiotics, of sign substitution, of the intellectual game of truth-value and museological authenticity", to cite Jonathan Friedman (1992b:845). "It is a question of existential authenticity of the subject's engagement in a self-defining project." In 1995 I asked an old Ndebele woman about the fate of Lobengula. "I cannot say that Lobengula died", she answered. She continued:[2]

> My father-in-law just told that Lobengula disappeared. By then people were telling lies. There were some people who tried to find his grave. ... My father-in-law used to get beaten about it, because he knew that Lobengula didn't die, and up to now nobody knows where his grave is—not even one person.

During the colonial era, Mudimbe (1994:xii) writes, Europe submitted the world to its memory. The representation of the Ndebele past is still to a large degree subsumed by the European past and today Ndebeles struggle, as Pathisa Nyathi puts it, to present themselves to the world.

References

Beach, David, 1990, *Zimbabwe before 1900.* Gweru.

Bourdillon, Michael, 1991 (1976), *The Shona Peoples.* Gweru.

Breutz, P.L., 1975, "Die Südost-Bantu", in Baumann, H. (ed.), *Die Völker Afrikas und Ihre Traditionellen Kulturen.* Vol. 1. Wiesbaden.

Census, 1992, 1994, Zimbabwe National Report. Harare.

Child, Harold, 1969, *The History of the amaNdebele.* Salisbury.

Cobbing, Julian, 1976, *The Ndebele under the Khumalos, 1820–96.* Lancaster (Ph.D. thesis).

Cooke, C.K., 1992 (1986), *The Matopo Hills.* Harare.

Friedman, Jonathan, 1992a, "Myth, History, and Political Identity", *Cultural Anthropology,* 7:2.

—, 1992b, "The Past in the Future: History and the Politics of Identity", *American Anthropologist,* 94:4.

Glass, Stafford, 1968, *The Matabele War.* London and Harlow: Longmans.

Hughes, A.J.B. & van Velsen, J., 1954, "The Ndebele", in Kuper, H., A.J.B. Hughes & J. van Velsen, (eds), *The Shona and Ndebele in Southern Rhodesia.* London. (Ethnographic Survey of Africa: Southern Africa 4.)

Jones, N., 1945, *My Friend Khumalo.* Bulawayo. (Under the pseudonym Mhlagazanhlansi.)

Kuper, Adam, 1982, *Wives for Cattle.* London: Routledge & Kegan Paul.

Levi-Strauss, Claude, 1966, *The Savage Mind.* Chicago: University of Chicago Press.

Lindgren, Björn, 1998, "Ndebele Identity as a Practice of Naming: Negotiation of Social Position in Umzingwane, Zimbabwe", in Andersson, Thorsten, Eva Brylla och Anita Jacobson-Widding (eds), *Personnamn och social identitet/Personal names and social identity.* Stockholm: Royal Academy of Letters, History nd Antiquities.

Livingstone, David, 1857, *Missionary Travels and Researches in South Africa.* London.

Lye, W., 1985 (1980), "Early History and Upheaval", in Lye, W. & C. Murray, (eds), *Transformations on the Highveld: The Tswana and Southern Sotho.* Cape Town.

---

[2] Interview with Mrs Mloyi in Nkayi district, 5 June 1995.

Moffat, Robert, 1940 (1835), *Robert Moffat's Visit to Mzilikazi, 1829–1860*. Witwatersrand. (Oppenheimer Series 1:1.)

Mudimbe, V.Y., 1991, *Parables and Fables: Exegesis, Textuality, and Politics in Central Africa*. Madison, Wisconsin: Univeristy of Wisconsin

Press.

—, 1994. *The Idea of Africa*. London and Bloomington: Indiana University Press.

Murdock, G.P., 1959, *Africa: Its Peoples and Their Culture History*. New York.

Nyathi, Pathisa, 1994, *Igugu Likamthwakazi Imbadi Yamandabele 1820–1893*. Gweru.

Rasmussen, Kent, 1977, *Mzilikazi*. Harare.

—, 1978. *Migrant Kingdom: Mzilikazi's Ndebele in South Africa*. London: Collings; Cape Town: D. Philip.

Schapera, Isaac, 1953, *The Tswana*. London. (Ethnographic Survey of Africa: Southern Africa 3.)

Sicard, Harald von, 1975, "Das Gebeit Zwischen Sambesi und Limpopo", in Baumann, H. (ed.), *Die Völker Afrikas und Ihre Traditionellen Kulturen*. Vol. 1. Wiesbaden.

Warmelo van, N., 1974, "The Classification of Cultural Groups", in Hammond-Tooke, W.D. (ed.), *The Bantu-Speaking Peoples of Southern Africa*. London: Routledge & Kegan Paul.

Gender Dimensions in the Images of Africans in Commercial Works of Art

I. Bolarinwa Udegbe

Introduction

Psychologists have emphasised that first impressions especially unfavourable ones, exert more influence on people's judgement of others than subsequent information (e.g., Rothbart & Park 1986, Friedman 1983). The implication is that perceptions of Africa by people in other continents are strongly influenced by the type, content and slant of their first impressions. Only few Europeans have had direct experience of Africa through visits to parts of Africa or encounters with African communities in Europe. The majority on the other hand have had indirect experience through documentaries, news, literature, or works of art.

Unfortunately, many of the impressions of Africa created in myths, religion and reflected in arts, mass media, literature philosophy, history and even in the sciences have been negative. Africa has been depicted as underdeveloped and beset with problems. The peoples have been reflected as uninhibited, primitive, often engaged in wars, ritualistic, superstitious, festivity loving, etc. Pelrine and McNaughton (1988) observed that many aspects of attitudes formed several hundred years ago when explorers first started encountering Africa's sculpture remain intact today. Like art from the South Seas, American Indian, and Far Eastern cultures, African art is viewed as products of strange and uncivilised societies. However, not all these images have been created by colonialists, missionaries or travellers; rather some of the images have been the reflections—sometimes magnified, more often distorted—of Africans themselves.

Art is one of the three most specialised forms of communication (McCall 1975), it is not surprising therefore that traditional art forms, particularly sculpture, is one of the ways that African traditions are studied and portrayed. Traditional African art, dominated by figure compositions, served cultural aesthetic functions such as religious or ritual functions and historical functions in a memorial context to past kings or ancestors (e.g., Dark 1975, Olopade 1980, Parrot 1972). Contemporary African art, which did not emerge until decades after traditional art had become known, and also dominated by figure compositions, is different from traditional art in that it is mainly for entertainment. It is also different from artworks from Europe and America in that while the latter emphasise the outside experience of artists the former produces images related to traditional African background. However, since traditional African sculpture belongs to the past, contemporary art may be seen as carrying on the function of providing information about the African way of life.

Very few studies have been carried out on contemporary art. Those available have been devoted to catalogues of exhibitions and monographs on certain outstanding individual artists and works. Also, attempts to classify the artworks based on training avenues, themes or periods have shown inconclusive trends (e.g., Oyelola 1976). A recent attempt by Adepegba (1995) noted four tendencies based on forms: discernible images of experience and ideas; naive visions encouraged and fossilised; abstractions beyond common understanding and revisitations of traditional art forms. This classification was mostly a qualitative description of some outstanding published works or pieces and did not provide empirical information on the pattern of themes and images present in contemporary African art. Indeed, the topic of interest has not been approached by much social scientific research.

Because there is a marked growth in the production and importance attached to artwork locally and internationally, the assumption in this paper is that contemporary art objects may serve as a first point of contact for many people outside the continent. Further, they may serve to provide information which confirms first impressions. To what extent therefore does African art, particularly that produced for commercial purposes prompt negative images of Africa? Unfortunately, because negative or unfavourable first impressions are more resistant to change, they are much harder to override. In addition, like stereotypes, first impressions consist of knowledge structures that guide the way individuals process information and also perpetuate themselves by orienting the individuals toward information that confirms their impressions (Weitin 1989, Feldman 1985).

Given these serious implications of first impressions, and consequently the possible sources of the impressions, there is a need to examine in depth, the roles they play in production and reproduction of images of Africa. This study was therefore interested in the images of Africa being portrayed in contemporary artworks. Unlike previous studies which have been limited to works of known artists or which examined the works from stylistic perspectives, this research focused on the apparent meanings in the images. This approach was adopted in order to examine the dominant images that are being transmitted about Africa to local and international communities. Since contemporary African artists rely mainly on European buyers, the pattern of images portrayed will tend to reflect the images of Africa produced and reproduced in Europe. Finally, many of the previous studies on this topic have not examined gender differences in the images being produced. This therefore constitutes another major focus of this paper.

Method

Study Site

The study was carried out in Ibadan city, one of the largest traditional cities in West Africa. The Yorubas are probably the most prolific wood carvers in West Africa (Olopade 1980) and Ibadan is the largest Yoruba city. Being a large commercial and traditional city, it is likely to have pieces from neighbouring areas. Indeed, discussions with the dealers revealed that the art objects in the shops came not only from local Yoruba sources but from the Benin-city area, Northern Nigeria and a few pieces from other parts of West Africa e.g. Ghana and Mali. Commercial works of art—carvings and paintings —are usually found in big hotels, conference centres, shopping centres and markets. For the purpose of this study, the selection of locations and shops was based on a consensus from initial pre-study enquiries made to dealers and relevant informants. Altogether, twelve shops were visited in various locations.

Data collection

In each of the shops visited, all carvings and paintings for sale were examined. In cases where there was more than one piece of the same art object in the same shop, only one piece was used for the study. The carvings, mainly contemporary pieces included thorn carvings. In addition, only portable pieces (which were a majority) were included in the study, large pieces such as door-posts or door panels and antiquities (rare pieces, usually, not displayed or sold) were excluded. The African paintings studied included framed and unframed works of various sorts such as oil, water, pen, ink and spray paintings.

Data collection involved making a record of the art object in each shop. Details of the sex, activity, images and themes reflected in the pieces, activities ascribed to the figures, features displayed and other relevant descriptions were recorded for each object, in consensus with the dealer. Therefore, in essence, the apparent meaning (from the perspective of the observer) of the objects was recorded, It must be noted however that for many of the carvings, the dealers were sufficiently informed about the themes displayed based on their contact with some artists. Many of the paintings and some carvings also carried titles or were catalogued by dealers, which made it easier to identify their themes, particularly those of semi-abstract and abstract works. Data collection in each shop ranged from two to five hours depending on the quantity of the stock. Information obtained from dealers was recorded in Yoruba or pidgin English (for non-Yoruba dealers), translated to English and finally subjected to content analysis.

The works were analysed piece by piece by addressing issues of themes and images. A piece may consist of a single focal figure (e.g., a horse rider, a woman pounding or an antelope grazing) or more than one focal figure (e.g., a set of twins, a couple, a group of people dancing, a group of elephants). But for the analyses of activities ascribed to the figures, the unit of analysis was each figure in the artwork. Generally, summaries of data were made using descriptive statistics—percentages and ranks.

Findings

Altogether, 600 pieces of artwork were used in this study, they were made up of 530 pieces of carvings (415 single figure pieces and 115 multiple figure pieces) and 70 paintings. Of these 5 per cent were abstracts or semi-abstracts most of which were easily discernible.

General themes and images

Table 1 summarises the broad categories of themes portrayed in the works and percentages and ranks of the themes reflected. On the average, each piece was interpreted as portraying one general theme, but, there were a few cases in which the pieces were perceived as reflecting two themes. For example, a woman with a child on her back cooking or performing a ritual was seen as fertility and cooking or fertility and religious themes. The works were grouped into four depending on sex of the focal figures (male, female, both sexes, and non-specific sex).

Table 1. *Percentages and ranks by sex of the themes displayed in the images portrayed in the sample of commercial art works* (ranks in parentheses)

Themes	Overall		Male		Female		Both sexes		Non-specific sex	
Traditional occupational activities	12.3	(1)	28.0	(1)	8.8	(5)	5.0	(6.5)	-	
Domestic activities and scenes	11.5	(2)	6.2	(6)	21.8	(3)	2.5	(10.5)	6.7	(4)
Animals	9.7	(3)	-	-	-	-	-	-	64.6	(1)
Music and dancing	9.6	(4.5)	19.1	(3)	5.0	(6)	12.4	(4)	-	
Fertility	9.6	(4.5)	0.0	-	24.4	(1)	2.5	(10.5)	-	
Femininity and beauty	8.6	(6)	0.0	-	23.1	(2)	-		-	
Religious and ritual scenes	8.3	(7)	11.8	(4)	11.8	(4)	3.3	(8.5)	-	
Royalty	7.2	(8)	20.2	(2)	2.5	(7)	3.3	(8.5)	-	
Mask/pendant heads	3.1	(11)	1.8	(9)	0.4	(9)	-		14.6	(2)
Journey (traditional and modern)	4.4	(9)	-		-		23.1	(1)	-	
Couple	4.2	(10)	-		-		22.3	(2)	-	
Environment	2.7	(12.5)	-		-		14.3	(3)	-	
Modern themes and concepts	2.7	(12.5)	-		-		5.0	(6.5)	11.5	(3)
Begging/despair	2.5	(14)	8.4	(5)	-		-		-	
Twins	2.4	(15)	0.6	(8)	2.5	(8)	6.6	(5)	-	
Others	1.7	(16)	3.9	(7)	-		-		-	

The five most dominant themes portrayed were traditional occupational activities (such as farmer, palm-wine tapper, carver, seller, warrior, and hunter)

(12.3%), domestic activities and scenes (11.5%), animals (9.7%), music and dancing (9.6%) and fertility (9.6%). The second most important (domestic activities and scenes) was usually reflected by women cooking, cleaning, presenting gifts or men playing games or eating. The third theme was the animal theme portraying images of animals such as elephants, antelopes, fish, reptiles, etc. Pieces reflecting the music and dancing theme consisted of scenes of drummers (see Plate 1), flutists or *goje* players and dancers. Fertility was portrayed by images of mother and child in various forms and activities, the most common being mother with child on her back or suckling an infant.

Other themes that were reflected included femininity and beauty (8.6%), traditional religious/ritual (8.3%), royalty (7.2%), journey (4.4%) and couple (4.2%). In many works portraying femininity and beauty, female sensuality and beauty were depicted by images of

Plate 1. Drummer

women in sensual poses, emphasising breasts and feminine features, and female faces and hairstyles. Religious themes consisted of images of deities, priests, worshippers and ritual scenes while royalty depicted images of kings, queens and chiefs. The journey theme depicted traditional forms of travel such as by canoe, on horse back and on foot, and modern means such as in cars, motorcycles and buses. The couple theme depicted a man and woman, usually busts in various traditional outfits.

The less dominant themes observed were environment (2.7%) consisting of village, market and forest scenes, modern concepts (2.7%) such as Christianity, football etc., begging/despair (2.5%) which reflects poor or old men, beggars or a thinking man and twins (2.4%). The others (1.7%) category consisted of objects with themes that were not easily discernible or precluded classification.

To what extent are there gender differences in the themes presented? Table 1 also shows the dominant themes reflected in works depending on the sex of the object of focus in the pieces. In works depicting males as the focus, as for the overall sample, traditional occupational activities (28.0%) constituted the dominant theme. The second theme was royalty (20.2%) while the third reflected music and dancing (19.1%) (for example, Plate 1). On the other hand, about a quarter (24.4%) of the female-centred pieces depicted fertility. The second dominant theme was femininity and beauty (23.1%). The third theme is domestic activities. This theme is often illustrated by women carrying babies on their backs.

In comparing the images of males with females, the findings suggest that about 60 per cent of the male images emphasised power (e.g., royalty and religious themes) and industry (traditional occupations). For females, about 70 per cent of the images emphasised fecundity, femininity, and subservience. For both groups religious themes are the fourth most dominant theme (see Plates 2 and 3). Where both sexes were the objects of focus, the dominant themes depicted were journey (23.1%), couple (22.3%), and environment (14.3%).

How are males and females portrayed in the artworks? In order to examine in closer detail gender differences in the images depicted in the works, Table 2 presents the activities (in percentages and ranks) ascribed to males and females in all the pieces.

Table 2. *Comparison of percentages and ranks of activities ascribed to males and females in the sample commercial art works* (ranks in parentheses)

Female				Male			
Domestic:	20		(1)	Occupational activities:	21.6		(1)
-cooking/cleaning		13.7		-farmer		6.3	
-farming/harvesting*		5.8		-palmwine tapper		5.6	
Motherhood	17		(2)	-traditional craft		5.3	
Bust/portrait - beauty	8		(3)	-hunter		2.1	
Wife/woman	7.8		(4)	-horse rider		2.4	
Occupational activities:	7.5		(5)	Man/husband	14.7		(2)
-selling		5.2		Musician:	14.0		(4)
-weaving/dyeing		1.5		-drummers		12.3	
-hair plaiting		0.9		-others (flutists, etc.)		5.1	
Sensual	7		(6.5)	Royalty	14.4		(3)
Dancer	7		(6.5)	Leisure/eating	6.5		(5)
Worshipper (ritual)	6		(8.5)	Priest (ritual)	5.5		(6)
Royalty	6		(8.5)	Messenger/town crier	5.1		(7)
Gift bearer	5		(10)	Driver (vehicle)/paddler	4.5		(8)
Deity/goddess	4		(11)	Mask/masquerade	1.0		(14)
Passenger	3		(12)	Deity/ancestor	3.8		(9.5)
Twin	2		(13)	Old man/beggar	3.4		(10)
Mask	1		(14)	Twin	2.4		(13)
				Passenger	3.1		(12)

Note: Figures in italics represent sub-totals
*farming/harvesting are traditionally perceived as domestic work for women

The unit of analysis is any discernible person in the artworks. The findings follow the pattern observed in Table 1. Of the images describing women's activities, about half depicted them in domestic (20%), motherhood (17%), beauty (8%) and wife/woman (7.8%) roles. For men on the contrary, 21.6 per cent of the activities in which they were depicted emphasised traditional occupations, while activities reflecting fatherhood (as against motherhood), and domestic roles prominent for women figures were absent in male images. Furthermore as earlier observed, men are portrayed in positions of higher status and power in themes such as husband/man, royalty (second and third

Plate 2. Two separate carvings showing
a woman carrying a calabash (left) and a
priest in a ritual scene

Plate 3. A female
worshipper in a ritual scene

most dominant images), priesthood and in leisure activities. This point is also emphasised in the kind of images portrayed of men and women in relation to the same theme:

(1) While men were mainly portrayed as musicians (14.4%) at festive occasions women were portrayed as dancers (7%).
(2) In ritual or worship scenes women were mostly worshippers (6%) while men were mainly diviners or priests (6%) (see Plate 2).

Table 3 shows percentage differences in images of males and females in terms of dressing. This analysis did not include paintings and thorn carvings.

Overall results showed that about a third (37.6%) of the images were presented as half dressed or nude, 35.4 per cent were fully dressed, while 27.1 per cent were not indicated or did not require dressing as in abstracts or busts. There were also marked gender differences in dressing. Results showed that 38.9 per cent of women were depicted as nude/near nude or half-dressed, as against 14.3 per cent of men. The majority of the men (60.2%) were fully dressed as against 16.8 per cent of the women. Hairstyles are symbols of beauty in African art while the breasts on females emphasise the nurturing role of women (Pelrine, 1988). Table 3 also shows that a majority of the women were depicted with African hairstyles while men (67.3%) were depicted wearing caps. Among the women, breasts were depicted prominently in 49.6 per cent of the images (Plates 2 and 3), outlined in 17.7 per cent, slightly outlined in 19.3 per cent and not indicated in 13.5 per cent of the cases.

Table 3. *Percentages showing gender differences in the images as depicted by mode of dressing for the sample of carvings*

		Female	Male	Total
1. Dressing (body)	Nude/near nude	38.9	6.1	24.9
	Half dressed	16.0	8.2	12.7
	Fully dressed	16.8	60.2	35.4
	Not indicated/not relevant	28.2	25.5	27.1
2. Dressing (head)	Hairdo	72.9	6.5	43.3
	Cap	1.5	67.3	30.8
	Headtie	3.0	0.0	1.7
	Haircut short	7.5	9.4	4.2
	Not indicated/not relevant	22.6	16.8	20.0

Discussion

This study attempted to examine in-depth the dominant themes in the images of Africa produced in commercial works of art, and the extent to which there are gender differences in the images. The findings revealed that the three most dominant themes in all the works studied were traditional occupations, domestic activities and animals. These themes accounted for about a third of the images produced in the works. In addition to themes depicting royalty, religious and ritual scenes, masks and twins, they constituted more than half of the images reflecting pre-colonial traditional African values, activities, and scenes. Such images include horse rider/warrior, *Sango*, *Osun*, diviner, tapper, masks, African mother etc. The animals images (e.g., elephants, antelopes, reptiles, birds, and fish) produced in the pieces tended to represent ideas from traditional art. Ben-Amos (1976) noted that animals served several functions in traditional art, ranging from sacrificial animals depicted as symbols of offerings (e.g., antelopes, mudfish) to those associated with authority (e.g., elephants, leopards, crocodiles) and those associated with the spirit of medicine and witchcraft (e.g., owl, chameleon). Since contemporary art pieces obviously do not serve religious functions, what then is the link between the images and the old traditional uses? Indeed, many of these images have been reported as common in traditional sculptures (e.g., Adepegba 1995) and closer details of the activities ascribed to males and females in this study suggest that many of the works in this group are revisitations or adaptations of traditional themes and ideas.

The main aim of this paper is to examine the gender dimensions of the images portrayed. First, it was observed that while females were predominantly presented as symbols of fertility, beauty and subservience, men were depicted as symbols of power, strength and industry. Furthermore, some activities were portrayed as exclusively female or male. For example females were the only groups presented as gift bearers, dancers (except in one case), and symbols of sexuality and fertility. On the other hand, only men were depicted in themes reflecting leisure, drivers and musicians. Second, the findings showed that the functions ascribed to males and females differed for the same themes: again, men were depicted in roles reflecting authority and activity while women were portrayed in less powerful and more subservient or passive roles. For example, women served as worshippers or bearers of sacrifices in ritual scenes while men served as priests. Third, women's hair styles were emphasised in three quarters of the images while men in almost all the cases were depicted dressed in caps except for representations of *Sango*. Some previous writings (e.g., Pelrine 1988) have suggested that African art depicts images of beauty with hairstyles, our findings also showed this tendency in the marked gender differences in mode of dressing.

While only a negligible proportion of male images was portrayed nude or scantily dressed, a substantial proportion of the female images were depicted nude. No doubt, if the intention was to present African images in stereotyped nude or near nude mode of dressing there would not have been such marked gender differences. In addition, the majority of the images of women in the sculptures, particularly those of women scantily dressed, prominently emphasised the breasts. Thus the findings seem to confirm the view that women's bodies are the single most exposed and abused objects in visual art (*Gallery* 1995). Furthermore, the images tend to portray African women relative to men as tradition bound, ignorant, victimised and domestic. Contrary to the observations (e.g., Badejo 1991) that Yoruba religious construct supports parallel or complimentary roles of women in traditional African societies, hierarchical or dichotomous structures are evinced in the commercial artworks in this research.

What are the implications of these findings and trends? First patronage obviously affects the themes and forms produced in the artworks and because art is now a thriving business in Africa, only a few artists can sacrifice promoter's and buyers' recognition and patronage for freedom of expression. It therefore seems logical to conclude that the trend in the images of Africa produced as observed in this research reflects the preferences of foreign (mostly European) buyers. The findings suggest that, although unlike traditional artworks these commercial art pieces may not serve religious or other cultural functions, they do heavily emphasise African religious practices and traditions. On the one hand, they may serve as objects of nostalgia or ethnic identity for Africans while on the other hand, they may present Africa as consisting of highly traditional and primitive societies. Also, the images provide only very little evidence of changing lifestyles and increasing secularisation. As Adepegba (1995:87) observed, "it seems that the direction of contemporary Nigerian art would

have been different if there had not been expatriate promotion and patronage".

Second, the findings also raise some questions: Do the images reflect realistic images of Africa in the various ways portrayed? To what extent do these
images reflect African day to day scenes and experiences? For example, are
Africans (from traditional and contemporary settings) mostly nude or half
dressed? What effects do these themes have on images produced of Africa?
What effects do the themes portrayed in commercial art have on Europeans
who have had direct, indirect or no direct contact with Africa? It appears that
in a bid to make the artworks attractive to buyers who are mostly foreigners,
"the unusual", "the strange" and "the different" are perceived as more attractive and thus more emphasised. The images seem not only to reflect preferences and perhaps stereotypes of the market but also auto-stereotypes of the
artists. Consequently, the production and reproduction of the images may
reinforce the stereotypes not only among the buyers and the artists but also
other Africans. This point highlights directions for further research: What
meanings do these themes have in African people's lives? To what extent do
Africans relate to the images portrayed?

Third, the images, like general stereotypic views about women in other cultures, tend to be marked in this research. The implication is that the uncomplimentary, more negative presentations of women not only tend to influence
attitudes to women, they also tend to influence the images presented of Africans generally. For example, while many of the women were portrayed scantily dressed as against the majority of the men depicted fully dressed, the
findings also revealed that overall, only a third of the males and females were
depicted fully dressed, and about two fifths were nude or scantily dressed.
This translates to an overall portrayal of a high proportion of nudity in the
images of Africans, which to some extent may be negative. Indeed, although
the images may reflect unique qualities of traditional African lifestyles and
values, they tend to produce or affirm ideas, beliefs or knowledge structures of
Africa, which may be negative or uncomplimentary.

Although this exploratory study has attempted to accommodate some of
the complexities in examining artworks, there are still limitations. For example, because artworks can be covert or overt, explicit or implicit, ambiguous
or readily discernible, their apparent meaning may not necessarily be consistent with the artists' intended meaning, This study was however limited to the
apparent meaning of the works based on consensus with dealers. In addition
the study may have benefited from a wider geographical spread (across states
and regions) of the shops. We do not know whether the present scope may
limit the ability to generalise the findings. These raise the question as to what
can be done to increase the chances of presenting complimentary images of
Africa without neglecting its rich traditions.

In conclusion, by carrying out an exploratory survey of themes in artworks, this study makes important contributions in documenting trends in the

distribution and relative importance of themes and images portrayed in contemporary works. Another major contribution is its focus on the specific areas of gender differences in the images portrayed. Finally, because few studies have focused on contemporary African art this research is an important contribution because of its focus on commercial works of art, which hitherto have been neglected in research in preference for works of renowned artists.

References

Adepegba, Cornelius Oyeleke, 1995, *Nigerian Art: Its Traditions and Modern Tendencies.* Ibadan: Jodad.

Badejo, Diedre L., 1991, "Oral Literature of the Yoruba Goddess Osun", in Olupona, Jacob O.K. & Toyin Falola (eds), *Religion and Society in Nigeria: Historical and Sociological Perspectives.* Ibadan: Spectrum.

Ben-Amos, Paula, 1976, "Man an Animal in Benin Art", in *Man* II, 2.

Dark, Philip John Crosskey, 1975, "Benin Bronze Head Styles and Chronology", in McCall, Daniel F. & Edna G. Bay (eds), *African Images: Essays in African Iconology.* New York: Africana.

Feldman, Robert S., 1985, *Social Psychology: Theories Research and Applications.* New York: McGraw-Hill.

Friedman, Howard S., 1983, "Social perceptions and face-to-face interactions", in Perlman, Daniel & Paul Chris Cozby (eds), *Social Psychology.* New York: Holt, Rinehart and Wineston.

Gallery,1995, Art Magazine from Gallery Delta, March No. 3.

McCall, Daniel F., 1975, "Introduction", in McCall, Daniel F. & Edna G. Bay (eds), *African Images: Essays in African Iconology.* New York: Africana.

Oyelola, Pat, 1976, *Every Man's Guide to Nigerian Art.* Nigeria Magazine special publications, No. 1. Lagos: Nigeria Magazine.

Olopade, O., 1980, "Ife Classical Art", in Isaac Adeagbo Akinjogbin (ed.), *The Cradle of a Race: Ife from the beginning to 1980.* Port Harcourt: Sunray.

Parrot, F.J., 1972, *Introduction to African Arts of Kenya, Zaire, and Nigeria.* New York: Arco.

Pelrine, Diane M., 1988, *African Art from the Rita and John Grunwald Collection.* Bloomington: Indiana University Press.

Pelrine, Diane M. & McNaughton, Patrick R., 1988, "African Art: Introduction", in Pelrine, Diane M. (ed.), *African Art from the Rita and John Grunwald Collection.* Bloomington: Indiana University Press.

Rothbart, M. & Park, B., 1986, "On the confirmability and disconfirmability of trait concepts", *Journal of Personality and Social Psychology,* 50, 131–42.

Weitin, W., 1989, *Psychology: Themes and Variations.* Pacific Grove Co: Brooks/Cole.

Jungle Drums Striking the World Beat
Africa as an Image Factor in Popular Music

Johannes Brusila

Introduction

Black musical forms have been aspects of Western popular culture since at least the middle of the nineteenth century, but the first breakthrough of Afro-American music in the larger part of Europe happened after World War I when jazz spread to even the more remote cities of the continent. A large part of the musicians, the cultural establishment and the intellectuals despised the new musical style, and contemptuous comments about "this new howling by Zulus with nose-rings, who tootle it on cars' signal horns, which have been robbed from white people" (Väinö Joensuu in Suomen Musiikkilehti 1925, quoted in Jalkanen 1989:338) were common.

At the same time jazz was seen more positively as both a fashionable craze from the metropolis and a primitive force with roots in the exotic Africa. Intellectuals and artists, who were tired of the old degenerated highbrow and popular art forms of the West, were eagerly looking for new impressions and experiences. The "ecstatic roar of the Negro-orchestras", as the Finnish writer Olavi Paavolainen described the sounds that made the young intellectuals dance, functioned as an exciting window-opener to a new world.

Some of the central European viewpoints on Afro-American popular music were already established in these first comments on jazz. In most cases the exotic African roots of the music were stressed, either because of the overall percussive sound of the orchestras, or because of the connections to dance and corporeal elements. But most of all because it represented a primitive force, an "Other", which functioned as an antithesis to the Western intellectual and controlled world. These viewpoints have lived on even if they have seldom had any stronger, analytical background. What is more important than the truthfulness of these images is however how and why some people have given Africa these meanings in the context of Afro-American popular music. And today, with increasing international contacts, an even more important question is: Has anything of this changed?

In my paper I shall discuss how these images were created in the first place when jazz came to Europe. After that I will try to describe how many of the basic premises of the argumentation concerning basic concepts such as African, American and European are even today vaguely defined and seldom stand up to a thorough analysis. I will also reflect on how the images of authenticity are being created (or recreated) today, taking into consideration the changes that have occurred due to e.g. media expansion and development, and finally through the creation of the concept "world music".

Jazz—music from darkest Africa

One can of course ask why older forms of jazz are taken up when discussing Africa as an image factor in the popular music of Europe. The answer is partly that the acculturation process, which took place in the popular musics of European countries during the first half of the century, laid not only the musical foundation for a large part of the national popular music styles to come, but also manifested certain cultural meanings related to identity that are still visible today. It is also precisely because the ideological aspects of the process had already from the start so little to do with musical facts, that it clearly shows how the external meanings of the music were created.

The first adaptations of Afro-American musical styles in Europe could be heard in Britain in the 19th century when minstrelsy became popular among the lower-middle class, but it wasn't until the 1920s that elements of Afro-American music and national popular music styles merged in larger parts of the continent. Pekka Jalkanen has made a thorough analysis of this development in Finland (Jalkanen 1989). What is striking is the complexity of the acculturation process and the strong emotions that were tied to the first confrontations with the new music. An example of this is an eyewitness report from Helsinki:

> In 1919 [should be 1922 according to Jalkanen] in a restaurant opposite the railway station in Helsinki—then called City-Brondin—one night a strange dandy could be seen. When step (fast march) was played, he beat his rattles without a break. He also changed to small drum sticks, with which he banged hollow wooden rattles on his sides, put a metal helmet covered with bronze on his head, a long extension on his nose and a whistle in his mouth, with which he whistled madly. The small orchestra shrieked tones as much as it could, but the air was constantly filled with the hellish noise raised by the drummer. It was then told that the name of this new ideology was jazz and that it came from the Negro countries. (Similä 1941:45–46, quoted in Jalkanen 1989:73)[1]

The music which was described in these words had actually very little to do with jazz, in fact it was an offspring of the German cabaret-tradition, but already at this point the ecstatic rhythmic approach and the idea of an African origin were stressed. It took some time before jazz in the range of styles being played in America became known to a wider audience. In the beginning of the century scores with Afro-American "jazzy" ball-room dances were spread among the lounge orchestras of the cities, but often the only connection to jazz was to be found in the names of the tunes. Radio and records eventually made

---

[1] See appendix for original text in Finnish.

it possible to hear American musicians and spread the idea of how to play jazz, but even then it took a long time before the repertoires of local musicians consisted of original jazz tunes. Personal improvisation in the style of American jazz musicians became common only after a couple of decades. (See e.g. Jalkanen 1989 for the development in Finland and Edström, 1988 for the development in Sweden.)

The Afro-American music and its impact on the European music caused strong counter-reactions within the national art organisations. The art music establishment in particular found it hard to adjust itself to the new situation. The reasons for this are partly to be found in the elitist aesthetic ideas of the conservative cultural elite, which saw the invasion of jazz as a corrupting threat to the people's unspoilt taste. On the other hand the aesthetic and educative aspects of the folklore critique against the new "cannibal-orchestras" could also function as a cover for the harsher economic reasons that lay in the background. A lot of the criticism that was published in for example the magazines of the musicians' unions can certainly be explained as pure protectionist measures. In many European countries the older musicians saw the new styles and the foreign musicians who performed them as a threat on the unstable market and did their best to ban them. (See e.g. Jalkanen 1989:198 about the musicians' union in Finland; Edström 1996:416 for Sweden; and Frith 1988:52 for Britain.)

The racist critique of jazz has basically been played down after the Second World War, but for example as late as in 1946 a Swedish college teacher wrote in his article called "The Jazz Attacks" these following lines:

> Jazz cannot be fully understood without taking in consideration three significant facts concerning its creation:
> It has been created by Negroes.
> It has been created by drunken Negroes.
> It has been created by drunken Negroes in a brothel environment.[2]

The African roots, the racial aspects (prejudiced genetic viewpoints), rhythm, corporeal spontaneity and sexuality were connotations given to jazz as it was heard for the first time in the more remote areas of Europe. The new Afro-American styles were however not only criticised because of these characteristics, in fact they were also praised because of them.

In the 1920s Paris became the centre of the new European "jazz age". For the younger intellectuals jazz was a primitive force of the black people and it was expected to have a fruitful impact on the degenerate European culture. The interest in the "wild" was a liberating reaction against Victorian puritanism, but at the same time this ambivalent thirst for exoticism often covered a racist biologisation of the "primitive".

---

[2] Quoted from Bruér and Westin, 1995:10. See appendix for original text in Swedish.

The symbol of this period was Josephine Baker, a black dancer from Saint Louis who became an overnight sensation in Paris in 1925. Baker had light brown skin, but instead of asking her to powder it, as would have been the case in USA, the promoters in Paris asked her to keep it as dark as possible in order to appeal to the audience (Nederveen Pieterse 1994:142–43). The European avant-garde artists saw Josephine Baker and Afro-American music as a direct expression of fundamental emotions and primitivism, which put it in advance of the new art movement. Composers like Stravinsky, Milhaud, Ravel and Weill also turned to jazz in search of new inspiration (instead of turning to European folk music as had been done during the national romanticism).

The new popular music of this period was given a most exotic image by both the popular music producers and marketing personnel, as well as by the intellectuals. Many songs and poems of the 1920s are filled with romantic pictures of foreign places, peoples, instruments and everything that could be described as exotic from a Western point of view. A large part of this exoticism is of course outdated now and it is hard to avoid laughing at the mixtures of deserts, jackals, islands, trains, banjos and flutes that can be found in lyrics and poems of the "jazz age" (see e.g. Yrjö Jylhä's poem "Saxophone" analysed in Jalkanen 1989:342 or Edström 1988:60–62 on one-step lyrics in Sweden). It is however obvious that in this case the realistic picture of a particular cultural environment or phenomenon was not (and is not) as important, as was the search for a generally understandable "Other", where the intellectual could project his images, hopes and desires (as well as fears) of an alternative primitive force. In this case the emergence of the new Afro-American music was more a factor that triggered off this projection, rather than a phenomenon that was analytically examined and found suitable for the purpose.

The images of African and Afro-American music as a spontaneous, primitive force, and as something sexual, corporeal and ecstatic have lived on during the decades that followed the first jazz-wave. Even today "black music" is still very much associated with these old images despite the fact that different forms of modern, urban Afro-American music have sprung up in the urban environments of the United States of America and are spread throughout the industrialised world (see e.g. Frith 1981:15–23).

The African origins (real or assumed) of many rock and pop styles have also been used as an argument by moralists who have tried to fight the new musical styles of the youth, be they jazz, rhythm & blues, rock, soul or rap. At the same time there has been a need among the white youth in America and Europe to identify themselves with blacks and their culture, which has been said to offer stronger experiences. This is personified in Sal Paradise, the main character in Jack Kerouac's novel "On the Road", when he walks in the evening through the coloured district of Denver:

wishing I were a Negro, feeling that the best the white world had offered was not enough ecstasy for me, not enough life, joy, kicks, darkness, music, not enough night. (Kerouac 1991:180)

What is often forgotten in this search for a spontaneous alternative life in black music is for instance the intellectualism of many jazz-styles, the impact of the white artists and audience on the development of jazz and rhythm & blues, the influences of European styles, and the closeness of the creator's world to the listener's own world. "Black music" is simply still an "Other" in relation to the white mainstream, be it in white America or Europe (see also Lilliestam 1996:49–51 for the European interest in Afro-American music).

The bourgeois brain and the black body of the "other"

The images associated with Afro-American music raise interesting questions concerning the creation and use of stereotyped and simplified concepts such as "African", "American", "Afro-American" and "European". It certainly would be a truism to say that Afro-American popular music was a result of the merging of African and Western elements which were brought to America by the African slaves and the European colonialists, or that it is possible to track down African elements in today's pop. But at the same time it would be a simplification to say that the Afro-American music was born after a fusion of two separate, homogenous and clean cultures. Unfortunately the latter is often the case and in this viewpoint the stereotyped image of Africa as the spontaneous, rhythmic spice is once again manifested as an opposite pole to the European intellectual side of the fusion.

Philip Tagg has questioned, in a rather provocative open letter to his fellow popular music researchers (Tagg 1989), the way in which even scholars seem to be taking for granted complicated terms like "Black music", "Afro-American music" and "European music". According to Tagg those definitions of "black" and "white" that connect the terms with for example racial aspects are bound to end up with racist conclusions, that is, seeing the musical expressions as a result of genetic aspects. An ethnic definition would in turn lead to a concept "Afro-American", which would also denote geographical, social and historical locations and phenomena, which are not especially "black" (the USA, the South, rural, urban, proletariat, certain cultural traditions etc.). As a logical conclusion Tagg moves on to ask what styles connected to the terms "black", "Afro" and "Afro-American" actually have in common musically.

Tagg analyses four elements that are usually mentioned as typical "black" or "African" traits: blue notes, call-and-response techniques, certain rhythmic structures and improvisation. He comes correctly to the conclusion that one can hardly call blue notes, call-and-response or improvisation as such exclusively "black" or "African". All of these are fairly common in different versions in music cultures around the world. On the question of polyrhythm Tagg for example states that, even if complex simultaneous metres on top of each other are not common in for example Europe, this kind of a rhythmic structure "would be a valid musical trait distinguishing one type of African music not only from European music in general but also from a lot of other African musics" (Tagg 1989:289). When it comes to syncopation, another "African trait", this is again a common feature of e.g. older Scottish folk tunes.

Neither Tagg nor any other ethnomusicologist is of course trying to rewrite history and simply wipe out the existence of an "African" or "European" element in much of today's popular music. On the contrary, what is relevant is to study the depth of this problem from an ethnomusicological point of view. The concept "African music" is already in itself a complex matter, because "there are more 'African' musics than Western", as Bruno Nettl has put it (Nettl 1985:44). If we wanted to know the exact origins of the different elements of a particular Afro-American musical style of today, we would first have to know what sort of improvisation, call-and-response techniques and rhythmic or melodic practices were common in the different parts of Africa and Europe in the seventeenth and early eighteenth centuries, and, secondly, which slaves and colonialists settled where, and how their styles merged during the following centuries. Needless to say we are dealing with a vast area of research.

Recently many ethnomusicologists have rather stressed the similarities than the differences between the musical styles of the Africans and the Europeans—a certain overlapping between two cultures is after all a primary condition for a fusion between them. The functional connections of the music in for example religion, work songs, dance music, festivals and oral traditions must have formed several bridges between the cultures (see e.g. Martin 1991:28–29). There must also have been structural elements that were common. According to van der Merwe, for example, the "blue-notes" of the Afro-American blues-tonality probably were born from a synthesis of West-African music, Afro-Arabic savannah music, British folk music and European middle class light music of the late 19th century (van der Merwe 1996:65).

The strengthening of a simplified bipolar view with "African" and "European" as almost contradictory terms hides the deeper stereotyped images where Africa stands for the spontaneous, rhythmic and danceable, and Europe for the structuralised, melodic and intellectual. These ideas seem to follow the thoughts of those European folklorists who at the turn of the century tried to refine the folk culture by arranging it according to the aesthetic principles of the bourgeois conservatory ideology. A lot of this purified music, which was produced for stage performances with written scores, played by semi-professionals on modernised instruments, most certainly lacks a lot of the spontaneity, complexity of rhythmic structures, corporeality and sexuality, which are seen as African traits. This should however not be seen as if European culture lacked these qualities completely.

Altogether corporeality has been given several peculiar connotations, both in relation to music and rhythm as well as race and sex, which in turn once again shows the underlying patterns of Western thought (see Frith 1996:123–44 and McClary and Walser 1994 for excellent discussions on this topic). There is a tendency for a romanticising of the body as something, which is left after reason and civilisation have been flung out. The background to this can be found in a long tradition of Western thinking where mind and body have been separated into a dichotomy in which reason and aesthetics have been tied to the mind, and feeling and hedonism have been connected to the body.

Following this model European music is naturally seen as intellectual and the African-derived styles as physical, even if this has little to do with reality since both repertories draw upon both mind and body (see McClary and Walser 1994:77). Talking about an opposition between spontaneous creativity and intellectual structuralism makes no sense of what the musicians in fact do. Calling the most complex forms of African polyrhythm unrestrained, ecstatic or unstructured shows little if any understanding of the music itself, or why and how it is created. In many ways the musics that are described as European polyphony or African polyrhythm are equally intellectual and strict.

Body, rhythm, sex and race are closely tied together in the romantic way of defining African culture as the body, the "Other" of the bourgeois mind. The primitive, innocent noble savage can thus be held up against the sophisticated or over-civilised because he is closer to the uncorrupted human essence. This is, as Frith explains, important to understand if we want to get to the heart of claims about Afro-American music, rhythm, and sex:

> The logic here is not that African music (or African-derived musics) are more "physical", more "directly" sexual than European and European-derived musics. Rather, the argument is that because "the African" is more primitive, more "natural" than the European, then African music must be more directly in touch with the body, with unsymbolized and unmediated sensual states and expectations. And given that African musics are most obviously different from European musics in their uses of rhythm, then rhythm must be how the primitive, the sexual, is expressed. (Frith 1996:127)

Bearing in mind this logic it is easy to understand and put the European reactions against African-derived musics in the right context. The harshest criticism against the different Afro-American musics is usually based on a fear of what is seen as primitive and sexually tempting, and the criticism is usually directed explicitly against the rhythmic character of the music. The supporters of African-derived musics have on the other hand often completed the circle by stressing the primitivism of the rhythm, which is seen to make the music some kind of a manifestation of uncivilised spontaneity, of a mystified subconscious and unrestrained sexuality.

"Authenticity" in reality

The European reactions towards Afro-American music form an interesting pattern of rhetorical shifts in music commentary following each other and partly co-existing side by side. This could first be seen in early jazz criticism, but the reception of many later genres follow the same stages (the classification presented here is based on the shifts which have been sketched out in Frith 1988:57–58). When a particular Afro-American music style is spread among the Western audience for the first time it is treated as primitive and more negatively as gimmicky. After this the survival of the music seems to depend on a rapid assimilation into tried and tested forms of "good" music. Soon however these adapted forms are seen as "commercial" and they are criticised for sapping the music of its distinctive energy and truth.

The latter reaction however leads to several problems. When the music is taken from its original context of creation and mediated and distributed in a new environment to a different audience one certainly can ask if it can be unaffected by all the contextual changes. The supporters of the mediated Afro-American styles have met the critical argument concerning the risks of this mediation or "commercialisation" with the counter-argument that the best of these styles have still managed to stay "authentic" despite the changes. According to the fans this has happened because of the music's ability to touch real emotions, or as Frith has put it in the case of British inter-war jazz lovers: "the answer was to make the music a matter of feeling, expressive of personal not social identity, of sensual not cultural need" (Frith 1988:58).

It is ironic that by using "personalisation" and "sensualisation" the fans are in fact covering their underlying expectations and desires, which are clearly socially as well as culturally structured. The search for "primitivism", "direct expression of fundamental emotions", "sincerity", "playing from the heart" is once again an example of the bourgeois culture's need to find and define an "Other", in many ways ideologically not far from the folklorists search for a "true soul" in folk music during the 19th century.

The question of commercialism versus authenticity is often approached along the lines of racial tensions, where "blackness" is seen as an authentic force, which can be destroyed by "whiteness". Often this has explicitly been focused on the commercial production of music, which is seen as separating good music from bad music, especially as the music industry traditionally has been in the hands of white Western people. The music consumed by a mass audience is also seen, by virtue of the electronic mediation alone, as inferior to the music of a more select group.

It is worth taking up some of the problems concerning this angle of approach. Charles Hamm has done it using the historiography of ragtime as an example of how one thread of jazz scholarship has seen jazz as an authentic black art, threatened by, but always superior to, the products of the white-controlled music industry and media (Hamm 1995:11–17). Hamm correctly criticises this idea because, even if we would not want to dispute the Afro-American roots of jazz and the fact that the best jazz musicians have been black:

> to suggest that the argument that only a certain repertory played by certain black musicians is authentic, and that the genre has otherwise been subverted by media exploitation and appropriation by inferior white musicians, distorts two aspects of the history of popular music; the critical role played by the mass media in the development of jazz and other genres by black musicians themselves; and the historical reality of repertories created by white musicians and accepted by contemporary audiences and performers as 'jazz', even if these were stylistically different from the music of black performers. (Hamm 1995:14–15.)

Critics, fans, musicians and scholars have often constructed their own preferred music as a "pure" alternative to what has been perceived as manipulated products and black music is certainly not an exception. These normative statements include an idea of the development of a musical style from "authentic folk culture" to "industrial mass culture". What in fact happens is not always such a big change in the ways music is made than in the ways it is interpreted. The people who use the concept "authenticity" to distinguish their preferred music from some other music often read as sociological facts what are in reality ideological experiences. Feelings of "community", "creativity" and "honesty" are read into the music so that it is made to match participants' own cultural desires (see Middleton 1990:140 and Frith 1981). No Afro-American music (just as no intellectual response to it) has developed in a vacuum without any interplay with commercially mediated musics, nor have any intellectual responses to the music grown from an empty space.

The European relationship to African music has to a large extent been coloured by this same idea of authenticity. It can be seen in both a fear of the cultural imperialism of the West and in a need to interpret the existing forms of popular culture as either "pure" or "commercial". Quantitative analysis of the flow of music in the media-sphere shows that the threat of the transnational media corporations is a very real one. This has supported the imperialism thesis which sees the Western based industry as a force of exploitation and homogeneity trying to weaken the local traditional cultures.

In the 1990s several researchers have however revalued the old assumptions of cultural products being clearly traditional or modern, or strictly local or international in today's media-world. It has become evident how complicated it can be to present value judgements when it comes to the new musical expressions that are produced, distributed and consumed within the technological sphere, or to use Garofalo's words:

> It isn't that this music is somehow less 'authentic' than other musics, it's that our feelings about authenticity—like our copyright laws and theories of culture—have not kept pace with technological advances. (Garofalo 1992:24)

The old perception of globalisation and homogenisation as an inevitable tide of American junk drowning authentic cultures, is also more often seen as an exercise in metropolitan self-criticism than an informed account of what is happening. In the case of music, both the new and the old views concerning authenticity-versus-change and local-versus-global have been actualised to an even higher degree as the popular music styles of the third world (often from Africa) have found their niche in the Western music media.

World music—whose music?

The biggest shift in distributing and marketing African music in Europe seems to have happened at the end of the 1980s, when the concept "world music" was introduced. The term was invented in 1987 when a number of British independent record companies and DJ's wanted to create a category for artists such as Youssou N'Dour and Le Mystère Des Voix Bulgares, who were being played on radio programmes but were hard to find in record stores. By using the concept world music the companies wanted to establish a classification that would make it easier for producers, marketing personnel, radio companies, magazines and consumers to find their way to these musical styles that were becoming more popular in the Western world. In America "world beat" had already been used earlier as a promotional label in much the same way. (See e.g. Anderson 1995 and Sweeney 1991 on the launching of "world music", and Goodwin and Gore 1990 on "world beat".)

The broad definition of world music of course makes it impossible to find any musical similarities between the styles that are filed under it—already trying to find them in for example the musics of Youssou N'Dour and the Bulgarian female singers would be a waste of time. It is also important to remember that even if the creation of this new market label happened at the same time as a lot of non-western popular music styles were reaching the Western market, these styles were in fact nothing new, not even necessarily for European fans.

Already from the beginning of this century Western popular music had been influencing local music cultures around the world and at the end of the 1980s there was nothing new about the different acculturated styles that had been born as a result of this development.

What makes world music so interesting is how this concept has managed to find its place on the market despite its heterogeneous character. Following the ideas of modern marketing strategies one might say that the label has helped to create a marketable image for a product and in doing so it has not only made this music better known. It has also created certain images about what this music is like—images that do not necessarily have any common musical ground, as already mentioned.

Ever since the creation of the concept, world music has been criticised as being once again a thread of Western media imperialism and musical colonialism. When the British music industry people held the meeting in 1987 where they decided about the general term, only one music promoter who was born in Africa and living in England was invited. He however refused to take part because other Africans and Asians living in Great Britain were left out, and according to him this trend has unfortunately characterised the use of world music in the music industry ever since (see Kotirinta 1995).

Despite the introduction of the market term world music the music industry did not manage to merge the different sectors of the business under one umbrella. Even the millions of immigrants living in Europe have often been more or less outside the market. Many concert promoters have been forced to work hard to overcome barriers in connection to the music's contextual surrounding and the different expectations of the European and African audiences. Just the ticket prices and the geographic location can be a problem in the ghettoised urban environment of the European cities. At the end of the 1980s the same split was very clear in the phonogram market. The white audience bought compact discs with leaflets, written by (white) Europeans, explaining the music for the (white) European listener. At the same time many immigrants for many years kept listening to cassettes that had been brought by friends and relatives, or had been imported by some small entrepreneur from the same country of origin as the consumer. The national music businesses can in fact be very protective in relation to foreign music and musicians. Immigration laws, the Western copyright system and laws about how large the proportion of national products must be on national media all contribute to the barriers between the European industry on the one hand, and immigrants as well as non-Europeans on the other.

Considering these facts we must at least agree that despite the creation and use of the concept "world music", there still seems to be a gap between the white Europeans and immigrants as well as their home countries in the third world. The critical statement that world music is a creation of white Westerners for white Westerners is clearly relevant and we might even go as far as to claim that the successful use of the marketing term is evidence of this. It is the white Westerner who finds the classification relevant and finds the products he/she is looking for under this label when he/she consumes the music. If we use marketing slogans we might say that world music has managed to create an image which has sold well and met the needs of the consumers. And what are these needs? Joe Boyd of Hannibal Records, who produces a lot of world music, has described the British world music market in the following way:

> It's providing new sounds for a bored culture ... Now there is a clearly perceivable market for African music and that market is inescapably Guardian and Independent readers. White middle class culture has run out of inspiration. The normal sources to plunder are exhausted and white middle class culture is incapable of inventing anything. When this has happened before they tended to adopt working class culture and the biggest source of that musically, American Rhythm &

Blues and country, has been plundered dry. (Kershaw and Stapleton 1988:64, 67, quoted in Mitchell 1996:74)

What we find here is once again the Western bourgeoisie looking for an "Other", something exotic, spontaneous and exciting that would differ from the own intellectual culture which is believed to have lost these qualities. Or to use Richard Middleton's words:

> The 'natives' are very often pictured in Western versions of world music as stereo-types, as world music Others, who have this kind of authentic culture which we in the Western world have lost. (Middleton 1996:22)

This idea of authenticity in connection with world music resembles a lot of the views that were discussed in the previous section. The Western way of looking at the music bears strong marks of folklorism and especially of the way in which black culture has been explained earlier. In this "ideological" sense it draws on e.g. the folk music movement and the roots oriented rock music, in which authenticity, the connections to folk culture and a contempt for com-mercialism have always been evident. Frith has stressed how this continuation is often tied to the journalists who explain the music in the media. Many of the DJ's and journalists who present world music are in fact old rock and folk music fans who became bored with the conventions of the old styles at the end of the 1980s and turned to world music in search of authenticity (Frith 1994).

It is not easy to come up with exact demographic figures on world music consumers throughout Europe. But, bearing in mind Boyd's comment above, it is probably possible to make some assumptions based on two surveys which were made among the audiences at two WOMAD festivals in Finland (WOMAD—World of Music Arts and Dance). The research from 1992 gives some basic data about the audience (Jalava 1992). According to the survey a typical member of the audience is likely to come from a university town, to have higher education and to be an active consumer of culture. These answers are not very surprising if we think of the demographic statistics of those who listen to for example American college radios, which have been main sources for world music in USA.

A smaller survey at a WOMAD festival in Finland in 1989 gives informa-tion on what the audience found interesting in world music. Three main as-pects were frequently mentioned: the rhythm ("danceability", "the beat"); that it is "different" ("exotic", "new", "variation", "an alternative to disco and commercial pop"); and authenticity ("genuine", "honest", "real feeling", "truthfulness"). It is also descriptive that the audience especially preferred African, Afro-Latin and other "rhythmic" genres when asked about what kind of world music styles they liked. (Kurkela and Laakkonen 1989.)

This search for authenticity in a distant, "exotic" culture outside the West-ern world is in many ways based on a myth (this has been stressed in e.g. Frith 1994). The whole Western environment of consumption is naturally very far from the original context of the non-Western traditional music. In fact it is not surprising that those music styles that have been born in a context which bears the greatest resemblance to the Western consumer's context, are the most popular (dance music for restaurants and clubs, radio pop etc.). A large part of the world music and the industry which is mediating it seems to be like a tight-rope walker balancing between the need for authenticity (genuine, untouched by the West) and recognisable elements (familiar for the consumer in the West).

In a lot of the African music which has found its place on the world music market of Europe the authenticity-code is not so much based on a true reproduction of Africa as on a reproduction of the European images of Africa. To put it another way, one might say that the "tradition" is made to serve not so much local African as European needs. There are numerous examples of how the African musicians have had to adapt to these foreign norms and values and I will only briefly take up a few of them here.

The basic idea of African music as something that is tied to race (genetics) and geographic location seems to live on among the audience and business personnel of many European countries. For example several bands who play African music in the Nordic countries have complained that it is harder for a band which includes white members and plays in the North to get gigs than what it is for a band from Africa with only black members (see e.g. Sondlo 1996). The European audience also expects an African band to wear certain types of folklore clothes, masks, have female dancers in skirts and play drums in order to be regarded as a "real" African band (see e.g. Lange 1995:102 and 107–08, Impey 1992:119–20 and 173–74).

On a musical level the idea of authenticity puts the performers in complex situations where they have to think of both their musical tradition and the Western audience's ideas of it, as well as of their own creativity. A career abroad can lead to a conflict between both the expectations of the African home market and the international world music market. A lot of the Third World pop styles that have become popular in Europe, e.g. Central African soukous and South African mbaqanga, are in fact old fashioned in their home countries, but are still performed by musicians who have found a Western audience for this kind of music. In other cases popular musicians have lost (at least temporarily) their support in both Europe and Africa because they have been said to have lost their "roots". An example of this is the Zimbabwean band "Bhundu Boys" who got a record deal with WEA International and subsequently made a modernised record "True Jit" with partly English lyrics in London. The record never made it in either Great Britain or Zimbabwe, because the band had become "more British than the British themselves", as one production manager in Harare put it.

The fact that African rhythms and the beats of Afro-American musical styles can be heard throughout the world should of course make most African musicians and African music lovers in Europe happy. It is an undeniable fact that the introduction of the concept world music has increased the availability and awareness of musics from non-Western countries, but it has also contributed (even if unwillingly) to the strengthening of many preconceived ideas on Africa and African music.

Paul Simon's Graceland is probably in economic terms the most successful record in the category of world music (or "world beat" in America). If we look at Graceland from today's perspective we find that the political debate surrounding Simon and his South African background musicians during the cultural boycott of South Africa in many ways confused the other issues of the project. A more general aspect is stressed by the South African ethnomusicologist Andrew Tracey, who writes that Graceland contributes to:

> the perpetuation of popular stereotypes, e.g. that Africa provides the rhythm section, the body of the pop music world, while Europe provides the melody, the head. Another is that it is the Black man's job to help the White man do his thing. History repeats itself: musically and artistically nothing has changed. Is African music only good for backings, not frontings? (Tracey 1987:3)

It seems that a lot of the old images of African music, which are as old as the roots of the earliest forms of Afro-American popular musics, are being reborn in new contexts, and world music does not necessarily change this trend.

Conclusion

The introducing of jazz into the European musical vocabulary became an important step in what later became modern national popular music styles of this century. It seems that just like Afro-American music has, a lot of the early conceptions and simplifications regarding the Africanisms in music have also become very common in our culture. Many of our central terms and definitions are taken for granted even if they are seldom analysed in detail. Behind the stereotyping lie long, complicated processes of crossing cultural influences, acculturation and hybridity. The new situations in the history of population groups have always created a need for new objects for identification, as well as a need for opposing images.

The roots of our models for explanation are to a large extent found in the European folklorist ideals and a Western search for an "Other". This is not only characteristic of our way of looking for authenticity in African music but also for our way of approaching many Afro-American musics. It seems that modern music media have greatly helped in spreading this image and the invention of the concept world music has not changed the situation. The development of the Western music activities and the international music industries change the surroundings, but a lot of the basic underlying ideas remain the same.

This chapter is a slightly revised version of a paper submitted to the seminar "Encounter Images in the Meetings between Europe and Africa" in November 1996.

References

Anderson, Ian,1995, "World Music—sopiva kauppaluokitus", *Musiikin Suunta*, 1/1995, pp. 27–28.

Bruér, Jan and Lars Westin, 1995, *Jazz: Musik, människor, miljöer.* Utbildningsradion & Svenska rikskonserter.

Edström, Olle , 1988, "Hur schottis blev bonnjazz (eller hur svensk foxtrot besegrade jazzen, eller har afro-amerikansk musik funnits i Sverige?)", in Pekkilä, E. and V. Kurkela (eds), *Etnomusikologian vuosikirja 1987–88*, pp. 54–83. Suomen etnomusikologinen seura.

—, 1996, *Göteborgs rika musikliv.* Skrifter från Musikvetenskapliga avdelningen, No. 42, Musikhögskolan, Göteborgs universitet.

Frith, Simon, 1981, "'The magic that can set you free': the ideology of folk and the myth of the rock community", *Popular Music*, 1, pp. 159–68.

—, 1988, "Playing with Real Feeling—Jazz and Suburbia", in S. Frith, *Music for Pleasure, Essays in the Sociology of Pop*, pp. 45–63. Cambridge: Polity Press.

—, 1994, *"The Naked and the Dead": World Music and the Politics of Authenticity.* Paper presented at the seminar "Methodologies in Popular Music Studies" at the Department of Folk Tradition, Tampere University. Unpublished.

—, 1996, *Performing Rites: on the value of popular music.* Oxford: Oxford University Press.

Garofalo, Reebee (ed.), 1992, *Rockin' the Boat: Mass Music and Mass Movements.* Boston: South End Press.

Goodwin, Andrew and Joe Gore, 1990, "World Beat and the Cultural Imperialism Debate", *Socialist Review*, Vol. 20, No. 3, pp. 63–80.

Hamm, Charles, 1995, *Putting Popular Music in Its Place.* Cambridge: Cambridge University Press.

Impey, Angela, 1992, *They want us with salt and onions: Women in the Zimbawean music industry.* Ph.D. Dissertation, Department of Anthropology, Indiana University.

Jalava, Katja, 1992, *Kulttuuritapahtuman paikalliset vaikutukset: Maailmankarnevaalitapahtuma Seinäjoella.* Helsingin yliopisto, Maaseudun tutkimus- ja koulutuskeskus, Raportteja ja artikkeleita 17.

Jalkanen, Pekka, 1989, *Alaska, Bombay ja Billy Boy: Jazzkulttuurin murros Helsingissä 1920-luvulla.* Suomen etnomusikologisen seuran julkaisuja 2, Helsinki.

Kerouac, Jack, 1991, *On the Road.* Penguin Books.

Kershaw, Andy and Chris Stapleton, 1988, "Back in the High Life", *Q*, September, pp. 62–68.

Kotirinta, Pirkko, 1995, "Maailmanmusiikki taisi tulla jäädäkseen—toisin kuin termin keksijät uskoivat", *Musiikin Suunta*, 1/1995, pp. 33–35.

Kurkela, Vesa and Anu Laakkonen, 1989, "Värilliset pipot päässä soitellaan", *Musiikin Suunta*, 2/1989, pp. 47–56.

Lange, Siri, 1995, *From Nation-Building to Popular Culture: The Modernization of Performance in Tanzania.* Bergen: Chr. Michelsen Institute.

Lilliestam, Lars, 1996, "The Sounds of Swedish Rock", in Hautamäki, Tarja and Tarja Rautiainen (eds), *Popular Music Studies in Seven Acts: Conference proceedings of the Fourth Annual Conference of the Finnish Society for Ethnomusicology (1995).* Department of Folk Tradition, Tampere University and Institute of Rhythm Music, Seinäjoki.

Martin, Denis-Constant, 1991, "Filiation or Innovation? Some Hypotheses to Overcome the Dilemma of Afro-American Music's Origins", *Black Music Research Journal*, Vol. 11, No. 1, pp. 19–38.

McClary, Susan and Robert Walser, 1994, "Theorizing the Body in African-American Music", *Black Music Research Journal*, Vol. 14, No. 1, pp. 75–84.

van der Merwe, 1996, "The Italian Blue Third", in Hautamäki, Tarja and Tarja Rautiainen (eds), *Popular Music Studies in Seven Act*. Department of Folk Tradition, Tampere University and Institute of Rhythm Music, Seinäjoki.

Middleton, Richard, 1990, *Studying Popular Music*. Milton Keynes: Open University Press.

—, 1996, "Who May Speak? From a Politics of Popular Music to a Popular Politics of Music" (including discussion following the presentation of the paper), in Hautamäki, Tarja and Tarja Rautiainen (eds), *Popular Music Studies in Seven Acts*. Department of Folk Tradition, Tampere University and Institute of Rhythm Music, Seinäjoki.

Mitchell, Tony, 1996, *Popular Music and Local Identity: Rock, Pop and Rap in Europe and Oceania*. London: Leicester University Press.

Nederveen Pieterse, Jan, 1994, *Hvidt på sort: Illustrerede fordomme*. Copenhagen: Mellemfolkeligt samvirke.

Nettl, Bruno, 1985, *The Western Impact on World Music: Change, Adaptation, and Survival*. New York: Schirmer Books.

Paavolainen, Olavi, 1929, *Nykyaikaa etsimässä: esseitä ja pakinoita*. Helsinki: Kustannusosakeyhtiö Otava.

Similä, Aapo, 1941, *Rikkaruohoja musiikin kukkatarhassa*. Helsinki.

Sondlo, Cecil Inti, 1996, "Få Afrikanska toner ljuder högt i Sverige." *Dagens Nyheter—På Stan*, 9–15.8.1996, p. 9.

Sweeney, Philip, 1991, *The Virgin Directory of World Music*. London: Virgin Books.

Tagg, Philip, 1989, "Open letter: Black music, Afro-American music and European music", *Popular Music*, Vol. 8, No. 3, pp. 285–98.

Tracey, Andrew, 1987, "A word from the editor", *African Music*, Vol. 6, No. 4, p. 3.

Appendix
Quotations in original languages

(1)

"Vuonna 1919 (po. 1922, PJ) nähtiin Helsingin asemaa vastapäätä olevassa ravintolassa—jonka nimi oli siihen aikaan City-Brondin—eräänä iltana ihmeellinen komeljanttari. Kun soitettiin steppiä (nopeaa marssia) hän löi helistimiään lakkaamatta. Sen lisäksi hän vaihtoi käsiinsä pienet rumpupalikat, joilla hän kalkutteli sivuillaan olevia onttoja puuhelistimiä, asetti päähänsä pronssatun metallikypärän, nenäänsä pitkän jatkon ja suuhunsa pillin, johon hän huikeasti vihelsi. Pieni yhtye kirkui säveltä minkä jaksoi, mutta ilman täytti koko ajan rummunlyöjän nostattama helvetillinen meteli. Kerrottiin silloin tämän uuden aatteen olevan nimeltään jazzia ja sen olevan kotoisin neekerimaista."

(2)

"Man kan inte förstå jazzen utan att taga hänsyn till trenne betydelsefulla fakta beträffande dess tillkomst.
Den har skapats av negrer.
Den har skapats av berusade negrer.
Den har skapats av berusade negrer i bordellmiljö."

Beyond Black and White

Reinterpreting the "Norwegian Missionary Image of the Malagasy"[1]

Karina Hestad Skeie

The image of a map

A special map decorates the wall in my office. It is a colour copy of the most famous missionary map in Norway: Captain Landmark's "*Missionskart over Madagaskar*" from 1892.[2] The first edition of this missionary map was issued in 1890. In 1890 10,000 copies were sold to people all over Norway in less than one year.[3] One hundred years ago this map decorated walls in private homes, in Christian assembly houses and in schools all over Norway.

I had seen miniature copies of this map in black and white several times, ascertaining somewhat condescendingly that it confirmed all my expectations of missionaries and their stereotypical images of the Malagasy-Norwegian encounter: Madagascar divided into colour-zones, graphically depicting the missionary encounter as an encounter between light and darkness. The first time I entered the Norwegian Missionary Society's archives in Stavanger and saw the original missionary map I was totally taken aback. First, by its size: 70x90 cm—Madagascar in a scale 1:1,826,000. What details! Suddenly I could see that it was an actual *map*; geographical areas, towns, rivers and mountains, their names written with accuracy and correct spelling. I went closer. There it was, at the centre: Imerina—the land of the Merina people around the capital Antananarivo; to the south of Imerina: Betsileo; and then Bara with the Isalo mountains. On the west coast: the vast Sakalava land, with large areas of "unknown land". I spotted a number of red "dots": Norwegian Mission Stations. Betafo, Manandona, Morondava, Manombo, Loharano, Fianarantsoa and all the other familiar places. In certain areas, especially in Betsileo, the red "dots" were many and lay close to each other. In other areas

---

[1] The research from which this paper draws, is and has been supported by a student and a doctoral fellowship from the Norwegian Research Council. This is a revised version of the paper presented at the Helsingör-workshop 15–17 November 1996. In addition to valuable discussions with fellow workshop participants in Helsingör, I also received important feedback at the London School of Economics' Malagasy seminar in January 1997, where I presented parts of this paper. I am grateful to Hilde Nielsen, Rita Astuti, Santiago Alvarez, Ingvild Hestad, Asbjørn Dyrendal and Rolf Welde Skeie for reading and commenting on various drafts of the paper.

[2] Capt. Landmark was the captain of the Mission Ship "Eliezer". For twenty years in the nineteenth century "Eliezer" brought missionaries to and from South Africa and Madagascar, the two mission fields of the Norwegian Missionary Society at the time.

[3] My source: Nils Kristian Høimyr, Norwegian Mission Society Archives, Stavanger. Reference printed in *Norsk Missionstidende* (from now on referred to as *NMT*) No. 20, 1890, p. 400.

there were merely one or two. There were black crosses too: British Mission Stations.

At this point I remember taking a step back, in order to take in again the sight of the full-size map. How beautiful it was! Patinated in an off-white-brown with Madagascar floating in a deep green Mozambique Channel and Indian Ocean, the missionary-map aspect was somehow not as predominant as it had been on the smaller black and white copies. Both the black, the light grey, and all the shades in between had got a patina of brown. Still, it *was* beyond doubt that this was not just any ordinary map but a *missionary map*, because of the division into colour-zones. The explanations on the original read:

> Light grey: "Where Christianity has gained entry to the extent that pagan power is broken in the exterior."
> Dark: "Those areas where paganism predominates, but where nevertheless some Christian congregations have been constituted. Mission is carried out here and there."
> Black: "Those areas where all indigenous inhabitants are pagans, and where so far no mission has been implemented."

In the upper left hand corner was a map of Zululand and Natal, the other "mission field" of the Norwegian Missionary Society at the time, divided into the same colour-zones as Madagascar. Around every red spot was a lighter zone, as if the Norwegian Mission Stations were light towers shining in a dark, black night.

Looking at the map in my office, I wonder what 'Madagascar' and 'Zululand' the Norwegian Christians thought they knew.

The purpose of this paper

This will deal with the Norwegian Missionaries in Madagascar, and some of the images of 'Madagascar' and 'the Malagasy' which we find in their writings. The first Norwegian missionaries came to this large island off the east coast of Africa in 1866. Since then, the Norwegian Mission Society (NMS) has carried out mission work in several areas of the island.[4]

The main focus in this paper is on the missionaries' images of 'the Malagasy' in two types of published missionary material: the *Norwegian Mission Magazine* 1866–1895, and some books of missionary author Johannes Einrem. I will discuss the different genres, which this material represents, and briefly relate it to the non-published missionary material in the Norwegian

---

[4] First and foremost, the Norwegian Mission has been substantial in the highland region called Vakinankaratra. However, quite early they also extended their fields to the west coast, east coast, Bara and Betsimisaraka areas. There are still a considerable number of Norwegian missionaries on the island, who are now employed by the Malagasy Lutheran Church (FLM) and paid by the NMS.

Mission Society's archives in Stavanger. My point of departure is the Mission Map, which graphically represents the missionary encounter as the encounter between light and darkness. This image has functioned as the paramount missionary image of the European-African encounter well beyond Madagascar. I will show that the image of light and darkness is very prominent in the texts of the Norwegian missionaries in Madagascar. Importantly, however, there are other images of Madagascar and Malagasy people in this material; images which on important points contradict and contest the images and the power relations of the black and white stereotype.

The postcolonial critique has been important in showing how the Christian missionaries, knowingly and unknowingly, functioned "as agent, scribe, and moral alibi" in the European colonising project (Comaroff 1991:88). Indeed, missionaries have been criticised for being the most radical agents of change on the colonial scene (Beidelman 1986); they literally set out to enlighten the dark, pagan, African mind, and in doing exactly this, they paved the way for the European colonisation of the African consciousness. Not so much by converting people to Christianity, but by engaging the African peoples in long-term conversations on European terms, forcing the Africans into European cultural categories (Comaroff 1991).

Following G. Prakash's invitation "to return to the history of colonialism, without rehearsing the naturalisation of colonialism as History" by examining stories *beyond* the history of successful colonial domination, this paper is an attempt to search for some of the "failures, silences, displacements and transformations" (1995:6) produced in the daily discourse between the Norwegian missionaries and the Malagasy people, and reproduced in the Norwegian missionaries' texts from "the field". These stories have important implications both for our understanding of the relationship between the missionaries and the Malagasy, and for the reception history of the missionaries' texts in Norway.

The stereotype: Encounter between light and darkness

Despite all I did to describe the many details of Landmark's Map of Madagascar, this map is admittedly first and foremost a *missionary map*. It graphically represents the missionary encounter as the encounter between light and darkness. Through this map, and through the different accounts from the missionaries "in the field", it is generally agreed that the missionary movement was preponderant in shaping the Image of Madagascar for generations of Norwegians (Simensen 1995:138). The monthly periodical *Norsk Missionstidende* (*NMT*), which was the Norwegian Missionary Society's magazine, had a considerable circulation; 10,000 in 1885 in a population of about 1,9 million, made the Mission Magazine larger than the largest newspaper in the country at the time (Simensen 1995:141). Usually stories from the magazine were read aloud at different local associations working for the mission (Jørgensen (ed.)

1992:69), which implies that the missionary tales from "the field" reached even further than the 10,000 Mission Magazine subscribers.

In addition to the *NMT*, there were articles in other periodicals, and a considerable number of very popular books by missionary authors, ranging from the more scientifically oriented such as L. Dahle's *Madagascar and Its People*, to novels and collections of "small stories from the field". Johannes Einrem, G. A. Meling and G. Nakkestad were among the most prominent of the latter category.[5] Einrem was the most productive and the most read missionary author in Norway at the beginning of this century (Borgenvik 1979:13).

Reading the printed texts, we can immediately conclude that the image of light and darkness is very prominent. The following story 'from the missionary's everyday life' is typical of some important types of light and darkness stories:

> "Late one Saturday evening, as I returned from a school-inscription ('Skoleindskrivning'), Abel came running, smiling and happy: "Mother wants to be baptised. She is very ill. Please, come and baptise her!"
>
> It was dark inside the hut where she lay. (...) "What do you want, Rampizafy?" "I need salvation." "From whom?" "From Jesus, who saves from sin; He has redeemed me." "Do you believe in him, then?" "Yes, I believe in him."
>
> The desolate hut was turned into God's temple, with the angels of God entering. Hence: "There is joy in heaven when a sinner has turned around; Angels down to earth descend, sent by the mercy of God!"[6] And strangely! As the holy water of baptism ran over her head, she rose. The lame woman could rise up, fold hands and—together with us—kneel and praise God's mercy!
>
> Later, a Sunday evening as I returned from a minor congregation, I visited her. She was happy like a child who is going home. She knew that the end was near. The following day she died." (*NMT* No. 11–12, 1891, p. 215)

The story of Rampizafy's baptism is an account of how the light of God conquers the darkness of ignorance and sin; the darkness of "paganism". The old, sick and unbaptised woman lies in a dark, humble hut. But as the holy water of baptism is sprinkled on her, it is as if a miracle happens before the eyes of those present (as well as before the reader's eyes). The humble and dark hut becomes the temple of God. The miracle of salvation even extends to the healing of physical handicaps; the lame woman is able to rise and kneel.

Apart from the baptism, we learn remarkably little about Rampizafy and Abel. In fact, they both act and talk like stereotypes, rather than ordinary people with ordinary feelings.[7] It is as if in the context of conversion, nothing else really matters. Significantly, the story of Rampizafy is almost identical to

---

[5] Towards the end of this paper, I will discuss a number of Einrem's books.

[6] Probably a quote from a Christian hymn: "Der er Fryd i Himmerige, Har en Synder sig omvendt; Engle ned til Jorden stige Af Guds Miskundhed udsent!"

[7] It is virtually impossible to translate part of the dialogue between the missionary and Rampizafy into Malagasy. I thank Maurice Bloch for pointing this out to me.

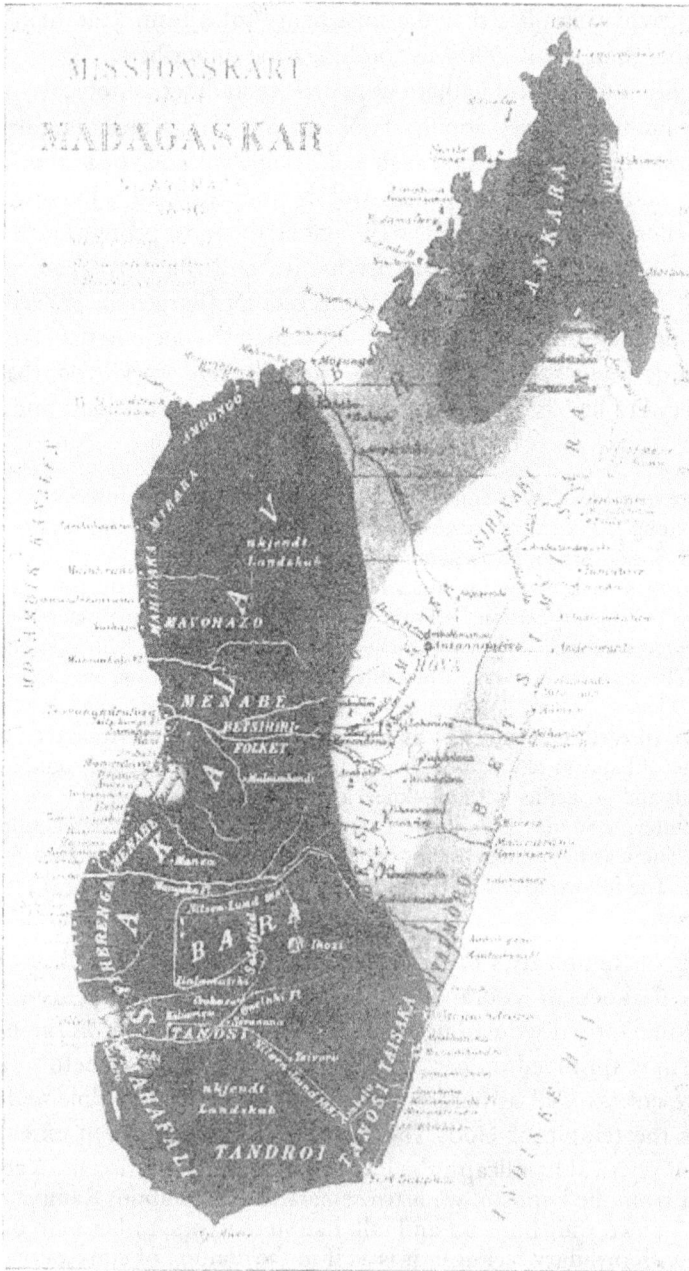

Black and white copy of Captain Landmark's Mission Map of Madagascar 1890.
(Birkeli et al. *Det norske missionsselskaps historie i hundre år*. Vol. IV, p. 144)

a lot of other stories from the missionary's 'daily life' in the Mission Magazine. These stories have the same basic structure, to the extent that they have to be understood as specific genres.

The story about Rampizafy combines two major Mission Magazine genres: conversion stories and deathbed stories. The purpose of both genres is to edify the already convinced supporter—to confirm and not to inform. Like in all other conversion stories, the story of Rampizafy's baptism creates an image of conversion as a result of an individual's conscious choice between two opposing religions, Christianity and "Paganism".[8] When the choice has been made and the person has converted he or she experiences a fundamental spiritual transformation, a change that is confirmed through external signs in this case a miracle. This genre is thus constructed on a series of oppositions; Christianity and 'Paganism', 'Christians' and 'Pagans', light and darkness.

The story about Rampizafy is also a deathbed story. And like all Christians, Rampizafy is, thanks to her conversion, able to meet death "happy like a child who is going home". The death of Christian converts stands in clear contrast to the image of the pagan's death. Missionary Engh tells about an occasion where he was called to a deathbed:

> Questions were posed at me from everybody present: "Is he going to live?" As I answered in the negative, unless God chose to do a miracle, some were very offended; the custom is, you see, to let each other believe ('indbilde') that even he who most visibly battles with death, is not going to die, and this with the strongest expressions like "If this person dies, you may very well bury him on my head."

Engh very accurately describes a strong Merina and Betsileo[9] taboo against pronouncing the word 'death' in the house where there is a mortally ill person.[10] His *interpretation* of this taboo is important: "Poor people! When death visits their houses, they have no better protection than such lies."[11] I have argued elsewhere (Skeie 1994) that the missionaries in their writings for the NMT systematically interpret Malagsy customs to fit the underlying presuppositions of their own world view. The image of the pagan's death is very important in this connection.

---

[8] This particular image of course fits perfectly with the general ideal of conversion found in missionary material well beyond Madagascar. The similarity to British missionaries for instance in South Africa is so fundamental, that one may claim that the two cases are almost identical in this matter. See Comaroff 1991.

[9] The Malagasy groups which live in the highlands around the capital Antananarivo.

[10] The taboo is meant both to protect the ill from the inherent negative power in the word itself and to protect relatives and friends from suspicion of witchcraft. Only witches want other people's death, and to state openly that a person is going to die, is tantamount to wanting this person's death.

[11] Letter from Engh, Betafo, 9 March 1871, printed in *NMT* No. 9, 1871, pp. 335–36.

[It is] distressing to experience that the old [people] grow old in sin with no hope for the life to come, and then in the end, to hear the bereaved relatives' delinquent screams around the lifeless body.[12]

There is something wild in their sorrow, which often feels terribly heavy. It is palpable: they have nowhere to go with their grief. Still, they feel impelled to express it, and this results in many of these forms that seem so horrible to us.[13]

The same wild despair comes to the fore in 'pagan' funerals. Instead of a calm dignity (such as at Christian funerals), there is a terrible noise;[14] drums are beaten and instruments played, accompanying the howls and screams from the professional mourners and the relatives of the dead, who are all intoxicated by alcohol.[15] One missionary describes a funeral where at one point, the professional mourners enter the open tomb to cry inside it. There they "in their own way pray to their deceased: 'Oh Father, oh Mother, fetch me, take me, so that I may live with you' and 'Give me many descendants, wealth and a long life!' What ironic play with death!"[16] According to the same author, the professional mourners, usually older women, often faint from the combination of the suffocating smell inside the tomb and their exalted state, upon which they have to be carried or helped out.[17] Such and similar descriptions of 'pagan funerals' together with the missionary interpretations, effectively create an image of Malagasy people living in hopelessness, misery and a terrible fear of death. Details like the noisy processions, drums and music, howls and cries and the use of alcohol, all effectively underline the savageness and unrestrained behaviour at the indigenous funerals. The wildness of the Merina/Betsileo creates the perfect antithesis to the civilised, restrained behaviour, which characterises Christian funerals:

It is with an odd, extraordinary feeling one stands by a Christian's litter, surrounded by a flock of pagans. The contrast between the wonderful belief and hope of the Christian and the pagan's empty, dark view of death and eternity stands out so clearly.[18]

It is the missionary's vocation to tell people about this wonderful belief and hope, to call people "from darkness to His [God's] wonderful light".[19] Indeed

---

[12] Letter from Dahle, Antananarivo 2 January 1886, printed in *NMT* No. 7, 1886, p. 130.

[13] Letter from Dr. Thesen, Antananarivo, report from the year 1890, printed in *NMT* No. 14, 1891, p. 277.

[14] Letter from Wetterstad, Soavina, 2 February 1892, printed in *NMT* No. 15, 1892.

[15] Letter from Engh, Betafo, 9 March, 1871, printed in *NMT* No. 9, 1871, pp. 336–39; letter from Nilsen, Loharano, 4 July 1885, printed in *NMT* No. 19, 1885, pp. 366–67, and letter from Th. Olsen, Soatanana, 27 July 1892, printed in *NMT* No. 21, 1892, pp. 414–15.

[16] Letter from Nilsen, Loharano, 4 July 1885, printed in *NMT* No. 19, 1885, pp. 366–67.

[17] Ibid., p. 367.

[18] Letter from Stueland, Fandriana, 18 July 1879, printed in *NMT* No. 23, 1879, p. 446.

[19] Letter from Svendsen, Fianarantsoa, 29 December 1887, printed in *NMT* No. 11, 1888, pp. 209–16.

the justification for the mission is that non-Christians live in terrible fear in darkness, only waiting to be freed (by the missionary) from the grip of the prince of darkness.

It is important to underline that within this specific Evangelical Christianity, everybody who is not a Christian, lives in darkness, fear and misery. Because of the disobedience of Adam and Eve in the Garden of Eden, misled by the evil spirit called the Devil, mankind is born with original sin, and is constantly subject to God's wrath and punishment. To die in this state means going to hell and suffering eternal damnation. Original sin applies equally to all, irrespective of nationality and skin colour. And without the salvation from Christ, the relationship with God, pivotal for man's happiness and well-being, is impossible. The justice of this situation is indisputable. Man was created with the ability to choose, was trusted, but betrayed the trust: he chose to disobey the good commandments of God, and suffers justly as a consequence of his action. In many Evangelical movements from which several of the missionaries came, the intense urge to seek salvation came after an equally intense experience of sinfulness and of having justly been abandoned by God, often conjoined with very strong fears of death and hell.[20] The fundamental experience of despair and hopelessness, together with that of the bliss of salvation, have been seen as an important motivation in the missionary candidates themselves, creating the urge to become missionaries.[21]

Within this framework mission is not merely a matter of life and death; it is a matter of *eternal life* and *eternal death*. The light of Christianity and the darkness of Paganism are the ontological categories around which the dichotomy moves. In this particular construction of the world, there are no nuances, no differences in perspective, and no shadows in between. The metaphors depict a dualistic world of light and darkness, where the missionary as well as his mission, emerge as torches in the dark. In this sense the story of Rampizafy and similar light and darkness stories, do not transmit actual *encounter* images, because they are first and foremost images about the mission, about the mission's ideology and the justification for its efforts. Actual encounter images would have to transmit something of 'the other', not merely contain the counter-image that serves to define 'the self'.

I have deliberately placed emphasis on the missionaries' religious ideology, what they would have called their faith in God and his salvation, thus distinguishing between the missionaries' religious and their civilising objectives.[22] It

---

[20] See Fuglestad and Simensen: *Norwegian Missions in African History*, Vol. 1, chapter 1.

[21] See ibid., p. 34. For the time being I choose to take this at face value, not discussing the differences in the accounts given in applications for the missionary school, and the source-critical problems involved in making use of them.

[22] When other missionary studies, like Beidelman 1982 see the religious and the civilising objectives as indissolubly linked, I presume this is because *their* missionaries do not operate with this distinction in their texts.

is clear from my material that although Christianity and 'civilisation' are perceived as two sides of the same coin, the religious objective is usually understood as the most important and primary of the two.[23] The missionaries somehow seem to think that when people convert to Christianity, some features of civilisation will follow as a matter of course. What these features of civilisation more specifically are, is not something the missionaries agree on, however. While the missionaries' understanding of 'civilisation' and the connection between Christianity and 'civilisation' are constantly negotiated issues,[24] the religious objective is the one thing they do agree on.

Selection and genres

Before we go further in our analysis of encounter images in the Norwegian Mission Magazine, we have to take into consideration the special nature of this source. Before we can even begin to consider what the prominence of the black and white image implies, whose image this really is (the missionaries' or the home public's) and the relationship between this image and other images found in the Magazine, it is crucial to be aware of the fact that the missionary accounts in the Norwegian Mission Magazine are revised extracts from the missionaries' frequent letters and reports to their Norwegian superiors.

The main bulk of missionary accounts in the Mission Magazine, are taken from the missionaries' half-yearly and annual reports and their letters to the mission leaders in Stavanger. From time to time the Mission Magazine also printed extracts from the missionaries' private letters to family and friends. For the purpose of our present argument, however, it is sufficient to concentrate on the letters and reports.

The half-yearly and annual reports give brief outlines of the type of work carried out during the year, statistics (the number of baptisms, marriages, funerals, services, communions etc.), and often also the missionary's opinion on the state of affairs in the congregation and the mission's immediate geographical surroundings. The genre 'report' requires objective, factual information, and as the missionaries become familiar with the genre, their reports become more and more similar and less and less informative and elaborate.[25]

The letters concern many of the same things as the reports; however, they are often more elaborate, include more ethnographic descriptions and episodes

[23] Letter from Rosaas, printed in *NMT* No. 18, 1882, p. 336; letter from Dahle, Antananarivo, 9 May 1871, printed in *NMT* No. 11, 1871, p. 425.

[24] This is an important point for negotiation and ambiguity between the missionaries which will be important to look into. Is it possible to decide the primary influencing factors for the missionaries' stand in such matters; European background, education, contact with other missionaries (both Norwegian and other nationalities), little contact with other missionaries/Europeans? Is it possible to see any difference in opinion over time?

[25] Interestingly, Johannes Einrem's reports represent one important exception to this rule.

from the missionaries' daily lives, as well as personal information about the missionary and his family.

In addition to the inherent constraints of the genres, there were a number of other influencing factors on the content of these letters. Firstly, all the letters were written to "the Honoured Heads of the Mission". I have not found indications in the early letters that the missionaries were conscious of the fact that their letters might be published in the Magazine, although it is clear that a substantial number of these letters were published more or less edited, either in full, or summarised. However, from the beginning of the seventies and onwards, some of the missionaries indicate that they know their letters are likely to be published.[26] Knowing that their letters were for other eyes besides the mission leaders', is bound to have influenced both the choice of topics and the way in which the missionaries wrote about them. Secondly, we may assume that there were sometimes differences between what the missionary in the field found important and what information interested the mission leaders at home.[27] It is likely that the missionaries would, at least to some extent, give the type of information that they thought the mission leaders (and the home public) were interested in. A third important influencing factor is the fact that the letters and reports from the individual missionaries (apart from the private letters) were sent *via the missionaries' local supervisor*.[28] It is very likely that in some important respects this was a more immediate influencing factor than the thought of the mission leaders at home.[29]

The editing practice of the Norwegian Mission Magazine concerned both language (spelling/grammar) and content.[30] Although it is true that a lot of the letters were printed more or less in full, and that many of the language corrections and/or omission of certain paragraphs, did not directly alter the meaning of the original letter, it is also the case that some letters were so heavily edited that the printed extract in no way can be seen as representative of the original.

---

[26] Some for instance, write their letters to "the Honoured Heads of the Mission and the Friends of the Mission", others explicitly state that some details are not to be published.

[27] Letter from Borgen to Pastor Dons, Tamatave 18 August 1870 (NMS Hjemmearkiv, Box 132, Jacket 6).

[28] In the first years, bishop Schreuder in South Africa was the superintendent. After Schreuder's resignation from the NMS in 1869 and L. Dahle's suggestion of a more democratic restructuring of the local mission organisation in the field had been accepted with some changes, the missionaries elected their supervisor from among themselves. Lars Dahle was the unchallenged leader until 1887, when he was called back to Norway in order to become the new Secretary General of the Norwegian Mission Society. After Dahle, Chr. Borchgrevink was elected superintendent.

[29] One thing was the position and personality of the supervisor; Lars Dahle, a strong and dominant personality in every respect, was more feared than loved according to E. Birkeli, a historian of the NMS (*Det norske missionsselskaps historie i hundre år*, Vol. IV, p. 132). Another important factor, was the relationship between those missionaries living and working close to other missionaries and those who lived isolated from other Europeans. There were strong social mechanisms within the missionary community ensuring that the individual missionaries behaved according to the generally accepted norms.

[30] My findings support those of the historian Pier M. Larson in this respect (Introduction in The Larson Catalog of the Madagascar Holdings of the Hjemme-Arkiv 1866–1899).

The most influential editorial device, however, was the selection of letters. Why were some letters printed? Why were some letters not printed? Why were the letters of some missionaries printed more often than letters from other missionaries? Although some missionaries undoubtedly wrote stylistically better and more interesting letters than others (interesting for whom, one must add), this cannot account for the entire editorial policy on this matter. For obvious reasons, the leaders of the mission were bound to be more interested in ethnographic details and "real life stories" which, directly or indirectly, supported and legitimated the overall goal of the mission: to convert people to Lutheran Christianity.

So far there have been no attempts at systematising the discrepancies between the original letters in the Norwegian Missionary Society's Archives, and the printed extracts in the Mission Magazine.[31] At the same time, there has been a tendency to rely almost exclusively on printed material, especially the extracts in the Mission Magazine, in the two major studies concerning Norwegian missionaries in Madagascar: S. Tobiassen's: *Kulturkollisjon* (1971) and *Norwegian Missions in African History: Vol. 2: Madagascar* edited by Fuglestad and Simensen (1986). This has important implications for both works. As far as the latter study is concerned, the main problem is precisely that it is too limited to do justice to the role the nineteenth century Norwegian missionaries played in certain areas of Madagascar. The main problem with Tobiassen's study is not the point it tries to make—that the Norwegian missionaries in Madagascar have to be understood as part of the wider colonial discourse. The problem is that this study ends up with a distorted depiction of the relationship between the Norwegian missionaries and the Malagasy, because it only focuses on one aspect of this relationship: the clashes and the misunderstandings due to the ethnocentrism of the Norwegian missionaries.

Given that the printed extracts from the missionaries' letters and reports were selected and edited by people in Norway for a Norwegian public, it is not surprising that we find a lot of light and darkness stories in the Mission Magazine. The Norwegian Missionary Society was a private organisation, which depended entirely on the mission supporters' financial contributions to keep up its work overseas. In this respect the image of light and darkness can be seen not only as the *ideological* basis for the Mission Society. In a real sense it would also be its financial lifeline. The image would be crucial in order to "sell" the mission at home, and the Mission Magazine was the most important line of communication between the Society and its supporters. Against this background it becomes quite significant that there in fact are *other* images in the Mission Magazine, images of Malagasy people and the relationship between the missionaries and the Malagasy that on principal points contradict

---

[31] This is something I hope to undertake as part of my present doctoral project: 'Conversion and Conversations. Discourses on Christianity and Tradition in Inland Madagascar 1866–1895'.

and contest the image of the missionary encounter as an encounter between light and darkness.

Contradicting implicit images

Through the conversion and deathbed stories, we have seen the creation of a world where the primary division goes between 'Christian' and 'Pagan'. Christians, both the missionary and the Malagasy convert, are happily saved and fundamentally transformed, while the poor pagans live in constant fear and misery only waiting to be saved from the grip of the prince of darkness by the missionary. Conversion not only happens according to clear-cut categories of 'Christianity' and 'Paganism'; the very categories 'conversion', 'Christianity' and 'Paganism' are identical to the *missionary's* understanding and definition of these categories. Thus, when the Malagasy individual unquestioningly and gratefully 'converts' from 'Paganism' to 'Christianity', he/she simultaneously submits himself/herself to the missionary type of 'Christianity'.

The many printed reports of the missionaries' everyday lives tell a completely different story. In a letter from 6 January 1870, published in *NMT* No. 6, 1870, p. 259 pastor Stueland writes:

> As far as Christianity's deeper requirements are concerned, most Malagasy are too superficial, too easily contented with the external: one keeps the Sunday and attends the services; that makes one a good subject of the Queen and—a Christian. This is what many people think, and live accordingly.

Stueland and the other Norwegian missionaries soon discovered that the Merina and Betsileo contested the missionaries' understanding of 'Christianity', what it meant to be a Christian, and their models of conversion. By the time the Norwegian missionaries arrived in Madagascar, Malagasy vocabulary and concepts of 'Christianity' had long been established[32] (Pier M. Larson 1997). Christianity was known as 'the worship': *ny fivavahana*, a Malagasy word which historically drew upon a continuity with long-standing traditional ways of Malagasy spirituality and worship (ibid.:13–22). While Christian converts during the first decade of LMS evangelisation in Antananarivo were known as "the believers" (*ny mpino*), the Christian converts had long been referred to as "the prayers" (*ny mpivavaka*). This had important implications for the notion of what it meant to be a Christian: rather than being fundamentally associated with belief and creed, the Malagasy notion was that "the essence of being Christian lay in the nature of what one did" (ibid.:17).

---

[32] The London Missionary Society (LMS) had started mission work in the capital in 1820, as a trade-off with the Merina king Radama I, who wanted the missionaries' technical and literary skills (Bloch 1986). In 1835 all European missionaries were expelled from the country, a ban that was lifted only 5 years before the first Norwegians arrived. When the Norwegian missionaries came to Madagascar in 1866, there was an influential and growing minority of Christian converts.

From 1869 and until the French occupation in 1895, *ny fivavahana* is fundamentally associated more with the Queen and the Merina state, not primarily with the European missionaries.[33] In 1869, the Queen, Ranavalona II, and her husband, the Prime Minister Rainilaiarivony, were baptised, and Christianity became the new state religion.[34] No matter what notions the missionaries had about Christian conversion as an individual's choice between two mutually exclusive religious systems,[35] the connection between Christianity and the Merina government meant that conversion to Christianity became a necessary condition for acquiring and/or keeping political and religious influence, and a sign of political loyalty to the Queen for ordinary subjects. As a result of the Queen's conversion, the number attending church services increased from about 17,000 in 1868 to around 153,000 in 1869.[36]

This situation was both good and bad for the missionaries. As one of them states:

> One certainly has to thank the Lord for paving the way for the preaching of the Gospel among this people; however, sadness is the only reaction when hearing of the lack of judgement with which the Government acts concerning the worship. One feels tempted to wish that the Government were less "favourable" towards Christianity, as that would undoubtedly create less hypocrites among the Malagasy Christians, than what is the case today.[37]

From the beginning, force made people build churches and attend Sunday services. The state churches were built through *fanompoana* (corvée labour),[38] and were usually used as schools during the week.[39] Because of this, and because the Merina government used the lists of students as enrolment lists for the army on several occasions,[40] the Christian Church and the school became inseparable from the hated institution of corvée labour (*fanompoana*) in most people's minds. "The same, sad experience is made almost everywhere: that people look upon the worship of God as a kind of *Fanompoana*; another reason why they hate it, because they think—quite reasonably—that they already have enough *Fanompoana*".[41] In a letter from pastor Vig 26 July 1889,[42] he reports that people are afraid to attend services on Sundays. The government

---

[33] Bloch 1986.

[34] Their conversion was highly politically motivated, rising from the need to control an already influential and rapidly expanding Christian minority (Bloch 1986).

[35] Cf. the conversion stories above.

[36] Ellis 1985, p. 17.

[37] Letter from Stueland, Fandriana, 2 July 1872, printed in *NMT* No. 12, 1872, p. 465.

[38] Ellis 1985, p. 19.

[39] Ibid., p. 19.

[40] Scarborough and Fuglestad, "A Note on the History of Education in Vakinankaratra and Neighbouring Regions 1870–1907", in Fuglestad and Simensen (eds), 1986, p. 101.

[41] Letter from Wilhelmsen, Soavina, 25 January 1875, printed in *NMT* No. 8, 1875, p. 287. The same point of view, that people look upon adherence to Christianity as *fanompoana*, is expressed by several people, among others: Egenæs, Ambohimasina, 5 October 1874, printed in *NMT* No. 2, 1875. Minsaas, Fihasinana, 5 August 1885, printed in *NMT* No. 24, 1885, pp. 472–73.

officials use such opportunities to send people to the hard, and dangerous *fanompoana* in the copper mines far away from home. Others complain that they thought that if they took up this worship they would no longer have to do military service.[43] However, when the military service continued to be as hard as ever, they could no longer see any point in the new faith.[44] Instead of improving people's situation, Christianity had only made things worse. Even the missionary understood why many returned to their old pre-Christian gods:

> (...) the hard corvée-labour, (which) takes most of peoples' time and power, Sundays and weekdays. People are constantly occupied, which leaves little spare time to seek the soul's salvation, had they wanted to. Gold is now the engrossing interest. Mammon worship has now become first priority, and as a consequence the idol-worship, which was burnt off before but was not burnt out of the heart, has restored its honour and glory. That this is how things are is not strange. People feel that since the time of the adoption of Christianity as state religion they have not become any happier, and the corvée-labour, instead of diminishing (...) has increased every year. People are about to collapse under its burden. Protection for life and property weakens every day, and justice has turned into a pure money speculation. People say to each other: do not even consider to prove yourself right if you do not have any money; the time has passed when even the poor could prove themselves right. Robbers and the so-called Sakalava, who, beside the blackmail carried out by the Chiefs and Officers, wreck the country and ruin its people, are the ones who are free and powerful.[45]

The intrinsic connection between Christianity and the Merina government certainly meant that the missionaries had relatively little influence on how the new worship was perceived. Unless they were associated with the government type of Christianity, the Norwegian missionaries were unable to get converts in the highlands. Outside the highlands, they had difficulties getting converts *because* of their association with the Merina government. The nineteenth century is a period of great Merina expansion, which was to culminate with their almost total control of the entire island at the moment of the French colonisation in 1895. When the missionaries approached new geographical areas outside those already under control of the Merina, they were met with great suspicion and perceived as representatives of the Merina government.[46] It did not improve matters that most missionaries spoke the Merina dialect. In the last years of the Merina state, it became more and more problematic for the mis-

---

[42] From Masinandraina. Printed in *NMT* No. 20, 1889, p. 392.

[43] In fact the Merina government had promised that *pupils and teachers* at the schools would be relieved of other forms of *fanompoana* (in other words: the school was seen as *fanompoana*), including military service. This promise was first made in 1874 and then in 1882, but at a later stage the government broke its vow (Gow 1979, p. 130).

[44] Letter from Vig, Masinandraina 21 January, printed in *NMT* No. 15, 1880, pp. 297–98.

[45] Letter from I. Nilsen, Manandona, 14 February 1891, printed in *NMT* No. 19, 1891, p. 371.

[46] See for instance letter from Bjertnæs, Ivohitsidy 15 February 1895, printed in *NMT* No. 19, 1895, pp. 364–70.

sionaries to be so closely associated with the increasingly corrupt, exploitative and unjust government.

Compromise and constant negotiation characterised the missionaries' daily lives, also in religious matters. For example in my study of the mortuary rituals in the highlands in the latter half of the nineteenth century, I have shown how the missionaries had to make considerable concessions when it came to Merina/Betsileo funerary practices, including the periodic, and to the missionaries fundamentally pagan, ritual exhumation and re-wrapping of corpses[47] (Skeie 1994). The devout Christian converts' practice in these matters showed that 'Christianity' and 'Paganism' were far from the clear-cut missionary categories of the conversion and deathbed stories. Instead of unquestioningly taking over the missionaries' definition of 'Pagan' and 'Christian', the missionaries' understanding of proper and improper conduct for a *mpivavaka*, the converts themselves contested and redefined these categories and the boundary between them through their actions.

The implicit images, which emerge from the descriptions of the missionary's daily life of Malagasy people, of the missionary and of the relationship between the missionary and Malagasy people, contradict the corresponding images emerging from the light and darkness image. Instead of the passive, stupid, non-rational and easily influenced child of the stereotype, 'the Malagasy' actively, cleverly, rationally negotiates the message of the missionary. In this relationship, the missionary's power and influence is considerable, but nevertheless limited. Negotiating proper and improper conduct for converts, the missionary not only persuades but is himself persuaded. Negotiating the categories and the boundaries defining 'Christian' and 'Pagan', the missionary not only influences but is himself profoundly influenced. And this is the point where yet another story emerges: a story where the light and darkness image re-enters the missionaries' texts but tells a different story than that of European domination and superiority. However, before we approach *that* story, we will examine some images of Madagascar and Malagasy people by the most popular and prominent missionary author in Norway this century: Johannes Einrem.[48]

Beyond black and white

Einrem came to Madagascar in 1893, where he spent 40 years working as a missionary, for 30 of which he lived on the island. During this period he wrote 28 books and more than 260 articles and essays which were published in different newspapers and periodicals (Borgenvik 1979:14–15). Many of his

---

[47] The *famadihana* ritual, also called the ritual of the turning of the dead. Cf. Maurice Bloch, *Placing the Dead*, 1971, for a modern study of this ritual.

[48] I thank Kirsten Sødahl for inspiring me to read Einrem.

books were reissued several times; "Through My Green Glasses" six times, the last time as late as in 1960.

Johannes Einrem's first book was issued in 1912: "Through My Green Glasses. From Madagascar". Except for the first two books, all his other books were first issued by other publishers than the Norwegian Missionary Society, Einrem's employer.[49] The fact that Einrem wrote "directly" to his Norwegian readers, and not via the Missionary Society, is an important difference between his texts and the missionary texts we have been looking at so far. Another important distinction between Einrem's texts and the other missionaries' letters and reports, is the fact that Einrem's texts are *fiction*. Einrem said that he chose to write fiction, because only a more elaborate genre than 'letter' and 'report' enabled him to give a truthful picture of the complex world he participated in and observed (Borgenvik 1979:17–20).[50]

Although Einrem is unique in his writing of fiction and in the amount of his literary production, the images of Madagascar and Malagasy people he produces are very representative of the general images we find in the Mission Magazine and other missionary publications. There are plenty of light and darkness images in Einrem's stories. There are also plenty of examples of the way in which he combines his religious ideology with the traditional European value-system at the time: the Malagasy in general are uncivilised, natural people, like children, governed more by feelings than by a rational mind. There are, however, also plenty of examples in Einrem's writing of images *beyond* the black and white stereotypes. The bits and pieces of information mentioned in passing, stories on related issues seen from different points of view, contradictions and inconsistencies between the different images he draws up, the changing social and cultural patterns over time—all this leaves the loyal and persistent reader with many-sided images of Madagascar and Malagasy people.[51]

First and foremost Einrem writes about people who live in a specific geographical and sociocultural context. These are people with virtues and vices, humour and wit, some of them are clever, others are dumb, and some are unpretentious, while others are pompous. These are not people who come smiling and tell about their mothers who are about to die (cf. the story about Rampizafy's baptism). In Einrem's stories all kinds of people have feelings and reasons for their actions; reasons he offers and reasons they give him. Christians are good and bad, just as pagans are both good and bad.

Einrem gives an often harsh and realistic picture of Malagasy life. Importantly, this picture does not serve primarily as a backdrop for Einrem's mis-

---

[49] A selection of his books was later issued by the Norwegian Missionary Society as 'Einrem's collected works'.

[50] For our present purposes we will take Einrem at face value.

[51] Interestingly, the same is true for the archival material. It is systematic and extensive reading which makes visible the many images beyond black and white.

sionising urge, as a demonstration of the 'harsh realities of Paganism'. There is an intrinsic tension in Einrem's writing between his strong statements on the "darkness of Paganism" and the positive attitude and deep understanding he shows for traditional Malagasy religion and culture.[52] Einrem goes very far in trying to make people and their attitudes and reactions comprehensible to a Norwegian reader. He systematically uses positive terms for religious specialists in the traditional religious realm.[53] The function which most missionaries label 'sorcerer', Einrem prefers to distinguish as 'priest', 'prophet' or 'doctor', according to context. The negatively loaded Norwegian terms, are systematically reserved for those who exploit, trick and deceive their clients (ibid.:270). The devoted 'Pagans' are described with understanding and sympathy. On this point Einrem goes one step further than most other missionary texts. Describing a conversation with an old man, Einrem relates that he is left without answers when the other confronts him: Don't *you* honour and respect your father, mother and your ancestors? Is not *your* teaching the teachings of *your* ancestors and *your* forefathers? Would Einrem consider breaking with this teaching and instead convert to *his* teaching? He too honoured and respected his forefathers and kept their prescriptions (ibid.:270–72).

In another story Einrem describes his arrival in a little village late one evening. A persistent drum accompanied by monotonous and mournful singing is heard from the other side of the village. Einrem follows the sound and stops in front of an open door. In the dim light from a lamp he sees 5–6 young girls sitting on the floor, drumming, clapping their hands and singing: "E-e-meloke-e, meloke-e, meloke-e! Aza ilaozan' jaza Inenibe malala-e!" Einrem translates: "In Norwegian this means something like: oh, we have sinned, sinned, sinned! Please do not punish us by leaving us, beloved grandmother." When the girls spot the missionary on the threshold, they stop singing and look anxiously at Einrem, as if they are afraid they have done something wrong. "They knew who I was, and now I had probably come to reprove them. About what they seemed not to know." Einrem greets them and is invited in. They offer him a seat on the drum. On a bed lies an old white-haired woman. Dying. "Grandmother was ill, they told me. – And you sit here and sing to her, I said. How kind of you to do that". (...)

> Later that night I reflected on the fact that I had commended these young girls for sitting there like pagans do singing for the dying. I had even asked them to continue. Was it perhaps wrong of me? What if I had prohibited them, frightened them into silence, what would I have gained? They knew no other song. And they sang to comfort and please the ill, to show their love. And the ill lay there and lis-

---

[52] This fact is also commented upon by J. Borgenvik (1979, p. 276), although I read more into it than he apparently does.

[53] The medicine man is called 'the priest' or 'the learned specialist'. The diviner ('Ombiasa') is called "a sacrificial priest and soothsayer" and also "trained doctor and soothsayer according to old Malagasy science".

tened to these familiar words and expressions. She had herself taught them how to sing and loved the song. These soft, sonorous notes soothed and coddled. It was as if her lovely grandchildren embraced her and chased out the fear. Although her eyes were closed, everything around her became brighter and brighter. For she was loved. Perhaps lay therein an unconscious notion of the great loving arms which so readily wanted to embrace her. For it is love which brings light. The way it comes is of less importance. Do we dare to say that God met her and embraced her in her grandchildren's love?

Therefore I thanked God for what he had led me to say tonight. For having helped me not to tear down and deprive. (Einrem 1925:60–64)

This story raises a number of interesting questions. In it Einrem redefines the ontological categories of light and darkness. They are no longer identical to the absolute light of 'Christianity' and the absolute darkness of 'Paganism'. Instead, light is love and darkness is non-love: "For it is love which brings light. The way it comes is of less importance." Thus, God can be present also in the Pagans' love for each other. The question is: Where does this leave the missionary? Has the missionary a role to play in God's great scheme of love? If yes, is the missionary's role much the same as in the scheme of Christianity versus Paganism? How can Einrem on the one hand go so far in understanding the other that he realises that what he represents "tears down and deprives"—and yet remain a missionary?

The missionary map revisited

Before we can begin to answer the questions Einrem's stories raise, and before we can establish to what extent other missionaries beside Einrem experience a strong tension between the clear-cut dichotomy of their ideological imperative and the ambiguities and contradictions of the daily experiences, we have to go *beyond* the *printed* missionary material, and *systematically* study the *archival* material. We need to study the archival material in its different forms: Not only the missionaries' *original* archival letters and reports to the Mission leaders on which the Mission Magazine is based, but the missionaries' private letters to family and friends in Norway, their private letters to missionary colleagues both in and beyond Madagascar, the missionaries' letters to and letters from Malagasy people, their personal diaries and their station diaries, and the detailed transcripts of the missionaries annual conferences to discuss and plan their work.

It is too early for me to provide definite answers and conclusions to what the archival material reveals. However, initial readings of all the missionaries' uncensored letters, with the petty things, the boring routines of most ordinary days alongside the odd special episodes, the frustrations, the health problems, the successes and the failures, the joys and the sorrows, sustain and further add to the complex picture of the missionaries' daily discourses with Malagasy people, already indicated by the implicit images of the printed extracts. Perhaps most importantly: the original archival letters make the individual missionary more visible. In their struggle to cope with and make sense of the discrepancy between their ideological notions of themselves and their work, the missionaries had different individual strategies. In this negotiating process, the prominent light and darkness image appears to take on other implications for some: Is this image the last straw of faith which some missionaries cling to, the only thing which legitimises their struggles, their illnesses and pains, their isolation? Is the image of light and darkness some missionaries' mark of protection from losing the grip and "going native"—in their own eyes, in the eyes of fellow missionaries, mission leaders, family and friends in Norway? Is the prominence of light and darkness images in some missionaries' writing in fact an indication of how profoundly they were influenced through the encounter with the Malagasy?

It should be obvious by now why it is not possible to talk about one single Norwegian missionary image of 'the Malagasy'.[54] Even the image of light and darkness, so fundamental to missionary accounts well beyond Madagascar, seems to mean different things for different missionaries when studied more closely.[55] The existence of more than stereotypical images in the printed missionary material, in my opinion, makes it difficult to argue that the missionary accounts merely confirmed existing stereotypical images in Europe, as far as the reception of missionary accounts in Norway is concerned. If J. D.Y. Peel is right in claiming first, that there is a tendency to rely on *printed missionary material* well beyond the Norwegian missionaries in Madagascar and, secondly, that a proper source criticism of published missionary material in general is as yet virtually unattempted (1996:70), it seems more important than ever to reinterpret the missionary sources in order to understand more of the history of European and African encounters. Just like the colour original of Landmark's missionary map simultaneously transmitted light and darkness *and* colours and complexity, the Norwegian missionary material both from Madagascar, and *beyond* Madagascar, tells stories *both* of the implementation of European colonial power and of its transformations, displacements, failures, and silences (G. Prakash (ed.) 1995:6). The missionaries' texts from the field were constrained in different ways; by genres, by potential and actual readers, and by the individual missionary's opportunity, ability and wish to express what he/she experienced. When the missionary texts, despite these

---

[54] Cf. the title of Simensen's article on the subject 1996.

[55] The fact that Hanna Mellemsether elsewhere in this volume reaches very different conclusions concerning the African images in the texts of Norwegian missionaries to Zululand, supports, in my opinion, the point that the local African context profoundly influenced the missionaries' understanding of themselves, the Africans and their mission work. In fact, I think the local African context was more decisive in important respects than the missionaries' Norwegian background.

constraints, succeeded in moving beyond black and white, we owe it to the missionaries—and to ourselves, to let these stories be heard.

References:

Beidelman, Thomas Owen, 1982, *Colonial Evangelism: A socio-historical study of an East African mission at the grassroots.* Bloomington: Indiana University Press.

Birkeli, Fridtjov, 1949, *Det Norske Misjonsselskaps historie i hundre år. Vol. 4: Madagaskar Innland, Vest-Madagaskar, Øst-Madagaskar.* Stavanger: Dreyer.

Bloch, Maurice, 1986, *From Blessing to Violence: History and ideology in the circumcision ritual of the Merina of Madagascar.* Cambridge: Cambridge University Press.

Borgenvik, Johannes, 1979, *Bajonetter og demoner på Madagaskar: Fransk okkupasjon og gassisk samfunn i Johannes Einrems forfatterskap.* Oslo: Luther.

Comaroff, Jean and John, 1991, *Of Revelation and Revolution: Christianity, Colonialism, and Consciousness in South Africa.* Chicago: University of Chicago Press.

Einrem, Johannes, 1912, *Gjennem grønne briller: Historier og skildringer fra Madagaskar.* Stavanger: Nomi.

—, 1914, *I sol og vind: Paa Madagaskar.* Stavanger: Det norske Missionsselskaps forlag.

—, 1918, *Ravola.* Bergen: Lunde.

—, 1921, *Mangarano.* Bergen: Lunde.

—, 1922, *Mot solrenning.* Bergen: Lunde.

—, 1922, *Brorhjel— Selvhjelp.* Bergen: Lunde.

—, 1924, *I skumringen.* Bergen: Lunde.

—, 1926, *Vaffelland.* Bergen: Lunde.

—, 1926, *Under dødsskygge.* Bergen: Lunde.

—, 1930, *På utferd.* Bergen: Lunde.

—, 1939, *Gamle minner.* Bergen: Lunde.

Ellis, Stephen, 1985, *The Rising of the Red Shawls: A Revolt in Madagascar 1895–1899.* Cambridge: Cambridge University Press.

Fuglestad, Finn and Jarle Simensen (eds), 1986, *Norwegian Missions in African History: Vol. 2: Madagascar.* Oslo: Norwegian University Press.

Gow, Bonar A., 1979, *Madagascar and the Protestant impact: The work of the British missions, 1818–95.* London: Longman.

Jørgensen, Torstein (ed.), 1992, *I tro og tjeneste. Det norske misjonsselskap 1842–1992. Vol. 1.* Stavanger: Misjonshøgskolen.

Larson, Pier M. Catalogue of the Madagascar Holdings of the Hjemmearkiv (1866–1899).

—, 1997, "'Capacities and Modes of Thinking'. Intellectual and Cultural Engagements in the Early History of Malagasy Christianity, 1820–1836", *The American Historical Review/ American Historical Association* (New York), Vol. 102, No. 4, pp. 969–1002.

Norsk Missionstidende (NMT). Stavanger: Det norske misjonsselskap 1870–1920.

Peel, J.D.Y., 1996, "Problems and opportunities in an anthropologist's use of a missionary archive", in Bickers, Robert A. and Rosemary Seton (eds), *Missionary Encounters: Sources and Issues.* Surrey: Curzon Press.

Prakash, Gyan (ed.), 1995, *After Colonialism: Imperial histories and postcolonial displacements.* Princeton: Princeton University Press.

Simensen, Jarle (ed.), 1986, *Norwegian Missions in African History. Vol. 1: South Africa 1845–1906*. Oslo: Norwegian University Press.

—, 1995, "The Image of Africa in Norwegian Missionary Opinion, 1850–1900", in Rian, Øystein et al. (eds), *Revolusjon og resonnement: Festskrift til Kåre Tønnesson på 70-årsdagen den 1. Januar 1996*, pp. 137–50. Oslo: Universitetsforlaget.

Skeie, Karina Hestad, 1994, *Religious and Cultural Identity in Times of Change. Beliefs and Rituals around Death among the Merina of Madagascar 1866–1895*. Unpublished Cand. Phil. thesis, History of Religion at the University of Oslo. Spring.

Tobiassen, Svein, 1971, *Kulturkollisjon: Norske misjonærers møte med Madagaskars innland 1867–1883*. Oslo: Pax Forlag.

Gendered Images of Africa?
The Writings of Male and Female Missionaries

Hanna Mellemsether

Alongside the Malagasy and the Bengali people, the Zulu are the most renowned people in Norwegian mission circles. From my own childhood I recall images of Africa formed by readings in mission journals and Christian children's magazines. We were told about the hero missionary Hans P. Schreuder who suffered and sacrificed everything for the poor, naked children of a far away Zululand. Horror stories about human sacrifices, exploitation of women and children and other monstrous practices. I heard stories about how the witch doctors abused a terrified people, and saw pictures of the brutal and cruel Zulu king in all his regalia. But also: idyllic stories about 'saved' Zulu children: happy, black faces over bodies covered in summer dresses from our local Norwegian clothes shop, visualising the victory of civilisation and Christendom over heathendom. I remember visits by black men to the local meeting house, bringing feathers and awe-inspiring spears, and artefacts from the witch doctor's medicine chest. These converted heathens were put forward as trophies, proof of Christianity's victory over heathendom. All this was part of MY first image of Africa, a collage of light and darkness, of pride, resistance and humiliation. This image was rooted in the values and world view of the 19th century 'Norwegian mission to the heathen'. This world view survived for a long time in relatively closed religious communities in Norway, communities that seem to have been structured on different realities than the outside world.

Martha Sanne

This image of Africa from my childhood, came to my mind when I was working on a historical analysis of texts written by a Norwegian woman who became a missionary among the Zulu people in Natal, South Africa. The woman was Martha Sanne (1852–1923), a teacher of deaf children in Kristiania (Oslo) for 12 years before she was called to 'Zulu'[1] when she was in her thirties.

I would like to thank J. Kwadwo Osei-Tutu and Karina Hestad Skeie, as well as the commentators at the Helsingør conference, for commenting on an earlier draft of this paper.

[1] 'Zulu' was used by the missionaries both for the people and the area they worked in. 'Zululand' was also used for the area, even where the mission stations were south of the Tugela river.

In Kristiania Martha Sanne belonged to the middle class with a bourgeois culture and values. Her social network included people that could be said to be part of a cultural elite at the time. To the dismay of her closest friends she changed this seemingly safe and easy lifestyle for a very uncertain and risky life in 'darkest Africa'. Miss Sanne joined a small inexperienced Scandinavian mission organisation Den Frie Østafrikanske Misjon (The Free East African Mission) DFØM. Despite fragile health she stayed in Africa from 1889 until her death in 1923.[2] She became the first Norwegian woman to run her own mission station, and during her active years as a missionary she wrote numerous articles in missionary journals, she wrote diaries and private letters describing her work and her way of life.[3]

Miss Sanne was one of a few Norwegian women missionaries in Africa at the time, and one of the rare female voices in the public discourse on missionary work. In comparing her texts to texts written by her male counterparts in the Norwegian missions in Zululand, I wanted to see if gender made any difference when the missionaries created their images of Africa for the Norwegian public. I was looking for specific female markers in Miss Sanne's texts, markers of marginality, subordination and compassion that were supposed to mark women's writings in Miss Sanne's time. And I found such markers in her overall writing. In her private letters and personal diaries,[4] she is concerned about keeping up her relations to neighbours and friends, discussing her physical and spiritual health. Food and clothes also are given due consideration in these texts. Here she also expresses humbleness and shortcomings, and in her later years also en increasing marginality to her social and professional contexts.[5] But both in letters and in her diaries she relates almost exclusively to *white* people. It is mostly in her public texts that we find representation of or interaction with Africans. These texts are obviously of a different kind than her private texts, most notably is the seeming lack of gender markers. In comparing her texts to other texts in other missionary journals, texts written by men, I was surprised by the homogeneity both in content and form, whether the writers were men or women, lay or clergy.

---

[2] DFØM was later to become the Det Norske Misjonsforbund (DNM). DFØM/DNM was an independent non-Lutheran organisation, grown out of the revival movement that swept Norway and Scandinavia around the middle of the 19th century.

[3] The letters and some of her original diaries are found in Riksarkivet in Oslo: RA PA410 DNM Box 39. Other diaries are published in an edited form in Thomassen, Magda: *En av de få— Afrikamisjonær Martha Sannes dagbokoptegnelser og brev*, DNM's forlag, Oslo 1929.

[4] I distinguish between her private letters to friends and her personal diaries, which supposedly are meant for her eyes only. However, some of the entries in the diary are clearly drafts of articles and letters and therefore not personal as such.

[5] This marginality Miss Sanne expresses in her later diaries is caused by the fact that her role as a missionary is taken over by 'capable men'. Due to increasingly bad health she is forced out of direct missionary work into a sort of 'relieving officer' service—helping other missionaries and their families in practical matters.

The mission journals

The texts I am using in this work are Miss Sanne's articles in *Missionæren*, which was the mouthpiece of the DFØM, later DNM. Miss Sanne was one of the biggest contributors during the first years, maybe because she was an extremely good writer, giving life to individuals and visualising both the African landscape and the people. Another reason that she wrote most frequently could be that while her male colleagues travelled far and away, looking for places to evangelise, Miss Sanne and her female colleagues stayed more in one place and kept up the work at the main station.

In addition to *Missionæren* I have worked with texts in *Norsk Missions-tidende*, (NMT) the journal belonging to the 'big brother' in the Norwegian mission: Det Norske Misjonsselskap, NMS. In NMT we almost exclusively hear male voices, when the occasional woman wrote it was detailed descriptions of their work in school and domestic activities in strange and often difficult circumstances.[6] The majority of the articles in NMT were of a different kind. Most texts are reports from the different mission stations in South Africa and other countries. We find reports from the missionary meetings and from general mission meetings. These reports give us a good impression of the work the missionaries did, how many people were baptised, how the school proceeded etc. Only occasionally did the missionaries portray individual Africans to illustrate the work they were doing, and how well or badly they succeeded in their mission.[7]

The mission journals are part of the colonial discourse along with texts produced by globetrotters, scientific expeditions, colonialists and others who wrote about colonised people. But since Norway never was much of a colonial nation, it was the missionaries who produced the bulk of these colonial texts from Africa, India and China. And more important, the missionaries wrote for a public that would only rarely read geographical or scientific description or even travellers' writings, namely the lay uneducated people in all areas of Norwegian society, many of whom were women who subscribed to the mission journals. In that way the articles written here would be very important

---

[6] From 1884 to 1925 they also included a monthly journal: 'Misjonslesning for Kvindeforeninger' (MFK Mission reading for women's associations) which was meant for women (only) and was sent to those who specially subscribed to it. After 1925 MFK became part of NMT and was sent to everybody who subscribed to NMT.

[7] In her paper 'Beyond black and white: Reinterpreting the Norwegian Missionary Image of the Malagasy' elsewhere in this volume, Karina Hestad Skeie gives a divergent interpretation of the missionary sources from mine. One reason for this different view might be the different histories of the mission in Madagascar and in Zululand. But the main reason for the contradictions seems to be that Hestad Skeie deals with an earlier period in the mission history. In 1903 the General Secretary of NMS, Lars Dahle, sent a letter of instruction to the missionaries, advising them how to write letters to the journal. (NMS-Archives Stavanger, Box 142–11: letter from L. Dahle, May 1903). The same Lars Dahle who became General Secretary in 1889, single-handedly edited the journal NMT for 14 years, and then with an assistant until he retired in 1920. (Dahle, Lars: 1923:49). This led to uniformity in the published articles, very "objective" stories which gave less space for anomalies.

contributors to the way 'ordinary' people perceived Africa and the Africans. The journals played an important role as the mouthpieces of the active missionaries and the leaders of the mission organisations. The genre they belonged to as literature for moral upliftment and religious inspiration put particular restraints on the text, and did not allow for any critical or divergent views on morality, religion and mission practices.[8] Given the purpose of these texts, writing for a mission journal meant that it was necessary to balance criticism with an optimistic view of the people they were sent out to work among. On the one hand, the texts should legitimate the missionary project: "a main function of information was thus to prove the need for evangelical work" writes professor Simensen in a recent article (Simensen 1996:138). This would produce texts much in line with the general picture of Africa portrayed in 19th century colonial discourses; the continent of darkness and barbarism, of inhuman exploitation of people by brutal leaders, and as the continent of fear; fear of evil spirits and cruel leaders. But on the other hand, missionaries also had to provide an economic and spiritual basis for their own work and make their public contribute towards their expenses. This would necessitate a more realistic picture of positive possibilities and of 'progress' as seen by the missionaries. This balancing act sets the missionary texts apart from other colonial texts, although we must bear in mind that the missionaries shared the European view of the superiority of their own civilisation and the need to 'uplift' 'heathens'.[9]

The mission ideology

Common to the mission ideology presented in the mission journals, whether NMS or DFØM, is the belief that the 'backwardness' of a people was as a result of sin, and only God could improve their lives. By bringing Christianity to the people, their culture would be 'civilised' and 'purified' by the force of the gospel alone.[10] The most important thing, for Martha Sanne as for all missionaries, was to spread the gospel: "... it's only that, which can save their souls and bring them from Darkness to Light" *(Missionæren*, No. 11, 1892).* To be able to spread the gospel, the missionaries had to create an environment that made the people receptive. It was necessary to teach them 'order and discipline' and Miss Sanne started with some needlework, hygiene and some housework "which is the most suitable both for boys and girls" (*Missionæren*, No. 11, 1892). But not too much education, that would spoil their souls and

---

[8] Lisbeth Mikaelsson discusses the genre of mission literature in her article: "Kvinner, kall og skrift - belyst ved livsskildringer av kvinnelige misjonærer" i Anfelt (ed.) 1992:167–91.
[9] Yet, the missionaries were very critical of the increasingly secularised European culture, and the results of the growing materialism and greed in colonial politics.
[10] In NMS this strategy started to change from the end of the 1800s. From seeing preaching of the gospel to individuals as the only way, they now put more emphasis on creating an autonomous Lutheran church in South Africa, and in that process education of an African clergy became more important.

brace their hearts against the gospel. In the hands of the Africans, the technology that knowledge constitutes, would be dangerous, and destroy their morals: "The Kaffirs are yet not mature for any development, and we see here as other places, that knowledge only makes them pompous and arrogant" (*Missionæren*, No. 11, 1892). We may well understand how this arrogance and pompousness could be a hindrance to the missionaries' work, pompous and arrogant people are not very receptive to a religion where humbleness is most important. Examples like these were expressed in various forms in almost any mission society around the turn of the century, and portrayed Africans as passive 'captives' in a static system of 'Darkness'. The actors were the missionaries, they were delivering the Africans into a 'Light' that is not only Christianity but also 'development' and 'civilisation'. In the missionary narratives the white missionaries are whatever the Africans are not: mature, masculine, modest, civilised and empowered. The most obvious picture of the Africans in all missionary texts is that of children in line with the paternalist language of the time. Both male and female texts portray Africans as 'children' needing 'discipline' and 'civilisation'. Miss Sanne maintains that the Africans are treated like children, because "... that's what they really are, even though they are quite big and developed. ... The Kaffirs, as a people, have no wish to be uplifted, they are a dull, idle people; when they have a pot full of food and can squat around the fire to keep warm without doing anything, they are perfectly happy" *(Missionæren*, No. 15, 1893). And to the extent that Africans are given a voice at all in the missionary narratives, the missionary's paternalism has penetrated the language in which they present themselves: "We are still like children: When someone tells us: 'Do this or that', we wish to obey, but are not able ..." ("Johane" in NMT, No. 9, 1916).

The 'laziness' of the Africans, and the fact that they are quite happy without the European civilisation angers the missionary. *Ora et labora* is an unknown value to the Africans. To the missionary who is raised within a culture where 'labour dignifies the man', lack of ambitions is provocative. Martha Sanne often stresses in her articles in *Missionæren*, how important it is to teach the Africans to work for privileges they get at the mission station: "By nature they are terrible beggars" she writes (*Missionæren*, No. 15, 1893). Therefore it is necessary to discipline them. When she teaches the girls to make their own dresses, she makes them work at the stations as compensation, or they are told to bring something, e.g. a pumpkin or mealie. She struggles with the African logic: the girls ask her why Martha herself doesn't make their dresses on her sewing machine, that would be much quicker and save them a lot of unnecessary work.

Public versus private texts

In her *public* texts, Miss Sanne is very sympathetic towards the Africans she is working with. She describes her pupils with humour and warmth. She focuses mostly on her teaching and that includes her teaching in domestic work as well as her preaching in men's huts and at beer-drinking parties. The individual African comes to life in her writing. She expresses much love and care for them, and takes great pride in her pupils. Describing pupils in her school like Ujubile, Uqigi or Zakayedwa she shows both understanding and leniency, even pride. Uqigi is the *"pearl"* in her school, and Miss Sanne misses her when she is not present. Ujubile is "not so bright, but attentive and observant". Zakayedwa is described as "a slim, nice little boy, clever and eager to get to school, walking through rain and sunshine, never absent without reason and he has a lot to tell" (*Missionæren*, No. 15, 1893). But these people are always portrayed as exceptions, and are seen as results of the work done by the missionaries. Through the help of God, and the missionary, they have conquered their evil and destructive 'nature'. In her articles, Miss Sanne shows contempt, not for the African individual, but for the heathen culture that 'darkens their hearts and souls'.

This view of the 'terrible nature' of the Africans (Zulu and Africans are used without distinction in her texts) is even more present in her private letters and diaries. As a people they are 'lazy', 'sly', 'untrustworthy' and most of the time up to no good. With few exceptions, the individual African is described as being dirty, demanding and ungrateful towards her and her work. She sighs and moans over how ineffective and bothersome the Africans in her neighbourhood are. All the time they pester her with questions and demands, without ever giving anything back.[11] We see how the mistakes and errors of her servants lead to generalisations on Africans as a 'difficult' and 'unmanageable' people.[12] The most striking difference between her public and her private texts is that in her private texts she has hardly anything positive at all to say about the Africans. The positive descriptions she gave of some of her pupils in the published texts, are absent from her diaries, here she mostly mentions blacks when there is something bad or troublesome to write about. But there are exceptions. A few times Africans working for her are mentioned with gratitude and even some respect. One exception is uLoise, who is her close co-worker and helpmate during a long period of time. Miss Sanne calls uLoise 'my man' because uLoise does all the hard work the delicate Miss Sanne cannot manage on the mission station. Other exceptions are 'Johan' and 'Hilda' who are kind and helpful. Common to all the exceptions are that they are Christians, they are humble, they are obedient to her orders and demands, and they admit their shortcomings. As Johan willingly admits to Miss Sanne's complaints about the Africans: "Our people are not so diligent as you white people".[13]

---

[11] See e.g. private letter 10.08.1903, no recipient, letter 22.08.1903 to 'mutter' (a colleague), diary entry 14.1.1906 from Mooi Plaats, Swaziland.
[12] See e.g. diary entry 6.9.1905 from St. Lucia Lake.
[13] Diary entry 14.1.1906 from Mooi Plaats, Swaziland.

A feminine discourse?[14]

The fact that Martha Sanne seems to show more solidarity and compassion with the Africans in her public texts than in her diaries and letters, may be because of the expectations placed on female writers at the time. Sara Mills argues in her study of women's travel writings, which men and women write differently because they take part in different discourses. Women are involved in the discourse of femininity in addition to the colonial discourse, and that informs their texts in another way than men's:

> Given their general lack of effective intervention in their own culture, women were denied the possibility of drawing on the predominately male discourse of Orientalism with the ease that male travellers had, since they were more strongly positioned by the conflicting discourse of 'femininity'. That is not to say that they escaped the constraints of colonial discourses, but rather that the constraints upon them were different in kind. (Mills 1991:96)

The feminine discourses at the time expected women to be caring, sympathetic, and to focus on relations with others and on domestic activities and values. To show feelings and empathy like Miss Sanne did in her public texts was seen as essential to femininity. Miss Sanne had broken away from the connection that defined her as feminine, as she herself chose to travel alone to the dark and dangerous Africa against the advice of her friends in Kristiania. Her public texts can therefore be seen as a strategy to show that she is feminine, despite the masculine position she holds in the mission organisation as leader of her own mission station. By stressing accepted female markers in her public texts, she can have a position of power in relation to the Africans, without having her femininity threatened by that position. She remains within the bourgeois ideal of 'mother' or 'social mother' that her unmarried position allows.

Male voices

But Sara Mills has not included missionary narratives in her analyses of colonial vs. feminine discourse. If one looks at missionary texts, the picture is not that clear-cut, because texts written by male missionaries carry much the same markers as those Mills labels feminine. The 'images' of Africans produced by male missionaries are very much like the ones I found in Martha Sanne's texts. The male missionaries also write about and with, emotions and feelings. They express empathy and solidarity with their 'clients' just as much as Miss Sanne did. As an example we can look at an article written by the Rev. Blessing

---

[14] Discourses are *"ways of referring to or constructing knowledge about a particlar topic of practice: a cluster of ideas, images and practices, which provide ways of talking about, forms of knowledge and conduct associated with a particular topic, social activity or institutional site in society"* (Hall 1997:6). A discourse is open-ended and incomplete, overlapped and limited by other open-ended, incomplete discourses. See also Doty 1996:6.

Dahle (NMT, No. 23, 1910). Blessing Dahle worked for NMS and is one of few missionaries who can compare to Miss Sanne when it comes to good narratives. Blessing Dahle writes an informal report about his work at the mission station at Eotimati. In this article he introduces his co-workers, the evangelists and teachers employed by the NMS. We get to know Isai Mavundhla who is about 40 years old, and "an incarnation of manliness". In the expression 'manliness' Dahle includes that Isai is always candid and straightforward in his speech, "something that can't be said about all the natives". He is an eager evangelist, a man with "strong feelings and great energy". *En passant* he mentions Isai's wife, who is also an eager evangelist. Abel Mpanza is Isai's opposite; quiet and gentle. But he too has lots of backbone; he walks through thick and thin to do his good work. Natanael Yengwa is tall and thin, works without being told, or without extra payment. The best man of them all is Abraham, a young unmarried man of 28 years and "a living proof of what a black man can become". Implicit in these comments is that through the help of God and the missionaries the African 'nature' can be turned around. Abraham is a quiet man: "unostentatious and patiently teaching English words as well as the multiplication table". And then there's Johan Biyela, a chief and an evangelist: "Johan is a noble man, spontaneously one calls him by his family name, Biyela. His facial features are more like a European and there is something noble about all his person". His wife, Gunhild speaks Norwegian and they have four clever children in school and "a nice home, where one often finds Gunhild by her Singer sewing machine". Note that Johan Biyela, the noble man, is NOT called by his family name in Dahle's text. Most Africans are not given a family name at all in the missionary narratives, a fact that makes it extremely difficult for a historian to trace these people in official archives.

In this article Blessing Dahle tells us what a man should be: humble, patient, honest and hard working, with deep feelings and lots of backbone. That is how the missionaries see themselves, and that is what they want the Africans to be. Johan Biyela is created in the missionary's image: he looks like a European, and his wife even speaks Norwegian and like many Norwegian wives, she has a Singer sewing machine. The same identification could be made with the couple Miss Sanne portrays, Jakobe and Anna (with no family name): "She is honest and fair in her own way, and is angered by injustice. Jakobe her husband, works in Durban. When she talks of him, her eyes sparkle, she loves him very much. On Sunday she wore a nice, blue dress and a white shawl, a gift from Jakobe" (*Missionæren*, No. 37, 1892). The European ideals of romantic marriage, European fashion and right-minded people are to seen as universal values. This is how the missionaries' vision of the future African is, after 'Darkness' has been conquered by 'Light'. It is not hard to understand how Norwegian readers could relate to the descriptions of these people, who through the works of God, the missionary and the mission people in Norway, have become images of themselves.

A mission discourse

I find that the images of Africa created by men and women in the Norwegian mission societies, carry few of the gendered markers Sara Mills discusses in her study of women in the colonial discourse. More than being forged by the feminine discourse at the time, I will argue that the images created by Martha Sanne in the mission journals were coloured by the mission discourse. Because of her participation in the mission to bring the gospel to all people, she had the power given by God to express herself in public.[15] That commission gave her confidence to participate in a public arena without consideration of her gender.[16] Therefore there would be no need for her to legitimate herself as an actor in a predominately male field, by writing within a specific feminine discourse.

An additional explanation of the seemingly 'ungendered' mission texts can be found when looking at ideological aspects of the mission discourse. The Norwegian mission movement originated in the evangelical revivals that stirred most parts of Norway in the second half of the 19th century. This religious movement contained other notions of 'masculinity' and 'femininity' than the understanding of the words that was constructed in the social world of industrialisation and modernisation. Evangelic religion, also labelled 'the religion of the heart', allowed expressions of emotions, humbleness and tears, also for the men. These expressions did not belong to the accepted masculinity in the social world of the 'modern' 19th century, neither do they in the 20th.[17] The blurring of the gender lines leads to a language based on equality, brother- and sisterhood. What we think of as feminine practices and properties were expected from all missionaries, they were expected to be emotional, self-sacrificing and humble regardless of gender. Anyone working for a mission society was thus expected to be more caring and sympathetic to the people they worked among, than their colonial counterparts would be.

This ideology results in a language of equality and brother/sisterhood among humankind that is an important part of the mission discourse. The ideological base of the mission discourse differentiates the missionaries from the general colonial discourses at the time, it does not entirely separate the two. The mission discourse, the missionaries, their texts and their practices occur in a colonial reality and thus within a colonial discourse. At certain points one can see that it was not always easy to keep up to the mission ideology of equality. In the increasingly race segregated South Africa in the 1920s

---

[15] DFØM was one of the few religious organisations at the time that used both male and female evangelists in their work. It was the conviction of one of the founders, Fredric Franson, that both men and women had a duty as well as a right to spread the gospel (Mellemsether 1995, ch. 4 and 5).

[16] About the possibilities for women within religious organisation see Cott 1984.

[17] For a discussion on the evangelical religion in the early stages in America see Smith-Rosenberg 1985. On masculinity, femininity and religion see Davidoff and Hall 1987, Part I.

the relationship between the missionary and his African congregation became a topic at several missionary conferences. Many missionaries in South Africa came from a settler background, which put them in a somewhat pressed situation between colonial and mission interests. The danger of being drawn into the broader colonial discourses on race was something the missionaries and their organisation became increasingly aware of. In the late 1920s, the Mission's Home Board in Norway had to point out to the missionaries that to discriminate between Africans and Europeans was 'unchristian', and against the role of a missionary. The missionaries were told to 'walk in the footsteps of Jesus', and not to adapt to the practice of the white colonialists who did not even shake hands with black people.[18]

In addition to the ideological constraints on the missionary narrative discussed above, the public, the readers of the mission journals all over Norway, also had expectations of another kind. Before the turn of the century, mission journals were one of few windows open to the outside world that were available to many people in Norway in the era before TV and radio. The largest journal, NMT had in 1870 6,500 subscriptions. Women's mission groups would subscribe to NMT, around the turn of the century groups like that had about 90,000 members. In their mission meetings, the journal would be read aloud, the articles were discussed and the missionary as well as the 'heathens' were duly prayed for. The mission journals and the missionaries that were on leave in Norway, had a function much like today's CNN: if the reports were not so fresh, it was the closest to direct reporting one came at the time. In times of important international crises "... (e)veryone wanted to hear news ...",[19] even people outside the mission circles came to listen to the missionaries. But even without crises and wars, people wanted to know. They wanted exotic stories from an alien culture, they wanted to know how the missionary first met the 'heathens', and of wonders and miracles in the mission field. To the devout missionary the people became too narrow-minded and too little interested in general mission strategies and development. People wanted first and foremost to hear about the Norwegian Mission, about 'what WE do', not mission as such (Nome 1943:50f). Thus it was their own contribution these people wanted to know about. They wanted to know what their own money, prayers and humble work in the Lord's vineyard had resulted in. In that way they created a direct connection between themselves and the 'proper' mission work in the far away countries; they created themselves as actors.

The individual missionary would contribute to the collage of African images with his or her personality. Missionaries with higher education would paint the picture in other words than the lay missionary, but without neces-

---

[18] NMS Archives Konferanserapport 1927, Svarskrivelse til konferanserapport 1927 [Written reply to conference report].

[19] NMS Archives Hjemmearkiv Boks 848A Legg 1.

sarily giving a totally different picture. The kind of work a missionary did would also flavour the images they presented; a housewife or a midwife would write about her work that took place among women. The male missionary, being a minister and administrator more than an evangelist as the mission developed, would to a great extent have his own image of Africans created in interaction with the male African evangelists, teachers and clergy. This would give the narratives of men and women missionaries different themes, but not necessarily different or gendered views on the Africans.

Conclusion

The image of Africans that was created by the missionaries around the turn of the century, was not one single image, but consisted of a collage within the polarities of Light/Darkness, Christian/Heathen. Neither was this image created by the missionaries alone. The public, the recipients of the mission narratives put the images to work and created a picture of the Africans in their own image at the same time as they created themselves.

The mission journals played a crucial role within the mission discourse, giving voice to the powerful, the knowing, the mastering race of predominantly white males, but also white middle-class women. The mission discourse as part of the wider colonial discourse, created images of Africa and Africans in a language of paternalism blended with the religious ideology of brotherhood and equality. This language transcends the gender divisions between the writers and generates, together with other constraints on the text, uniformity in the missionaries' writings about Africa and Africans.

In the mission discourse, a Christian African was more 'equal' than a non-Christian. The image of the Christian Africans was created in accordance with European standards—the more the African tried to become like the Europeans in appearance, practices and ways of thinking, the more 'equal' he/she was. The missionaries included black people in the family of humankind, but it was a hierarchically ordered family: white missionaries as parents and black Africans as children. But this ordering also implied that the blacks could 'grow up' to adulthood, a step up the evolutionary ladder as the missionaries saw it. And here the ambiguity and contradictions within the mission discourse become importunate: Spiritual equality is one thing, but economic, social and cultural equality is another. The missionaries' texts give no evidence of friendship, social equality or even economic partnership between white missionary and a black person. On the contrary, occasions when blacks are invited home to the missionary are so rare that the missionary takes good care to mention if they were allowed into the kitchen or the living room.

In the political and economic life of South Africa the languages of race and class are coming together more and more as the 20th century advances. In this reality, the missionary discourse and the struggle to create an image of the spiritually equal African, becomes increasingly weighed down by its own contradictions as the black demands for cultural, economic and political equality are persistently kept out of focus by the missionaries.

References

Cott, Nancy F., 1977, *The Bonds of Womanhood: "Woman's Sphere" in New England, 1780–1835*. New Haven/London: Yale University Press.

Dahle, Lars, 1923, *Tilbakeblik paa mit liv- og særlig paa mit missionsliv. Bind 3: Fra min avreise fra Madagaskar 1887 indtil min avsked, mars 1920*. Stavanger: Det norske missionsselskaps trykkeri.

Doty, Lynn Roxanne, 1996, *Imperial Encounters. The Politics of Representation in North-South Relations*. Minneapolis/London: University of Minesota Press.

Hall, Catherine and Leonore Davidoff, 1987, *Family Fortunes. Men and women of the English middle class, 1780–1850*. Chicago: University of Chicago Press.

Hall, Catherine, 1992, *White, male and middle class. Explorations in Feminism and History*. Cambridge: Polity.

Hall, Stuart (ed.), 1997, *Representation. Cultural Representations and Signifying Practices*. London: Sage in association with the Open University.

Mellemsether, Hanna, 1995, *Kvinne i to verdener. En kulturhistorisk analyse av afrikamisjonæren Martha Sannes liv i perioden 1884–1901*. Skriftserie 1/95 Senter for Kvinneforskning, Trondheim.

Mikaelsson, Lisbeth, 1992, "Kvinner, kall og skrift, belyst ved livsskildringer av kvinnelige misjonærer", in *Kjønnsidentitet, utvikling og konstruksjon av kjønn*. Skriftserie 1/92. Senter for Kvinneforskning, Trondheim.

Mills, Sara, 1991, *Discourses of difference. An analysis of women's travel writing and colonialism*. London: Routledge.

Nome, John, 1943, *Det norske misjonsselskap i hundre år*. Bind II: Det Norske Misjonsselskap i Norsk Kirkeliv, Fra syttiårene til Nåtiden. Stavanger.

Simensen, Jarle (ed.), 1984, *Norsk misjon og afrikanske samfunn. Sør-Afrika ca 1850–1900*. Trondheim: Tapir.

—, 1996, "The Image of Africa in Norwegian Missionary Opinion, 1850–1900", in Rian, Ø. et al. (eds), *Revolusjon og resonnement*. Oslo.

Smith-Rosenberg, Carroll, 1985, "The Cross and The Pedestal", in *Disorderly Conduct: Visions of Gender in Victorian America*. New York: A.A. Knopf.

Encounter Images in the Meetings
between Finland and South-West Africa/Namibia

Raisa Simola

One could imagine that if someone writes about Africa today, (s)he does not make the same mistakes as earlier writers did since the accumulation of information about Africa is much larger now than it was in the past. One could imagine that the black-and-white attitude of colonialism, the Manichean aesthetics made famous by JanMohamed,[1] is no longer valid. Or in Edward Said's words:

> ... whereas Conrad wrote *Nostromo* during a period of Europe's largely uncontested imperialist enthusiasm, contemporary novelists and filmmakers who have learned his ironies so well have done their work *after* decolonization, *after* the massive intellectual, moral, and imaginative overhaul and deconstruction of Western representation of the non-Western world, *after* the work of Frantz Fanon, Amilcar Cabral, C.L.R. James, Walter Rodney, *after* the novels and plays of Chinua Achebe, Ngugi wa Thiong'o, Wole Soyinka, Salman Rushdie, Gabriel Garcia Marquez, and many others.[2]

Unfortunately, however, by and large it is as if these books had never been published: according to Said, many contemporary novelists and filmmakers just continue the old tradition of cultural imperialism. But we Finns have never colonized Third World countries like, for example, Britain, France or America—Said's example countries—have done; consequently, shouldn't our encounter images in the meetings between Finland and Namibia/South-West Africa, for example, be sounder? The work that I'll place under scrutiny here is *Kotimaata kohden* by Esra Elovainio,[3] written and illustrated by Martti Pentti, published by the Finnish Missionary Society in 1993. However, before that I will talk briefly about the early missionary and scholarly work on Namibia.[4]

Namibian research

The Finns have been pioneers in Namibian[5] research. The Finnish Missionary Society that was founded in 1859, chose as its target area the former Ovam-

---

[1] JanMohamed, 1983.
[2] Said, 1994:xix–xx.
[3] ["Towards the Homeland"].
[4] This will be based mainly on Seppo Rytkönen's article "Suomalaiset Namibiaa tutkimassa" (Rytkönen, 1994:117–29).
[5] From now onwards, I will use the word "Namibia" both as a geographical area and a state; however, the word "South-West Africa" is used only in its historical meaning of a colony.

boland, the northern part of Namibia. The impulse to that choice was given by the Rhenish Missionary Society which concentrated its own work in Hereroland and Namaland, the central and southern parts of Namibia. The very first Finnish missionaries who arrived in Ovamboland in 1870,[6] participated in research on the Ovambo languages and cultures. The main aim was to translate and produce religious literature. Martti Rautanen, the grand old man of Finnish missionary work, translated *The New Testament* in 1893 and the whole *Bible* in 1924 into the Ndonga language. The Finnish missionaries were also the first to describe and research the people and cultures of Northern Namibia; among them was Martti Rautanen. We shall also mention Pietari Kurvinen's *Seitsemän ensimmäistä vuotta lähetyssaarnaajana eli iloja ja suruja Afrikasta* (1877–1889).[7] Again, among those Finnish missionaries who started to collect and study Ovambo folklore was Martti Rautanen. Further, we have to mention August Penttinen and Emil Liljeblad who collected Ovambo prayers, incantations, fairy tales, myths, riddles and proverbs. Later Matti Kuusi, using the existing collections, published his well-known books *Ovambo Proverbs with African Parallels* (1970) and *Ovambo Riddles: With Comments and Vocabularies* (1974).

The international research on Namibian history is quite young. Its beginning was in colonialist history writing, according to which the history of Namibia started when the colony was occupied.[8] In addition, it was emphasized that violence and struggles between the "tribes" were characteristic of precolonial Namibia. Later, anticolonial and Marxist explanations appeared.[9] For example, Heinrich Loth's study of 1963 dealt with the struggles of the Namibian people under the leadership of Jonker Afrikaner against centralized state building, and the resistance to the Europeans who were led by the Rhenish Missionary Society. Horst Drechsler for his part emphasized the brave struggle of the Namibian people against the German colonizer. He also pointed out how the German colonizers systematically took the land and cattle from the Hereros and the Namas, especially in 1893–1902. The work was based on original sources but it concentrated on the central and southern parts of Namibia. Interest in the history of precolonial Namibia as well as Namibia's oral tradition has arisen in the 1970s and has grown since.[10]

While it is quite common that there are no literary sources available written by Africans, the historical research work has been based on the sources

---

[6] Six of them were missionaries: Botolf Bernhard Björklund, Pietari Kurvinen, Martti Rautanen, Karl Leonard Tolonen, Karl August Weikkolin and Karl Emanuel Jurvelin; three were laymen, craftsmen: Juho Heinonen, Erkki Juntunen and Antti Piirainen.

[7] ["The Seven First Years as a Missionary or Joys and Sorrows in Africa"]

[8] Heinrich Vedder's work *Das alte Südwestafrika. Südwestafrikas Geschichte bis zum Tode Mahareros 1890* was the first important work concerning Namibian history. It was published in 1934 in Berlin. (Vedder, 1934).

[9] See First, 1963; Loth, 1963 and Drechsler, 1966.

[10] See for example Williams, 1991.

written by outsiders, mainly Europeans. The European settlement and German colonial economy from the beginning was concentrated in the middle and southern parts of present-day Namibia. Further, while the eurocentric history writing was interested in the European activities in Africa, it is clear that the northern part of Namibia that was outside German colony was not in the focus of scholarly interest either. It is here that the first Finnish missionaries arrived in 1870. It is from these times that the Finnish Missionary Society has continuous literary material concerning Ovamboland. The peculiarity of that part of Africa for the Finns lies in the fact that the Finns were the first European settlers in North Namibia and the first to write about that area as well. All in all, the Finnish research work on Ovamboland comprises a chapter of its own in the historiography of Namibia.[11]

The fictive story

The booklet *Kotimaata kohden* by Martti Pentti, which is in strip-cartoon form, consists of 50 pages. On each page there are generally fourteen picture-texts. Thus, the publication consists of about 700 picture-texts. The main protagonist is already mentioned in the title of the book: Esra Elovainio. He is a Finnish missionary. He and his family—Esteri Elovainio, his wife, and Esa, their little baby—are in the center of the story. Another family living on the same small missionary station in Africa also consists of three members: Johannes and Martta (Marjatta) Huttunen and their little baby Hilja, who is born at the beginning of the story.

The story starts with descriptions of life around the missionary station. After the small hospital has been built, Esra leaves with Abraham for the town called Bromvoel to buy medicine. He also fetches mail that has come from home. One message comes from the Missionary Society in Finland, and it invites Esra home on vacation. Now, Martta and Johannes have to take on the tasks and duties of Esteri and Esra, who start their long and exciting journey home. Meanwhile, the experiences of Martta and Johannes in their new roles are related. Esra and Esteri are welcomed by the Finnish Missionary Society, and they meet Esra's relatives. Esra describes his experiences in Africa to the Finnish congregations as well as to Finnish schoolboys. Meanwhile, a new young couple, Hilma and Semi Saastamoinen, whom the Elovainios have met on their way back to Finland, have arrived in Kashona, and start learning the native language. Semi has brought a little printing machine with him. Johannes and Martta face a new challenge when an African comes and asks for their help in the village of Ombambo where there is "a lot of illness and igno-

---

[11] Besides Finnish research works, the only scholarly study on North Namibian history is the dissertation by the South African historian E.L.P. Stals (1969). Before Stals, the Finnish missionary Erkki Lauermaa had published the first Ovambo history in the Ndonga language (Lauermaa, 1949). Another Finnish scholarly work on the Ovambos is Peltola, 1958. Later Finnish academic studies: Eirola, 1992; Salokoski, 1992 and Siiskonen, 1990.

Theme 1. *"All the blacks look the same"*

– Has anybody heard from Esra, I wonder if he is alive?
– Yes, when they go abroad you never know.
– But I heard from Kakombo that a letter had arrived ...

– And then our choir sings to the honor of brother Esra and sister Ester.

rance". Johannes writes to Esra that the Huttunens would like to build a "Lord's House" and a small missionary station in the Ombambo area but in this case, the Elovainios would be needed in Kashona. The Elovainios are ready to go back; everything only depends on the board of the Finnish Missionary Society. While Johannes baptizes Saara (earlier: Kalimba), the previous nanny of the Huttunens in Kashona, the Elovainios start their journey back to them, back to Africa. In addition, Saara and Abraham decide not only to step into a Christian marriage but Saara wants to become a nurse and Abraham a teacher.

"Kashonaland" is fictive; however, in the first picture it is stated that the place is "somewhere in Africa". Most evidently this "somewhere" is the former Ovamboland in the earlier South-West Africa. The signs are many: the dry savannahs, the isolation of the missionary station, the apartheid system of the nearest (fictive) town Bromvoel, the silhouette of another town on the Atlantic ocean where the characters board a ship to leave for Finland,[12] the

[12] The silhouette of the fictive town reminds one of the Namibian town of Swakopmund. Oral observation was supplied by Harri Siiskonen, 25.9.1996.

existence of the "Hottentots" and "Bushmen" in the area, and of course, the dominance of the Finnish missionary people in that area. Further evidence may be found outside the text: Martti Pentti, the writer and illustrator of the book, has had family members working in Ovamboland.

Just as the setting of the story has been made "vague", this is also the case with the timing of the story: the years of the events are never mentioned. Again, however, it is possible to determine the appropriate time setting. For example, the ox wagons, steam and sailing boats, gradually expanding mission work, modest missionary buildings, acquiring the first printing-machine,[13] crowds of "pagans" and the whole pioneering atmosphere are signs of the "old times", perhaps the beginning of the 20th century. The exact timing is not important, but one detail is: the book, which was published in 1993 and which is, at least among Finnish missionary people, quite popular,[14] is set in those old pioneering times. We return to this fact later.

Descriptions of whites and blacks

It is significant that the description of the whites and the blacks in *Kotimaata kohden* is different. The whites are in the limelight; and they are seen in more nuanced terms than the blacks. Our three perspectives on the issue are: naming, appearance, and character traits.

All the whites (eight) that live in Kashonaland are given names in the story, even the two little babies. Although the eight white people live among the entire Kashona people, only a few of these are given names and extended descriptions. Shimbungu the Witch and his son Kakombo are the most important black persons for the missionaries in Kashonaland: the former is their biggest enemy and the latter their greatest black helper at the missionary station. Shimbungu's wife and baby are shown once but their names are never mentioned. Kalimba is the black girl who becomes the nanny for the Huttunens' little child. In the story, space is given to Kalimba's connections with the white missionaries but not to her connections with her own family: Kalimba's family members are neither shown nor mentioned. The guide of the Ombambo village, who takes Martta and Johannes Huttunen to his village, is shown in several pictures but is never given a name.

The writer is careless in his use of the words "people" and "tribe" since he uses the expressions "Kashona people" and "Kashona tribe" interchangeably. Also, he talks about the "Hottentots" and "Bushmen" instead of the Khoi-Khois and the Sans. He uses the Finnish expression "poppamies" which is a Tarzanist name for the witchdoctor.

---

[13] *Osondaha*, the first Christian journal has continued to appear since the early 1900s. Information provided by Harri Siiskonen.

[14] Information provided by the bookshop of the Finnish Missionary Society, Helsinki, in spring 1996.

The features of the whites are illustrated as more nuanced than those of the blacks. In fact, it is difficult to see differences in the faces of Kakombo, Kalimba and the Ombambo guide. The small differences in the heads of the black characters are shown in the hairstyles. It is conspicuous that the shape of the heads of the blacks is almost without exception round. Coincidence or not, but the shape of the heads of white people is typically not round—except the heads of the little children. The similarity in outlook of blacks and white children may hint at the childlike mental skills of the blacks. In addition, the 'similar look' of the blacks is underlined in the group pictures. We may compare that even as members of a group, the whites have recognizably different features from each other. (See the pictures.)

In *Kotimaata kohden*, the character traits of the whites are more varied than those of the blacks. Esra, Esteri, Martta and Johannes are all personalities. The whites are described on several occasions in their everyday life, solving many little problems when spreading Christianity and Western education among the natives. The natives are shown on fewer occasions, and hardly in any other contexts than those of learning to read, adopting the new religion, and helping the missionaries. Kakombo and Kalimba and the Chief, Matako, become the individualized converts. Their conversions are mentioned very briefly: "Little Esa is looked after by Abraham, earlier called Kakombo, the industrious son of Shimbungu the Witch. He adopted his new name along with his new religion." It is also briefly mentioned that Kalimba has taken the name of Saara when being converted. The conversion of Chief Matako is then disclosed on the last page of the story: he drinks coffee (a sign of adopting Finnish culture!) with Esteri Elovainio and lets Shimbungu the Witch know that he has moved over to the other side and Shimbungu is now alone with his "pagan" thoughts. The implication of this evidence of the conversions is clear: Christianity wins since it is The Religion.

However, Shimbungu the Witch is different from all the other people. His language is humorous in its concreteness: "Leijonan leukaperät sentään!" [Oh, the jaws of a lion!]; "Puhvelin pusku sentään!" [Oh, the butting of a buffalo!]. In addition, his inability to understand the biblical and abstract language of the missionaries makes him funny if not ridiculous. But most important: his appearance is mean and evil and his thoughts and acts are even worse. In fact, the Manichean aesthetics of the booklet is seen most clearly in the contrast between Christianity and the "paganism" embodied by Shimbungu. There are situations where Shimbungu's bad thoughts and Esra's good thoughts clash with each other, and the innocent missionary wins. Shimbungu's evil at its extreme is shown when he uses black magic on Esra Elovainio; and Shimbungu's superstitiousness is shown in the situation when Esra falls ill—from mosquito bites—and Shimbungu believes that the cause has been his black magic. In addition, while the fearless missionaries present the model of fearlessness to the natives, Shimbungu's aim is to use fear as a method of subjugating the natives to his will. The defeat of his world view is most evident at the end of the story. Indeed he is a manifold loser: he has totally lost his son Abraham (previously Kakombo) to the Western religion and civilization; and even Chief Matako has given up supporting his views. The previously powerful witch has lost most of his power to the Christians.

Politics of whites and blacks

The white missionaries live in the isolation of Kashonaland, and it is evident that they are almost completely indifferent to the politics around them. Apartheid prevails no further than in the near-by town. The violent nature of the military people in the service of apartheid is presented; however,

Theme 2. *The bad character of the story: A witch and pagan*

the main reason for this motif in the booklet seems to be that it makes the story more exciting, and shows the power of fearless and non-violent Christian behavior. The soldiers of apartheid lay down their guns after having realized that Esra and Abraham are not armed; and these may safely go about their business. After Esra and Abraham have returned to Kashonaland, they do not consider it worthwhile to debate the apartheid system, even less taking some positive action against it. On the ship heading towards their homeland several people with colonialist and racist views present their ideas in Esra's and Esteri's presence. When a white man says: "The most important thing is that they keep our tea plantations productive", Esteri is sitting close to him and just smiles pleasantly. Esra, when asked to tell about "your funny Kashonas", does not feel hurt by the patronizing expression referring to his friends, nor does he react against it. Instead, he answers using a biblical phrase: (in Kashonaland) he has come across both "righteous" and "godless" people.

Yet another politically sensitive occasion is shown, when Esra rescues a considerable number of people. The "Hottentots" stop the train and threaten the passengers with their guns, but Esra fearlessly walks towards the armed "rebels" and solves the predicament—simply by talking with the attackers. The scene deserves to be looked at more closely. Esra says: "Don't trust in violence, don't put your hopes in stolen things." The "Hottentot" answers: "You could read that to those of your people who have taken our cattle, our pastures and everything. And now as the last nuisance we have got that smoking eyesore which drinks all the water from our last cattle's well." And—lo and behold—the very same evening a well is built at the nearby railway station for the "tribe". The implication of the text is that the "Hottentots" are happy now and the whole political issue raised by the "Hottentot" has been solved, thanks to Esra's wisdom.

Manichean world view

It's worth at this point comparing *Kotimaata kohden* with Chinua Achebe's *Things Fall Apart*: Chinua Achebe's most famous novel, *Things Fall Apart*, appeared as long ago as 1958. He describes the influence of the first Christians on some of the Igbo societies. The image he gives is not black-and-white. The Christian missionaries have a good influence on Igbo society in eradicating some of the cruel customs of traditional Igbo society. In addition, one of the two missionaries in the novel is willing to learn to understand the rich traditional religion. There is a theological discussion between Mr. Brown, the white missionary, and a black man. *Kotimaata kohden* is a complete contrast. The metaphysical world of the natives is never discussed—except the evil of black magic. The following quotation is illuminating: "The feared Shimbungu the Witch and our missionary friend Esra Elovainio get to the point and discuss profound questions. But Shimbungu does not seem to find any meaning in the answers." The missionary is wise; the native who does not understand his discourse is stupid. The missionaries have religion; the natives have only superstitions. On the other hand, in *Things Fall Apart*, the white missionaries are shown as having a bad influence on traditional Igbo society. In fact, they are part of the colonial project, part of cultural imperialism. *Kotimaata kohden* is a very different book. The missionaries impose Western culture— for example names, dress, hairstyles, music—on the natives; but the self-premise of this cultural mission is never questioned. And world politics seem to be beyond the frontiers of Kashonaland: the missionaries are presented as totally independent not only of apartheid but of the colonial project as well.

The world view of *Kotimaata kohden* is Manichean: Europe is civilized and Christian, while the Ovambos are pagan and uncivilized. Thus, Ovamboland has to be Christianized and civilized. It is as if times had not changed much for Martti Pentti, the narrator-writer, since Rudyard Kipling wrote in 1899:

> Take up the white man's burden
>   Send forth the best ye breed
> Go, bind your sons to exile
>   To serve your captives' need ...[15]

The Finns who go to Ovamboland certainly carry the heavy burden of the white man; the missionaries, even if they have some minor weaknesses, belong to the "best breed" in their deep involvement in the missionary task. Even if the Finnish missionaries do not literally take the natives as their "captives", they take their minds into "captivity". A power-image is used several times in connection with the defeat of Shimbungu the Witch. And conversely, the nar-

---

[15] This is the first verse of Kipling's famous "White man's burden", Rudyard Kipling, *Times*, 4 February 1899.

Theme 3. *The white people are never quite alike—They alone have personalities*

–Our countrymen are at least good chaps or what do you think, dear?
–The main thing is that they keep the tea plantation profitable.

–The Lord does not allow even an old person to experience hunger but he does not
allow the lusts of the ungodly come near.

Our missionary Esra Elovainio has returned with his family from an exciting work
abroad to the Kashonaland savannah. The mission people celebrate in his honour.
Raakel, the aunt of Esra, concludes the celebration by a prayer with kneeling.

rator or the white missionaries never feel empathy with this man whose family links have been broken and who witnesses the falling apart of the world view of his community. The most interesting thing in the last line of Kipling's verse, however, is the combination of the "captives" and the servile attitude of the whites. There is no doubt that in *Kotimaata kohden* the missionaries feel superior to the natives: they feel righteous and that only they possess the truth; but their method of getting their ideas through induces them to take the role of servants. They themselves, or the narrator-writer do not see any connections between themselves and the imperialism Edward Said talks about. They just serve the natives' needs. However, in their "servile" attitude towards the natives and their struggle against the "spiritual evil only" the missionaries at the same time are part of the colonialist and imperialist project.

Why has Martti Pentti not told about the present-day missionary work, why has he chosen "those old times" instead? There may be at least two reasons. First, the work of pioneering missionaries is much more challenging as a topic, more exciting, and exotic, even more marketable. When Esra during his holiday in Finland visits a high school, he starts telling the boys about the nature in Africa, and in the course of his talk describes some exciting incidents. Whether he tells about anything else, too—that is left unsaid. But what is told—that fits perfectly into the tradition of the travelogue. So many writers have been interested in, not so much the culture of South-West Africa, but the natural surroundings: they have been interested in the Wild South West which has had to be tamed.[16] And when it concerned the (often superficially seen) culture of the indigenous people, this was to be "tamed" as well. Second, the Manichean world view with its enemy-images may in general influence the positive attitude of the wider Finnish public towards the Finnish missionary work. Indeed, perhaps the bad Shimbungu Witches serve even today as an impetus for Christian people to support missionary work.

When compared to the 1990s, the 1970s and 1980s almost witnessed a boom in writings on Africa by Finnish novelists.[17] Different as these novels of the 'boom' were, the emphasis in all of them was put on the white characters. And almost by implication: none of them concentrated, for example, on the political or cultural resistance of the struggles of the blacks. However, these writers were interested in Africa, and some of them certainly increased the awareness of Africa and its life and culture among the Finnish public. *Kotimaata kohden* is one of those very few fictive publications of the 1990s telling about the encounter of Finns and Africans, and indeed may reach a large audience—which are the major reasons why it has deserved attention here.

---

[16] See: Dorian Haarhoff, *The Wild South-West. Frontier myths and metaphors in literature set in Namibia, 1760–1988.* Witwatersrand University Press, Johannesburg, 1991.

[17] See Raisa Simola, "The Image of Africa in Fiction in Finnish", in T.G. Ramamurthi (ed.), Harish Narang (guest ed.), *Africa Quarterly*, Vol. 34, No. 3, 1994. Special issue. *Mightier than Machete*, Indian Council for Cultural Relations, New Delhi, India 1994, pp. 89–102.

Unfortunately, the image it offers is basically Manichean. Or, as an art teacher put it: "I did not like the overall tone of the book. It is a pity if it is meant for the children, since it certainly does not increase education in internationalism nor understanding between different cultures."[18]

References

Drechsler, Horst, 1966, *Südwestafrika unter deutscher Kolonialherrschaft. Der Kampf der Herero und Nama gegen den deutschen Imperialismus (1884–1915)*. Berlin.

Eirola, Martti, 1992, *The Ovambogefahr. The Ovamboland Reservation in the Making. Political Responses of the Kingdom of Ondonga to the German Colonial Power 1884–1910*. Rovaniemi.

First, Ruth, 1963, *South West Africa*. Harmondsworth.

Haarhoff, Dorian, 1991, *The Wild South-West. Frontier myths and metaphors in literature set in Namibia, 1760–1988*. Johannesburg: Witwatersrand University Press.

JanMohamed, Abdul R., 1983, *Manichean Aesthetics. The Politics of Literature in Colonial Africa*. Amherst: The University of Massachusetts Press.

Kipling, Rudyard, 1899, "The White Man's Burden", *The Times*, Feb. 4, 1899.

Lauermaa, Erkki, 1949, *Afrika ¡Uuningininomutenja*. Helsinki.

Loth, Heinrich, 1963, *Die christliche Mission in Südwestafrika. Zur destruktives Rolle der Rheinischen Missionsgesellschaft beim Prozess der Staatsbildung in Südwestafrika (1842–1893)*. Berlin.

Peltola, Matti, 1958, *Suomen lähetysseuran Afrikan työn historia. Sata vuotta suomalaista lähetystyötä 1859–1959, II*. Kuopio. [The History of African Work by the Finnish Missionary Society. One Hundred Years of Finnish Missionary Work 1859–1959, II].

Pentti, Martti, 1993, *Kotimaata kohden. Esra Elovainio*. Helsinki: Suomen Lähetysseura.

Rytkönen, Seppo, 1994, "Suomalaiset Namibiaa tutkimassa", in *Tieten tahtoen*, Studia Carelica Humanistica 3, Joensuun yliopiston humanistinen tiedekunta, Joensuun yliopiston monistuskeskus.

Said, Edward, 1994, *Culture and Imperialism*. New York: Vintage Books.

Salokoski, Märta, 1992, *Symbolic Power of Kings in Pre-colonial Ovambo Societies*. Lic. thesis, University of Helsinki.

Siiskonen, Harri, 1990, *Trade and Socioeconomic Change in Ovamboland, 1850-1906*. SHS, Helsinki. Serie: Studia historica (Helsinki); 35

Simola, Raisa, 1994, "The Image of Africa in Fiction in Finnish", in Ramamurthi, T.G. (ed.), Harish Narang (guest ed.), *Africa Quarterly*. Vol. 34, No. 3, pp. 89–102. Special issue. *Mightier than Machete*. Indian Council for Cultural Relations, New Delhi.

Stals, E.L.P., 1969, *Die Aanraking tussen Blankes en Ovambo's in Suidwes-Afrika, 1850–1915*. Johannesburg: Archives Year Book for South African History.

Vedder, Heinrich, 1934, *Das alte Südwestafrika. Südwestafrikas Geschichte bis zum Tode Mahareros 1890*. Berlin.

Williams, Frieda-Nela, 1991, *Precolonial Communities of Southwestern Africa. A History of Owambo Kingdoms 1600–1920*. Windhoek.

---

[18] Päivi Mähönen, University of Joensuu, Finland.

Monkey Business in the Congo

Nicolas Martin-Granel

To illustrate what I mean by "monkey-business" let me start with two anecdotes from the Congo. The first is about when I arrived in this country in 1990 and heard some white people say openly: "As soon as we go home they will climb the trees again". This shows that today's racism can even surpass the colonial stories of Conrad and Céline. The other anecdote shows how the racist image has been assimilated even by those who were victims of it. It is about the use of the "symbol". The writer Sony Labou Tansi tells us[1] that primary school teachers in the colonial days hung a tin of excrement around the neck of weak pupils who made errors in French or refused to speak this language, the sign of "evolution". But the "evolution" of independence has not managed to eliminate this infamous symbol. A young colleague at University told me that in his school they hung a monkey's skull around the neck of poor students—a "symbol" that could not be more symbolic.

Let us remember what the word "symbol" meant from the start. The ancient Greeks used the word "*symbolon*" to denote a piece of wood, which was divided into two when guest and host parted. Each kept his piece till they met again and could check that the pieces fitted together. The monkey skull serves as a sign of recognition of what has tied the white slave trader or coloniser to the black native in Central Africa. The native received the whites, often fighting for his life, and in return he got this symbol of inequality and racism. The wounds of this unfortunate confrontation are not healed, and the insult remains in the monkey symbol, a symbol, which does not, as in Greek, denote recognition and friendship, but ignorance and xenophobia.

I will give an example of how persistent this monkey syndrome is.[2] This is what Sony Labou Tansi said in 1987:[3]

> In Kinshasa they were made to believe that to be regarded as a human being you needed a certificate of development; it means that from that day you are like a white man. You were educated and had left the monkey stage (...) In the countryside those who cultivated the soil were monkeys. That is how it was. And those

---

[1] See my "Discourse de la honte", *Cahiers d'Études africaines*, 140, XXV–4, 1995, p. 764.

[2] A syndrome coming from the tradition of proverbs. It is said about egoists, for instance, that they "stick to their job as a monkey sticks to his fruit" (*La Rue meurt*, 63, 6/1/95). In the same magazine the same image is used about aged heads of state: "Lately, our aged leaders have had the misfortune to end up on the operating table (...) let us, friends, pray for these old men and ask them to stop playing the monkey dying with his fruit." (*La Rue meurt*, 151, 19/9/96).

[3] In a series of radio interviews with the journalist Apollinaire Singhou Basseha in "Voix de la Revolution Congolaise".

who came to town kept looking at themselves as developed and kept considering those who stayed in the village as monkeys.

This shows how colonial racism has been assimilated and imitated by "developed people", who reproduce the prejudices of their teachers. Non-urbanised social groups are denoted by the pejorative term "villagers", and since they do not speak French, their language is called "pidgin". But the author does not mince his words, and is not ashamed of calling things by their right names. Behind the words "villager" and "pidgin" he finds and reveals the primitive insult. The reproduction of the insulting metaphor now used about his brothers and even about himself, leads to what we might call "internalised racism".

Congo—cradle of the monkey-man

Africa is called, both in the South and the North, the cradle of humanity. This image has become a cliché, spread under the cover of science. Since the famous Lucy was discovered, archaeologists, anthropologists and palaeontologists have never stopped bending over this cradle, filling it with their findings and conflicts. Over their shoulders other people read the text about the origin of mankind and spread the good news about the transition from bestiality to humanity, from monkey to man.

With this transition the scientific popularisation creates a mythological vulgate. There is for instance the famous "missing link", giving substance to the mythical idea of a natural evolution, occurring without mutations, from animals to human beings. One might even say that the human species is mixed up with animals and restored to its original animal shape. This confusion is evident in scientific terminology: zoologists or primatologists are hardly separated from anthropologists or ethnologists.

This kind of confusion is promoted by the idea of the jungle as the primitive ecological niche. How could one separate the primates from men in the shades of the deep wild forest? That is the law of the jungle, where all are alternately hunter and game.

A whole literature from the North, with its ecological concerns and racist prejudices, is bending over the African cradle of humanity. But sometimes these two ideological frames are superimposed on each other, like in the following short text, certainly not literary, but offering a symptomatic digest of the stereotypes on which literature thrives.

It is an advertisement for Toyota cars, which was published some years ago in French weeklies. What you see first is not, as could have been expected, the image of Japanese technology, but a group of zebras, a safari cliché. The subtitle is a pastiche of oral traditional tales: "Here are the zebras, who saw the lion, who saw the man, who had a Toyota". Then comes the story of this man, a legendary martyr of ecology:

But the Toyota man is a game-keeper in the Maasai Mara reserve in Kenya. He knows that if things go on like this, there will soon be no more to see in the beautiful reserves in Africa. Elephants, rhinos, gorillas are disappearing. ... And soon, if we do not take care, tens of species will only be found in encyclopedias as "extinct".

The Toyota man tracks down poachers who deal with ivory and other trophies; he is risking his life, for the ethnologists and gamekeepers who have been murdered by these traffickers are countless. The Toyota man knows all about the fauna he is set to protect and about the reserve and the Maasai living there.

This defence of the natural heritage is somewhat surprising, meant to promote polluting machines, manufactured in a country, renowned for its huge imports of ivory. But even more disturbing is the use of "ethnologists" with reference to the fauna. It may be an error of writing or translation, but it reveals a remarkable confusion and raises a crucial question—whatever are these ethnologists doing among the zebras? Studying gorillas as an ethnic group? Unless the gamekeepers keep an eye on the Maasai, a species at risk of disappearing like the other animals in the reserve? No doubt the word "reserve" causes the same difficulty in distinguishing between animals and human beings as between natural and social sciences. The Toyota man seems to know all about animals and human beings and feels at home both with ethologists and ethnologists.

This advertisement can thus be seen as an exemplary fable. The ideo-ecological tree conceals the forest with its diverse species of trees or animals, and even the forest inhabited by men of equally diverse cultures. Zoophilia, the infantile disease of ecologism, mixes up all these forests into one unique and mythical place—inferno or paradise—at the same time cradle and grave for the subhuman or superhuman animal. This forest could just as well be that of the Congo, the Maasai then being replaced by the Pygmies.

The forest that hides the monkey

Let us first remember that the word "forest", i.e. the King's own forest, comes from medieval Latin. Originally it denoted a hunting area, or "a vast, deserted area, where wild animals breed". Man ventures there only to live "as a creature of nature".[4]

But the "great medieval theme of the savage man" reappears today, and this reappearance occurs in Africa, the last primitive place still existing to Westerners. Where are the ancient forests, if not in the heart of Africa? More exactly in the Congo even though this Congo does not correspond to any precise geographical entity and only exists in the "psychological topography" of

---

[4] Quoted from J. Le Goff, "Le Désert-Forêt dans l'Occident Médiéval", *Traverses*, Minuit, 1980, pp. 23–33.

the explorer. The Congolese forest forms a vague whole whose contours seem to be drawn in the colours of dream and adventure.

It is in the first place a *terra incognita*, a kind of African Amazonas, represented on 19th century maps of Africa by a white spot. Or else it is black, the local colour, which stands out naturally as a generalisation! This is suggested in the introduction to Michael Crichton's novel *Congo* (p. 9): "In fact, Africa is called the black continent for one single reason: the vast humid equatorial forests of its central part". Later, the author explains that what the ancient Egyptians called the Land of the Trees was "a mysterious place, covered by forests, so thick that in broad daylight it was as dark as at night.[5] Strange creatures lived in the eternal obscurity, including little men provided with tails and half black, half white animals". Here, one can sense all the romantic mystery of the name of the Congo, beyond the sober geographical title, as the author emphasises: "In fact, in 1979, the word Congo denoted technically the hydrographic system of the river Zaire, which was however still called the Congo by the geologists, for reasons of familiarity but also because of its romantic connotation". We shall see later how the Congo was made into a novel, and a film.[6]

However, travel books may also depict the real Congo in more realistic colours. The country is neither white, nor black; it takes its natural green colour, as ecology demands. The author of the book *Au Congo jusqu'au cou*, Patrice Franceschi, writes:

> Having been fascinated for a long time by "green spots" in general, and those of Central Africa in particular, I decided towards the end of 1974 to launch an expedition with three of my old friends from Africa into the least known region of Northern Congo. (p. 9)

This book has an intriguing title: "Up to the Neck in the Congo", as it reads in English translation. The further presentation on the cover is equally fascinating, in its journalistic grandiloquence: "The Babinga-Pongo Expedition (June–October 1975), or the Initiatory and Exceptional Adventures of Four Frenchmen of 20 among the Pygmies in the Equatorial Forest".

However young, this modern adventurer discovers nothing new; he follows the medieval novel whose trails lead to the repelling, yet alluring heart of the forest, to "these far off places where man meets adventure and other men—even wild men that he at first sees as animals but who contend that they are human beings". This is doubtless why, as Francheschi naïvely explains,

---

[5] No doubt this black mythology is the origin of the title of Joseph Conrad's novel *The Heart of Darkness*, maybe even Céline: *Voyage au bout de la nuit*, at least where its African episode is concerned.

[6] Talking of romantic films, one must also remember Coppola's interpretation of *The Heart of Darkness* in *Apocalypse Now*, as well as *Poto-Poto* (Pygmalion, 1991), a novel written as a film scenario for Erich von Stroheim—both works using the image of the forest as a green inferno.

"the expedition was soon called Babinga-Pongo (Babinga=Pygmy, Pongo= fight, survive, but also the word for gorilla)" (p. 10). Let us for a while ignore this play on words, which is designed to make us doubt the humanity of the Pygmies, who are compared, according to the law of the jungle, to apes. We shall return to this important detail, but let us now go back to the young explorers, as can be expected, lost in the forests of the Congo.

This forest does not always have the same beautiful green colour as it had on the map. It is a forest, changing colours like a chameleon according to the moods of the beholder. At first, "we discovered a whole universe of nuances, ranging from wonderful to revolting" (p. 112). Nature is fine when it can be kept at a distance and be described in clichés: "a display of trees, creepers, roots, flowers. A huge fresco, of a shimmering green which assumes all the nuances the mind can imagine" (p. 95). The forest is just as wonderful as the smile of the Pygmies, "tinged with naïvety and innocence", and so much the more wonderful in the eyes of the traveller, who thinks of "all those who would have liked to travel and maybe this instant are bumping into each other in the subway like pale and busy ants" (p. 57). But as soon as the real ants of the forest enter the scene, darker colours take over: "the jungle is not a hell because of the big animals. Hell, that is the insects, thousands of tiny and voracious insects, who sneak into everything and force one into a constant fight, day and night, all the way to obsession" (p. 94). Céline had already spoken of this obsession of the voracious ants with a literary feeling we can share. But here, in *Up to the Neck in the Congo*, the jungle is conjured up as hell for the white man, and never leaves the stereotypes and metaphors: "immense dark cave" (p. 206), "obscure cave with thousands of deceitful and treacherous ramifications" (p. 207), "Dantesque universe" (p. 213), etc.

The travel book, like fiction, does not escape the basic myth of the deep Congo. This myth has a double origin, literary and colonial, going back to Conrad as well as Stanley. The author goes up the river from the Atlantic coast, while the journalist-explorer comes from the east. The Congo basin is somehow encircled by a pincer movement from two sides, the east and the west, by these two fathers of occidental exploration. One has to follow their footsteps; the routes they cleared for the first time are to be used by future travellers from the North, whether they are journalists, writers, religious or scientific missionaries, or even characters in books, and sometimes all of them at the same time. Gide and Naipaul in their travel notes recall Conrad,[7] while Lennart Hagerfors, a Swedish writer, who spent his childhood in the Congo, uses Stanley as main character of his novel, *The Whales of Lake Tanganyika*.

---

[7] Even the name is enough to transmit, from one traveller to the other, a mythical aura to the journey: "Conrad! I shiver when I read, in André Gide's words, that he crossed the same mountains on foot in 1890 as my train is climbing and that he describes in all their horror in his Heart of Darkness. (Philippe de Baleine, *Voyage espiègle et romanesque dans le petit train du Congo*, Presses Pocket, 1993, p. 20.)

The two roads to the interior cross each other in Graham Greene's works:[8] a well-known artist goes up the river to bury his fame "in the heart of darkness", while in the other direction, an unscrupulous journalist comes to suffuse the river with the false light of the colonial cliché: "the eternal forest lies dormant along the river banks where nothing has changed since Stanley and his little troop [...]". The journalistic cliché melts all forests into one, inevitably African, unavoidably Congolese.

This monochromatic vision of the forest leads us to the two branches of the African Amazonas, which serve as backgrounds to two contemporary novels, *Congo* by Michael Crichton, and *Brazzaville Beach* by William Boyd.[9] Crichton approaches the forest from the east and thus gives us a version marked by the first steps of the white conquistador Stanley; Boyd's forest is close to the Atlantic coast and has an atmosphere of Conrad's "return to the first ages of humanity". But their titles place them in the same imaginary land, a Congo without borders, where night merges with day, Maasai with Pygmy, man with monkey, even the gorilla with the chimpanzee.

The monkey, man's hidden face

Like Nature, the forest hates emptiness and the romantic forest even more so, since it needs characters to move in its monotonous scenery. Gide's butterflies are too ephemeral, Francheschi's Pygmies give too much an impression of being "animals in the Zoo" (p. 58). The monkey is obviously best placed to imitate—one might even say "ape"—what men normally do in novels (kill, let themselves be killed, love or hate ...); so he will play the leading rôle in the forest. Apart from the fact that he, as a native, is the most likely inhabitant, he also has old and convincing merits for the rôle. Before we try to find out for what functions our two novels have recruited gorillas and chimpanzees, it would be proper to remember that they just return to their service.

The first travel book from Africa mentioning men/monkeys goes back to Greek antiquity. It is the famous *Hanno Periplus*, Hanno's Travels, in which a modern commentator[10] sees "the model exploration, punctuated by the linear time concept of the great voyages, governed by the subtle change from exotic alienation to the shock of absolute otherness". The maximum of strangeness in this fantastic story is found at the end of the journey:

> During three days from there, we sailed near raging currents. We arrived at a bay called the Southern Horn. Deep in there was an island, similar to the previous

---

[8] *La saison des pluies*, Presses Pocket, 1960 [*The Rainy Season*].

[9] Published in French as Michael Crichton, *Congo*, 1995, Paris: Editions Magazine/Pocket, and William Boyd, *Brazzaville-Plage*, Paris: Le Seuil, 1991. The references in this text are to the French translations.

[10] Christian Jacob, "Aux confins de l'humanité: peuples et paysages africains dans *le Périple d'Hannon*", *Cahiers d'Études africaines*, 121–22, 1991, pp. 9–27.

one, with a lake, inside which was another island, full of savages. The women were most numerous. Their bodies were hairy and the interpreters called them Gorillas'.

Three short notes on these Gorillas.
– The text looks at them not as animals but as human beings of the female sex, just like another mythical tribe, the Amazons.
– The adjective "hairy", referring to an abnormal hairiness of their bodies, is the same word in Greek as is used for thick forests.
– The word "gorilla" is not found anywhere else, except in this text. This is probably an error by the copyist, writing "Gorillas" in stead of "Gorgadas", i.e. "Gorgons", other monstrous creatures of Greek mythology: "A very old tradition places the abode of the Gorgons and the place where Perseus met Medusa in the south west of Africa."

But myths, constituting the "mythical scenery" of the modern novel, lead a hard life. It is therefore not difficult to recognise Medusa, the first of the Gorgons, in the story Crichton tells us in *Congo*. Only the means and the weapons have been changed: the modern Perseuses are men of science—if only science fiction—and they defend themselves with the most sophisticated weapons against the new Medusas, creatures who are so much more terrifying as science, in spite of computers, cannot identify them and has to use the ancient name for them in the term "gorilla-like":

> This is why the expedition developed differently, that is into an even more dangerous situation. His first movement of renouncement disappeared when he remembered the video screen and the grey "gorilla-like" thing, which he thought of as a new, unknown animal. (p. 196)

After twenty centuries (Hanno's voyage is from the first century BC) the same thing is repeated, in the desire to explore "the limits of humanity". Before we get to the latest cases, I would like to mention intermediate variations on the theme man/monkey. The first, from the colonial era, is a short story published in Brussels, in 1900. The principal character, Gim, arrived in Europe "in his twelfth year, without identity papers, but with his little red heart, his black animal heart". The rest is as openly racist:

> This rare trinket, this flower of exotic flesh, a thing between monkey and man. (...) funny little beast, from a country where humanity ended, where the distinction between man and monkey was so slight that it was not worth speaking of.[11]

Let us speak no more of this. The second example is more ambiguous, for in its Rousseau-like tone it recalls "the fashionable savage" and starts a primi-

---

[11] Quoted by Marc Quaghebeur, "Texts from darkness", *Papier blanc, encre noire*, Bruxelles: Labor, 1992, pp. VII–XCIV.

tivist and ecological movement before it even existed. This is what Gide wrote in 1914[12] (*Les caves du Vatican*), where Lafcadio says:

> On the run towards a new world: let us leave Europe. ... If there is still in Borneo, in the deep forests, a surviving anthropopithecus, let us calculate down there what future a possible humanity has.

Gide is thus the forerunner of a literature we might call anthropopithecological. Moreover, he adopts as a travelling companion in the Congo a little monkey, called Dindiki, whose death is to become an absolute tragedy for him.

As for Stanley, in Hagerfors' *Les baleines du lac Tanganyika*, the monkey is the double metaphor of the white man having finally lost his arrogant conquering capacity. This is what happens to Shaw, the narrator, whom Stanley recruited for his expedition and whom he blames for losing his dignity as a "civilised" man:

> –Africa has worn you out, Shaw ... you have not fulfilled your mission. You have not conquered a continent, it has conquered you; it has taken your body and your mind.
> –Yes, I am finally lost. (p. 169)

This human rag, half mad and near complete "decivilisation",[13] can easily see the metamorphosis Livingstone had been subjected to:

> The young men supported an old man who looked like a chimpanzee. His legs were bent and skinny, his arms thin as if they had been drawn out. His hair and beard were grey and shaggy, his mouth opened and closed without a sound. (...)
> One of the Arab boys took the right arm of the old man and made him stretch out a hand which looked like a claw. Stanley took it between his two hands, fell to his knees, kissed the claw-like paw and pressed it to his cheek, crying.
> Stanley got back to his feet, slowly.
> –Doctor Livingstone, I presume.
> The old man burst into laughter, it sounded like barking, but panicked immediately. Stanley laid the stiff and apelike arm of the old man around his shoulder and led him back to his hut. (p. 187)

In this negative vision, which goes against the historical anecdote, hierarchies are reversed: superman becomes sub-human, the hero becomes a monkey. Even the great Stanley does not escape transformation into an animal, which is the law of the jungle. And when his rifle misses its target and the game slips away, the narrator notes: "I think this was the first time he was ashamed of not being an animal". But the monkeys are about to become human:

---

[12] André Gide, *Les caves du Vatican*, Paris: Gallimard Folio, 1999, p. 188.
[13] To use the name ("decivilisation" novel) as Pierre Halen (*Le petit Belge avait vu grand. Une littérature coloniale.* Bruxelles, Editions Labor/Archives et Musée de la littérature, 1993) calls this sub-genre of the colonial literature, whose prototypes were the "African" novels of Conrad and Céline.

> The monkeys have something of Stanley. They will always exaggerate. As soon as they see us, they start to howl about the decline of the world and the fall of the celestial bodies. (p. 178)

It is exactly this paradoxical ascent of monkey towards man that fascinates some of the novels and stories published in recent years. Let us just recall two novels from the eighties, which certainly do not place the monkeys in the Congo, but which use a theme exploited more fully in the "depth of the Congo"[14] by our two "Congolese" novels.

In *White Spirit*[15] the action takes place somewhere in Africa, on a banana plantation; the author introduces "three innocent characters" one of whom is Alexis, the chimpanzee. The note overleaf says about him that "he does not know he is a monkey".

The same year as the French translation of *The Whales of Lake Tanganyika* (original in Swedish: Valarna i Tanganyikasjön), Michel Rio's admirable novel, *Les Jungles Pensives*,[16] was published in France. Part of the summary on the cover is enough for our purpose:

> Africa 1913. A young biologist (the narrator) disembarks in the Ivory Coast to lead a scientific expedition whose mission is to study the behaviour of the chimpanzees in their environment. (...)
> Europe 1914. The elite of the superior species has declared a war of extermination on itself. The narrator, having left the comprehensible savagery of nature, enters the boundless savagery of civilisation. From an observer he is made into the toy of History. The murder, cleverly planned, is never-ending. No wonder the jungles are pensive.

Thus, between the supposedly "savage monkey" and "civilised man" a parallel is drawn, from which ethical, philosophical and scientific thoughts are fed into the novels. The most obvious result of this change of perspective is that the border between the human species and the monkey is confused.

In *Au Congo jusqu'au cou*, where the reflections on the man/monkey theme never go beyond the naive stereotypes we normally meet in travel books,[17] the young explorers meet a chimpanzee, whose mate they have wounded. Their reaction is to anthropomorphise the animal: "We have the cruel impression of having a man in front of us, at the same time furious and desperate". Otherwise, the reader gets the impression that they compare eating

---

[14] In the leaflet of a local travel agency produced for expatriates in Brazzaville one can read: "Discover the picturesque Eden of the Depth of the Congo" (*Confort Voyages*, May 1996).

[15] Paule Constant, *White Spirit*, Paris: Gallimard, 1989.

[16] Michel Rio, *Les Jungles Pensives*, Paris: Balland, 1985.

[17] See also *Voyage espiègle* ... quoted above. There we find, in a paternalistic or amused tone, all the clichés, from the gorilla raping white women, to the wild poachers shooting their "cousins", not to forget the theft of gorilla babies. The author of this post-colonial travel book writes in Paris Match.

monkeys, as the people in the jungle do, to cannibalism. This seems to be a kind of mortal sin, inevitably punished by being transformed into an animal:

> We are caught by a kind of madness (...) We feel we are becoming merciless beasts (...) To drink we have to crawl down to the river like animals. (p. 233)

Two portraits of monkeys as characters in novels

But the monkey stories in the novels *Congo*, 1980, and *Brazzaville Beach*, 1990, have more substance. It is intriguing to find certain analogies in those novels, apart from the titles.

First of all, they write from the very beginning about the humanistic idea of the relation between the Self and the Other. Crichton refers to a disillusioned remark by Stanley, who places the man of action among the moralists:

> The more experience and understanding I get of human nature, the more I am convinced that the most essential part of men is purely animal. (p. 7)

As to *Brazzaville Beach*, the author goes all the way back to the ancient Greeks, quoting Socrates:

> The life that is not examined is not worth living. (p. 9)

So, there is a moral to these romantic fables.

Secondly, it should be noted that the monkeys are used as characters all through the novels. This means that they are regarded as individuals, provided with a name, a psychology, a language and a behaviour. ... This is not the case in *Les Jungles Pensives*, where the monkeys are an anonymous nomadic group, true to their species and to the laws of nature. Evolution leads them to the threshold of becoming human beings, but they remain mere objects for study by men.

But our two "Congolese" novels let them over this threshold[18] and look at them as real, with the scientific caution of primatology:

> It was recognized, without the shadow of a doubt, that in future every anthropoid would have his own unique personality. (*Congo*, p. 61)

In *Congo* a female gorilla from a Californian laboratory is the star. This is how "she" greets Elliott, her scientist, while Karen Ross, a pure scientist, is looking:

---

[18] An intermediary can be found in another "Congolese" novel, Pierre Lestrade, *La Montagne des Singes*, Paris: Phebus, 1993 [*The Monkey Mountain*]. Gorillas, identified as individuals and given names, live in a "neutral space between man and monkey, forest and village. Where the gorilla lives he gives something to the forest which is neither animal nor human. They are sure to tell you they are inoffensive. I would rather say they are unpredictable, like we all are." (p. 240) Moreover, in this Stanley-like forest, strange things happen: "Had this gorilla not become a mutant, endowed with an aggressivity like that of men?"

He opened the door, stretched out his arm and said: "Good morning, Amy".

A huge black shape jumped in through the door and fell into his arms. Ross was surprised at the size of the animal. She had imagined something smaller and cuter. Amy was as big as an adult woman.

Amy kissed Elliott on his cheek with her big lips. Her head looked enormous beside his ...

"Is Amy pleased today?, he asked.

Amy's fingers moved rapidly near his cheek, as if she was chasing away flies. (...) and Ross realized that Amy was speaking. She talked with a surprising speed.

So, Amy has feelings, language, but also as we shall see, the capacity to dream and make judgements: she knows she is a monkey, she knows her limits like those of others. The laboratory assistant can be nothing but a "stupid human", when he irritates her by saying "how ugly he is", thus ignoring both her sex and her dignity. As to the mysterious, monstrous hominids, half gorillas, half men, or perhaps neither one nor the other, that she is supposed to identify, they are, in her language, "evil things".

In accordance with her status as a character in the novel, Amy has in fact a specific narrative programme. That is to "serve as the interpreter for, or perhaps even the ambassador of, humanity in its contacts with wild creatures". When the computers break down in the field, when all the science and technology of (white) men reveals itself as incapable of identifying the missing link between man and animal, the primate is the last resource. But a kind and domesticated primate, who collaborates with men against the Others, wild and wicked primates.[19] Amy, as a privileged informant to men, is the first eth(n)ologist among the monkeys.

Congo is more of a scientific spy thriller than a science-fiction novel. The action takes place in 1979, but its techno-science is supposedly from the end of the century. The fiction is within the limits of scientific verisimilitude. In the novel can be found today's ethological knowledge, such as it appears for instance in two other works published in 1990.

The title of the first one is in itself a whole novel: *Les hominides non identifiés des forêts d'Afrique*.[20] The author, Jacqueline Roumeguere-Eberhardt, places her story in the surrealist sphere. The preface is written by a certain B. Heuvelmans whose titles (Doctor of Zoological Sciences, President of the International Society of Cryptozoology) are supposed to give scientific warranty

---

[19] One might ask whether this is not a racist horror image typical of a certain America. In Stephen King's last book, called *Le singe*, Paris: Librio, 1994 [*The Monkey*] a fur toy is enough to create terror. With Hal, the adult, the "damned object", with "its ageless smile" provokes "a feeling of nearly instinctive disgust". This disgust is compared to that which could be provoked by the first inhabitant of the forest: "as if he had just discovered a murderous Pygmy"; "he was alive, writhing in his hands like a revolting Pygmy"...

[20] Jacqueline Roumeguère-Eberhardt, *Les hominidés non identifiés des forêts d'Afrique* ["The Non-identified Hominids of the African Forests"], Paris: Robert Laffont, Collections "Dossiers X".

to these fantastic ramblings about the African yeti. The second, *Destins de singe*,[21] is written by two academics, one a primatologist and one a veterinary. Two chapters, called "The Peace of the Gorillas" and "Chimpanzee Hunting", contain all the primatological details of our two novels, *Congo* and *Brazzaville Beach*, as if the fictive characters came directly from scientific study objects.

Both novels have as protagonists a couple made up of the observer (man) and the observed (monkey); and to meet the demands of romance, the couples consist of beings of different sexes. In *Congo*, we have seen what kind of ties exists between Peter Elliott and Amy, "his" laboratory gorilla. In *Brazzaville Beach* the scene is the opposite. In the advertisement, Hope Clearwater is introduced as "a young, beautiful and learned ethologist". As the narrator, she presents in the very first lines of her story, Clovis, the male chimpanzee who is at the same time the neutral object of her research and of her feelings. She reacts with a completely feminine sensitivity:

> I never felt particularly friendly with Clovis, he was too stupid to inspire real affection, but he has always had a place in my heart, mainly, I think, because of his instinctive way of covering his private parts when he was nervous or worried. An endearing attitude, I feel, which showed a natural vulnerability, altogether contrary to his usual moods: arrogance or total egocentricity. (p. 19)

Clovis belongs to a small group of chimpanzees, called the "southerners" because they have separated from their relatives of the North and settled on the southern bank of a river, jokingly called the Danube by the primatologists who observe them. But for the monkeys this river is not a joke. It is a real frontier that the northerners' troops silently cross to make surprise attacks on their southern "brothers" and exterminate them with extreme and cunning cruelty, worthy of that which previously seemed to be the privilege of mankind.

The last survivor from the south is called Conrad, a name which has not been chosen by chance. His terrible death indicates the end of the (civil?) war of the chimpanzees, but also the end of the novel. Hope is there, incapable of stopping the massacre, but "pleased to have been there to end Conrad's suffering", by giving him the coup de grâce:

> I crossed the little river to look for Conrad. I found him, covered with blood and crouching under the thorn bushes. His right hand was torn off at the wrist, and he raised the stump towards me in a parody of aggression. His face was red and pulpy, slashed by Darius' nails and fists. But these brown eyes looked steadily at me. Accusing? Pleading? Hostile? Stupefied?
>
> I went down on all fours behind him so that he would not see me, and shot him directly in the head. (p. 345)

---

[21] Christine Desportes et Bernard Thierry, *Destins de singe*, Paris: Acropole, 1990 [*The Destiny of the Monkeys*].

This literally *sympathetic* act might be called "humanitarian" even if the term is used here about an animal and seems to be used too often about human beings suffering like beasts. With this act the narrator abandons her scientist's reserve and neutrality to eliminate in the moment of death the distance separating her from the animal. "On all fours" she is finally capable of understanding him.

This rapprochement is in fact suggested a little earlier, when she tries to drive back the assailants:

> "Go away, I cried, waving my revolver. Run! Run!" But what was a revolver to them, Homo Troglodytes? And what was I? Just another strange biped monkey, showing off, threatening, and noisy. (p. 344)

This passage shows the allegorical ambition of the novel. This story of the monkeys could be a fable or a philosophical tale of man in the twentieth century, which has invented "humanitarian" compassion as well as the violence of "genocide".

As a kind of conclusion one would like to give to the Congo itself the right to reply to all this romantic anthropopithecology produced in the North.

First, as a reply to *Brazzaville Beach*, here read[22] as a novel about decivilisation, it must be stated that the transformation of man into animal is not only a *topos* of western literature. It can also be found in an authentic Congolese fable, cited in the novel of Sony Labou Tansi, called—very significantly for our theme—*L'anté-peuple:*[23]

> As the legend has it, the monkeys were members of a tribe, which had fled, thousands of years before, from the taxes of a merciless government. They had asked their ancestors to intervene. The ancestors then transformed the tribe into monkeys, to save them from evil.

Concerning *Congo*, it is necessary to mention the immediate scathing reaction of the Congolese press. It reacted not so much to the words of a book, which had already been available for some years in the bookshops as to the film adapted from the novel by John Marshall in 1995. It deals with the *image* of the Congo as a modern and civilised state. A first article[24] is summarised on the front page of the oldest local newspaper, a Christian weekly, which is highly and justifiably respected:

---

[22] About the division between human and natural sciences, see also "These words that hide the forest..." my article in *Journées du Département de Littérature et Civilisations Africaines*, devoted to "Quarante ans de littérature congolaise" (1993), soon to be published by Editions l'Harmattan.

[23] Sony Labou Tansi, *L'anté-peuple*, Paris: Le Seuil, 1983 [*The Ante-People*] p. 174.

[24] "Hollywood makes billions, attacking the Congolese", *La Semaine africaine*, 2069 from 2/5/95, pp.1 and 9. It should be emphasised that it is exceptional for this magazine to put an article about culture on the front page, let alone illustrated with a photo (a baby monkey behind bars). It should also be said that the author, Jérémie Dongala, lives in the US where he has a high position in an international organisation.

In the US, the Congolese are "considered" as murderous gorillas. This is the story of a film, which makes fun of us: "Congo".

The same indignation is found in a second article published in the most widely read satirical weekly in Brazzaville:

It is as surprising as it is annoying that the Congo, as a geographical, historical, and political concept, in the make-behave of the American film-maker John Marshall—of Jurassic Park (sic)—only inspires if not pejorative at least bestiary (I nearly said bestial) ideas. But why complain if we do not make an effort ourselves to improve our public image inside as well as outside the country? (...) Sébastien Kamba should consider avenging our honour frustrated by this identification with the symbol of King-Kong.[25]

So now the symbol occurs again, definitely symbolising primitive racism. However, if the two articles agree about the collective shame inflicted on their country, they differ significantly about the reasons for this *denigration*.

The article in *La Semaine Africaine* analyses in detail how the film lines up "all possible racist prejudices against black people, here represented by the Congolese", and proposes a functional explanation:

With films like *Congo*, the American audience understands that it is not worth while throwing money to cannibals and African gorillas, particularly not to those of a country like the Congo.

But he loses himself in conjectures trying to understand the notable absence of reaction from his Congolese compatriots to such an insulting film.

The article in *La Rue Meurt* might give an explanation to this criminal silence. He sees in the film an allegory of the recent fratricidal war whose trauma would be literally impossible to express if not in the shame of a racism shared with the Other. *Congo* illustrates the lack of humanity—of all humanity.

Whether it is a coincidence or not, this film, dealing with the life of gorillas, seems to come at the right moment, considering the exceptional cruelty that these primates show in certain sequences. Have we Congolese not ourselves proved to be barbaric during the pogroms of December 1993? In fact, these animals have no monopoly on violence. This is the truth.

Thus we are reminded of the question Hope poses, in *Brazzaville Beach*, seeing herself as *Homo Troglodytes*, "just another strange biped monkey" ... Obviously there is something in the novel about desperate and de-civilised westerners in "the heart of darkness", that corresponds, from the heart of the

---

[25] "*Congo* fait du cinéma" [*Congo* made into film], *La Rue meurt*, 96 from 31/8/95, p. 4. Sébastien Kamba is the most famous Congolese film-maker.

self-same darkness, to a certain popular discourse on internalised racism.[26] The one explains the other, and vice versa. And the *symbol* is reconstructed—in what we call at present the intercultural.

---

[26] This is evident in the "popular" magazine (*Le Vagabond*, 6/93, talking of "Senile Delinquence": "Our fathers are much more our gorillas than our parents"), as well as in the official discourse (The Head of State, 18/7/96, answering to a toast from the French president, talking of the "hominisation of the negro").

The Development Gaze
Visual Representation of Development in Information Material from Danida

Hanne Løngreen

My intention was, originally, to write about the uses of development communication in Danish-supported development projects in the Third World.

But reading through material from the Danish national development agency, Danida, searching for projects where participatory development communication was in use, my attention was again and again drawn to the uses of photographs and visual representations in the material produced by the Agency. I became increasingly interested in the uses of photographs and visual representations in this material. One question became more and more pressing: What images were produced of development and the 'Others' by the uses of visual representations in the material? Instead of focusing on a description and a record of the content of participatory development projects, I decided to look closer at the uses of visual representations in the material which the national Agency produced, and especially the material produced to inform the public about its work in the Third World. The pictures and photographs in this material could be read as statements about the Agency's construction of meaning in regard to development and its attitude towards the 'Others'.

The intention of this article is therefore to try to define some general characteristics of the visual representation of development in a selection of information material from Danida. The intention of this article is not to make a quantitative or representational investigation of all the material produced for the public by the Agency. Instead the aim is to make an analysis of a few items of the material produced to find some tendencies in the way the Agency expresses its view of development and its attitude towards the 'Others' through the material and especially through the visual representations. The question to be answered here is therefore 'what is' the visual representation of development and not a description of 'how' and/or in 'how many' ways development is visually represented. The aim is to interpret not to describe. This article takes as its point of departure a humanistic interpretative study on a micro-level.

For a longer period I have been very interested in questions about visual representation.[1] In my latest work with these types of questions I have espe-

---

[1] In *Blændværk, brændvidde og mentale billeder. Visuel kommunikation om den tredje verden* (1988) I looked at the different stereotypes which were produced of the 'Others' and especially of

cially been interested in how meaning is produced in the field of tension between the global and the local in visual representations. There is no doubt that the social context is reflected in the production and representation of social practices in photos. To this can be added that these visual representations develop into cultural encounters when they appear in cultural situations different from the cultural context in which they are produced (Løngreen 1992).

It could be interesting to examine these types of cultural encounters in the field of tension between the global and the local in relation to the representation of development. In my previous work I have tried to find evidence for the global and the local in the visual representation. It would be interesting to trace what is happening with specific themes as for example development in the field of tension between the global and the local in visual representation produced by institutions, which work with and within development. How is globalization reflected in the visual communication? How is the meaning of development constructed in the perspective of globalization? Is it possible to identify a specific mode of representation and in relation to this is it possible to construct a certain 'gaze' embodying this representation?[2]

Globalization

A changing view of the role of economy in the world has emerged among academics. Among others Lavie and Swedenburg (1996) call attention to the fact, that the condition for the global political economy is the division of the world into Center and Margins (Lavie and Swedenburg 1996). But as Lavie and Swedenburg point out the boundaries between Center and Margins are getting blurred because the Western economic power is no longer fixed to specific locations as it is becoming increasingly detached from places of production because of the constant hunt for cheap labor, low taxes etc.

Appadurai (1990) is also critical towards the traditional explanation of the global economic power. He no longer finds that the world can be understood in the old center-peripheries models (ibid.:296) and introduces five dimensions to understand the global cultural economy or what he calls the disjunction between economy, culture and politics. The five dimensions he introduces are: a) ethnoscapes; b) mediascapes; c) technoscapes; e) ideoscapes and f) finan-

---

black Africans in pictures in the newspapers, magazines, product packaging etc. One chapter was about the historical development of the different representations of the 'Others'. Proceeding along these lines I looked closer at the meaning behind an example of an advertisement from an African magazine in *Cross-Cultural Communication in Connection with Advertising in Africa* (1993). This work was followed by the production of information material for the Danish exhibition 'White on Black' at the Danish National Museum (1994). Finally I used the perspective of the construction of meaning in the field of tension between the global and the local in an analysis of two advertisements from respectively Denmark and Kenya in *Visual Communication in the Field of Tension between the Global and the Local* (1995).

[2] As will become clear later I am inspired by John Urry's (1990) work on the Tourist Gaze. Also among feminists some theorists are working with a 'gaze' concept. See e.g. Laura Mulvey (1989), *Visual and Other Pleasures*, Basingstoke, Macmillan.

scapes. The five dimensions are interrelated but in relation to finanscapes he writes "... even an elementary model of global political economy must take into account the shifting relationship between perspectives on human movement, technological flow, and financial transfers, which can accommodate their deeply disjunctive relationships with one another" (ibid.:298).

Both Lavie and Swedenburg, and Appadurai stress the necessity to reformulate the understanding of the power of the global economy. The global economic power can no longer only be understood as pure structure but has to be seen in a broader context. Economic power together with ideology and culture has to be understood as integrated parts of the globalization process. Globalization is therefore not only another word for global accumulation of capital but also implies significant cultural components. This intermix has consequences for the construction of meaning of the relationship between 'Us Here' and 'Them Out There'.

Edward W. Said (1978) talks about a series of imaginative geographies where the world is divided into different spaces that reflect the division of the world into separate worlds having different meanings and roles. Thus we are talking about a First and a Third World.[3] To Said's notion of an imaginative geography, where the world so to speak is described from a horizontal view, Benedict Anderson's (1983) notion of 'imagined communities' defines how the meaning of the specific worlds are constructed and have come into existence in a 'mental geography'. Anderson examines how national identities are formed and have come into existence. Both Said and Anderson are from different perspectives engaged in the analysis of the construction of meanings. By finding and analyzing different texts (literature and historic texts) they reach their conclusions through interpretation of the mental images on geography and communities.

With globalization the world is changing. The rapid change is speeded up by the media. The media become the messengers of the multiplicity of the world. This multiplicity is not only a global condition, but also a characteristic of the regional and local situation. As the media have become messengers, the cultural and social practices are marked by complexity and differentiation. The world is at one and the same time distant and very close. We are talking about the neutralization of space (Hannerz and Löfgren 1994).

It seems as if globalization means homogenization of the national cultures along very standardized patterns. Through consumerism the world is becoming 'Americanized'. Even if these standardizations seem to be alike all over the world, it is possible to recognize hybridizations between the uniforming global 'Americanization' and local variations. This is what Ulf Hannerz calls 'creoli-

---

[3] Before the fall of the Wall it was easier geographically to point out a Second world. Although the Wall has broken down it is still possible of talking about a second world as a mental construction both for the First World and for the former 'Second' world.

zation' (Hannerz 1992). With both the dissolving of the boundaries and the compression of time and space new spaces of meaning are produced.

Globalization, development and the media

We might have expected that information about development projects and processes in the Third World would be more noticeable in the field of global-ization. This seems not to be the case.

Although the media are important messengers they are not capable of be-ing the messenger of development processes in the Third World. Because of the focusing on news by the media, the media are oriented towards sensations. As for development projects this means that we only hear about projects that are failing or have severe problems. Development projects and development processes become equal to lack of success. The news about successful projects very seldom finds its way to the news media. When we learn about develop-ment projects this kind of information is mixed with the overall focus on the Third World as a place of coups, crises and natural catastrophes.

What does this connote in relation to globalization? The Third World seems to be a place situated outside the globalization process. This becomes clear when we look at globalization as Robins is discussing it. He boils glob-alization down to: "Globalization is about the compression of time and space horizons and the creation of a world of instantaneity and depthlessness. Global space is a space of flows, an electronic space, a decentred space, a space in which frontiers and boundaries have become permeable. Within this global arena, economies and cultures are thrown into intense and immediate contact with each other—with each 'Other' ..." (Robins 1991:33).

In this light the situation for producing information about the 'Others' has a lot of obstacles. This is underlined when we look at information material produced by institutions outside the vehicle of commercial and national broadcasting corporations or 'the creators of the universal cultural space' (Robins 1991:30).

The status of this kind of information material is distinctive because it is produced *outside* the information flows of the commercial and national broadcasting media systems. This type of material obtains its own meaning in relation to the institutionalized media flow and in relation to its own position as data about both the sender-institution itself and about specific selected topics.

This, in double-meaning, marginalized position of the 'Others'—*outside* the content of media and *outside* the vehicle of the dominant media institu-tions makes the presentations of the 'Others' worth examining. Is it possible to define a specific gaze that could define both the 'Others' position in the overall visual world and define the very way of representing them? In the following I will try to trace this line by looking closer at how development influences the social practices in the Third World and how this is shown through the visual representations of these practices.

The Gaze

John Urry (1990) is in his book *The Tourist Gaze* working with the way the social practices, defined as tourism, have come into existence. The social practices of tourism are reflected in the manner certain places in the world are constructed as places for leisure and travel. With the definition of place comes a mode of defining and looking at the world, which Urry defines as the Tourist Gaze. Along these lines I have been working with the possibility of defining a Development Gaze. Is it possible to work with a notion of a Development Gaze and hereby explain the visual representations in pictures and photographs in information material produced by national development agencies and particularly by the Danish Agency?

Trying to use Urry's concept the Tourist Gaze as a model for elaborating a Development Gaze has some obvious problems. First and foremost tourism as a social practice is characterized by pleasure and holidays. To work in a developing country has nothing to do with either pleasure or holidays in the sense connected with tourism. To go away as a tourist has also something to do with consumerism—to go away on holiday is to consume products which are both material (goods, dinners etc.) and non-material (museum visits, service etc.).

Because of this it is obvious that it is not possible to completely compare the social practices of tourism and development work. Nevertheless both practices have something in common and that is the activity of going away to places which are far away and different from the places where we live our everyday life. And both social practices have something to do with reducing the distance between 'Us Here' and 'Them Out There'. In the process of going 'Out There' we are confronted with the differences of our everyday life and the everyday life of 'Them Out There'. Their everyday life becomes objects to the gaze of the tourist—or to the gaze of the development worker. The 'Others' change into objects to be studied by 'Us Here'. In this process we ('Us Here') are the subjects.

As Urry points out, there are "many professional experts who help to construct and develop our gaze as tourist" (Urry 1990:1). The same can be said of the concept of a Development Gaze. There are many agents in defining and constructing the Development Gaze. At the national-state level, governments and foreign ministries are the prime instruments in the definition of development because of their active dealing with these types of questions. At the level of social movements it is also possible to identify several types of agents, namely NGOs and other movements based on voluntary or paid labor.

At both levels the media are the place for distributing the meaning of development i.e. both within and outside the vehicle of commercial and national broadcasting corporations. To this can be added, as I have dealt with earlier, the commercial and national media's own construction of development or rather the media's orientation towards the Third World as a place to find sensations.

We may say that both the tourist and the development worker have the same basis in an ideology specific for the world of 'Us Here'. The ground for both gazes is a discourse on 'Westernness'.

The Development Gaze

Although the social practices of tourism and development work are not identical, it might be fruitful to work further with a concept of a Development Gaze along the lines introduced by Urry on the Tourist Gaze.

The question is then, what is specific for the Development Gaze and the social practices of being a development worker?[4]

a. To act as a development worker is to be characterized by being 'modern'. Being 'Out There' is characterized by the constant encounters between different cultures and different phases in social and economic development. In the case of the Third World the encounters could be distinguished by the meeting of the (post-)modern and the pre-modern point of view.

b. As the tourist "relationships arise from a movement of people to, and their stay in, various destinations. This necessarily involves some movement through space, that is the journey, and a period of stay in a new place or places" (ibid. p. 3). This description covers both the development worker and the expert who are visiting development projects in the Third World.

c. The development worker stays in sites "which ... (are) outside the normal (Western) places of residence and work. ... There is a(n) ... intention to return 'home' within a ... period of time" (ibid., p. 3. My insertions).

d. In contrast to Urry's fourth paragraph the places where the development worker finds himself are connected with paid work. The contrast to the paid work at 'home' in the West is the contrast between both cultures and the social and economic conditions. The social practice of the development worker in the Third World is defined by cultural encounters and often also cultural clashes. In contrast to the tourist these cultural encounters and clashes are the development worker's working conditions and not only situations to be noted from a distance.

In addition the encounters with the locals are institutionalized through the set-up of the development program. The development worker and the local meet because of this set-up and not because of other types of social interactions. The social practices produced by this can be said to be imbued with the notion of the prevailing ideology of development.

---

[4] In the following definitions of the social practices of development work and of a Development Gaze I am following the characteristics of the Tourist Gaze presented in Urry 1990:1–3. In this presentation I have left out the specific characteristics of tourism.

e. Only very few people in modern societies become engaged in social practices of development. There is a very strict selection of these people. They represent different types of occupations and are highly paid. The difference in social and economic position between them 'Out There' and the development worker is very much emphasized by this.

f. The selection of places for development work is made from different parameters. There are of course specific social and economic reasons for development support. Moreover the selection of places and nations is based on international and national appraisals of levels of basic needs and national gross income per capita. The selection is affected by political influences both nationally and internationally. Furthermore the development process is either started or supported by the West. It is worth taking into consideration that there is a difference between aid and development support.

   Here the media also play a role, as it is through the media that the Western societies become aware of crises in the Third World. This is often the case for aid programs too, as we have recently seen it in connection with the different crises in Africa (Ethiopia, Rwanda, Sudan, and Liberia).

g. The development gaze is directed towards features which are 'pre-modern' and which separate them from Western ways of living.

h. The development gaze is constructed through these markers. The categories of development are constructed through the collection of photographs of everyday life situations and views in the Third World. The material produced by development agencies presents markers of development such as 'Danish road project', 'health clinic' to name just two.

i. Development professionals develop different sorts of techniques and approaches to development. They are often supported by academics who are interested in development from a theoretical point of view. They meet at conferences or the academics are involved with the working out of reports about specific projects.

j. Unlike in the case of tourism there is an obvious power-relation between 'Us Here' and 'Them Out There'. In development projects we ('Us Here') are always those who give support to the 'Others'. This has consequences for the ways in which we look at each other. Even though we are talking about participatory development projects there is always an element of control. To legitimate the use of funds in development projects it is necessary to legitimize the use of funds to persons who have given them such as private sponsors or taxpayers. The development relation therefore becomes bureaucratic and accordingly some sort of administration always springs from development projects.

   From this we can see that there is a major correspondence between the construction of a Tourist Gaze and a Development Gaze. This means that there is a potential to use Urry's definition of the Tourist Gaze as a model for a Development Gaze. With this the Development Gaze can both be defined as a social practice as well as a specific way of representing this very practice through visual representations.

As I have now introduced the concept of a Development Gaze, I will in the following examine its explanatory power in relation to the visual representations and photographs in the information material from Danida.

The Development Gaze and the Danida material

Before looking more closely at the Danida material it is necessary to briefly outline recent developments within the discussion of identity and postmodernism. I think this is necessary because the Danida material can be looked upon as an illustration of a previous stage in the theoretical discussion about identity, culture and postmodernism. This previous stage was characterized by a very dichotomous view of what happened in the cultural encounters between the 'Others' and the West. In one version the Western hegemony simply overwhelmed the other cultures and destroyed them. This version was prevailing in theories about cultural imperialism.

Another version saw a tendency towards hybridization, which meant that the cultures melted together and became a hybrid. Yet another version saw the cultures from the point of view of the 'Others' and talked about 'creolization' (Hannerz 1992).

Recent theories are occupied with what they call the Third Timespace. This space is characterized by the creation of a cultural identity by ethnic groups within the Western world. It is especially the 'Others' within the Eurocentre that are formulating these new forms of identities (Lavie and Swedenburg 1996).

When examining the Danida material I use the theories which have the dichotomous view. I do this because the Third Timespace theories are more concerned with ethnicity and race and the construction of these within postmodern societies than with the representation of 'Otherness' in the Eurocenter. The Third Timespace theories focus on the 'Others' within the Eurocenter, I am interested in the 'Others' placed outside the Eurocenter.

The Danida material

The Danida material I am going to examine consists of three small pamphlets about Danida in Zambia, Bangladesh and Central America respectively.[5] They have all the same uniform layout with the use of the same colors, and with texts built up on the same themes. In all the pamphlets there are facts about the country or region with indexes of population, national gross income, and a map with the major cities.

The texts are about the development problems of the countries and projects which Danida is involved in. The tone is objective and sober.

---

[5] *Danida i Zambia* (1995), Udenrigsministeriets informationssekretariat, København; *Danida i Bangladesh* (1993), Udenrigsministeriets informationskontor, København; *Danida i Mellemamerika* (1995), Udenrigsministeriets informationssekretariat, København.

The visual representations

Each pamphlet has a front photo and four other photos. All the front photos display scenery from the country/region the pamphlet is about: a boy planting rice on the Bangladeshi pamphlet, a Guatemalan market woman on the Central American pamphlet and a car on a road on the Zambian pamphlet.

The four other photos in all the pamphlets are divided between photos from factories, scenes from villages, different Danida projects, people on a street and a photo of a rainforest.

All the photos are categories, which means that they present generalized scenes and social practices. The text following all the photos is for instance 'a Zambian village', 'a village in Nicaragua', 'a health clinic', 'Danish road project', 'they learn to read in Noakhali', 'rainforest', 'Managua'. Besides being categories of these features the photos also become categories of nationalities, geographic areas and gender. The photos are through this not only categories but also signs of development.

Because of the photos being categories the places and people represented in the photos are homogenized—all villages in Zambia are like this. The name of this particular village is without interest. You see one and you have seen them all. Because the village has no name we do not have to involve ourselves. The village and the villagers are anonymous, we have no relationship to them. And when we have no relationship we do not really bother about them. The distance between 'Us Here' and 'Them Out There' is untouched.

Another element, which confirms this, is the fact that the identity of the 'Others' is anchored to specific locations. The 'Others' are attached to the culture of the place, they can never be detached from their cultures.[6] In contrast the Western identity is detached from place and has in the modernization process become increasingly individualized. The pictures are comments on differences as they are displaying persons, behavior and nature that are chosen because of their 'Otherness'. Displaying the 'Otherness' also indicates that this is not 'home'. The photos do not represent 'home'.

The difference in the state of identity results in a disruption of simultaneousness in both the contrasting meaning of being individuals in social practices and in diverse phases of societal development. The 'Others' live in premodern societies.

Living in pre-modern societies means that the society is collective in contrast to the Western individualism. An example of this can be seen in the photo 'they learn to read in Noakhali'.

In addition to the pre-modern societal situation the Third World is seen as a place in a timeless state (Lavie and Swedenburg 1996). Time has something

---

[6] We can see this when the 'Others' migrate to the Eurocentre. Here their identity will always be that of the place where they originally came from. A Pakistani will always be a Pakistani even though he/she has lived in the Eurocentre for generations.

to do with progress and expansion. That the Third World is in a timeless state is stressed by the 'Others' way of dressing. When the 'Others' are dressed in anything other than their traditional clothing, they dress in a synthetic and old-fashioned way from a Western point of view.

Development under these conditions means the introduction of factories that can support the prevalent pre-industrialized production of simple products. The factories are not producing advanced products, such as for example electronic components, but chairs and textiles. The first level of industrialism is from single production to mass production of pre-modern products. In the three pamphlets we therefore also have photos from this type of factory.

These photos are contrasted with the photos of the villages. The villages are representations of authentic unspoiled life. You may even say that this life is a representation of reality. This life has a feeling of aura. Some governments in the Third World are romanticizing[7] this aura and turning it into business. The set up of National Cultural Villages where the authentic African life is exhibited is an example of this. I would say that this romantic gaze is underlined in the photos of the villages but especially on the front photos of the Bangladeshi and Central American pamphlets.

In a way the romantic gaze is also indirectly emphasized when we look at the photos of the factories. The photos of the factories differ from the photos of the villages. In the factories the social practices are organized and regulated. Some of the work presented is collective in the sense that two or more persons are working together. The Zambian textile factory is different. Here the workers are placed at a distance from each other—like small islands in the sea. Although the production process is collective—all contribute to the total production, the working process is split up in individualized units. The photo of the Zambian textile factory is in contrast to the front photos. Modernity does not have an aura.

Conclusion

I think it is possible to define a Development Gaze that can conceptualize the way Danida visually represents development and the 'Others' in Danida's use of photos in the selected material examined here.

The main element in the visual representation of the Development Gaze is the categorization of the 'Others', which underlines the distance between them and us. The distance is especially crucial when we combine the categorization with globalization. In the globalization process the world has become compressed. But it seems as if this compression does not include the Third World and the 'Others'. Instead of compression the distance is widened. This is done

---

[7] Also Urry uses the concept of a romanticized gaze.

by the stressing of the pre-modern social and economic conditions of the 'Others'. This places the 'Others' outside the globalization process.

I think the process of extending the distance between the Eurocenter and the Third World and the 'Others' marks a phase in the postmodern development of this relationship. With the increasing multiculturalization of especially Western Europe where the 'Others' no longer only live outside Europe but also within it, 'Us Here' have to produce distance to emphasize power. Producing this distance means that 'Us Here' have to formulate that there is a distance between 'Us Here' and 'Them'—not only 'Out There'—but also 'Within Here'. This is done by emphasizing race and ethnicity.

When we look at the 'Others' outside the Eurocenter race and ethnicity are not used as explanation for distance between 'Them' and 'Us'. Here the explanation for the distance is the contrast in social and economic development, the difference between a pre-modern and post-modern societal situation.

I think that my argumentation can be confirmed by drawing Robins into the discussion. Robins (1991) shows that there are different ways of conceptualizing the 'Others'—the 'Others' exist within and outside the Eurocenter. According to Robins there seems to be a hierarchy of 'Others'. He mentions two classes of 'Others', but as I see it we can talk about three, namely by adding a third class of 'Others' who are not only placed outside the Eurocenter and the globalization process but who are more specifically the poor in the Third World.

By this the Development Gaze stresses the power-relation between 'Us Here' and the 'Others' outside the Eurocenter. It is 'Us Here' who are ruling the 'Others' and who select the areas for development. The power-relationship is even emphasized because of 'Us Here' being absent in the photos. It is 'Us Here' who manage the gaze, who define the Development Gaze.

The Danida material does not break with the traditional way of representing the others or the traditional way of representing development issues.

This conclusion is by no means revolutionary. The arguments could have been foreseen. But from this conclusion a question arises: How is it possible to visually represent the present paradigm within development programs, namely development seen as a participatory process? How is the meaning of the participatory development processes constructed? Will the different types of social practices within this paradigm be reflected in the visual representations in photos taken from this type of development program? How is a new visual discourse on development constructed?

References

Anderson, Benedict, 1983, *Imagined Communities*. London: Vertigo.

Appadurai, Arjun, 1990, "Disjuncture and Difference in the Global Cultural Economy", in Featherstone, Mike (ed.), *Global Culture*. London: Sage.

Danida i Bangladesh, 1993, Udenrigsministeriets informationskontor.

Danida i Mellemamerika, 1995, Udenrigsministeriets informationssekretariat.

Danida i Zambia, 1995, Udenrigsministeriets informationssekretariat.

Hannerz, Ulf, 1992, *Cultural Complexity*. New York: Columbia University Press.

Hannerz, Ulf and Orvar Löfgren, 1994, "The Nation in the Global Village", *Cultural Studies*, Vol. 8, No. 2.

Lavie, Smadar and Ted Swedenburg, 1996, "Between and among the Boundaries of Culture: Bridging Text and lived Experience in the Third Timespace", *Cultural Studies*, Vol. 10, No. 1.

Løngreen, Hanne, 1988, *Blændværk, brændvidde og mentale billeder. Visuel kommunikation om den tredje verden*. Arbejdspapirer nr. 8. Institut for Sprog og Internationale kulturstudier, The University of Aalborg.

—, 1992, "Billeder på tvärs af kulturer", in Lundström, Jan-Erik och Berit Sahlström (eds), *Talspråk, Skriftspråk, Bildspråk: En Antologi*. SIC 35. Tema Kommunikation, University of Linköping.

—, 1993, "Cross-Cultural Communication in Connection with Advertising in Africa", in Arntsen, Hilde (ed.), *Media, Culture and Development I*. Department of Media and Communication, University of Oslo.

—, 1994, *Hvidt på sort—illustrede fordomme*. Copenhagen: Nationalmuseet.

—, 1995, "Visual Communication in the Field of Tension between the Global and the Local", in *Proceedings of the Fifth International Conference on Marketing and Development*, Concordia, Montreal.

—, (work in progress), *Discourses of Development Communication*.

Morley, David and Kevin Robins, (1995): *Spaces of Identity*, Sage, London.

Mulvey, Laural, 1989), *Visual and Other Pleasures*. Basingstoke; Macmillan.

Robins, Kevin, 1991, "Tradition and translation: National culture in its global context', in Corner, John and Sylvia Harvey, *Enterprise and Heritage*. London: Routledge.

Said, Edward W., 1978), *Orientalism*. London: Penguin.

Urry, John, 1990), *The Tourist Gaze*. London: Sage.

I Often Tell People I Have Been to Africa …
Swedish-African Encounters through the Aid Relationship

Anna Wieslander

Evaluations, studies and reports bear witness to changes, planned or unplanned, brought about by aid from the North to African countries. But how were people affected by this work? What impressions did Swedes bring home, and did their experiences change their attitudes—and their own society? And Africans who became immersed in the Swedish society—did they sink or swim? Part of this study deals with some individuals involved in the massive post-war programmes for international development and co-operation.

One basis of this study is the interviews I carried out in 1981 with around 80 Swedes working in four African countries (Mozambique, Tanzania, Zambia, and Ethiopia) about their work, motives and attitudes. Some of the interviews were collected for a book.[1] Many of those interviewed made Africa and development cooperation their career, one had a breakdown, but most returned to their ordinary jobs. In this study I examine how a number of the people interviewed look on this meeting with Africa years later.

In 1990, I met and interviewed Africans—at the grass-roots level, as counterparts in aid, as administrators and researchers—from the same four countries (except that Mozambique was replaced by Tunisia) to see how Swedish aid had affected them.[2] Some of the Africans interviewed received their education in Sweden in the early days of the aid relationship. In this study we see how their stay in Sweden influenced their lives, but also what other Africans experienced in the encounter with Swedes and Swedish aid in Africa.

Examples of the image of Africa are also quoted from my recent study on the relations with Africa of a Swedish medium-size community, Halmstad. The study was done for the Swedish Foreign Ministry, as part of their Partnership Africa Programme.[3]

Some of my interviewees had lost faith in aid as such, but feel that it is an important means for people to meet and learn from each other. The question is whether the roles as "donor" and "receiver" are still fixed, after more than 35 years, or whether this contact has led to a real exchange, on equal terms. This study gives some examples of the kind of interpersonal exchanges that can be found in organisations, churches and schools.[4]

---

[1] Wieslander, 1982.
[2] Wieslander, 1993b.
[3] Wieslander, 1998.
[4] All interviews made in Swedish have been edited and translated by the author.

Swedish international development cooperation

Aid as such is a consequence of the European colonial image of Africans. It presupposes Africans as "the other", as "they", who need help from "us" to be admitted to the international arena. This feeling of benevolent superiority was the basis of the Swedish national aid programme when it started in the fifties, and the first efforts were characterised by naivety and optimism.

Sweden started her commitment through contributions to the UN and its agencies after the war. In the 1950s and 1960s, Swedish churches and organisations pressed for an increased Swedish involvement. Their motives were expressed in terms of international solidarity, but their knowledge of the world was not extensive, and their experience of development limited to Sweden.

The goals for an official aid programme were laid down by an Act of Parliament in 1962. It stated as the main goal helping to raise the standard of living of people in the poor countries of the world, and assuming that this would be achieved through support to economic growth, economic and social equality, economic and political independence and democratisation. These goals remained unchanged until 1988 when environment was added and 1996 when the gender issue was incorporated.

In the early days of the aid relationship, Sweden like other donor countries invited young students from the South to its universities on scholarship programmes and sent out an increasing number of experts, at first mainly through the UN, but with the growth of a bilateral programme bilateral experts too. This interpersonal exchange was concentrated to Africa.

The scholarship programmes ended in the early seventies, replaced by, among other things, support to local institutions and the training of staff in Swedish supported projects. The number of long-term experts employed directly by SIDA[5] increased till the end of the 70s. Today most Swedes working in Africa are employed by consultancy firms working on Sida contracts, or Swedish volunteers sent out by NGOs but financed by Sida.

Since the start of international cooperation, Sweden has changed, for better and for worse. A number of these changes can be seen as direct results of the aid relationship, especially Swedish people coming back from Africa with new ideas and ambitions.

Most of these changes have added something to Sweden, new institutions, new firms, new organisations etc. But while the aid relationship has also often helped in constructing new institutions in African countries, it has contributed at the same time to the destruction of systems, values, and ideas.

---

[5] SIDA, in capital letters, refers to the Swedish International Development Authority. Since 1995 it has been re-organised and is written Sida.

Africans studying in Sweden

One important change in Sweden is that the homogeneous Swedish society of the post-war-period has become a multicultural one, with an increasing part of the population of foreign descent. The small group of African students were among the first foreigners in Sweden.

The scholarship funds initiated at Swedish universities in the late fifties were made up from contributions from all the students. Quite a few African students were admitted at the existing four Swedish universities. Scholarship programmes were soon questioned in most donor countries—and indeed also in the countries of origin of the students—often seen as a costly way of educating young citizens of "new" countries. While most of the African students in the end benefited from their Swedish education for their careers at home, some of them chose to remain in Europe after completing their studies.

Eunice Corbin from Liberia studied medicine and is now a doctor—in Sweden. She sees the arrival of the African students as a privilege—for Sweden. But it was sometimes tough for them as pioneers in a country where few had seen black people before.

– This contact with the South, she says, means that Sweden is no longer so secluded and isolated.

But she feels that the climate is getting harder.

– I wonder where the solidarity of the sixties is now, she says.

Rupiah Banda, Zambian politician and businessman, started his studies at Lund University before Northern Rhodesia had become Zambia. Immediately after obtaining his degree he was appointed ambassador of his country to Egypt, a career somewhat more rapid than that of many fellow students in Sweden. In 1990 he was the Mayor of Lusaka and comments on his years in Sweden:

– It was very interesting—there I was, directly from colonial Africa, and was fully accepted as a person in Sweden. That strengthened my self-confidence. And your system was so interesting—a balance between capitalism and socialism that every country has then tried to copy. Without Sweden I would not have become the man I am today ...

Billy Modise, a South African student leader who also found his way to a scholarship in Sweden, was deeply involved in student politics during his studies. After some years with SIDA in Uppsala he joined the UN, worked for the Swapo Institute in Lusaka, became the ANC representative in Stockholm before he finally went back to South Africa.

He recalls the frustration of the African students at Lund University.

– The Swedish students felt they had a right to tell us where to stay, what to study and how to behave, since they paid our scholarships, he says.

Nevertheless Billy thinks scholarship programmes are a good idea.

– Education, says Billy, is and will always be the best way to support poor countries, for it is a key to the future. In Africa we cannot content ourselves with only studies at our own universities—we need, just like you, people with a world perspective.

Kebede Tato from Ethiopia followed a course in Earth Sciences in Uppsala. He stayed in Sweden for quite a long time, but went back, and in 1990 he was in charge of the Soil Department in the Ministry of Agriculture in Addis Abeba. Later he became a SIDA consultant in Southern Africa. In the seventies he worked in ARDU, a SIDA-supported project for Integrated Rural Development in his home country:

– It was a fantastic period, he says. We Ethiopians were all young and enthusiastic, and so were the Swedes, all spirited by the same ideas. Everything we did was new in the country, from planning and accounting to agricultural extension. Our goals were change and improvement, and we had concrete agricultural problems to solve!

An early evaluation of the scholarship programmes found that some of the African scholarship holders had stayed on in Sweden, and that few of the others had then reached positions suitable to their education. But, twenty years later, as my interviews show, many of them had important positions, often very relevant to their studies in Sweden.

If this is compared to the Swedes who have worked in Africa, we find that some few of them stay on in Africa, forming new relations, and finding new jobs. Most of them return home, and some are able to use this experience in Sweden, with Sida or other organisations. But in general, an African experience does not lead to promotion in Sweden—in certain contexts it is regarded as a waste of time.

Swedes working in Africa

A study[6] about the attitudes of Swedish aid workers to their jobs and to Sida, among other things, looks into the reasons why Swedish people take up this kind of job. The following often-overlapping motives were found:

– Their parents were involved in aid.
– They look for adventure.
– They want to broaden their minds.
– They see it as a challenge.
– They want to contribute to change and fight injustices.
– Ideology and solidarity are important for some.
– Christian values are important to others.

But the motives changed when they went out a second time. Now they mention money, acknowledgement, a good life for the family, and the love of the climate and the warm human contacts.

---

[6] SIDA/AUGUR Marknadsanalys AB, 1993

However, Africa has had a strong influence on the lives and attitudes of the Swedes who worked there. One says: "I am in fact a Congolese—my skin is white, but my mind is black".

Africa changed my view of Sweden

In 1981 Folke Albinsson was working at the Cooperative College, Lusaka, Zambia, as an advisor to the Director and a Deputy Director.

He says his early view of Africa, as that of any Swede at that time, was based on the few pieces of information they got from missionaries—exoticism, jungles, dangerous animals, a thrilling continent—attractive, but also strange and threatening.

– But we looked at Africa then, he says, as a continent of poverty, disease and misery, but the idea was also conveyed to us that it was possible and indeed necessary for us to help change this situation.

In the sixties a political dimension was added to this commitment. Awareness was developed of the effects of colonialism and oppression, and the role Europe—including the Swedes—had played in Africa. Nyerere's writings, the Arusha Declaration and Education for Self-Reliance convinced Folke that Adult Education could be important for a country like Tanzania.

– So, he says, my image of Africa, before going there in 1969, was a mixture of exoticism and the belief that we had a mission, a possibility to help the Africans.

Folke first worked for four years in Tanzania in adult education and later spent three years in Zambia. After that a period of work at home, before he settled for another long period of Adult Education in Ethiopia. His image of Africa has now become modified.

– First of all, he says, I no longer see Africa as a unit, an entity. I see the difference between the countries, and I no longer speak of Africans in general. This change is important in the perspective of peace and civilised co-existence in the world. Generalisations must end and we must see that "we" and "they" are alike, and have more to share than to fear.

– The feeling of exoticism is long gone, but I enjoy meeting people in Africa who are more spontaneous, vital and generous than we are. This attraction to life in Africa, has become part of my life.

– Like most others, I believed that change would be rapid, an attitude which characterised the whole aid concept. I have now realised that modernisation is a slow, lengthy and difficult process.

– Before, my only point of reference was Sweden, which has now become one among all other countries. This creates a kind of alienation, a crack in the mirror. Even though this means a loss of my spontaneous relationship to Sweden, I see it as a privilege to have been a guest in many worlds.

– Africa also gave me a new attitude to Sweden. I saw my country as part of the world's upper class, a kind of manor house, where everything was nice, peaceful, well organised, well regulated. I also found that Sweden had become a materialistic paradise, but that no one seemed to have time to enjoy that.

An interesting job—and some grey hair

Hugo Berch worked in the Zambian Ministry of Agriculture in 1981, coordinating a large project for Integrated Rural Development, supported by SIDA.

He had been among those who started a radical student group for increased international aid at Lund University in the sixties. After graduating, his first job abroad was with the UN in Uganda in the mid-seventies. Returning home, after Zambia, in 1982, he became a partner in a consultancy firm, working in forestry and agriculture for Sida and the European Union, for example.

Hugo considers himself lucky. His work in Africa led to a totally different life than could have been expected.

– I have profited a lot as a person. I have got a more interesting life—and some grey hair ...

– In Africa particularly I learnt much from my contact with people who were warm and joyful, in spite of all their pressing problems. I have also got a new way of looking at the world, a huge network of contacts, and a lot of new knowledge. In winter I take different consultancy jobs, and spend most of the summer on the farm. The international assignments have made it possible and indeed necessary for me to make the production of my own agricultural land more ecologically sound, and this is now of primary importance for me.

– Africa taught me the sense of a long perspective, and of how much we are alike. We in Sweden may seem to live in a different historical epoch, yet I always see parallels between Africa and my farm. When a Guinean farmer expresses his thoughts, I can sense it is exactly what my Swedish neighbour says. This has made life so much more interesting.

Hugo thinks Sweden as a whole has profited from its international commitment.

– Development cooperation became our entrance fee to the world, he says. Before we just had a few commercial ties to the South. I also feel that Sweden has become more multicultural through the aid programme. Thousands and thousands of Swedes have had their first contact with the world outside Europe through friends and relatives who worked abroad.

If I had known ...

In 1981 Eva Carling lived in Kibaha, a regional centre for integrated development supported by the Scandinavian countries and in 1970 handed over to Tanzania. Eva's husband was an adviser at a Teacher Training Centre, but she could not get a job of her own. She had a newborn baby, three other sons to care for and a household to run. These were difficult years in Tanzania, as well as for herself.

– If I had known how difficult the practical things would be, she says, I do not think I would have agreed to go. Now I am happy I did not know, for once you are there, you manage and see new possibilities in life.

This family was stricken by disaster a few months before going home. Their six-year-old son died of malaria. Eva does not put the blame on Africa, or on their decision to go there. Her feelings about Africa are strong, even after fifteen years, but not negative.

– I often tell people I have lived in Africa, and the impressions I convey are so vivid that they are surprised when I say we were there for only two years. Those years meant a lot to me. I still often think in Swahili, and many striking expressions come to my mind, again and again.

– I feel that I grew old in Africa, much more rapidly than at home. All life cycles seem so rapid there. Everything grows faster, ecological development seems to progress at a much higher speed. Whatever man builds is soon covered again by nature, so potent and sometimes violent. That is thrilling, but frightening.

Eva was impressed with African nature and wildlife, and also with the encounter with different cultures and people with a different background, many without any formal education.

– I learnt a lot from them, she says, and their ways of looking at life. It helped me to get rid of the unconscious snobbishness one has, coming from a culture where education is a matter of course. People seemed to look at things in a more matter-of-fact way, to have the gift not to be angry and upset about life's adversities.

The stay in Africa also meant a new perspective on Sweden.

– I realised how well organised Sweden is, and how we decide and organise things together. I was also struck by our relative lack of large income differences. It was distasteful to be as privileged as we were in Tanzania. Not only was it unfair, but it also often made us scared of those who might be jealous. Inequality is very detrimental for development.

– I was also made to see the negative sides of our culture. I felt we were too self-centred and seemed to think we were invulnerable. I also realised how immense our contempt is in the North for people of the South. Thanks to our Tanzanian experience, I think our family is fortunate to have become less prejudiced than ordinary Swedes.

– So our stay in Africa was positive, in spite of everything. We profited much more than those we were supposed to help. The important thing about aid is for people to meet; I no longer think aid furthers "development".

Eva certainly did not profit professionally from her African experience, but the stay added a new dimension to life.

– It is fifteen years ago, and yet it all seems very close, she says. Those years were important, and I left a big part of myself in Tanzania.

Every morning a new promise

– Africa can be said to have given my life its direction—my family and a lot of my professional life, says Per Iwansson.

In 1981 he was about to leave Mozambique after three years of challenging work as an architect, employed by the Africa Groups of Sweden. He wanted to go home, to make up his mind about the future. Once back in Sweden he decided to stay—but life wanted something different. Like many other young volunteers he didn't find a job on his return. Instead he developed a research project, related to his Mozambican experience. His research took him back to Mozambique, where he now found his wife. A consultancy job for UNHCR led to his present work in Bosnia for UNHCR and SIDA. So, his years in Mozambique have unintentionally led to his present professional activities.

– Once committed to Africa you cannot help loving it, he says. One thing is the remarkable ease, in spite of all the hardship, in society and relations. Then there is the nature, an atmosphere to live and relive for ever. Somebody wrote about Africa: "Every morning a new promise, cool, fragrant, teeming with sounds, before the sun starts to burn."

– Africa, in spite of all its enormous and unexploited resources, symbolises today more than before the poverty of the South. But in the long run Africans must be accepted by the world society. Sooner or later we will benefit from the contacts we have made. Many people do not seem to believe that, but I do. The African countries will surely become important in the world economy one day.

– But till then we just cannot let poor people in Africa die—it is not right! So, aid must continue, and if, as now, it is cut down, the bulk of it should be directed to Africa, which is poorest.

– What I learnt is hard to say, he concludes. Maybe a little more humility. Africa conveyed a perspective on how fortunate we are in Sweden.

What am I doing here?

Terttu Häggström stayed for more than four years in Kitwe, Zambia, as a nurse tutor, and later as Head of the Nursing School. In 1981 she was well adjusted in her job and had many interesting insights into life in Zambia. She recalls one important aspect of what Africa taught her:

– I was teaching psychology to my students, she says, and I was talking about old age. I told them how we take care of our old people in Sweden, building fine separate homes for them, etc.

– One of my students just shook her black head in contempt and asked: "But who teaches your children to live then?"

– I got very upset. I thought: What am I doing here, bringing my western ideas into a cultural context, which is built on values, we subconsciously know we lack.

– This question is now part of my present research into nursing care for stroke and dementia patients. Age, in our culture, is regarded as decay, not as wisdom. In our nursing care, respect for the elderly is rare, because in Sweden only science is of importance. This was one thing I learnt in Africa.

Terttu returned to Sweden after her years in Zambia, but she continued her international commitment with consultancy jobs in Vietnam. Africa had been an important step.

Zambia also taught her to revise her idea of friendship.

– I naively wanted to make friends in the new country, she says, but on my own terms. My friend Mary cried on the evening before our departure. She said: This is what my friends warned me of—you go home and just leave me behind. I learnt, for life, that friendship is a serious, mutual responsibility.

She was struck by the ease with which Zambians accepted white people, when in remote villages in Sweden a black person would have been something very exotic.

– We were always accepted, she says. I am very sad to see that people of different cultures are not met with the same respect in our country today.

Africans looking at the Swedes

Since I found that the content and nature of contacts differ, in my interviews in 1990 with people in Tunisia, Ethiopia, Tanzania and Zambia, I divided, the Africans, "recipients" as some call them, into three categories, the target group, counterparts and leaders.

The target group, whose conditions are supposed to be improved by aid, often have little direct contact with the expatriates. Many of them do not even know about the aid projects, unless they are directly involved. They like expatriate visitors who are kind and generous and help their neighbours, and often ignore them otherwise.

Ato Dubaro, a farmer from the hills near ARDU, a SIDA-supported project and beneficiary of its services since the mid-sixties says he has never heard of the Swedes.

– Well, people came here and said they would civilise us, he says, with some irony. And we use some of their advice still, if we can afford to. I don't know about aid. But if ARDU got aid, we farmers have also profited, for ARDU did a lot of good to us. At least it never did us any harm.

The *counterparts*, who have the daily contacts, suffer most from the inequalities built into the relationship, which expose the flagrant injustices of the world economy. While a Swede working in Africa may not have a standard of living higher than that at home, his economic situation may well be ten or twenty times better than that of his African colleagues. Many seemed to take the differences in living conditions as a matter of course, maybe out of an inherited feeling of inferiority, based on the colonial experience. But evaluations show that many Africans are impatient.

A study[7] was done in Kenya, Tanzania and Zambia, based on interviews with Scandinavians as well as Africans. It is very critical. Much of the criticism deals with donor planning, for example, that the experts are often a condition for other resources and that the existence of qualified local personnel is not properly analysed.

African counterparts complain that they have no power or control over the expatriates, that the salary differences are too great, and that only expatriates have access to all resources.

Some experts are said to be excellent, but the majority are either considered not being needed or not very efficient. Many work hard, but few are capable of transferring competence. Only twenty percent are said to have good work relations.

These results are confirmed in a UNDP study from 1993, *Rethinking Technical Assistance*. These findings have led to cuts in recruitment in all Scandinavian countries. But there are now consultant firms instead—with as many people.

A Zambian psychologist, Naboth Nculube, expresses the attitudes of African counterparts in aid as follows:[8]

– Expatriates, even volunteers, have a good car, good housing and good working conditions. The counterpart has nothing. This creates frustrations with our elites. When experts stay on in their luxury, even if they are not useful, our own people start to wonder what is the use of their long and costly education. Today there are more expatriates in Africa than in the colonial time. What is it all about—a new kind of colonialism?

However, many Africans seem to see this difference in standard as normal. An Ethiopian in charge of a workshop in an Ethiopian project is not too upset, stating that the salary of the consultants is not for paid by his own government. The main thing for him is that his Swedish counterpart is useful:

– In a while he had learnt how things function here, he says, and we could work well together on a technical level. And he was very useful—when you bring a white person along, it is always much easier to get the resources you need from the central administration.

Many are tired of talking about the blatant differences in living conditions, but hold back their irritation. Some, like an Ethiopian, think it is better that people meet on unequal terms, than that there are no contacts at all.

– Isolation is a prison, he says, and in prison you can survive, but not develop.

Very many also have pleasant memories of their Swedish colleagues:

– I like them, for they are so practical, says an Ethiopian. They do things, they teach and they work very hard. They work with their own hands, and do

---

[7] Forss, 1988.

[8] Wieslander, 1993b, p. 230

not stand beside and just watch, like the Ethiopians used to do. But the Ethiopians learnt from the Swedes, and that was so nice.

Of the third category, *people in leading positions*, those in charge of the budget think there are too many expensive experts.

– All in all, says one, what they achieve is never in proportion to what they are paid.

Those directly in charge of aid activities can be more positive.

– We need them for inspiration in modernisation, says one, but then of course they must inspire the right things.

Swedish "efficiency" can be negative.

– Ethiopians, says one, get used to the idea that only experts from abroad have the know-how. When the Swedish expert leaves nobody knows how things work.

Quality and equality

I think, like some of my informants, that an important part of aid is "for people to meet". But the quality of the encounter is of paramount importance. This is too often ignored.

An attempt was made in SIDA's support to Instituto Industrial de Maputo, Mozambique, to improve the quality of the encounter.[9] A local consultancy firm was engaged to organise an introductory training for newly arrived Swedish consultants to the Institute, together with the local teachers. This was followed up by a number of seminars, where Swedish aid was introduced, goals of the project were discussed and differences in cultures were highlighted. In spite of language difficulties the results were encouraging. The Mozambican teachers expressed satisfaction at being treated on equal terms with the Swedes, and at finally understanding the aims of the Swedish support. The Swedish teachers felt the seminars had helped integration and had somewhat changed their attitude to the development of local competence. This proved, however, to be an isolated example of taking the encounter in aid seriously.

One may, finally, ask why there is not a more widespread antagonism in Africa to all these foreigners, who disrupt societies and disregard indigenous ideas and thoughts. Maybe it is because they have to accept the foreigners, maybe the foreigners are sometimes useful. But I think there is also a unique capacity in Africa for looking at people as individuals, not as representatives of a group. As one informant says: "We look at you as individuals, and hate or love you for what you are worth".

---

[9] Wieslander, 1993a.

Is true exchange possible?

Is mutuality in the aid relationship possible? Has a "development cooperation" developed a cooperation where the actors are not "donors and receivers", but where the goal is exchange and mutual benefit? There is a new trend in the relationship between Africa and Sweden where this is concerned.

The present Partnership Africa programme, initiated by the Swedish Foreign Ministry, has had a study[10] carried out, where all the different relations between Sweden and sub-Saharan Africa are covered, including commercial relations, tourism, institutional cooperation as well as those of the civil society. Exchange between schools, churches, cultural associations or NGOs, to name a few examples, have existed for a considerable time. One case is the exchange organised by the Farmers' Association between farmers from Töreboda, Sweden, and Kibaha, Tanzania. In 1990 I met Domenic Palanjo, head of the dairy farm at Kibaha. He had spent nine months in Sweden and says he learnt a lot.

– Unfortunately, he says, I cannot use much of it. Here in Tanzania we do not have machines like you do.

This programme was abandoned long ago, but similar ones have been organised later, such as those by the Swedish Cooperative Centre in other countries. Other organisations have tried other initiatives.

Mission in return

The missions represent the oldest relationship between Sweden and Africa. The Swedish (Lutheran, state) Church mission, SKM, is one of the biggest NGOs, working with a great number of churches around the world. SKM handed over the management and ownership of the schools and hospitals it built to the local sister churches quite early and now administers its aid on requests from these churches.

When asked in 1988 what Tanzania could do to help Sweden in return, the first African bishop in a Lutheran diocese in Tanzania, the late Bishop Kibira of Bukoba, laughed and said:

– Sweden, so rich, what can *we* do for *you?* But he added:

– Well, only old people seem to come to your churches. Perhaps we could help by introducing more life and rejoicing, so that young people would become more interested and come back to your churches.

His hopes for an exchange were not great, for he added, sadly, that the interest of Swedish priests in listening to his sermons on a visit to Sweden had been very weak. But some churches have no doubt been inspired to introduce more "life and rejoicing" into the divine services, making them look—and sound—like those of the Lutheran Churches in Tanzania.

---

[10] SIPU International/SIDA, 1997.

SKM also tried in the late 1980s to create mutuality in the cooperation through a programme called "Mission in return". Swedish parishes were invited to describe problems they would like to solve with the presence of missionaries from the South. Thus a number of youth leaders, deacons and priests were invited from 1991 to Sweden to spend some years in a Swedish parish. This exchange created much better contact than the occasional African visitors, appearing as "decorations" at events in parishes around Sweden.

Some of these "return missionaries" were never integrated in Swedish society, but some were much loved. Quite a few found innovative ways of making immigrants in Sweden come to the church, a group that Swedish church people often try to reach in vain. In some cases this exchange created a commitment that has led to "friendship parishes" in Africa. The programme as such has not been repeated but continues in a new form.

Adult education, Tanzania

In 1975 the idea was introduced of creating Tanzanian Folk Development Centres, FDCs, based on Swedish folk high schools. The aim was to train young villagers, who could not go further in the formal school system, so that they could make a living in the village. Over fifty schools were started. Their principals were invited to Sweden to study Swedish folk high schools on the spot. They were sent out to different schools to see and learn. The results of these visits varied. In many cases the reception of the Tanzanian guest was half-hearted and led to no further cooperation.

But in some cases sister schools were established, and exchange programmes organised, even to the extent of sending Swedish students and teachers to work camps at schools in Tanzania and inviting Tanzanian teachers and students to visit Sweden. At several Swedish schools shops were established to sell goods imported from East Africa. The few schools that specialised in development studies made the best use of this exchange.

Other examples of exchanges

While many Swedish NGOs have now moved their focus to the Baltic states, some still have an active interest in Africa. Some organise seminars, with equal participation from Africa and Sweden. The Africa Groups of Sweden have taken numerous other interesting initiatives. So, for instance, students of medicine in Gothenburg support their fellow students in Mozambique in an exchange programme, where Mozambican students come to Gothenburg as trainees, and vice versa. A similar programme is organised by the School of Nursing in Örebro whose students support a nursing school in Maputo. Numerous Friendship Associations arrange programmes in Sweden or in Africa, publishing newsletters and starting exchange programmes. Many members of these organisations are Swedes who have worked in Africa, often their children too who maintain the commitment.

My study of relations between the town of Halmstad and Africa shows that some schools, study organisations and churches have developed exchanges with African communities, sometimes utilising aid resources. One example is SKS, the study organisation of the Lutheran Church, which is developing a network for mutual learning and understanding between Swedish and immigrant women workers and women in South Africa.

But there is still some way to go before there is an exchange on equal terms between Swedes and their African counterparts. Swedish schools, organisations and churches tend to look at themselves as donors, implying an attitude of superiority, which does not seem to have changed with the intensified contact. The image of the African is still, in the memory of many Swedes, characterised by the "Negro" on top of the savings box in the mission house. When a coin was put into the box, the black doll nodded "Thank you!" There is little evidence in Sweden of a readiness to change this image, and learn from Africans.

On equal terms?

Sweden has become multicultural during the period of aid relations. But while Swedes in Africa are often better off abroad than at home, the majority of Africans in Sweden are unemployed. And they are sometimes met with complete ignorance. A well-educated Somalian lady, on arrival in Sweden, was surprised to be taught how to flush a toilet and turn on the electric light.

Nevertheless, individual people on either side have developed in the encounter staged by aid. This goes to show that the encounter is a means to change attitudes and prejudice. Whether this might one day lead to greater mutual respect and benefit and to more equality, remains to be seen. So far, in spite of increased contact, our images of each other still reflect the old stereotypes of inequality.

A real change in the relationship demands a change of attitudes on both sides. Official Sweden is offering a partnership. Maybe Africans would welcome it. Meeting a Tanzanian literacy group in 1990 I asked if they had heard of Sweden. Yes, they had; they knew Sweden had contributed tape-recorders long ago and funds for easy readers. I asked if they had wondered why the Swedes would bother to help people in a far-off country. Most of the women were embarrassed and just giggled. But one of them said:

– Yes I have. I think you are humanists, and want to help us.

– Fair enough, I said, and will you help us in return one day?

There was more giggling, but the same lady said, very seriously:

– Why not? Maybe one day we will help you with our ideas like you help us with yours. Our countries have become friends through your help. And the thing about friendship is you exchange gifts. And then you give what you have—it can be both things and thoughts.

References

Forss, Kim, 1988, *Effectiveness of Scandinavian Technical Assistance Personnel*. Stockholm: SIDA.

SIDA/AUGUR Marknadsanalys AB, 1993, *Biståndsarbetares syn på svenskt bistånd*.

SIPU International/SIDA, 1997, *Review and Analysis of the Interchange between the Swedish Society and Sub-Saharan Africa*, Study for the Ministry of Foreign Affairs, Final Report.

Wieslander, Anna, 1982, *Ett slags gåva: Biståndsarbetare berättar*. Stockholm: Informations-byrån, SIDA.

—, 1993a, *Nu förstår vi äntligen helheten*. Stockholm: Division of Human Resources (PU), SIDA.

—, 1993b, *Var kom skruvmejseln ifrån? Mottagare & medarbetare i det svenska biståndet*. Stockholm: SIDA.

Wieslander, Anna, 1998, "More than we think—less than there should be: A study of relations between Halmstad and Africa", in Kayizzi-Mugerwa, Steve, Adebayo O. Olukoshi and Lennart Wohlgemuth (eds), *Towards a New Partnership with Africa*, pp. 232–47. Uppsala: Nordic Africa Institute.

Valentin Y. Mudimbe
Africa remains the absolute difference—An interview

Valentin Mudimbe: In order to understand "Invention of Africa", we can use a number of entries, levels of interpretations which were made by scholars, journalists and anthropologists, in order to define the specificity of Africa. We have levels of comprehension and understanding the history of the West; its everyday life, practices and its ethno-philosophy, and indeed the practice of disciplines such as history, sociology, theology and the philosophical level in its two dimensions.

I distinguish the *semiological* from the *hermeneutic* form. The first is understood as the totality of skills and knowledge that allows one to describe what one is seeing in social science. The second as the totality of skills and knowledge that allows one to read meanings.

That is the first entry; the levels of interpretation of what is going on in a given society, which thus could qualify Africa as abnormal. We can also see that abnormality or difference, by using a model, the mode of production. In France particularly, people like Catherine Coquery Vidrovitch, Claude Meillasoux and Emmanuel Terrey, conceived "the lineage mode of production", to qualify the specificity of Africa on the basis of the Marxist legacy, and the concept of "mode of production". This specificity of difference was tabulated and described in a systematic comparative study, which at the economic level was used to oppose the relationship existing between processes of production and social relations of production in the West. At the super structural level they conceived of opposing spaces: a political space in which there was a dialectic relationship between the organisation of production, that is in other terms the organisation of power, and the political discourse in the West vis-à-vis in Africa.

And finally we have the intellectual configuration and the concrete speculative processes. And this comparison, which was a comparison made by highly politically motivated people back in the 1950s and the 1960s, and who were working for African independence, were qualifying Africa out there as the absolute difference, as the absolute difference to European society itself.

But there again the model we are referring to, to quote Michael Foucault, is a European model in which we can distinguish internal or external procedures of integration or exclusion. Finally we can identify the procedures establishing people who can speak with competence about society itself.

In the internal procedures I focus on the distinction between reason and reason, between reason and madness, between normality and abnormality. It is the distinctions we can refer to in order to understand the whole enterprise of characterising cultures and societies.

We are more critical of that distinction today in social sciences and in philosophy. Yet out there, when we look at papers, news and the common sense in Europe, Africa remains today the absolute difference. And when you read some new books on Africa, you will find the same presuppositions that we find in travellers' narratives of the 18th or the 19th century.

Mai Palmberg: In certain popular literature or popular journals, it seems as if there is even regression towards, if one can say so, more primitive images than one has seen in the past 20 years. Do you have such an impression at all?

VM: Well, I have the bad habit of not reading journals and papers and not go-

248

ing to movies. Yesterday I went to see a movie on Frantz Fanon. It is the first movie I have seen since August 1970. And I do not watch television in the United States. So I live in a world in which the perceptions of otherness do not exist. And what I apprehend and my understanding of what is going on come from my reading of books. And my impression is that there is a coming back of the idea of the *primitive* because of the political and economic catastrophes that can be seen in Africa today.

Personally I do believe that this coming back of the negative images of the 19th century; images which justified colonisation as a way of assimilation, as a way of conversion to civilisation and to Christianity, can be reduced to what I call "the original sin". There is a subject, someone apprehending himself as a subject, and looking at an object, object of knowledge or an object of domination. And in this process, what we find, is a signification: the object is in actuality a human being. And that human being is reduced to its difference as an object. And that is what we call in our language "the original sin".

And in "the original sin" the subject tends to forget that to perceive is to be perceived. The European who is actualising the African as that object which is fundamentally different, forgets that he is being perceived also by the African. And also signified, redefined and reduced to the object represented by the mediation of his body and his behaviour.

MP: In all encounters one can figuratively speak of either looking through a window or looking in fact only in a mirror. That is, either really seeing the other or only seeing the self, or constructing the self through the image of the other. Can seeing the other really be achieved? And what are the obstacles and the prospects?

VM: I have responded already to that question by referring to "the original sin". I prefer the metaphor of the mirror, because in conceiving *the other* what one is perceiving is a body. And it is only

through the perception of that mediation, represented by the body, that I can conclude that there is something like a consciousness and intelligence in *the other*.

Thus in the perception, in the understanding, in the effort to empathise with *the other*, in fact I am projecting *my own self*. And perhaps we could say that the main problem of anthropology, at least of African anthropology, has been for the West a search for *itself*, the origins and the understanding of this absolute commencement.

MP: Our book, which this interview is for, is premised on a perhaps unwarranted generalisation of *us* in Europe, and *them*, meaning *those* in Africa. If we want to question this generalisation are there any other important clusters of *us* and *them* we should rather use?

VM: The opposition between *us* and *them* reproduces the basic opposition between *the I* and *the other*. And what you do by going from *the I* to *the we*, is literally speaking a sociologisation of the Cartesian cogito. And thus we have a relationship, that we can reduce to a square; *I, we, other, they*. And in this square *the other* and the *they* constitute the radical opposition of *the I* and *the we*. We can comment on a concrete relationship existing between *the I, we* and *the other, they*, which are relationships of opposition of antagonism of reduction of signification.

We can also move from this violent relationship to something else, which is happening economically today, and which is frightening. It is the globalising world in which we are living today. A mode of production that is planetary, and this mode of production is not only characteristic of one nation, but of multinationals. They are now organising this planet; they are reducing all of us, Africans and Europeans, to objects producing according to the demands of multinationals. And thus, I think the century which is coming, will be completely different because of this globalising system.

MP: In a recent lecture you were talking about the postulates of right to dominance, which were expressed in the enunciation by the Pope as early as in the 1400s. That this also means that racism started as early as that?

VM: Well I do not know about that. You know, it is possible to go for example to the Roman Empire. And Rome is a good illustration because people from different origins were living there; from the north of Germany for example, from the south of Africa and so on. And slavery then for example, was not based on the colour of the skin of the people. And to compare that type of society to let us say the 14th or 15th century of European society or of our present day society, is tricky because we are dealing with radically different societies. Instead of using history I want to think of what racism is about, and what universalism is about.

And thinking about it in terms of research that I have been doing, and in seminars that I have been teaching (and I have been teaching in Stanford and in Berlin on theories of inequality, theories of difference) I would say that there is a paradox. We should look at universalism as a racism. Universalism comes from somewhere, from a locality, from a tradition, from a language, from a philosophy, and poses itself as normality to all other cultures, societies and individualities. And in doing so, what it is promoting is the power, the imperialism of a given local experience. I am not inventing it, I am referring to a collective work done by Etienne Balibar from France and Immanuel Wallerstein from the United States.

But on the other hand racism is the apprehension of oneself as norm, more exactly looking at oneself as particular and incarnating an otherness. That incarnation disparts its negativity, then it wants to be universal. And so particularism in its own limitation is an ambition to universality.

MP: I want to refer to a discussion on this, which was held in conjunction with a book fair in Gothenburg here in Sweden two or three years ago. There was a session on human rights and all of those involved were universalists except one on the panel, who was talking about cultural rights. And I made a small intervention and I said that if it is so that human rights emanate from the French revolution or whatever, then we should just be very thankful to the French.

But there was a lot of opposition to my comment: one lawyer from Spain said that it is not at all true that it is a Western concept. When the declaration of human rights was enacted or adopted by the United Nations, both the Chinese and the Indians and other representatives said that this emanated from their particular ideology and philosophy. And a politician from Sweden told me off by saying that there is only one thing that is Western about human rights, and that is our claim that it is Western. So could it be true that it came from several localities?

VM: Well, it is possible to find in different traditions the concept of human rights. It is true that in China or in America there was a philosophy that has a conception of human rights. But these conceptions, and this is my point, are completely different from those of the enlightenment. And secondly, the enlightenment also succeeded in imposing this perception thanks to the French Revolution. A concept of equality and fraternity for example imposed itself, not only philosophically but also politically, and we are dependent on that. But this should not allow us to forget the shortcomings when we look at the writings of someone like Condorçet who was sincere, who was a revolutionary, who was for the rights of the slaves and women—and yet we find passages which are sometimes astonishing, in which he writes explicitly there are people who are more equal than other people! So we should take that critically and understand that our thinking today on human rights is inscribed in a history, which is political and philosophical, and accept the fact that it has been institutionalised thanks to the legacy of the enlightenment.

MP: Is there any concept of Africa that is not externally defined?

VM: Is there a concept of Europe that is not externally defined? Europe defines itself but it is also being defined from a Chinese, Japanese or African viewpoint. All of us we define ourselves, our identities, by assuming and accepting the fact that we are beings for others. And what is true for an individual is also true for a culture. We inhabit our cultures, our traditions, in the way we inhabit our bodies. We are perceived and thus defined by other people.

MP: I was struck in Ghana by the way people said "... this is not African and this is African tradition and so on ...". I am wondering how much the conception, or the concept African, is a reflection of the reflection of the Western concept of Africa?

VM: I think that in all societies you find a definition of yourself, which is a definition that you should be understood as a comparative. One defines oneself vis-à-vis someone else; it might be an individual, it might be a culture. And Africans ... let us put it in this way; the concept of Africa is an invention. We can go back to the end of the 15th century and the encounter with Europe, when the continent is qualified. And its characteristics are given in books and in papers as if Africa is unified. And with that African cultures, which were different, collapsed. Despite their differences, with their own traditions, their own languages, they have been brought together. That is what is called an invention. It is a perception. And in the 19th century that continent is going to be colonised by Europe. And unified by Europe, the frontiers are going to be delimited by Europe also.

This invention created something new, which was not there before. But despite that newness a new consciousness of belonging to a continent was indirectly created, perhaps I should say directly created. That is how in Ghana or in Senegal you meet people defining themselves as "we Africans". It is interesting because it should be possible to ask: what is that exactly? And to which invention are they referring; to the tradition, the culture to which they belong? Was that tradition qualified as African and by whom and since when? Or are they referring to the Africa invented and organised by the coloniser? That is not impossible.

[The interview was made in Stockholm on November 25, 1998 by Mai Palmberg.]

Terence Ranger
I did not set out to deconstruct—An interview

Mai Palmberg: One can perhaps say that your research has to a very large extent been about deconstructing African and European images of Africa and African history. What motivated you?

Terence Ranger: I did not set out to deconstruct, I just increasingly found that the mental structures that were being used to describe African society did not fit with realities. I suppose my deconstruction of the idea of ethnicity did have some kind of political motivation as well because I disliked the way in which both inside Africa and outside it, conflicts were routinely ascribed to ancient tribal hostilities. In the little book that I published in Zimbabwe called *The Invention of Tribalism in Zimbabwe* I actually started off very explicitly with this. It was distressing and ridiculous that tension within Zimbabwean politics, what happened in Matabeleland etc. could be described by the Guardian in terms of thousands of years of tension between the Ndebele and the Shona. So what one wanted to do in a way was to deconstruct. Of course that has turned out to be more complicated than I expected because you can say that the whole idea of a bounded tribe is partly the creation of the imposition of boundaries, and partly the creation of language work. It is only partly, as I first of all set off to say, the invention of various European classifiers.

So then you have to say that it is filled with meaning by African classifiers and by people who come more and more to feel that they really are Kikuyu or they really are Shona. Thus even if you can say that this is a relatively recent concept and that identity groupings were very different in pre-colonial Africa, one then comes back to the fact that ethnic identity has become increasingly important in 20th century Africa. So when I wrote *The Invention of Tradition* I did it very much in terms of the initial invention. And then when I wrote *The Invention of Tradition Revisited* I did it very much in terms of the African imagining. Anyway it was largely a historical intellectual process for me and partly related with my work on missions, mission evangelism, mission ethnography and mission language work, but there was also a political motivation to try to escape from the irrationalism of explaining everything through tribal conflict. And when I gave a lecture like that in the Saint Antony's series Lady Dahrendorf said to me "How strange, it is all quite different from what we thought and yet somehow the same". And that is the problem with it. But my own belief is that the sense of identity is very situational and that you are not caught in an inevitable tribal or ethnic identity, but it has been constructed. And it can be deconstructed, it goes side by side with many other identities.

MP: This also touches upon the question of the self images of educated Africans who are possibly influenced by these images created in Europe.

TR: I think one has to go back and talk about educated Africans who by contemporary standards were not very educated. These key figures were the first catechists and teachers of the missions, and who brought certain of the principles of classification as part of their commitment to Christianity and as part of their shared involvement in creating the written languages. The way that African languages were turned into written languages was not miraculously achieved by missionaries working alone. Both parties brought very important things to it, the Africans brought the vocabulary and the syntax and so on, the missionaries brought principles of linguistic classification. And these ideas of being able to see order where hitherto there was only practice were attractive to some of these early missionary catechists and evangelists. Using the newly created written languages, they engaged in what Wyat Mac Gaffey has called the ethnographic encounter, where they were reporting back upon the beliefs and practices of groups who shared the language but which hitherto had been unknown to these catechists and evangelists, and so in this kind of way they were categorising. And of course they had every motive for doing so, they thought of enlarging the scale of the African unit, making available this marvellous tool of a written language and so on. From the very beginning they were participating critically in the business of defining units and identities.

They did become apparently subordinate to European missionaries but in fact were extremely influential leaders. Because the people who helped create the written language in the first place fanned out then through the area of mission influence. A great example is Buganda where the Ganda speech is carried out to new areas as the missions expanded. It happens in eastern Zimbabwe too where the Manica speech originally is created by people in one chieftainship and is then carried out to others.

These evangelists and teachers with the new written language, and ideas of classification, are beginning to write the first histories, and the first ethnographies. From the end of the 19th century or the beginning of the 20th century, they are filling in these bounded concepts. What they are doing is creating bounded areas, which keep out travelling rainmakers, or travelling witch cleansers and the like. Because the new Christian evangelists and teachers have located bases of power: the village, with the village school, and so on. So from the very beginning these kinds of people who subsequently are marginalized because they are not very educated,

nevertheless play the kind of role that Steven Feierman describes in his *Peasant Intellectuals*, they are a kind of organic intellectuals.

Later on their sons become considerably more educated and begin to use different classificatory systems. John Iliffe in *A Modern History of Tanganyika* says that even inventing a nation was exactly the same process as inventing a tribe and was done by the same sort of people —another generation but the same sort of people. There is a tension then between those who were enlarging that invention still further and those who still are deeply committed to the original invention of these bounded identities.

Obviously the idea that it was all done by native commissioners and missionaries and so on would be very crude. So in this kind of way you have a deep implication, to use Basil Davidson's favourite word, on the part of Africans with Europeans. European missionaries are only very imperfectly aware of all the initiatives the evangelists and teachers have taken and in the standard mission histories they see themselves or their predecessors as the takers of all these initiatives. I think in the whole history of nationalism in Africa you have a process of discovering where your boundaries are going to be which is very similar to this earlier process of carving out bounded tribes. Because if the first educated generation is thinking of a kind of Pan-African or Pan-southern African identity as well as an ethnic one, the idea of a territorial nationalism, is something that comes very late in the day. You first discover what the practical boundaries are, and then somewhat belatedly you have to put a lot of imaginative effort into giving that some cultural meaning and historical meaning.

So you see these processes of moving from much wider networks of interaction to significantly bounded units, first of all creating localities or tribal groups and then creating territorial nations. In east central and Southern Africa you see this process going on. Now obviously it is true to say that the nation is an artificial concept, is an import. The person who says this most vigorously is Eric Hobsbawm in his *Age of Extremes* book where he sees it as impossible that a nation can emerge in Africa. I think that the imagining of a national boundary was just as much an artefact in Europe as it was in Africa. But it may well be, that people did not have long enough to imagine their nations, but still it seems to me that in effect African nations became units of identities. Whether you feel a Tanzanian, if you feel a Kenyan or a Kikuyu or a Zimbabwean or an Ndebele depends very much on the context. You have these hierarchies of identity and then you move to and fro. So one of the things that people are studying is precisely the African construction of these identities and one can say, and it is certainly true, that both the idea of tribe and the idea of nation are European ideas, but infused with African meanings by this process. John Lonsdale has, in the most complex way, explored this process of the way that an ethnicity or a nation becomes objects of disagreement and debate amongst Africans and come to have enormous richnesses of meaning that would be impossible for the first European designers of the blueprint to have imagined.

The reason that cultural nationalist leaders came down on the territorial nation as a unit was initially an entirely practical one. For example, in the most recent of my books I show the Zimbabwean Methodist leader, nationalist politician Thompson Samkange, in correspondence with Doctor Banda. And Thompson is taking a very Pan-Southern-African attitude. What he is saying is that there is really a single Congress movement. But it has different manifestations in a Nyasaland Congress and in a Rhodesian Congress, but wherever you are you should support that local manifestation. So if you are a Southern Rhodesian in Nyasaland you should join that Congress and if you are a Nyasa in Southern Rhodesia you join that Congress. And it is against

this Pan-African idea to start branches of your own territorial Congress in other countries. And Dr Banda initially agrees with that entirely, but then of course it becomes critical to the Nyasaland Congress to have rebates from their migrant workers. And after federation it becomes so critical for Nyasaland to make its own independent case. And then ultimately in Southern Rhodesia it becomes clear that there is such a tremendous difference between the colonial official territory and the settler state. There is also such a difference between the settler state of Rhodesia and that of South Africa. And ultimately the only tactical way to operate is on the territorial level. And what Banda says, "... trust me ..." he says, "... let us lead the federation, let us break up this unit and then once we have achieved our independence we will assist you." And of course he did not.

So it seems to me that the idea of a Zimbabwe or whatever it was going to be called, as a distinct national unit, a majority rule unit, or the idea of Malawi or Zambia is actually quite late, from the 1940s maybe, particularly sharp in the 1950s. Prior to that the influence of the South African National Congress had been profound partly because of labour migration. There were many people living in the territories to the North who still went on thinking of themselves as South African ANC members. People say to me "well I was a loyal ZAPU member but the ANC was my brother, my mother and father". You have this kind of idea, and then with a real sense of loss people begin to say we have got to focus on the national unit. Then when they do begin to focus on the national unit you have the problem: well there are things called nations, and this is going to be our nation. If it had been the whole of Southern Africa then there would have been some kind of common principles of Africanity. Now it is a smaller unit and in a sense we have to justify this in cultural terms.

So in Tanganyika you say we magnify that which we have in common, the Swahili language, in a kind of secular nationalism, we are not going to allow any one tribe to become dominant and on the whole they succeed remarkably well. In Malawi you say "What is our historical cultural point of reference?", well it is the Chewa Empire, and this involves the subordination of the North. And today they are seriously talking about calling the country Nyasaland again rather than Malawi. Because it started off as a Nyasaland African Congress, banned in 1959, the leaders detained, and then out of this turmoil there emerged the Malawi Congress Party. Now there are many people in Malawi today who say, "... we do not want that name". That was an invented name, which tried to impose Chewa, a single cultural tradition upon us, Chewa dominance. Just as in what used to be Zaire they have now gone back to the name of Congo.

In Zimbabwe I have not heard people saying that they repudiate the name Zimbabwe. Although there was some debate when the first Zimbabwe African People's Union emerged, there were people writing in Matabeleland: "We ought to call it the Matopos National Union because the Matopos are the spiritual centre of the Nation."

Richard Werbner in *Tears of the Dead* talks about what he calls pseudo-nationalism, that is the temptation to try to shortcut the problem of how you arrive at cultural homogeneity. In Zimbabwe many people did not even know that they were Shona until the 1950s. But then politicians say the great majority of the country is Shona and it would simplify everything if everybody realised that this was true.

MP: Let us touch upon the question of myth and reality. For example in Angolan or should we say the MPLA version of Angolan history, Queen Nzinga is a very important figure. And you can look at Queen Nzinga in many different ways; you can look at her as a kind of symbol of resistance and so on, but there are also other ways of looking at her, as an oppressor and so forth. What should the

line really be? Should we sit by and say that these images are useful, or should we as intellectuals and together with our African friends and colleagues try to dispel this?

TR: Queen Nzinga is a very interesting example. I have never been to Angola but I was at a meeting in the United States where a black American woman was giving a paper on the heroines of African history, and how they have been neglected. And she used Nzinga, and she used the fact that Nzinga had repudiated slave trade treaties with the Portuguese and was an emancipatory figure. And Paul Lovejoy who was there, said that she only repudiated those treaties because she made more effective ones with the Dutch, and she was a great slave trader. And the Afro-American woman responded to him by saying "you are just a typical historian, you are relying on documents, which were written by Europeans, and I am relying upon the oral tradition of her people, which says that she was a heroine." It was an absolutely classic crux, it was at a conference at Santa Cruz about Black resistance, and Paul was outflanked in a way. I think it is a matter of great importance because ultimately, obviously all nationalisms need myths, and there are plenty of them in Europe: the invention of William Tell and all the rest of it. But what is important it is not so much whether they are true or false but what kind of heroes they are portrayed as. If you base your nationalism upon heroes, ultimately you cannot prevent people from seeing if they were people of power and exploitation and oppression.

Now this was the dilemma, which we often faced when we were at the History Department of the University College of Dar es Salaam, where we were trying to find what the roots of Tanzanian national unit were. And there was a lot of writing at that time about enlargement of scale in the 19th century. People who were able to create more effective units were regarded very favourably in Tanzanian nationalist history.

And there is this one character whom Aylward Shorter wrote about, The Breaker of Rocks, who was incorporated into this idea of the enlargement of scale. But at the same time he was obviously the most straightforwardly thuggish character; he had slave armies and when he was attacking a stockade, if his armies were repulsed he just sent in more slaves, saying: "Throw on more logs." And you know, the contradiction became apparent even at that time. You say, OK well Bismarck was a man of blood and iron, but nevertheless the contradiction between this kind of enlargment of scale and its anti-emancipatory implications really becomes very sharp. So it is a question of, you know the Swiss managed to invent a successful rebellious man of the people, and it is a question of finding, I suppose, the stereotype figure that represents that in some way. It is a very complicated interaction between academic history, geography and nationalist invention.

In the case of Zimbabwe it was not so much us, so called nationalist historians, but quite conservative historians, like Donald Abraham or the archaeologist Summers. They were working with oral tradition or with archaeology, and Summers was constructing the Zimbabwe ruin as the capital city of a great ancient state. Not because he was a nationalist, but because it was the tendency of archaeology to focus on those kinds of units. And Abraham who certainly had no sympathy whatsoever for modern African nationalism was creating a similarly oversimplified model from the oral material. And he was being profoundly influenced by marvellously manipulative African informers, by the medium of the Chaminuka spirit, and so on. And Abraham was writing about the Shona nation in the 15th century, about the capital city of the national state in absolute naïvety, really, because certainly the last thing he wanted to do was to hand this material to an anti-colonial nationalist movement.

When the Zimbabwe News had a special issue on ZANLA history, Mugabe wrote about how the spirit of ZANLA had been incarnated throughout history; he was going back to the Mutapa state and the rebel Mutapas and the exclusively Shona version of history, which was just there available so to speak. It did not even have to be motivated by a wicked, genocidal dislike of the Ndebele, because it was all there lying about in the work of the oral historians and the archaeologists and so forth.

To have a different kind of idea of a national past became very complicated. A bit earlier than that when Joshua Nkomo was the leader, he actually tried very hard to balance all varieties, so he would take his Shona-speaking allies to the grave of Mzilikazi or to one of the Mwali shrines, and he would go with them to the senior Shona spirit mediums and so on. He was trying very hard to keep all this in balance. And now again, since 1990 really, with the collapse of the one-party state idea, historians too are trying to produce this impression of complexity and pluralism and so on. But since Shona speakers are so much in the majority, and you've got this history offered to you of a coherent Shona imperial system, there is a great temptation to create your national history on that.

Obviously Mozambique cannot possibly do that because that long thin country has no precolonial historical coherence at all. And Mozambique has always been open to the irredentism of its neighbours. Dr Banda would have liked the chunk between Malawi and certainly the other side of the lake and that would have made very good cultural sense. And then Zimbabwe knows that there are Shona speakers right up to the sea, and if Cecil Rhodes had not been such a chicken then Zimbabwe would have had a sea coast and so forth. Mozambique had constantly to guard first of all against the colonial ambitions of Britain and Germany and so on. But in the more recent period there is this feeling that zones of Mozambique are really part of the cultural areas of other countries. When Mozambique constructs its national myth, it has to do so on a totally different basis, because it cannot possibly build on a core identity.

MP: I suppose that also in Angola and in the Congo as we now call it again, the temptation must be to centre the history on those societies or kingdoms which were centralised. And then for example in Angola, you leave out the UNITA territory.

TR: Yes and I think this has always been a real problem for Basil Davidson who wrote in *Black Mother* the influential early accounts of the Portuguese interaction with the kingdom of the Congo, which of course spreads into both Angola and Zaire, and was a large territorial entity. But at the same time Basil, in quoting Cabral, says that what must be done is to recapture history. Basil emphasises from the very beginning that that did not mean a return to the past, but a recapture of historical initiative. And somewhat disconcertingly to many Africans who relied upon him for "old Africa rediscovered" and for the "glorious African past", more and more he emphasised that there has been a rupture in the 19th century and that a return to the past was impossible. What was important was a recovery of political, economic, social and to some extent a cultural initiative. So his writing on Cabral is very interesting from that point of view. In a book like *The African Genius* he brings out very clearly this notion that he feels there has been a disruption, and even that it was a pre-colonial disruption caused by overpopulation, ecological crisis, Mfecane, the slave trade, and so on. And it is a viewpoint that Vansina for example, such a different historian from Davidson, in his *Path in the Rainforests*, Vansina takes the same attitude. Here is this great shaping tradition, which with the colonial conquest in this case, does come to an end.

Vansina takes the invention of tradition to very formidable extremes: "... customary law is the gravestone of tradition ..." he says, the Europeans invent identi-

ties. But that does smash up the flexibility in the dynamism of the tradition.

Nevertheless the people who have told us most about pre-colonial Africa are in fact the people who most emphatically insist that nothing is to be gained by any kind of return.

What I like better of course is Feierman's *Peasant Intellectuals* where he shows the continuous flexibility of cultural idioms that are available for modernisation rather than this idea of a tradition that comes to a disastrous end, and which then does not provide you with any sort of assistance. Obviously this is so in Zaire which is so huge that the idea of any single kind of history seems impossible. But there are number of countries where it does not seem impossible. Uganda perhaps, although obviously they put together such tremendous variety of different kinds of societies in Uganda that it became very difficult. Kenya is difficult because you have the coast, which is the leader, then becomes the periphery and so on. But you have places like Lesotho and Swaziland. Swaziland I suppose is an example where absolute enforcement of a single cultural identity is a kind of oppression upon any sort of minorities. Botswana is a very good case in point where none of the minority languages are allowed, because you have the advantage of Tswana. I have done some work actually on Kalanga-speaking groups in northern Tswana who effectively want to secede and they do not want to recognise the authority of Tshekedi who is the regent of the Bamangwato. And they are saying "look we are Kalanga" and Tshekedi says: "when I say you are Bamangwato I am not saying that you are Tswana by origin, the Bamangwato are made up of people of all over the place. That is because we are a nation, we are not a tribe we are a nation. You want to be a tribe". Of course the power relations are very unequal and they are genuinely being exploited, and so on. It is the same argument in the nation-state of Botswana where all these clever Kalanga from the north are in the civil service and they are at the university, but they cannot operate in their own language. And the argument is that Tswana is not a tribal language but a national language. Botswana is a good example of a country in which the power imbalances of the past still continue within a supposedly democratic system.

MP: In those countries which have gone through a war of liberation there is also another kind of imagery being created, and that is the imagery of heroes. Is this something that is functional and should be just seen as such or is it something that should be scrutinised?

TR: In the Zimbabwean case of course it has been enormously controversial. Norma Kriger has written an excellent piece about this in *Society in Zimbabwe's liberation war*. The Heroes' Acre in Harare is fascinating and kind of post-colonial, post-modernist exercise. At one level when you go there it is obviously powerfully shaped by the Korean influence. And it feels very much like an eastern European heroic monument, a monument of the personality of Mugabe and so on. At another level other people have felt that this is tremendously within Zimbabwean tradition, that under the Mutapa emperors in the 16th century there were places to which pilgrimages were made to the dead. And the Heroes' Acre is a kind of democratisation of that principle, because it is certainly not only ex-monarchs who were buried there. But the idea is that it is a central place where annually, the living king used to go to the hill where his predecessors were buried and communicate with them and the spirits would reply. Particularly in the early days of Heroes' Acre that is exactly what Mugabe did, annually on Heroes' Day he would go to Heroes' Acre and he would invoke the heroic spirits. Not only as an example but also almost as to signal moral danger to people who were not committed to the nation. So obviously what he was trying to do was to combine ideas of the great leader, of the sort of

eastern European-Korean idea of the great leader, with something that made sense in Zimbabwe in cultural terms.

Now notoriously this has not worked, and it has not worked for all kinds of reasons; one is that when you declare a chief a hero like Chief Tangwena all you get is a coffin with rocks in, because Chief Tangwena's people had buried his actual body in the cave with the other chiefs. And it has not worked with many of the non-chiefly heroes whose families would not bury them there. There are lots of people buried here compulsorily so to speak, like Herbert Chiepo. His widow thinks he is there with the people who murdered him. There is only one woman hero buried at Heroes' Acre, namely Sally Mugabe. Most Zimbabwean women historians would say that they have missed opportunities there.

The construction of the Heroes' Acre is very interesting. The balance between the politicians and the soldiers, the guarded character of this base which is not open to the public without a permit, are among so many issues that arise. At first it seemed like a brilliant modernisation of tradition, and then it has got more and more problematic. And it is really interesting to know when there is a changed regime as I suppose there is bound to be when Mugabe dies, whether Heroes' Acre will be kept up and maintained or whether it will pass. Of course it has great importance for the living because the widows, and the family of the heroes have pensions and there is a whole structure of support. And then there has been a whole question of whether this idea can be extended to another part of the country; can it be extended to Matabeleland, if so how? Essentially they failed there to create a new pilgrimage centre which has been an effective rival to the old. I think what is expressed there too is this enormous combined mixture of nationalist ideologies, the Zimbabwe Ruins which are evoked by the architecture of the Heroes' Acre, and the idea of the Royal Spirits.

MP: Let us turn briefly to another subject or another way that images shape people's minds, the way that we look upon history. There seems to be an accepted image that Africa today is in crisis. But then there is a questioned imagery of what it looked like before and what the contrast is. This is something you touch upon in your essay in *Post-colonial Identities*.

TR: Well, *Post-colonial Identities* as you know was edited by Richard Werbner and myself, and very good friends as we are we never cease disagreeing with each other. Dick in his excellent useful introduction was obviously very much taken with the utility of the idea of the post-colonial, and he seemed to me to be combining the very essences in which that term can be used.

What I was saying in the postscript was that I thought it was dangerous to reaffirm the idea of the post-colonial, which is as you say a state of crisis, a sense of anomie, a lack of belief in any narrative etc. etc. And I say it is dangerous partly because it does imply even without the contributors intending it to, some kind of contrast with the period where things were much more straightforward and stable, and by extension presumably the colonial period. I argue that if you were to use the same methods, and to ask the same questions about the colonial period that people ask about post-colonial Africa, it would all look much more similar than it does at the moment. Now you are contrasting the colonial social sciences and their product, not only with the realities of post colonial Africa but with the methodologies of post-colonial Africa. I am sceptical about the idea of post-coloniality and the uniqueness of this crisis and so on.

In the case of Zaire for example the Zairian papers say that things are falling apart, but we have been told by so many people that things are falling apart in the Congo over the last hundred years that, you know one cannot believe that they were ever really put together again.

This is all part, of course, of the other question that you asked; dominant media images of Africa in the West, the protests against this amongst the Africans but nevertheless the shaping of their own attitudes.

At the Keele conference there was a very interesting paper given about a boys' secondary boarding school in Uganda, and the way in which the boys were cutting themselves off from their bush parents, the village and the peasants and their enormous sense of themselves as modern people, side by side with an absolute adoration of the West. They are going to be like Europeans though many of them secretly think that they never can quite be like Europeans. Africans cannot quite make it, cannot quite be efficient, cannot quite establish order and so on. A very depressing paper in a way for this cultural subservience and this contempt of "we are all African". One finds this kind of thing all over the place, the exaggerated prestige of Western manufactured goods rather than local manufactured goods, the belief that education in Europe is infinitely superior to the locally offered education.

A positive national image based on whatever tendentious history, seems really important in all this as a kind of protection against these tremendous feelings of race failure and inadequacy. It does seem very important that people can feel well. The only great leader in the world today is Nelson Mandela, and everybody wants to come to Cape Town. Because otherwise the kind of increasingly dismissive Western stereotype is very easy to internalise. When people started off imitating Europeans at the end of the 19th century in the dance societies and so on, they were doing that in order to gain power. Because the belief was that you were reflecting the power struggle in and the forms of power. Now there is in many places this almost resigned feeling that Africa is never going to get power, it is sort of on the edges.

But let me just say in conclusion about images; I ran a seminar here two years ago called Images of Africa, and there were a whole series of extremely interesting papers. But by the end I realised, as I should have done from the start, that they were all European images of Africa and Africans; ethnographic photography, exhibition displays in early 20th century England, the making of landscape by colonial interventionists etc. etc. And hardly anything about African images: African images of Europe, African images of Africans, African images of themselves.

One of the great things for me at the Keele conference in May 1997 on "The Meaning of the Local" was Heike Behrens showing examples of marvellous studio photography in Mombasa. These studio photographers who were up-country people and who were taking slides of the country boys and women coming to town with a very particular style, marvellously colourful flat style, importing images like the jet plane taking off through the window of your living room and so on. And what one was seeing there was not ethnographic photography but African urban photography.

I was asked to go to Berlin for the conference on modernity, they asked me to do a paper on landscape and modernity and obviously what they expected was that I would say: well landscape is a notion imported by the external view, Africans have use-values, Europeans think of landscape and the creation of landscapes is another imperial intervention and so on. All of which is to some extent true and all of which I have said to some extent before, but then I thought: to hell with this. Why don't I try to find out what Africans think about landscape? I mean their comments on their environment are not restricted just to use-values or to particular trees and so on, so I did a long paper about the conjunctions which generate African propositions about landscape.

I am becoming increasingly restless with this marvellous sophisticated literature about colonial discourse, European creation of these images or that, even if it is true to say that these are then often in-

ternalised by Africans. And I am increasingly interested in work that enables one to see African conceptualisations.

[The interview was made by Mai Palmberg in Oxford in June, 1997.]

Select annotated bibliography

Petra Smitmanis

Abraham, Kinfe, *From Race to Class: Links and Parallels in African and Black American Protest Expression.* London: Grassroots Publisher, 1982. 258 pp.

Deals with black literature with an analysis based on the Marxist interpretation of social and historical events. The book is a critical survey of the major trends in the development of black literature. The book highlights the tragic drama of slavery and colonialism, looks at the situation for black literature in Africa, America and the Caribbean, the confusion about the concepts of race and class, and the task of modern black literature.

Achebe, Chinua, *Hopes and Impediments: Selected Essays 1965–1987.* Ibadan: Heinemann, 1988. 130 pp.

Deals with how literature and culture interact with the socio-political realities of the modern world. Examines the Eurocentric bias of the fiction and mores of the colonialist era and also in contemporary literary journalism. Achebe argues for greater recognition of the universality of the African experience and the specifically African novel. Achebe also argues that literature should contribute to our development as individuals and as members of a global community in need of inspiration and purpose.

Africa and the United States: Images and Realities. Boston: Department of State Publications, 1961. 212 pp.

This volume of essays includes 14 essays written as background papers to the 8th National Conference of the U.S. National Commission for UNESCO dealing with Africa and the United States. The essays treat topics such as African politics, education, women, research, culture and media. Contributors: Helen Kitchen, Wendell P. Jones, Betty George, Martin L. Kilson Jr., Adelaide C. Hill, Laura Bornholdt, John J. McKelvey Jr., Eric R. Rude, Lawrence E. Howard, William E. Moran, Roy Sieber, Alan Merriam, Dorothy B. Porter, Robert A. Lystad, Robert Hartland.

Alatas, Syed Hussein, *The Myth of the Lazy Native.* London: Cass, 1977. 267 pp.

This book deals with the origin and the functions of the myth of the lazy native, from the 16th to the 20th century in Malaysia, the Philippines and Indonesia. The central theme in the analysis is the functions this myth had in the colonial ideology. The author concludes that the images of the native as lazy were constructed by colonialism, and have been used as an impediment to the understanding of native life. The author argues that these images have been and still are influential.

American society of African culture, *Africa from the point of view of American Negro scholars.* Dijon: Présence Africaine, 1958. 418 pp.

This volume includes 22 essays divided into three parts, where the first part deals with analyses of African society. The following part deals with African art, dance and literature and the last part deals with the Afro-Americans' relationship to Africa. Contributors: St. Clair Drake, Martin L. Kilson Jr., Hugh H. Smythe, William Leo Hansberry, Lorenzo D. Turner, James A. Porter, J. Newton Hill, J. Eugene Grigsby Jr., Pearl E. Primus, Samuel W. Allen, Mercer Cook, Rayford W. Logan, James W. Ivy, Horace Mann Bond, E. Franklin Frazer, Hildrus A. Poindexter, W.E.B. Du Bois, John W. Davies, Adelaide Cromwell Hill, Dorothy B. Porter, Ulysses Lee.

Amin, Samir, *Eurocentrism*. London: Zed Books, 1988. 157 pp.

This book deals with the identification of the elements which have distinguished the thoughts and civilisation of Europe from those of its neighbours, and it explores the transition from metaphysical to scientific thought. The analysis of Europe's present intellectual ascendancy exposes many illusions Westerners have about the nature of their own culture, its roots, and what it really has to offer to the future. Amin questions the argument that it is only through imitation of the West that the rest of the world can progress. He considers as well the relative failure of third world nationalism and attacks its successor, Islamic fundamentalism.

Appiah, Francis, *The Importance of African Culture for Overall Development*. Statsbyggingsprosjektet Notater. Universitetet i Bergen. Bergen: Universitetet i Bergen, 1989. 24 pp.

The author discusses the concepts of culture and development. He then discusses the role of the state in development, and how culture has become institutionalised in Africa. He deals with questions such as: What is the history of culture and development in African states? In what way does culture affect development and how does development affect culture in African states today? The author then analyses how culture has been studied in relation to development and the position of African culture in post-colonial development.

Appiah, Kwame Anthony, *In my Father's House: Africa in the Philosophy of Culture*. London: Methuen, 1992. 366 pp.

Deals with what it is like to be African today from a political and cultural point of view. The issues of race and nationhood are treated, how they arose in African, Afro-Caribbean and Afro-American thought over the last century and a half. Appiah examines the idea of Africa to illuminate an African identity that extends into the continent's diaspora. Appiah considers the views of political leaders, writers and philosophers. He dissects the role of racial ideology in the development of Pan-Africanism showing how it has obscured the diversity of African cultures. Then he addresses the ideas of critics and writers, arguing that the project of constructing an African literature rooted in African traditions has obscured Africa's profound entanglement with the intellectual life of Europe and United States. In analysing from a variety of perspectives, philosophy, politics and the arts, Appiah challenges prevailing conceptions of the much discussed opposition between tradition and modernity. Finally he sketches the theoretical and practical possibilities of a reconsidered Pan-Africanism.

Arntsen, Hilde, (ed.), *Media, Culture and Development*. Oslo: University of Oslo, 1993. 252 pp.

Deals with various aspects of contemporary media in a cultural and developmental perspective. The contributions range from theoretical elaborations to policy discussion and case studies, with the focus on Southern Africa and Norway. The volume includes three parts. The first part deals with general theoretical and policy issues, the second part deals with the situation in Africa in general, and Zimbabwe in particular. Part three deals with the Norwegian situation.

Asante, Molefi Kete and Kariamu Welsh Asante, (eds), *African Culture: the Rhythms of Unity*. Trenton, N.J.: Africa World Press, 1990. 270 pp.

The book deals with the relationship of African cultural data to that of other regions in the world, as well as with African philosophical writings on culture that explain the unity of African thought or show the common philosophical approaches employed by people of African descent. The book suggests measures for reconstructing and re-energising African cultural unity. The volume is divided into four parts. The first part dealing with the ethnocultural motif, includes "Afrocentricity and culture" by Molefi Kete Asante; "The African world and the ethnocultural debate" by Wole Soyinka and "Cultural, political and economic universals in West Africa" by Aguibou Y. Yasane. The second part dealing with the artistic and intellectual tradition, includes "Communalities in African Dance, an aesthetic foundation" by Kariamu Welsh Asante; "African oral artistry and the new social order" by Samuel Osei Boadu; "The African intellectual and the problem of class suicide, ideological and political dimensions" by Maulana Karenga. Part three dealing with the concepts of cultural values, includes "African traditional education, a tool for intergenerational communication" by Felix Boateng. The last part dealing with cultural continua, includes "African-American historians and the reclaiming of African history" by John Henrik Clarke; "Quilombismo, the African-Brazilian road to socialism" by Abdias do Nascimento; "The concept of African personality, sociological implications" by Mwizenge S. Tembo; "The implications of African-American spirituality" by Donna Richards; "The African essence in African-American language" by Molefi Kete Asante; "The rhythms of unity, a bibliographic essay in African culture" by Molefi Kete Asante and Kariamu Welsh Asante.

Berghahn, Marion, *Images of Africa in Black American Literature*. London: MacMillan Press Ltd., 1977. 230 pp.

This book deals with the African image in Afro-American literature, in order to examine the development of the image of Africa from the period of slavery to the present. The author discusses the white image of Africa from the colonial period onwards, and the impact of the white image of Africa and Africans on the Afro-Americans' images of themselves. The author examines the African element in the culture of Afro-Americans, the literary work of DuBois, and the Harlem Renaissance. The book includes a useful bibliography.

Beyaraza, Ernest, *Contemporary Relativism with Special Reference to Culture and Africa*. Bayreuth African studies series, ed. Eckhard Breitinger. Bayreuth: Universität Bayreuth. Africa Area Studies Programme, 1994. 261 pp.

Associates relativism with subjectivism and critical metaphysics. Critical metaphysics, on the basis of "association of ideas" is taken as a platform from which concepts of both Africa and culture are examined. The book defends culture in Africa, but also demonstrates cultural dependence, retardation, distortion, and even death. It argues for cultural recovery and independence. Culture is conceived of not as a dead museum piece but as a living reality of the people.

Bjornson, Richard, *The African Quest for Freedom and Identity: Cameroonian Writing and the National Experience*. Bloomington, Indiana: Indiana University Press, 1991. 507 pp.

By tracing the evolution of literate culture in Cameroon and examining writing in its social, political, economic, and cultural context Bjornson shows how the concepts of freedom and identity have become the dominant themes in Cameroon writing. Bjornson relates the themes to the emergence of Cameroon as a complex modern state. He also shows that one of the most common themes is the individual's struggle to create a personally satisfying identity in spite of traditions and a corrupt, modern society. Bjornson also argues that a national consciousness can be seen in the shared systems of references made possible by the emergence of literate culture.

Björkman, Ingrid, *Mother Sing for me: People's Theatre in Kenya*. Zed cultural studies. London: Zed Books, 1989. 107 pp.

Deals with an examination of the performance of the Kenyan songplay "Sing for me, Mother", the conditions surrounding it, how it was received and the consequences the performance had. The performance, which contained traditional songs and dances, was prohibited by the Kenyan authorities. Björkman's interviews bear witness to the audience recognition of the drama's main themes: that the colonial oppression is still present and that the key to freedom lies in unity over ethnic boundaries.

Blaut, J.M., *1492: The Debate on Colonialism, Eurocentrism and History*. Trenton, N. J.: Africa World Press, 1992. 124 pp.

Blaut argues in this volume of essays that the rise of Europe began in 1492 and resulted from the capital accumulated in colonial activities, mainly in the Americas. The beginning of colonialism in 1492 resulted from global locational factors, not from any special qualities within European society. Therefore, colonialism explains the unique development of Europe. Commentaries on this argument are given by Andre Gunder Frank, Samir Amin, Robert Dodgson, Ronen Palan and Peter Taylor.

Boehmer, Elleke, Laura Chrisman, and Kenneth Parker, (eds), *Altered State? Writing and South Africa*. Oxford: Dangaroo Press, 1994. 137 pp.

This volume includes eleven essays dealing mainly with English language writing and criticism from different points of view. The essays treat topics like liberation and the crises of culture, criticism of resistance literature, narratives of South African freedom, construction of cross-border readers, short story journals, the romance form as an expression of racist fantasy, the role of the railway in South African literature, the deconstruction of South African urban space by Wally Mongane Serote, the concern of South African writers on reading Dick Coetzee's Foe, the struggle against apartheid by rural women in the novels of Lauretta Ngcobo and, Marxist reading of Athol Fugard's plays to treat postcolonial South Africa. Contributors: Njabulo Ndebele, Benita Parry, Graham Pechey, Lewis Nkosi, Stephen Finn, John Stotesbury, Michael Wade, Jane Wilkinson, Pamela Dunbar, Brian Worsfold, and Dennis Walder.

Boulding, Kenneth E., *The Image*. Ann Arbor: The University of Michigan Press, 1956. 175 pp.

This book deals with the concept of images. The book focuses mainly on the question of what determines the image. The author states that the image is built on the experiences the image possessor has, and that the image constantly changes due to new experiences and information. He argues as well that the image changes depending on the value of the information, if it is positive or negative. The concept of the image is analysed in connection with organisation theory, public or private content, history, science etc.

Breitinger, Eckhard, (ed.), *Theatre and Performance in Africa: Intercultural Perspectives*. Bayreuth African studies series, ed. Eckhard Breitinger. Bayreuth: Universität Bayreuth. Africa Area Studies Programme, 1994. 216 pp.

The book deals with how theatre for development, popular theatre and musical performance describe the social and political implications of cultural practices. It includes production analyses of Soyinka's plays, of how masquerades and semiotic analyses cover the aesthetics of performative arts in Africa. It also deals with how radical change in South Africa or democratisation elsewhere seeks expression in contemporary theatre, popular song, and even state controlled television.

Buchanan, William, *How Nations see each Other: a Study in Public Opinion*. Urbana: University of Illinois Press, 1953. 220 pp.

This book deals with the concept of stereotypes. The aim of the book is to outline attitudes which lie behind reactions between different people, and to explore the relationships between different views about human nature. The main part of the book is concerned with national surveys, based on questionnaires, of nine countries. By analysing these surveys a number of images of different people emerge.

Bugner, Ladislav, (ed.), *The Image of the Black in Western Art, I–IV*. Cambridge, Massachusetts: Harvard University Press, 1976.

This book deals with the image of the black in Western art through the centuries. It consists of four parts dealing with different periods. Part I: "From the Pharaohs to the fall of the Roman Empire". Part II: "From the early Christian era to the age of discovery", divided into two parts, 1. "From the demonic threat to the incarnation of sainthood, 2. "Africans in the Christian ordinance of the world (14th–16th century). Part III: "Africa and Europe: 16th to 18th century". Part IV: "From the American revolution to World War II" divided into two parts, 1. "Slaves and liberators", and 2. "Black models and white myths".

Cairns, Alan C., *Prelude to Imperialism: British Reactions to Central African Society, 1840–1890*. London: Routledge & Kegan Paul, 1965. 329 pp.

This book deals mainly with the intellectual and emotional reactions of the British pioneers who came in contact with Central Africa between 1840 and 1890. In the writings of these pioneers the African is seldom described as an individual, unless as an object of salvation, an obstacle to rapid travel, or as a faithful follower. The central theme in the book is race relations. Interesting is that the pioneers depended more on African society than the later colonialists did, and the absence of imperialism is an important factor in this book.

Campbell, Horace, *Rasta to Resistance: from Marcus Garvey to Walter Rodney*. Dar-es-Salaam: Tanzania Publishing House, 1985. 364 pp.

A detailed study of the Rastafari movement, which is at present the foremost Pan-African and Pan-Caribbean political force in the Caribbean. The development of the Rasta cause and resistance of the black people against the capitalistic system is traced back from the era of Marcus Garvey to the recent contribution of Walter Rodney.

Chatterjee, Partha, *Nationalist Thought and the Colonial World: a Derivative Discourse*. London: Zed Books, 1986. 181 pp.

This book can be read as a criticism of Western theories of Third World Nationalism. The author explores the central contradiction, which nationalism in Africa and Asia has consequently experienced: setting out to assert its freedom from European domination, it still remained a prisoner of European post-Enlightenment rationalist discourse. Using the case of India the author shows how Indian nationalism did effect significant displacement in the framework of modernist thinking imbibed in the West.

Chinweizu, *Decolonising the African Mind*. Lagos: Pero Press, 1987.

Consists of twenty essays, divided into five sections; Economics, History, Cultural Control Systems and Literature. In these areas Chinweizu is opposed to alien influence, which is the common theme in the book. He is arguing for recapturing the great African tradition.

Cohen, William B., *The French Encounter with Africans: White Responses to Blacks, 1530–1880*. Bloomington: Indiana University Press, 1980. 360 pp.

This book deals with the images of Africans created by the French after the earliest contacts in the 1530s to the 19th century. The author treats the writings concerned with the French reactions towards Africa, and claims that the French, among other things, thought that Africa and the Africans needed a white master. This idea was established after the encounters between the French and the Africans and the idea was included in the socio-political context. The author opposes the French claim of racial equality as dominant in French history and states the opposite.

Comaroff, Jean and John Comaroff, *Of Revelation and Revolution: Christianity, Colonialism and Consciousness in South Africa*. Chicago: University of Chicago Press, 1991. 414 pp.

This book deals with the colonisation of the Southern Tswana and with the encounters between the British missionaries and the Tswana people. The aim of the book is to write a historical anthropology of colonialism in South Africa. The book is divided into two volumes, where the first volume deals with the British images of the civilisation of the indigenous people and the relations between the British missionaries and the Tswana. The second volume deals with the missionaries' efforts to change the Tswana and their culture, and how the missionaries' efforts actually affected the Tswana.

Coombes, Annie E., *Reinventing Africa: Museums, Material Culture and Popular Imagination in late Victorian and Edwardian England*. New Haven: Yale University Press, 1994. 280 pp.

This book deals with the images of Africa mediated through exhibitions at the end of the 19th century to 1913. The book consists mainly of case studies to show the differences between the popular and the scientific images of Africa that existed. The exhibitions and the classification of material culture are analysed since the exhibitions were the prime information sources on Africa mediated to the public. The material culture is analysed as a stand-in for African societies during the period, and the author discusses the images of anthropology existing at that time.

Curtin, Philip D., *The Image of Africa: British Ideas and Action, 1780–1850*. Madison: The University of Wisconsin Press, 1964. 526 pp.

This book deals with the images of Africa that emerged in Britain in the 1780s to the 1850s. During this time the images evolved and in 1850 they were made permanent. The author argues that later images of Africa were based on these images and that they were still current in the 1920s. The author wants to show how the ideas behind the images from the 1850s were integrated within Western thinking about Africa. The author also discusses the relations between Africa and the West, and the role of ideas, such as those behind the images from the 1850', in meetings between different cultures.

Curtin, Philip D. (ed.), *Africa and the West: Intellectual Responses to European Culture*. Madison: University of Wisconsin Press, 1972. 259 pp.

This volume of essays deals with African intellectual responses to Europe. The different responses are concerned with any idea that may influence or change the society, ideas that can influence the feelings of ordinary people and ideas that can influence formal theories. The essays explore as well different themes in African intellectual history and different forms of reactions to the West, such as political or military reactions which are seldom recorded, the changing appearance of the individual, the acceptance of new ways of thinking or the fusion of new and old ways of thinking. Contributors: Philip D. Curtin, James W. Fernandez, Whatt MacGaffey, Jean Herskovits, Leo Spitzer, G. Wesley Johnson Jr., Harold Scheub.

Davis, Peter, *In Darkest Hollywood*. Athens, Ohio: Ohio University Press, 1996. 214 pp.

This book deals with the images of Africa mediated in films. The main focus is on the film images of South Africa, and mainly of the depiction of the black people through film history, and how the depiction has changed. The author discusses the importance and the impact of the film images of black South Africans, and what the created images reveal about the creators. The author argues that the film images of Africa show the images created during the colonial period.

Diemer, Alwin, (ed.), *Africa and the Problem of its Identity*. Frankfurt am Maine: Verlag Peter Lang, 1985. 279 pp.

This volume includes twenty-two essays dealing with identity from different points of view. The essays discuss questions such as the common African identity, the conflict between the established idea of Africa and the philosophical concept of culture and identity, and contemporary and future philosophical thinking. Contributors: Mona Abousenna, William E. Abraham, Peter O. Bodunrin, Bachir Diagne, Alwin Diemer, Paulin Hountondji, Tanella B. Kone, Mohamed A. Lahbabi, Issiaka Laleye, Richard M'baya, Allassane N'daw, Tshiamalenga Ntumba, Odera H. Oruka, Okonda w'Oleko Okolo, Olu J. Sodipo, Claude Sumner, Kwasi Wiredu, Christophe Wondji, Konate Yacouba, Walther Ch. Zimmerli.

Drag, Marianne, (ed.), *Media, Culture and Development*. Oslo: University of Oslo, 1993. 217 pp.

Deals with themes such as video production, popular theatre, oppositional discourses and development theory. All of the contributors move within the tradition-modernity continuum in Zimbabwe.

Dudley, Edward and Maximillian E. Novak, *The Wild Man within: an Image of Western Thought from the Renaissance to Romanticism*. Pittsburgh: University Press, 1972. 333 pp.

This volume of essays includes eleven essays dealing with the concept of "the wild man" from different points of view. The unifying theme in the book is primitivism, which was an important aspect during the period concerned. The author argues that the savage was regarded in a complex set of attitudes generated from the medieval period, he argues as well that the concept of the wild man influenced politics, education, anthropology among other topics. Contributors: Hayden White, Stanley L. Rose, Gary B. Nash, Earl Miner, Edward Dudley, Richard Aschcraft, Maximillian E. Novak, Geoffrey Symcox, Ehrhard Bahr, John G. Burke, Peter Thorslev Jr.

Eguchi, Paul Kazuhisa and Victor Azarya, (eds), *Unity and Diversity of a People: the Search for Fulbe Identity*. Senri ethnological studies. Osaka: National Museum of Ethnology (Osaka), 1993. 232 pp.

Deals with Fulbe identity in its various manifestations, past and present. The central theme in the volume is "what exactly constitutes the notion of Fulbe-ness and how pervasive has it been in Fulbe societies, geographically and historically". Much of the discussion concerns various dimensions and manifestations of this notion. Comparisons between the Fulbe's identity in western Senegal with that of the identity of the Fulbe in the eastern settlements in Sudan are made. The debate is focused on the outer peripheral boundaries and the inner core of Fulbe identity.

Fredrickson, George, *The Black Image in the White Mind: the debate on Afro-American character and destiny, 1817–1914*. New York: Harpers Row Publishers, 1971. 343 pp.

This book deals with the development of intellectualised theory and ideology of racism, and how these theories and ideologies were used to solve the "problem" of the black people in the United States in the 19th century. The book deals as well with racial concepts, images and various solutions to the "problem" proposed by people connected to the hard racism school. The author has concentrated on the relationship between racial doctrines, images of society and intellectual development, and historical conflicts. The author concludes that the racist attitudes towards blacks as inferior and different to whites had their origin in the institutionalisation of slavery based on race in the 17th century. He also concludes that the racist theory culminated in the 19th century due to the fact that the presence of blacks was a central fact in the sectional conflict, which resulted in institutionalisation of extreme racism, such as legalised segregation and disfranchisement.

Fuglesang, Minou, *Veils and Videos: Female Youth Culture on the Kenyan Coast*. Stockholm studies in Anthropology. Stockholm: Stockholm Studies in Anthropology, Stockholm University, 1994. 322 pp.

Deals with youth culture and their engagement with media, and the process of social transition from the perspectives of urban youth, focused on young women from Lamu Town in Kenya. Central in the female youth culture, argues the author, are romantic melodrama, fashion and dance, important sources of female pleasure. The study attempts to identify the practices by which young women enlarge their space for action and experiment with elements of style to express changing modes of femininity, modernity, ethnicity and religiosity. The notion of looking is treated with regard to the use and meaning of veils and videos, central in this culture.

Gabriel, John, *Racism, Culture, Markets*. London: Routledge, 1994. 212 pp.

This book deals with the connections between cultural representations of race and their historical, institutional and global forms of expression and impact. Gabriel examines the current fixation with market philosophies in terms of the crisis in anti-racist politics and concern over questions of cultural identity. He explores issues such as the continuing relevance of terms like black as a basis for self-definitions, the need to think about identities in more fluid and complex ways, and the need to develop a more explicit discussion of the construction of whiteness and white identity. The book includes case studies such as the Rushdie affair, the Gulf war, separate schooling, tourism in the third world, racism in the new Europe, studies that consider the role played by contemporary media and popular culture.

Gaines, Jane M., *Contested Culture: the Image, the Voice, and the Law*. London: BFI Publishing, 1992. 340 pp.

This book deals with the ownership of an "image", the author analyses copyright, trademarks, and intellectual property law, asking how the law constructs works of authorship and who owns our cultural heritage. Gaines asks whether an individual or a company can claim to possess the look of a face or the sound of a voice. The author shows how merchandising and the commercial exploitation of the image are not recent phenomena. She begins with the decision of the Supreme Court in 1884 involving Napoleon Sarony's photograph of Oscar Wilde, she then explores a number of examples of more recent time from a Dior magazine advertisement using a Jacqueline Onassis look-alike to decisions about DC Comic's Superman.

Goode, Kenneth G., *From Africa to the United States and then...: a Concise Afro-American History*. Glenview, Illinois: Scott, Foresman and Company, 1976. 192 pp.

Deals with the Afro-American dimension of American history, from its origin in West Africa to the present day. Includes chapters dealing with slavery, the labour movement, the struggle for civil rights among other topics.

Granqvist, Raoul, (ed.), *Culture in Africa: an Appeal for Pluralism*. Seminar proceedings from the Scandinavian Institute of African Studies. Uppsala: Nordiska Afrikainstitutet, 1993. 204 pp.

A collection of 13 essays on African culture. The first three essays deal with Zimbabwe from different aspects such as Zimbabwean church music drama, Zimbabwean students' response to electronic church propaganda, the African one party state. The other essays deal with topics such as the function and status of languages in Botswana, Kenyan popular literature, oral tradition's impact on Kenyan women's literature, African writers' neglect of the African heritage, Islamic architecture and art, Yoruba theatre, Bessie Head, the cultural and political appropriation of the legacy of Shaka and Dingane by different leaderships in the liberation struggle in South Africa and the involvement of indigenous writing in the political struggle in South Africa. Contributors: Raoul Granqvist, Olof Axelsson, Hilde Arntsen and Knut Lundby, Chenjerai Hove, Lars-Gunnar Andersson and Tore Janson, Bodil Folke Fredriksen, Ingrid Björkman, Adewale Maja-Pearce, Karin Ådahl, Kacke Götrick, Gillian Stead Eilersen, Carl F. Hallencreutz, Rose Petterson.

Harries, Patrick, *Work, Culture and Identity: Migrant Laborers in Mozambique and South Africa, c. 1860–1910*. Johannesburg: Witwatersrand University Press, 1994. 305 pp.

This book deals with the Mozambican workers who went to the sugar plantations, diamond fields, and gold mines of South Africa. The workers arrived with the values, signs, and rituals of authority they had learnt at home. It was through their encounter with other blacks, as well as Europeans and colonialists, that a new and dynamic culture emerged. This book is a history of the making of that culture, a story of the day-to-day life of the migrants as they travelled to work and lived their daily lives far from home. The first part deals with the origin and the early history of migration, the second part examines the changes during the first decade of mining on the Witwatersrand and the last part is concerned with the impact on migrant labour of the first fifteen years of colonial rule. The book focuses on the causes and consequences of migrant labour, the social history of the migrants, and their changing relations with employers and the state. There is also a discussion of the manner in which workers constructed new ways of seeing themselves and others through innovated rituals, traditions, and beliefs. Culture, identity, and interpretation are central themes in this book.

Harrow, Kenneth W., *Thresholds of Change in African Literature: the Emergence of a Tradition*. Studies in African Literature. New series. Portsmouth, N. H.: Heinemann, 1994. 370 pp.

Deals with the emergence of a literary tradition of the African spirit, influenced by earlier African oral tradition, by European writings, by changing social condition, and by African writings themselves, and particularly in the ways in which the emergent literature underwent change at each critical stage. The dynamics of literary change are analysed with theories of the Russian formalist, Kuhn and Derrida. A model of African literature is elaborated. The book includes analyses of works by some of the African novelist from the 1950s and 60s, and a study of the changes in literature in the period 1960 to 1990.

Hawk, Beverly G. (ed.), *Africa's Media Image*. New York: Praeger, 1992. 263 pp.

This volume of essays deals with the images of Africa mediated by the media in the United States. The images are remarkably coherent and the stories reported are easily accessible to, and easily understood by, the population as racial stories, wars, and famine. Stories dealing with African culture or African history are never reported. The volume is divided into four parts, where the first part covers the debate between Africanists and journalists, the next part consists of an overview of the media coverage of Africa, the third part deals with the media coverage of Southern Africa and the last part discusses the changing media coverage of Africa. The editor states in the introduction that the colonial images of Africa have become the media images of Africa, and the media is supposed to tell the truth. Contributors: Beverly G. Hawk,

Bosah Ebo, Stanley Meisler, William Hachten, Wunyabari Maloba, Robert J. Bookmiller, Kirsten Nakjavani Bookmiller, Minabere Ibelema, Rodger M. Govea, Jo Ellen Fair, Charles A. Bodie, Hassan M. El Zein, Anne Cooper, Lisa Brock, Julie Frederikse, Chris Paterson, Elaine Windrich, David Zucchino, Tami Hultman, Thomas Winship, Paul Hemp, Danny Schechter.

Helly, Dorothy, "'Informed' Opinion on Tropical Africa in Great Britain 1860–1890", *African Affairs*, Vol. 68, No. 272, 1969. pp. 195–218.

This article deals with the ways opinion and attitudes about tropical Africa were spread among those interested from 1830 to 1890 in England. Through the network the images already established were developed and strengthened. The author concludes that the network consisted of a small group of men, some of them active in the acquirement of a British empire in Africa.

Hentsch, Thierry, *Imagining the Middle East*. Montreal: Black Rose Books, 1992. 218 pp.

This book deals with the questions of how the Western perception of the Middle East was formed, and how these perceptions have been used by us as a rationalisation for setting policies and determining actions. Hentch sees our ideas of the other and our ethnocentrism as our whole way of viewing the world. He believes that the Middle East serves as a mirror to Western consciousness, as a point of reference. He argues that the images of the Orient vary and depend on at what time and under which circumstances the image is created.

Herman, Edward S. and Noam Chomsky, *Manufacturing Consent: the Political Economy of the Mass Media*. London: Vintage, 1988. 412 pp.

Contrary to the usual image of the press as investigative, the authors of this book argue that an elite lies behind the news. The authors analyse the way in which the marketplace and the economics of publishing shape the news. They focus on the question of attention, and how the press mediates a picture useful to the government and power groups in society. The book reveals the propagandistic function of the mass media and scrutinises the selectivity of the information promoted.

Husband, Charles (ed.), *'Race' in Britain: Continuity and Change*. London: Hutchinson, 1982. 329 pp.

This book deals mainly with the concept of race in contemporary Britain. In three chapters the historical context is discussed, where European attitudes towards the rest of the world from the 17th to the 19th century are treated, as well as impressions from the first English encounters with black people, and the origins of racialism through caricature pictures of blacks. The contributors to the history part: V. G. Kiernan, Winthrop D. Jordan, James Walwin.

"The Image of Africa", *IFDA Dossier*, No. 67, 1988. pp. 3–19.

This article deals with the image of Africa mediated during the famine crises in 1984/5. It is emphasised in the article that the West perceived the famine crisis as an event, and the only way to save the starving people was to send aid from the West. Nothing was reported about the efforts made by the Africans in the situation, instead the focus was on passive and helpless Africans. The article continues with an account of the result from the research about different images promoted at the time of the famine crises by the media, by NGOs and the image of Africa in the public mind in Denmark, the United Kingdom, West Germany and Ireland.

Images of the West. Zimbabwe and Copenhagen: Baobab Books and Images of Africa, 1996. 96 pp.

This volume of short essays deals with African images of the West, and different aspects of Western habits and culture. One of the central themes is identity, with emphasis on racial questions. The photographs accompanying the essays are important in the volume. Contributors: Yvonne Vera, Tahar Bekri, Jowie Mwiinga, Veronique Tadjo, Shimmer Chinodya, Dani Nabudere, Fatuma Ali, Alex Mukulu, Uazuvara Katjivena, John Eppel, Nuruddin Farah, Julia Odaka Mundawarara, Emmanuel B. Dongala, Charles Mungoshi, Taban Io Liyong, Sekai Nzenza, Adewale Maja-Pearce, Chenjerai Hove, Geoffrey Haresnape, Jamal Mahjoub, Viola

Mukasa, Okello Oculi, Munashe Mashiri, Wahome Mutahi, Florence Odwee, Tobias Zimidze, Bethuel Thai, Barbara Robinson, Theophilus Tefe.

Jordan, Winthrop D., *White over Black: American Attitudes Towards the Negro 1550–1812*. Williamsburg: University of North Carolina Press, 1968. 651 pp.

This book deals with the whites' attitudes toward blacks during the period when Europeans and Africans came to the American continent. Different kinds of attitudes are treated, intensive, conscious and unconscious. The book is concerned with the English and their attitudes at that time, the origin of American black slavery, central religious ideas, the thoughts of Thomas Jefferson among other topics.

Keen, Sam, *Faces of the Enemy: Reflections of the Hostile Imagination.* San Francisco: Harper & Row, Publishers, 1986. 199 pp.

This book deals with the twisted caricatures of propaganda posters, cartoons, and distorted images to show the mechanisms of enmity. The author argues that the images of the enemy have to be examined, how do we create them, and how do we identify the enemy? In the first part of the book Keen constructs a "phenomenology of the hostile imagination", examines the historical question of guilt and innocence, and tries to identify the archetype of the enemy. In part two of the book Keen examines the psychological roots of the habit of enmity and how the shadow projected onto the enemy can be reclaimed. In part three the variety of scenarios for the future of enmity is examined.

Kivikuru, Ullamaija. *Value Harbours or Instruments of Self-expression? Considerations on Mass Communication as Mediator of Culture in Peripheries*. Helsinki: Helsinki University, Department of Communication, 1989.

In the paper the author brings together three concepts, peripheralism, cultural identity and mass communication, to study the filtering of mediation mechanisms of mass communication in a peripheral society in view of cultural identity building.

Kivikuru, Ullamaija, *Tinned Novelties or Creative Culture? A Study on the Role of Mass Communication in Peripheral Nations*. Helsinki: Helsinki University, Department of Communication, 1990.

Deals with mass communication under peripheral conditions in societies outside the centres of global power. The book deals with questions like the characteristics of peripheral mass communication, the social function of peripheral mass communication, the significance of origin for mass communication, and the modes and genres and defence mechanism of mass communication. Part one deals with theoretical aspects, includes a general review of previous literature concentrating on the key concepts national and cultural identity, dependence, peripheralism and mediation. Part two includes five separate empirical case studies. It deals with the structural basis of mass communication in peripheries, presents media vehicles of Finland and Tanzania, deals with news transmissions, non-news mass communication, and mass communication receptions. Part three deals with conceptualisation, discusses the theses presented in part one through the experiences collected in the empirical excursions.

Lange, Siri, *From Nation-building to Popular Culture: the Modernisation of Performance in Tanzania*. Chr. Michelsen Institute Report. Bergen: Chr. Michelsen Institute, 1995. 182 pp.

Deals with Tanzania's efforts to use elements from ethnic expressive arts in political propaganda and in the creation of a national culture after independence. It analyses why nationalised traditional dances failed to work as national symbols, and further shows how certain central aspects of traditional ritual performance, aspects lost with the nationalisation and modernisation of the dances, are now being carried on in a genuinely new cultural form: commercial popular theatre to entertain the low-income masses in Dar-es-Salaam.

Lemelle, Sidney J. and Robin D.G. Kelley, (eds), *Imagining Home: Class, Culture and Nationalism in the African Diaspora*. London: Verso, 1994. 373 pp.

This volume of essays examines the image of Africa in the imaginations, cultures and politics of its New World descendants. The book is divided into four parts where the first part deals with the cultural politics of Pan-Africanism, the meaning of Africa in the Harlem renaissance, the African-American communist, the relationship between gender and Pan-Africanism, Rastafarians, Haitian social organisation, and black music. The next part deals with Pan-Africanism and black intellectuals, such as Adelaide Casely Hayford, W.E.B. Du Bois, C.L.R. James and Max Yergan. Part three deals with relations between Southern Africa and the U.S., the apartheid in the south of the U. S., Pan-Africanism and the politics of education, and Pan-Africanism and apartheid. The last part deals with Pan-Africanism as a liberation theory, and in connection with materialist thinking. Contributors: David H. Anthony, Barbara Bair, Patrick Bellegarde-Smith, Paul Buhle, Horace Campbell, Marsye Conde, Paul Gilroy, Barbara Harlow, Robin D.G. Kelley, Marian Kramer, Sidney J. Lemelle, Ntongela Masilela, Gersham A. Nelson, Kathy J. Ogren, Cedric J. Robinson, Ann Seidman, Lako Tongun and William H. Watkins

Leveson, Marcia, *People of the Book: Images of the Jew in South African English fiction 1880–1992*. Johannesburg: Witwatersrand University Press, 1996. 277 pp.

This book deals with the images of Jews in South African literary texts. The book focuses on the different authors' perceptions of and intentions with the images of Jews and their attitudes towards Jews. The texts analysed are written by mainly white authors of British descendants or British colonial writers, British Jewish writers, and some black authors writing in English. Important in the book is the aim to insert the literary images of Jews in the historical, mythological and sociological context. The author concludes that the literary images of Jews are based on negative stereotypes with connections to the treatment of Jews historically in society.

LeVine, Robert, et al., *Child Care and Culture: Lessons from Africa*. Cambridge: Cambridge University Press, 1994. 346 pp.

This book deals with parenthood, infancy, and early childhood in an African community, raising provocative questions about "normal" child care. By comparison between the Gusii people of Kenya and the American white middle class, the authors show how divergent cultural priorities create differing conditions for early childhood development. Combining the perspectives of social anthropology, paediatrics, and developmental psychology, the authors demonstrate how child care customs can be responsive to varied socio-economic, demographic, and cultural conditions without inflicting harm on children.

Ludwar-Ene, Gudrun and Mechthild Reh, (eds), *Gender and Identity in Africa. Beiträge zur Afrikaforschung*. Hamburg: Lit Verlag, 1995.

As part of the special research program "Identity in Africa: processes of its formation and change" a colloquium was held on the topic of gender and identity in Africa. A common issue was that of how far women are able to shape their social life without adjusting to the social rules developed by men, in the interest of men, whether this goal can be achieved and if so which social groups are most likely to succeed. The articles deal with topics like identity and continuity, possession cults, economic development and discrimination among others. Contributors: Beverly Stoeltje, Ute Luig, Heike Behrend, Anke Kleiner and Roman Loimeier, Karin Barber, Karim Traoré, Heidi Willer, Gabriele Zdunnek, Gabriele Wurster and Gudrun Ludwar-Ene, Christina Jones, Ana Maria Pessoa Pinto and Chuma Himonga.

Magubane, Bernhard Makhosezwe, *The Ties that Bind: African-American Consciousness of Africa*. Trenton, N.J.: Africa World Press, 1987. 251 pp.

This book deals with the historical significance of the relationship between black Americans and Africa. The book discusses the interpretation of the black man's response to certain cultural and historical premises, established by the white Americans, on which the black self-contempt was built. The author presents an interpretation and an analysis of the phenomenon of ambivalence persistent in the Afro-American consciousness of Africa and offers an exploration in the field of social identity as it affects people in the Diaspora. The book deals with the image of Africa in the Western world, analyses stereotypes about Africa, deals with the ideas of racism, the genesis of Africanism in the Afro-American community, the "Back-to-Africa" movement, the Italian assault on Ethiopia, Africa after World War II, and racism in South Africa and the Afro-American response.

Makinde, Akin M., *African Philosophy, Culture, and Traditional Medicine.* Monographs in international studies Africa series. Africa Studies Programme. Centre for International Studies. Ohio University. Athens, Ohio: Ohio University Press, 1988. 154 pp.

Deals with African culture, philosophy and traditional medicine. The history of African philosophy deals with unwritten philosophy and unknown philosophers, colonial ethnophilosophers and critical re-orientation in philosophy and the contemporary African philosophers. The following part of the book deals with the social and political philosophy of Obafemi Awolowo. The principles and practices of traditional medicine are treated in the last part of the book and the author discusses the question of treating traditional medicine seriously.

Marshall, Peter James and Glyndwr Williams, *The Great Map of Mankind: British Perceptions of the World in the Age of Enlightenment.* London: J.M. Dent & Sons Ltd, 1982. 314 pp.

This book deals with the attitudes towards, and the images of, the societies 'discovered' by the Europeans described in e.g. travel literature, journals and letters from the second half of the 17th century to the end of the 18th century. The book focuses on the images and attitudes towards societies in Asia, North America, West Africa and the Pacific. Among others, the writings of James Cook, J.R. Forster and William Smith are discussed and analysed.

Masolo, D.A., *African Philosophy in Search of Identity. African systems of thought.* Edinburgh: Edinburgh University Press, 1994. 301 pp.

Deals with the question of whether there is such a thing as an African philosophy. The author discusses whether the African lives by reason or by intuition and magic. He includes Francophone and Anglophone philosophers in the analytic and phenomenological traditions. He argues that the uses of philosophy, by African thinkers, has been to analyse the question of identity, in contrast to the objectivisation as the other. The author discusses the thinking of African philosophers such as Frantz Fanon, Aimé Césaire and Cheik Anta Diop as well as Alexis Kagame and John Mbiti. The author ends up with the conclusion that African philosophy has grown out of particular cultural circumstances and now embraces many different constructions of African reality, problems, and methods of acquiring meaningful knowledge.

Mazrui, Ali A., *The African Condition: a Political Diagnosis. The Reith lectures.* London: Heinemann, 1980. 142 pp.

To stimulate thought, argument and controversy Mazrui is using six fundamental paradoxes of the African predicament to examine in what condition Africa faces the 1980s. The following paradoxes are discussed; Africa was the earliest habitat and yet is the last to become truly habitable. Africans are certainly not the most brutalised of peoples and yet they are the most humiliated in modern history. African societies are not the closest culturally to the western world and yet they are undergoing the most rapid westernisation. Africa is by no means the smallest continent and yet it is almost certainly the most fragmented politically. Africa is not the poorest region of the world but technically the most retarded. Africa is the most centrally located continent, it is the most peripheral in political terms.

Mazrui, Ali A., *The Africans: a Triple Heritage.* London: Heinemann, 1986.

Deals with Africa as a continent with a triple heritage of three civilisations, its own inheritance, Islamic culture and the impact of western traditions and lifestyles. The influences of the triple heritage are present in the conflict between mankind and nature, in the tension between city and countryside, between soldiers and politicians, between the élite and the masses, between the secular and the religious, between a longing for autonomy and the shackles of dependency upon imported cultures.

Mazrui, Alamin, "Language and the Quest for Liberation in Africa: the Legacy of Frantz Fanon", *Third World Quarterly:* Journal of Emerging Areas, Vol. 14, No. 2, 1993, pp. 351–63.

Deals with language as an important dimension for mental liberation in Africa. Different theories on the impact of language are outlined, and different colonial language policies are treated. The author argues that neither the European nor the African languages are necessarily instruments of cultural bondage or cultural liberation. He believes that the psycholinguistic impact has had less to do with the deterministic power of language on human cognition than on the psychological alienation that results from racial and class domination, which is the base in Frantz Fanon's views on language, imperialism and liberation. The author discusses Fanon's theory of language and concludes that the language of liberation can only be a product of a thorough semantic revolution in each and every language that would demystify the process of decolonisation.

Mazrui, Alamin and Ibrahim Noor Shariff, *The Swahili: Idiom and Identity of an African People.* Trenton, N.J.: Africa World Press, 1994. 187 pp.

Deals with the identity of the Swahili. In the first part the authors argue that the Swahili entered the twentieth century with an ancient tradition, a centuries-old writing tradition and a visible homogeneity of culture, on which the Swahili identity was built. They attempt to demonstrate that the confusion around Swahili identity is a problem connected to Eurocentricity. They try to demonstrate the relativity in the concept of identity by giving concrete examples of criteria used by different people to determine who belongs to a group, the dichotomy of self–other. Part two deals with the confusion over Swahili identity, which has been influenced by distorted views on the Swahili language.

Mbaekwe, Iheanyi J.S., *The Image of Africa in Sweden before 1914: a Study of Six Types of Persuasive Ideas.* Lund: Lunds Universitet, Statsvetenskapliga institutionen, 1980. 187 pp.

This dissertation deals with specific images of Africa mediated to the Swedish population before 1914. The images studied are the affectional image, the literary image, the ethnographic image, the value socialising image, the relational image, and the political image. The materials used are educational books, travel narratives, ethnographic and mission literature, and newspapers. The author concludes that the general image of Africa was homogenous, based on stereotypes and clichés. The mediated image was mainly European, since most of the written material originated from other European countries.

McElroy, Guy C., *Facing History: the Black Image in American art 1710–1940.* Washington, D.C.: Bedford Arts, 1990. 140 pp.

This book deals with how American art has imagined and portrayed the Afro-American, and treated the identity of the black man from slave to citizen. The author argues that racial identity remains rooted in social assumptions. The book reveals the importance of black identity in the United States at present, and the ways Afro-Americans have been looked at over the centuries. Through analyses of art the different stereotypes of Afro-Americans and the black identity are revealed, as well as the opinion of blacks being inferior to the whites.

Mda, Zakes, *When People Play People: Development Communication Through Theatre.* Johannesburg: Witwatersrand University Press, 1993. 250 pp.

Deals with theatre used as a way of increasing popular participation in the development process. The book examines the experiences of training extension workers in the use of theatre-for-development, and explores the author's attempt to develop a new model of theatrical communication. The author argues that theatre in Africa has potential as a democratic medium for it can enable audience participation, integrate indigenous and popular systems of communication and use whatever local resources are to hand. The author concludes that if theatre is to play a role in the expression of development problems faced by people who are marginalised, a more carefully thought out methodology combining intervention and participation is needed.

Miller, Christopher L., "Theories of Africans", in *Black Literature and Culture,* ed. Houston Barker, A. Jr. Chicago: Chicago University Press, 1990. 328 pp.

Miller stages an encounter in every chapter between a critical or theoretical model, usually of Western origin, and a specific African context over which the theoretical model claims competence as theory in relation to the reading of African literature. Deals with the problem if it is possible for a western literary critic to describe African literature.

Mphahlele, Ezekiel, *The African Image*. Rev. ed. New York: Praeger Publishers, 1974. 316 pp.

This book deals with literary images of blacks, black identity and black consciousness. The relationship between Africa and the Diaspora is treated, the history of the Afro-American movement and the Afro-American relationship to South Africa. The literary images treated are white authors' images of blacks as well as black authors' images of blacks.

Mudimbe, V.Y., *The Invention of Africa: Gnosis, Philosophy, and the Order of Knowledge*. Bloomington, Indiana: Indiana University Press, 1988. 241 pp.

Deals with the questions of the meaning of being African, what is and what is not African philosophy, is philosophy part of Africanism? Mudimbe uses the African gnosis as a system of knowledge, and he is concerned with the process of transformation of different types of knowledge.

Mudimbe, V.Y., *The Idea of Africa*. Bloomington: Indiana University Press, 1994. 234 pp.

This book deals with the evolution of the idea of Africa in Europe, from antiquity to the 19th century. The author describes the forces in African art, the importance of early African writings. He treats Martin Bernal's Black Athena not too critically. He discusses philosophers such as Frantz Fanon and Amilcar Cabral, who he praises and Léopold Sédar Senghor, Kwame Nkrumah and Paulin Hountondji who he criticises.

Ndebele, Njabulo S., *Rediscovery of the ordinary: essays on South African literature and culture*. Johannesburg: COSAW, 1991. 160 pp.

The eight essays deal with Turkish tales in connection with South African fiction, new writings in South Africa, redefining relevance, popular culture and progressive formalism, the English language and social change in South Africa, progressive cultural planning, against pamphleteering the future and, the writers' movement in South Africa.

Nederveen Pieterse, Jan, *White on black: images of Africa and blacks in Western popular culture*. New Haven: Yale University Press, 1992. 259 pp.

This book deals with the development of Western stereotypes of black people over the last two hundred years. Its purpose is to show the pervasiveness of prejudices against blacks in Europe and America as expressed in stock-in-trade racist imagery and caricature. Reproducing a wide range of illustrations the book exposes the hidden assumptions of even those who view themselves as unprejudiced. Nederveen Pieterse analyses the representations of Western images of Africa and blacks from medieval times, through the colonial period to the present day. He examines the persistence of stereotypical images in the multicultural societies of the 20th century, and in their relations with Africa. The book includes a very useful bibliography.

Ngugi wa Thiong'o, *Moving the Centre: the Struggle for Cultural Freedoms. Studies in African literature*. New series. London: James Currey, 1993. 184 pp.

Deals with the need for moving the centre, between nations and within nations, in order to contribute to the freeing of world cultures from the restrictive walls of nationalism, class, race and gender. Between nations the need is to move the centre from its assumed location in the West to a multiplicity of spheres in all cultures in the world. Within nations the move should be away from all minority class establishments to the real creative centre among working people in conditions of racial, religious and gender equality.

Nixon, Rob, *Homelands, Harlem and Hollywood: South African Culture and the World Beyond*. New York: Routledge, 1994. 305 pp.

In the book the author examines the struggle against apartheid in connection with the ways in which American and South African culture have been fascinated with and influenced by one another. The possibilities and problems, with the images the Americans and South Africans have of one another, are discussed. The book analyses Hollywood representations of the struggle for liberation, the impact of the Harlem Renaissance on the Sophiatown writers, the banning and censorship of television under apartheid, Bessie Head's front-line state, Mandela and messianic politics, the sports and cultural boycotts, ethnic nationalism and multi-culturalism, and the culture of violence. The last two chapters in the book have connections with events in Europe, the impact of the fall of the communistic regimes on South Africa and the ethnic cleansing in former Yugoslavia in comparison to the Bantustans.

Ojo-Ade, Femi, *On Black Culture*. Ile-Ife: Obafemi Awolowo University Press, 1989. 279 pp.

Deals with colour and culture in literature. The volume includes essays on the subjects: Africa in diaspora: the Afro-Cuban writings of Lydia Cabrera; The church versus the shrine: Christianity, scourge of African society; Of man misery and Marxism: the black race in the work of Jacques Roumain; The literary translator, messenger or a murderer: a study of Oyono's "Une vie de boy" and Reed's "Houseboy"; Blackness, bane or boon: race and religion in Africa and the Antillean diaspora; Buchi Emecheta: second-class citizen, second sex, slave; From decolonisation to neo-colonialism: West African Francophone fiction; The political ideology of negritude and Senghor's notion of the civilisation of the universal; The African writer and cultural relativity.

The Poster Book Collective. South African History Archive, *Images of Defiance: South African Resistance Posters of the 1980s*. Johannesburg: Ravan Press, 1991. 181 pp.

This book consists of posters made by organisations broadly associated with the congress movement in South Africa. It includes about 320 posters which reflect the people that fought against the injustices of apartheid. The collection is a part of the history of the struggle that has to be told, and it can be analysed from the point of view of the images the collection mediates.

Said, Edward W., *Covering Islam: how the Media and the Experts Determine how we see the Rest of the World*. London: Routledge & Kegan Paul, 1981. 186 pp.

This book deals with the media image of Islam, and with how the media and the government and the business establishments have created over-simplified and misleading images of what Islam and Muslims are supposed to be like. The author describes the Western images of Islam as representing everything from anti-Americanism to an inferior culture, while Islamic countries respond by using Islam to strengthen the state structures or to rally the masses. Said analyses how the U.S. press covered recent events in the Middle East and argues that the press has created its own image of Islam.

Schapera, I., (ed.), *Western Civilisation and the Natives of South Africa: Studies in Cultural Contact*. London: Routledge and Kegan Paul, (1934) 1967. 312 pp.

The book was first published in 1934 and it deals with the so called Native question in South Africa at that time. The main purpose of the book is, referring to the editor, to give a picture of the Natives at that time in South Africa, to describe their living conditions, to describe changes in their traditional culture, to analyse their position in society and to depict how the Natives were looked upon by the European inhabitants. Contributors: I. Schapera, W.M. Eiselen, W.G.A. Mears, G.P. Lestrade, Percival R. Kirby, H.M. Robertson, J.D. Rheinallt Jones, W.H. Hutt, Edgar H. Brookes, R.F. Alfred Hoernle, D.O.T. Jabauu.

Schilder, Kees, *Quest for Self-Esteem: State, Islam, and Mundang Ethnicity in Northern Cameroon*. Research series, African Studies Centre (Leiden). Avebury: Aldershot, 1994. 283 pp.

Deals with Mundange ethnicity and culture, its main features and limits, cultural roots, local kinship structure. Deals as well with the history of the persistence of ethnicity, and the author argues that the Mundange group is a precolonial construct. The relationship between Mundange and Fulbe and the colonial impact on Mundange ethnicity are also treated. The last part of the book deals with Mundange ethnicity after World War II, the profile of the ethnicity, the relations with post-colonial society and with the Fulbe. Finally, the Mundange ethnicity expressions among educated people with governmental jobs are treated.

Silberman, Charles E., *Crises in Black and White*. London: Jonathan Cape, 1964. 370 pp.

Deals with the question of racism in the United States, and the black movement. One of the chapters deals with the images of Africa present in the United States.

Simensen, Jarle, "The image of Africa in Norwegian missionary opinion, 1895–1900". 1996. pp. 137–50.

The article deals with the images of Africa that existed among the Norwegian missionaries in the 19th century, and the thinking of Africa by prominent missionaries. The focal point is the Norwegian Missionary Society (NMS) and the Missionary school in Stavanger. A model of their images of Africa is constructed from missionary literature, textbooks, missionary correspondence. The image was dominated by the dichotomy between black—white, African —European, savages-civilised people, Africa was depicted as the most primitive region in the world. The images resulted from the rejection by the missionaries of African culture but also from their ambivalence to contemporary European civilisation. The Africa images of Lars Dahle (NMS) versus Hans P. Schreuder and Niels Astrup (another missionary society) are analysed and show that different images were prevalent at the same time in different missionary circles.

Taylor, John V., *The Primal Vision: Christian Presence amid African Religion. The Christian Presence.* London: SCW Press, 1963. 212 pp.

A missionary's writings on "what is happening in the spiritual conflict which is modern Africa". The author "seeks to establish the essentially African way of feeling the truth about things". The book mediates an image of Africa from a missionary's point of view during the time for independence in Africa.

Tiberondwa, Ado K., *Missionary Teachers as Agents of Colonialism: a Study of their Activities in Uganda, 1877–1825.* Lusaka: Kenneth Kaunda Foundation, 1978. 168 pp.

This book deals with missionary teachers and their education as instruments of destroying indigenous African values and preparing African minds for smooth reception of colonial values, and paving the way for complete colonisation. The author makes revelations on the collaboration between European trading companies and the colonialists on the one hand and missionaries on the other

Waterman, Christopher Alan, "Jùjú: a Social History and Ethnography of an African Popular Music", in *Chicago studies of ethnomusicology,* ed. Philip Bohlman and Bruno Nettle. Chicago: University of Chicago Press, 1990. 277 pp.

The book gives a detailed account of the evolution and social significance of a West African popular music. The origin of Jùjú is described, from the colonial capital of Lagos in the 1930s through independence and the oil boom in the 1980s. The author links changes in the music to the shifting Nigerian political economy and developing Yoruba nationalism. The book is complemented with an account of the contexts, social organisation, aesthetics, and symbolism of jùjú. Waterman explores themes of continuity and change, ideology in popular culture and style as a medium for publicly presenting and negotiating identity. He argues that musical practice can play a powerful role in reproduction and transformation of social order.

"What Museums for Africa? Heritage in the Future", in *What Museums for Africa? Heritage in the Future.* Abomey, Benin; Accra, Ghana; Lomé, Togo: ICOM, 1992.

The volume includes six parts dealing with different issues concerning museums and cultural heritage in Africa. The first two parts deal with experiences with "museum management" mainly in Africa and "personnel and training". The next two parts deal with "conservation, repose and exchange of the heritage within and outside of Africa" concerning mainly collections and "museums and research". The last two parts deal with "heritage and contemporary culture" and with "the museums as a tool for development".

About the authors

Johannes Brusila (FL) is curator of the Sibelius Museum at the Department of Musicology at Åbo Academy University, working in the fields of ethnomusicology and popular music studies. He has done fieldwork in Zimbabwe during several periods and written his licentiate thesis and articles on the music industry of Zimbabwe. Brusila is writing his Ph.D. thesis on the world music phenomenon, using three Zimbabwean case studies.

Annemette Kirkegaard is Associate Professor at the Department of Musicology at the University of Copenhagen. Her Ph.D. thesis in 1995, "Taarab na Muziki Wa Densi", is on popular musical culture in Zanzibar and Tanzania seen in relation to globalisation and cultural change.

Bernth Lindfors is a Professor in English and African Literatures at the University of Texas at Austin. He has written and edited a number of books on African literature and on the production of images of Africa and was for several years editor of the influential review Research in African Literatures. He has received a prize for the several volume work on Black African Literature in English. His recent book *Africans on Stage—Studies in Ethnological Show Business* (1999) has been highly acclaimed.

Björn Lindgren received a BA in Journalism at Stockholm University in 1991 and a M.Phil. in Cultural Anthropology at Uppsala University in 1996. He has carried out research on journalism, ethnicity, and gender relations in Zimbabwe since 1993, and is currently working on a Ph.D. thesis on Ndbele identity in Cultural Anthropology at Uppsala University.

Hanne Løngreen Associate Professor at the Department of Communication, Roskilde University, Denmark. Research interests: intercultural communication, visual representation of 'otherness', media in the Third World. Has written a number of articles on media and the Third World and intercultural communication. She has co-edited *Interkulturel kommunikation* (1993), *Samfundslitteratur and 'Kultur og kommunikation'* (1995).

Zine Magubane is Assistant Professor of Sociology and African Studies at University of Illinois at Urbana-Champaign. She is a sociologist and a graduate from Harvard University. She has also been a lecturer at the University of Cape Town (1996–97). Two forthcoming books are on *Postmodernity, Postcoloniality, and the Study of Africa* and *Bringing the Empire Home: Imagining Race, Class and Gender in Britain and Colonial South Africa.*

Nicolas Martin-Granel is a researcher in African literature, and has worked with the Centres Culturels Français in Mauritania and Congo-Brazzaville. He has published a book on Mauritanian literature, edited works of the Congolese author Sony Labou Tansi, has written articles on orality in African literature, and edited an anthology on black humour in African novels. He is presently working in Cameroon on the continuing education of teachers of French.

Hanna Mellemsether is a Ph.D. student at the Department of History, Norwegian University of Science and Technology in Trondheim. Her research interests are gender studies, South African history and the history of Norwegian mission and immigration to South Africa. Earlier published work are *Kvinne i to verdener. En kulturhistorisk analyse av afrikamisjonæren Martha Sannes liv i perioden 1884–1901*, Senter for Kvinneforskning, Rapport 1/95, Trondheim 1995.

V.Y. Mudimbe holds a position as Professor of Literature at Duke University, USA and as Professor of French, Comparative Literature and Classics at Stanford University USA. He has taught at the Universities of Louvain, Paris-Nanterre, Zaire, and at

Haverford College. His research interests are in phenomenology and structuralism. His publications include *The Invention of Africa* (1988), *Parables and Fables* (1991), *The Idea of Africa* (1994), and *The Tales of Faith* (1997); and has edited *Nations, Identities, Cultures* (1997), *Diaspora and Immigration* (1999).

Mai Palmberg is a political scientist from Åbo Academy University in Finland, and works since 1984 at the Nordic Africa Institute. She has written, among other things, on political developments in southern Africa, aids in Africa, and the images of Africa in school books.

Terence Ranger is Emeritus Professor of Race Relations and African Studies at the University of Oxford and visiting Professor of History at the University of Zimbabwe. His publications include *Voices from the Rocks* (1999), *Postcolonial Identities in Africa* (with Richard Werbner) (1996), *Are We not also Men?* (1995), *Peasant Consciousness and Guerilla War in Zimbabwe* (1985); and the edited volumes, *Soldiers in Zimbabwe's Liberation War* (1995), and *Society in Zimbabwe's Liberation War* (both with Ngwabi Bhebe) (1995) and *The Invention of Tradition* (with Eric Hobsbawm) (1992).

Raisa Simola (Ph.D.) teaches at the University of Joensuu, Finland. Her doctoral thesis *World Views in Chinua Achebe's Works* was published in 1995. She has been attached to the English department of the University of Texas at Austin. She is currently working on a study of Ben Okri.

Karina Hestad Skeie is research fellow at the Institute for Cultural Studies at Oslo University, Norway. She has done research on traditional Malagasy religion, on Malagasy and African Christianity, and on Christian missions to Madagascar. She is preparing a Ph.D. thesis on nineteenth century Norwegian missionaries to Madagascar.

I. Bolarinwa Udegbe is a senior lecturer in Psychology at the University of Ibadan in Nigeria. Her specialisation is women's studies, gender attitudes, leadership, socio-psychological aspects of gender issues in work place and impact on policy. She was awarded a senior Humanities fellowship in 1999 at the Institute for the Study of Gender in Africa (ISGA) in the James S. Coleman African Studies Center of the University of California, Los Angeles, where she worked on Nigerian proverbs as sources of conceptualisation and the meaning of gender.

Yvonne Vera has gained a BA, a Master of Arts and a Doctorate, all in English at York University, Toronto, Canada. She is the author of short stories and novels and both *Nehanda* (1993) and *Without a Name* (1994) were short-listed for the Commonwealth Award Africa Region. Selected again for her work *Under the Tongue*, Vera was awarded this prize in 1997. She now works as the Director of the National Gallery of Zimbabwe in Bulawayo.

Anna Wieslander has written several books, reports and articles on Swedish-African encounters through the aid relationship. She wrote a descriptive book about a town in Tunisia and has edited some books, among them an anthology of articles based on the Cairo conference in 1994. She also made a study of a project financed by Swedish assistance in Sri Lanka, a report about the contacts with Africa in a city in Sweden and, in 1999, a study on Swedes in Africa.

Selena Axelrod Winsnes has for many years been specialised on Ghana. A five-year residence in Ghana roused interest in African studies and resulted in her becoming an Africanist through studies at the University of Ghana at Legon and the Centre of West African Studies, University of Birmingham, UK. At the request of her professors at Legon, her knowledge of Danish led to what has become her specialisation—critical translations into English of published Danish primary sources for the transatlantic slave trade.

www.ingramcontent.com/pod-product-compliance
Lightning Source LLC
Chambersburg PA
CBHW080607270326
41928CB00016B/2954